PRINCIPLES OF HOSPITALITY LAW

FOURTH EDITION

ALAN PANNETT AND MICHAEL BOELLA

CASSELL

Cassell
Wellington House
125 Strand
London WC2R 0BB

127 West 24th Street
New York
NY 10011

British Library Cataloguing-in-Publication Data
A catalogue record for this book is available from the British Library.

ISBN 0–304–33574–6 (hb)
    0–304–33575–4 (pb)

Typeset by Keystroke, Jacaranda Lodge, Wolverhampton
Printed and bound in Great Britain by Redwood Books, Trowbridge, Wiltshire

CONTENTS

FOREWORD

Hospitality is now one of the UK's most important industries, employing over two million people and representing around seven per cent of our gross national product.

The industry embraces a vast range of different types of hospitality products and services. In the private sector these include hotels and other providers of accommodation, restaurants, public houses and bars, clubs, transport operations, residential care and leisure centres. In the public sector are included many different types of catering or accommodation services including hospitals, educational establishments, prisons and the armed services.

Irrespective of the particular sector we are in, we now find ourselves operating within an ever-changing and increasingly complicated legal environment. As the old legal adage states, 'ignorance of the law is no excuse'. Those who break the law now find themselves facing very heavy penalties, as well as very damaging publicity. This book sets out to ensure that no manager needs to remain in ignorance of the law.

In its first three editions this book has established itself as the leading text on the subject, so this new edition is very welcome. Its authors have set out to make the law understandable to the average manager, at the same time avoiding the dangers of over-simplification. As a consequence *Principles of Hospitality Law* is useful not only to those teaching or studying the subject but equally importantly to the busy manager working in the hospitality industry.

I am therefore very pleased to commend it to you, the reader, whether to use as a reference book to take off the shelf from time to time or to help you with your studies.

Jeremy Logie FHCIMA
Chief Executive
British Hospitality Association
London
April 1996

PREFACE

Principles of Hospitality Law succeeds *Principles of Hotel and Catering Law*, published in its third edition in 1992. This text is designed as a comprehensive guide to the many aspects of English law which affect the caterer, hotelier and restaurateur as well as all those concerned in the management of the leisure, travel and tourism industries.

Throughout this text we have been concerned to draw on practical examples of how the law affects the working lives of those within the hospitality industry. Source materials and practical examples have been employed to illustrate how the law relates to everyday management decisions. Whenever it has been possible to do so we have considered the relevant legal issues from a practical management perspective, rather than a narrow legalistic standpoint. This we have sought to achieve through appropriate case studies.

The primary use of this volume is as a source of information for students.

Principles of Hospitality Law is an ideal text book for all students of hotel and catering subjects and in particular those following NVQ Level 4 courses, Bachelor's and Master's degrees, the Hotel and Catering International Management Association Professional Certificate and Diploma courses, and many other hotel and catering courses with a law content.

Practising managers will also find *Principles of Hospitality Law* a useful and practical reference work.

We are most grateful to Croner Publications for permission to use material from their publications.

We take full responsibility for any errors, deficiencies or inaccuracies in, or omissions from, the text. The law as stated in this volume is that which was, to the best of our knowledge, in force on 1 April 1996.

Alan Pannett
Michael Boella
Brighton
April 1996

INTRODUCTION

The purpose of this text is to help students of hotel and catering management and people working within the catering professions towards a better understanding of those principles of English law which closely affect them in their day-to-day work in the hotel and catering industry.

The hotelier or catering manager will in the course of his or her work enter into many different legal relationships with other parties. The catering manager, for example, enters into a contract of employment with his or her employer. The catering business by which that person is employed enters into many different contracts, both with suppliers for equipment and stores, etc., and with customers for the provision of food, drink and accommodation. The catering business itself is regulated by various Acts of Parliament which impose duties and standards of conduct that must be observed. It is vital that the caterer, hotelier or restaurateur and his or her staff work at all times within the boundaries of the law. It is therefore of the utmost importance that these people understand the law and how it affects their work and the conduct of the catering business.

Figure A illustrates the various legal relationships in which professional caterers might find themselves. Each line in the diagram represents a relationship. These are just some of the most common forms of legal relationship which the caterer will undertake.

A sound knowledge of law is as essential to the professional caterer as is a knowledge of business management and the fundamental skills of the profession. Law affects the caterer in so many ways that he or she cannot afford to ignore it. The ways in which the caterer is affected by the law are too numerous to mention. However, two every-day situations may serve to illustrate how important it is to have a practical, working knowledge of the law.

Example A. The proprietor of 'Mamma's Pizza Restaurant' has employed Chris as a waiter for some four years. One evening, whilst serving in the restaurant, Chris is rude to a customer. The proprietor dismisses Chris then and there and without notice.

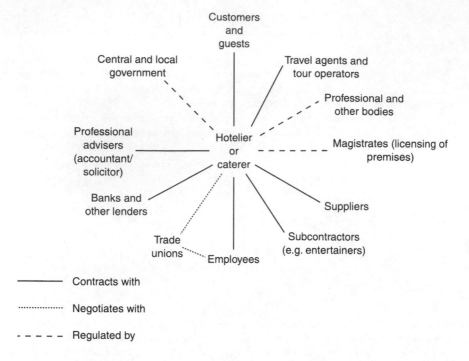

Figure A The legal relationships of a professional caterer.

This simple factual situation raises a number of legal questions:
(a) Has the proprietor the right to dismiss Chris summarily and without notice?
(b) Has Chris a contractual claim to any wages instead of working his notice period?
(c) Has Chris a claim for unfair dismissal?
(d) Has the proprietor any possible defence to a claim by Chris for either wages which may be owing to him or unfair dismissal?
(e) What remedy might Chris obtain if he succeeds in either of these actions against the proprietor? Can he claim his job back?

Example B. Mr Careless, the proprietor of The Barmy Towers Hotel, overbooks the rooms in his hotel, in the expectation that some guests may cancel and he will still have a full hotel. Mr Careless also states in his brochure that 'the hotel's restaurant provides internationally acclaimed cuisine and top-name cabaret entertainment. All rooms have sea views'. Mr Hapless books for a fortnight's holiday for himself, his wife and two children. On arrival he finds that the room which Mr Careless had confirmed would be reserved for the family has been double-booked. The Hapless family were placed in a room which was staff accommodation, overlooking the kitchens. The hotel's restaurant provided only poor-quality food and the top-name cabaret entertainment consisted of a local group of amateur singers.
(a) Is Mr Careless criminally liable for overbooking the hotel?
(b) Is Mr Careless criminally liable for the representations which he made in the brochure?

(c) Which form or forms of civil action might Mr Hapless bring against Mr Careless?

(d) Can Mr Hapless recover damages for his own disappointment and that of his wife and children, at the loss of their holiday?

A primary function of this book is to consider the principles of law which relate to the hotel and catering industry in the context in which they arise. This is in the hope that they will become clearer to those who work within the industry. The text deals with the important cases and statutes as they arise within the framework of the book.

It is the hope of the authors that this book will be of use both as an explanation of relevant legal principles and as a point of reference for dealing with legal problems as they arise in the context of the reader's work in the hospitality industry. However, this text is not a substitute for professional advice from a solicitor and should never be used as such.

ONE

Law and the legal system

1.1 INTRODUCTION

The purpose of this chapter is to outline the basic principles which form the foundations of the English legal system. We shall consider the respective roles of Parliament and the courts, and in particular we shall examine the jurisdiction and functions of those courts and tribunals with which the caterer is likely to come into contact in the exercise of his or her profession.

Before examining the institutions in which English law is rooted it is important to consider three fundamental classifications of law. There are a number of other different ways of classifying law, but the three classifications set out below are essential to a basic understanding of English law and the legal system within which it operates.

Civil and criminal law

Civil laws cover contract and liability in tort. These are matters of private arrangement between individuals; the state is not normally involved. Contract covers such things as the booking of a hotel room, the provision of a meal in a restaurant and the employment of staff. Tort considers such things as the caterer's liability for negligently prepared food which causes injury to the customer.

Criminal law on the other hand deals with matters involving the state and the enforcement of penal laws. In general, we think of the criminal law as the means by which individuals are prosecuted, tried and punished for the offences (e.g. theft, assault, etc.) which they have committed. The criminal law as it relates to the catering industry is more a means of regulating the standards of business practice; the Food Safety Act 1990 regulates the quality of food which is produced and served to the public, and it renders businesses which do not meet the standards required liable for prosecution and punishment. Breach of a civil law, in contrast to a breach of a criminal law, normally renders the person who has broken it liable to pay damages to the victim of the breach. It does not involve a prosecution or state intervention. Damages are designed not to punish the person in breach but to compensate for the loss sustained by the plaintiff. In certain situations a single set of facts and circumstances may give rise to both a civil claim and a criminal prosecution. An example of such a situation is where hoteliers overbook their accommodation. This may give rise to a civil claim for breach of contract on the part of the guest who is double-booked, and may possibly lead to the prosecution of the hoteliers for an offence under section 14 of the Trade Descriptions Act 1968.

Common law and equity

The Judicature Act of 1873 created a single Supreme Court comprising the High Court of Justice and the Court of Appeal, presided over by the Lord Chancellor. Today the High Court is made up of three divisions; the Queen's Bench Division, the Chancery Division and the Family Division. The work of the old Court of Chancery is today undertaken by the Chancery Division of the High Court and the modern equivalent of the principles of equity formulated in the old Court of Chancery are still used to provide remedies, e.g. injunctions.

Common law and statute law

Laws may be classified by reference to source. Statute law is enacted by Parliament, e.g. the Food Safety Act 1990, whilst case law is derived from judicial precedent established through the hearing of cases in the courts. Case law is also referred to as the common law, which describes the vast number of judicial precedents built up over the years through court decisions. Examples of case law and statute are to be found throughout this book.

1.2 LEGISLATION

Within the English legal system, which covers both Wales and Northern Ireland, but not Scotland, which has a separate and distinct legal structure, there are two principal sources of law: legislation and the common law.

Legislation refers both to Acts of Parliament (primary legislation) and to delegated legislation, otherwise known as secondary legislation, which is created under the authority of an Act of Parliament. The fundamental purpose of legislation is to create, amend or repeal law, thereby giving effect to the intentions of Parliament.

Legislation may be required for any one of a number of reasons:

1   To create new rights, an example of which is the Equal Pay Act 1970.
2   To raise revenue; the annual Finance Acts are passed to give legislative authority to the Chancellor's Budget.
3   To put into practice political policies, for example the Race Relations Act 1976.
4   Codification of case law; Parliament may pass legislation in order to give legislative effect to judicial decisions and bring together all of the law in one statute e.g. the Police and Criminal Evidence Act 1984.

5   Consolidation of previous legislation, for example the Employment Protection
    (Consolidation) Act 1978.
6   To cope with an emergency, for example the Drought Act 1976.

Primary and secondary legislation

Primary legislation

This form of legislation comprises Acts of Parliament. Parliament has unlimited
legislative power. This stems from the doctrine of parliamentary sovereignty, which is
a fundamental principle of English law. This doctrine means that a person cannot
question the validity of a piece of legislation through the courts. The function of the
courts is to interpret and apply legislation and not to question its existence; hence no
court can override an Act of Parliament.

The United Kingdom does not have a written constitution unlike many other
countries, e.g. the United States of America, therefore it is sometimes difficult for an
individual or organization to clearly identify the rights which it has under the law.
There has been political pressure in the last three decades for legislation in the form
of a Bill of Rights, which would set out individual freedoms and responsibilities.

A bill is normally sponsored by the cabinet and introduced into Parliament by a
cabinet minister. Not all bills are introduced in this way; any Member of Parliament
may, of course, personally introduce a bill. Bills are normally drafted by Parliamentary
Counsel. A bill may be introduced into either House, though non-controversial bills
are usually commenced in the Lords, allowing more time in the Commons for controversial bills to be introduced. Money bills (e.g. taxation) are always introduced in
the Commons. The first step in Parliamentary procedure is the introduction and first
reading of the bill. The bill is thereafter debated in Parliament at the time of its second
reading. It then enters the committee stage, when standing committees within the
House scrutinize the bill. Later it enters the report stage, when any amendments made
during the committee stage are reported to the House. The bill will receive a third
reading, and once passed by the Commons will be debated by the Lords in much the
same way. The bill, after being passed by the Lords, receives the royal assent, a mere
formality, whereby the monarch accedes to the bill. Thereafter, the bill becomes an
Act, and will have effect from the date of its publication, or any date thereafter stated
in the Act itself.

Certain legislation of the European Union has direct effect and forms part of the
United Kingdom's primary legislation.

Secondary legislation

Secondary legislation is the name given to the vast body of rules, orders, regulations
and by-laws created by subordinate bodies under specific powers delegated to those
bodies by Parliament. It is otherwise known as delegated legislation. The enabling Act
which grants the power to make secondary legislation will set out the procedures to
be followed when the secondary legislation is created. If the scope of the enabling Act
is exceeded or the procedures set out in it are not followed, the secondary legislation
thereby created is said to be *ultra vires* (i.e. beyond the power given). If the secondary
legislation thus created is found by the courts to be *ultra vires* it will be deemed to be
of no effect.

Statutory construction and interpretation

Not all the terms of a statute may be clear and unambiguous; hence they will need interpretation or construction. 'Interpretation' is simply the process whereby a meaning is assigned to the words of the statute, whilst 'construction' is the process whereby uncertainties or ambiguities in a statute are resolved. Ambiguity arises where, through an error in drafting, the words used in the statute are found to be capable of bearing two or more meanings. Uncertainty occurs where the court is not sure whether the statute was designed to cover the factual situation which is before it for decision.

The basic task of the judge when construing legislation is to ascertain Parliament's intention when passing the Act. There are three rules of construction which the courts might employ when construing a statute.

The rules of construction

The literal rule. Parliament's intention must be found in the ordinary and natural (i.e. literal) meaning of the words used in the statute. Where the literal rule may produce a perverse result, one of the other rules should be used in construing the statute.

The golden rule. In applying this rule the words of the statute will be interpreted according to their natural, ordinary and grammatical meaning, but where such an interpretation produces a manifestly absurd result, the words will be interpreted so as to avoid the absurdity.

The mischief rule. In *Heydon*'s case (1584) the court required that four questions should be considered when giving a meaning to a statutory provision:
(a) What was the common law before the Act?
(b) What was the mischief and defect for which the common law did not provide?
(c) What remedy had Parliament resolved to cure this defect?
(d) What was the true reason for that remedy?
Applying each question in turn to the words of the statute the court seeks to find the meaning of the words in the statute. This is also known as the purposive approach, since the courts are looking at the purpose for which the Act was passed.

European Community legislation

The various forms of European Communities legislation are provided for by Article 189 of the European Community Treaty. The Treaty forms the 'primary legislation' of the EU. Under the Treaty the Council and the Commission of the EU are empowered to make:
1   Regulations.
2   Directives.
3   Decisions.
4   Recommendations.

Regulations. These are generally applicable and binding in their entirety, and have direct effect upon all member states. Hence, regulations confer individual rights and duties which must be respected by the courts of the member states. An EC regulation in the United Kingdom does not require further legislation in Parliament for it to be enforceable i.e. it has direct effect. Furthermore, Parliament is limited in its actions, since it should not pass legislation which conflicts with the regulation. EU regulations are of some importance to the caterer since they cover matters such as wine labelling, egg labelling, vegetable grading and Euro sizing.

Directives. These, unlike regulations, do not necessarily have immediate binding force. A directive is addressed to member states within the EU but it is left to each individual government to decide whether or not to implement the directive. When a directive is implemented in the United Kingdom it is normally done by means of delegated legislation. A directive was, however, considered by the European Court to have direct effect, such as to confer rights upon the plaintiff in *Van Duyn* v. *Home Office (No. 2)* [1975] 3 All ER 190, although the United Kingdom Parliament had not implemented the directive by means of delegated legislation.

An important example of how an EC directive can affect UK law is to be found in the Product Liability Directive (1985), which brought about the Consumer Protection Act 1987 (see below); also the EC Directive on Package Travel, Package Holidays and Package Tours (90/314/EEC).

A member state which is in breach of Community law by failing to implement a directive may, in certain circumstances, be liable to compensate an individual who has suffered loss as a result of non-implementation, even though the directive in question does not have direct effect. An example of this is *Marshall* v. *Southampton and South West Hampshire Area Health Authority (No. 2)* [1993] 4 All ER 586 (CJEC).

Decisions. Decisions of either the Council of Ministers or the European Commission are merely a means of enunciating policies or initiating actions. A decision is binding upon those to whom it is addressed, and may operate to create individual rights which must be protected by the courts of the member states.

Recommendations. These do not have binding effect upon member states.

Whilst these various secondary forms of legislation are open to review by the European Court, and by the courts of the member states, the Treaties which form the primary legislation of the European Union are not. The Treaties are, however, the subject of interpretation.

The European Union

Much of English law, such as contract, tort, land law and criminal law is *not* affected by United Kingdom membership of the European Union. European Community law is concerned mainly with restrictive trade practices, competition law, agriculture, fisheries, etc. Where the business person working in the hotel and leisure industries is likely to encounter European legislation is in the areas of employment law, consumer protection and environmental legislation.

The primary EC legislation consists of the three core Treaties which established it, together with the Single European Act and the Treaty on European Union (the Maastricht Treaty). The provisions of these treaties are directly applicable in the United Kingdom without the need for further legislation from the UK Parliament, by virtue of s.2(1) of the European Communities Act 1972.

The Single European Act was signed in February 1986 and made important changes to the Treaties, and this was ratified by the United Kingdom Parliament in the European Communities (Amendment) Act 1986. The Single European Act added a new article 168A to the EEC Treaty. This Article provided for a new Court of First Instance of the European Communities. This court is attached to the European Court and has jurisdiction to decide certain categories of case brought by individuals and other legal entities. There is a right of appeal to the European Court from decisions of the Court of First Instance on points of law only.

Interpretation of European Community legislation

The European Communities Act 1972 joined the United Kingdom to the European Economic Community (EEC) as a member state, thus introducing a new and higher level of authority into the English legal system.

Section 2(1) of the European Communities Act 1972 provides:

> *All such rights, powers, liabilities, obligations and restrictions from time to time created or arising by or under the Treaties, and all such remedies and procedures from time to time provided for by or under the Treaties, as in accordance with the Treaties are without further enactment to be given legal effect or used in the United Kingdom shall be recognised and available in law, and be enforced, allowed and followed accordingly: and the expression 'enforceable Community right' and similar expressions shall be read as referring to one to which this subsection applies.*

By section 3(1) of the same Act the European Court is recognized as being the ultimate determinant of the principles of law laid down by the Treaties and subsequent EC legislation. Furthermore s. 2(4) European Communities Act 1972 provides that any Act of the Westminster Parliament shall be presumed not to conflict with EC legislation, and will be given effect only so far as it does not conflict with the EC legislation. We can see therefore that the English courts are bound to apply Community law.

Community law constitutes a distinct body of law interwoven with the national laws of member states. As can be seen from the case of *Costa* v. *ENEL* [1964] ECR (EC), within the Community's legal system Community law prevails over national laws of member states. Lord Denning remarked in *Application des Gas SA* v. *Falks Veritas* [1974] Ch. 31 (CA):

> *the Treaty is part of our law. It is equal in force to any statute. It must be applied in our courts.*

The effect of the Treaties and any given regulation or directive is ultimately a question of interpretation for the European Court.

It may seem that Community law is somewhat remote from us as individuals and is irrelevant to our daily lives. This is a serious misconception. Since the Articles of the EC Treaty have direct effect, they are capable of enforcement by individuals within member countries, just as if they were the laws of that country. Hence, where a particular company, individual or government is not observing Community law, the person who is adversely affected by this failure may commence an action to enforce his or her rights under Community law; this may have profound effects.

DEFRENNE v. SABENA A Belgian air stewardess, Ms Defrenne, claimed pay equal to
AIRWAYS [1976] ICR 547 that of male air stewards. Article 119 of the Treaty of Rome
(EC) provides that 'Each Member State shall ensure that . . . men
and women shall receive equal pay for equal work'. Belgium,
as a member state of the EEC, had not legislated for equal
pay. The European Court held that although Belgium had not legislated to give effect to Article
119, Ms Defrenne was entitled to pay equal to that of male cabin stewards. Article 119 took
direct effect and was enforceable through the courts of a member state.

GARLAND v. BRITISH The employers permitted all their employees to have certain
RAIL ENGINEERING travel concessions for themselves and their families. Male
LTD [1982] 2 WLR 918 employees retained these rights after retirement. A female
(EC) employee's husband and her family could not benefit from
the scheme after she had retired. When the case came before
the House of Lords a reference to the European Court was
made to determine whether the facts disclosed discrimination under Article 119 of the Treaty of
Rome. The European Court held that Article 119 covered pay and also included other forms of
consideration, whether payable immediately or in the future, provided the worker received it in
respect of his or her employment. The provision of special travel facilities therefore was covered
by Article 119. Since the travel facilities were provided on a more beneficial basis to male
employees, this constituted a breach of Article 119, it being the duty of the English courts to
apply Article 119, which overrode the English law. The Court of Appeal had held that s. 6(4) of
the Sex Discrimination Act 1975, permitting discrimination in relation to retirement, operated,
and the provision of travel facilities in this way did not amount to unlawful discrimination (see
[1979] 1 WLR 754).

MARSHALL v. This case concerned the effect of the Equal Treatment
SOUTHAMPTON AREA Directive (76/207/EEC). The applicant was employed by the
HEALTH AUTHORITY area health authority. It was the authority's policy, and an
[1986] 2 WLR 780 (EC) implied term of the applicant's contract of employment, that
employees retired at the age when they became entitled to
draw the state retirement pension, this being aged 65 for a
man and 60 for a woman. The applicant did not wish to retire when she reached the age of 60 and
that requirement was waived by the authority until shortly after her sixty-second birthday, when
she was dismissed. She claimed that she had been discriminated against on the grounds of sex
contrary to the Sex Discrimination Act 1975. The industrial tribunal dismissed the complaint on
the grounds that s. 6(4) of the Act of 1975 permitted discrimination arising out of 'provision in
relation to . . . retirement'. When her appeal to the appeal tribunal was dismissed, the applicant
appealed to the Court of Appeal. The court found that the authority was an emanation of
the state and referred to the European Court of Justice the questions of whether the dismissal of
the applicant after reaching normal retirement age for a woman constituted discrimination prohibited by Council Directive (76/207/EEC) and whether the applicant could rely on the directive
in national courts notwithstanding any inconsistency between it and s. 6(4) of the Act of 1975.

Held: 1. Article 5(1) of Council Directive (76/207/EEC) provided that the application of the
principle of equal treatment with regard to working conditions, including the conditions relating
to dismissal, meant that men and women were guaranteed the same conditions without
discrimination on grounds of sex, and the term 'dismissal' in that context included retirement in
accordance with an employer's policy. Accordingly, the policy of dismissing a woman employee
solely because she had attained the qualifying age for a state pension which was lower than that
for a man constituted discrimination contrary to the Council Directive.

2. Since the forms of the Council Directive were unconditional and sufficiently precise, they could be relied upon by an individual in an action against the state, but not against another individual. Accordingly the Council Directive could be relied upon by the applicant against the health authority.

This case is an important illustration of the direct applicability of European Community law in member countries. The issue of direct application of Directive 76/207 has more recently been debated in the European Court in the case of *Foster* v. *British Gas* [1991] 2 WLR 258, where it was held that provisions of a Directive which were capable of having direct effect could be relied upon by bodies made responsible by the state for providing a public service under state control where such bodies held 'special powers' in relation to such a function.

The *Marshall* case also serves to show how a case decided in the European Court may become a force to bring about change in national law within member states. Parliament enacted, in the Sex Discrimination Act 1986, provisions which have the effect of bringing UK national law into line with the Council Directive on which Ms Marshall based her case.

Section 2 of the Sex Discrimination Act 1986 amends s. 6(4) of the Sex Discrimination Act 1975 so as to provide that it is unlawful for a person to discriminate against a woman:
(a) in such of the terms on which she is offered employment as make provision in relation to the way in which she will be afforded access to opportunities for promotion, transfer or training or as provide for her dismissal or demotion; or
(b) in the way she is afforded access to opportunities for promotion, transfer or training or by refusing or deliberately omitting to afford her access to any such opportunities; or
(c) by dismissing her or subjecting her to any detriment which results in her dismissal or consists in or involves her demotion.
The Sex Discrimination Act 1986 is fully discussed in Chapter 9.

Lastly, the effect of EC legislation has been considered in the battle over Sunday trading. In *Torfaen Borough Council* v. *B&Q PLC* [1990] 2 WLR 1330 the European Court of Justice held that the validity of English Sunday trading laws depended upon replies to the following points:
• Did the Sunday trading laws pursue an aim which was justified with regard to Community law?
• Did the effect of the law exceed what was necessary to achieve that aim – did its effects on the free movement of goods exceed what was necessary to achieve that aim?
The European Court noted that:
(a) The provisions of the Shops Act 1950 prohibiting Sunday trading were designed to protect shop workers from having to work on Sundays – this was an aspect of economic and social policy within the jurisdiction of the member state's government.
(b) As to the effects of the prohibitions contained in the 1950 Act, the European Court held that this turned on the issue of 'proportionality' – i.e. if the aim of the Sunday trading prohibition could be achieved by other means which would have a less serious effect on the free flow of goods, then the law would contravene Article 30 of the Treaty of Rome.
Following the European Court judgment, the Cwmbran magistrates convicted B&Q of breaches of the 1950 Act, holding that the Sunday trading laws did not contravene Article 30.

In *Stoke-on-Trent City Council* v. *B&Q PLC* and *Norwich City Council* v. *B&Q PLC* [1991] 2 WLR 42 the High Court granted injunctions to the two plaintiff councils restraining B&Q PLC from trading on a Sunday. However, only one month earlier the High Court had reached a decision in *W. H. Smith Do It All Ltd and Payless DIY Ltd* v. *Peterborough City Council* [1990] 2 CMLR 577, which gave exactly the opposite result. Reference should also be made to the House of Lords decision in *Kirklees MBC* v. *Wickes Building Supplies Ltd* [1992] NLJ 967.

The issue of the validity or otherwise of member state legislation restricting Sunday trading will receive further review when the European Court provides guidance following another reference to it. Currently the English, French and Belgian courts all conflict in their interpretations of the impact of legislation restricting Sunday trading. Clear legislative reform is needed to overcome the inadequacies of the current position. In 1986 the Shops Bill, which sought to remove the prohibition, failed to be enacted.

1.3 THE COMMON LAW

The basic tenet upon which a common law system (i.e. the English legal system) is founded is known as the doctrine of precedent. Precedent here refers to judicial precedent, derived from cases decided within the hierarchy of the court structure. There are said to be three preconditions of a common law system based upon judicial precedent:

Reliable system of law reporting. The doctrine of precedent is bound up with the need for a reliable system of law reporting. Law reporting is required because those who wish to rely upon a previous decision of the court to further their own case must have a clear and reliable record of the decision and the reason for the decision in the earlier case. The rule is that any decision may be cited to a court provided that it is reported by a member of the Bar who was present when judgment was delivered. The member of the Bar present will report the case, and the report may be published in one of the official series of law reports (e.g. All England or Weekly Law Reports); such reports are considered a true record of the case.

Hierarchy of courts. A hierarchical court structure is essential to give to a particular case a level of authority; this will determine whether or not the case can be overruled by a decision of the same or a higher court, and which courts, if any, are bound by its decision. The English legal system has a rigid hierarchical structure.

An effective system of appeal. There must be a system of appeal throughout the court structure which leads to a 'court of last resort' beyond which there is no further appeal. The 'court of last resort' in the English legal system is the House of Lords.

Where the matter is one of European Community law the ultimate court to which an appeal may be made is the European Court. A reference can be made to the European Court from a court in the English legal system. Guidelines for the making of a Reference were laid down by Lord Denning MR in *H.B. Bulmer Ltd* v. *Bollinger SA* [1974] Ch 401 (at pp. 420–5). The discretion to refer the case or not belongs to the English court and not to the European Court. A party to proceedings cannot complain to the European Court about the exercise of the discretion one way or the other by the English court.

The first reference to the European Court by the Court of Appeal was *Macarthys Ltd* v. *Smith* [1979] 3 All ER 325 – a case relating to equal pay. A very recent example of a reference to the European Court by the Court of Appeal is the case of *R.* v. *H.M. Customs & Excise ex parte EMU Tabac SARL and others*, a decision of the Court of Appeal 1995 (unreported). This case relates to the importation of tobacco products for personal use through an agent based in the United Kingdom who purchases cigarettes etc. from a retailer based in Luxembourg paying local tax which is significantly lower than in the UK.

In addition to the existence of these three preconditions, the English legal system requires two further rules in order to function.

1   Superior courts in the hierarchy have the power to overrule decisions of inferior courts and in certain cases to overrule their own decisions. A superior court is one with unlimited jurisdiction such as the High Court, Court of Appeal or House of Lords. An inferior court is one which has limited jurisdiction, such as the County or Magistrates' Court.

2   Any common-law rule established by judicial precedent may be amended or removed by a statute passed by Parliament. This rule emphasizes the doctrine of 'parliamentary sovereignty'. Parliament is all-powerful, the supreme authority within the legal system. The role of the courts is to apply the common law and interpret statutes; the function of Parliament is to legislate and create law.

The English legal system is a composite of legislation and judicial precedent. These work hand in hand to provide the principles of English law which are applied in the courts. Neither precedent nor legislation is sufficient in its own right; common-law principles may need codifying in a statute, and a statute will need judicial interpretation to determine the scope of its operation.

Ratio decidendi and *obiter dictum*

Ratio decidendi

This amounts in plain terms to the principle of law contained in the decision of the court. In any given case the decision of the court will be made up of the following elements:

1   Findings by the court of material facts.

2   Statements of the principles of law applicable to the problem disclosed by the facts of the case.

3   A judgment by the court based upon 1 and 2 above (e.g. in a civil case an award of damages).

It is 2 which amounts to the *ratio decidendi* of the case. Hence, the *ratio decidendi* of a case may be defined as the statement of law applied to the legal problems raised by the facts as found, upon which the decision is based. Not every statement made in the course of a judgment is binding as part of the *ratio decidendi* of the case. Only that part of the judgment which is based upon the facts as found and upon which the court bases its decision forms part of the *ratio*. Other statements are discarded as *obier dicta*.

It is not always easy to identify the *ratio decidendi* of a given case. The problem is increased when considering the *rationes* of a Court of Appeal decision where three (or possibly five) judgments are given; in the House of Lords five (or possibly seven) speeches are given. The *ratio* of a given case is found (if the opinions of the judges are not unanimous) by identifying the majority viewpoint. This may not always be straightforward since, although there may be a majority decision, the reasoning used by each member of the majority may differ. The role of the lawyer when analysing a case is therefore to extract the principle(s) of law from the decision of the court.

Obiter dictum

A statement may be classified as an *obiter dictum* if it falls into any of three categories:

1   A statement of law based upon facts which either were not found to exist in the case or were found not to be material to the decision.

2   A statement of law which, although based on facts found to be relevant by the

court, does not form the basis of the court's decision, e.g. a dissenting speech in the Court of Appeal or House of Lords.

3   A statement which forms the basis of a decision of the court but which, although it would otherwise be considered as binding, is made in a court which is outside the hierarchy of the courts. Hence a decision of the Judicial Committee of the Privy Council (which is the ultimate court of appeal for decisions reached in Commonwealth courts) will not be binding as *ratio decidendi*; it falls into the category of *obiter dictum*.

Judicial precedent and the hierarchy of the courts

The authority given to a particular case depends upon the court in which the decision was made. According to the position of the court in the hierarchy other courts may be bound by the *ratio* of the case or may be in a position to overrule or amend it. Figure 1.1 represents the civil court structure and Figure 1.2 represents the criminal court structure. The dotted line in each diagram separates the superior courts from the inferior courts. Figures 1.3 and 1.4 illustrate the appeal structure in the English legal system. Figure 1.3 represents the appeal structure for civil cases, Figure 1.4 the appeal structure in criminal cases.

A traditional classification of the English courts is a division into 'superior' and 'inferior' courts. The superior courts are those within the structure of the Supreme Court of Judicature as constituted by the Judicature Acts 1873–5. This incorporates the High Court, the Queen's Bench Divisional Court, the Crown Court and the Court of Appeal (Criminal and Civil Divisions). The House of Lords is of course a superior court although it does not form part of the Supreme Court of Judicature. A feature which distinguishes superior from inferior courts is that superior courts are not limited in their jurisdiction, whereas inferior courts are limited both geographically and as to the subject matter of the dispute.

We must now consider the function and position of each court within the English legal system.

The House of Lords

The House of Lords is the highest English court. Decisions of the House of Lords are binding upon all other courts trying civil or criminal cases.

Since the Lord Chancellor's *Practice Statement* [1966] 3 All ER 77 the House of Lords has considered itself at liberty to depart from its own previous decisions when it appears right to do so. This replaced the previous rule in *London Street Tramways Co.* v. *LCC* [1898] AC 375 (HL), which held the House of Lords to be bound by its own previous decisions. The House has, however, departed from its own previous decisions in very few cases. The judicial attitude of the House of Lords may best be illustrated by this dictum of Lord Reid in *British Railways Board* v. *Herrington* [1972] 1 All ER 749 (HL), where he observed:

> *Our change of practice in no longer regarding previous decisions of this House as absolutely binding does not mean that whenever we think a previous decision was wrong we should reverse it. In the general interest of certainty in the law we must be sure that there is some very good reason before we so act.*

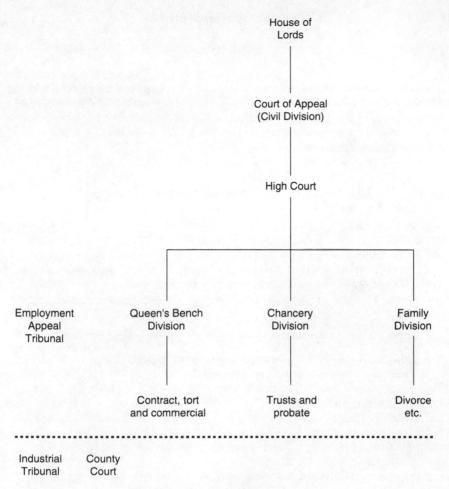

Figure 1.1 The civil court structure.

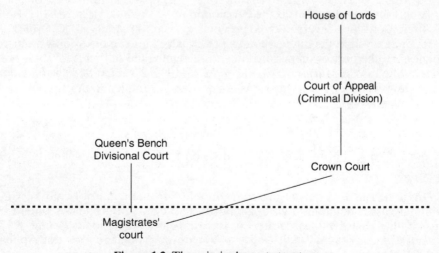

Figure 1.2 The criminal court structure.

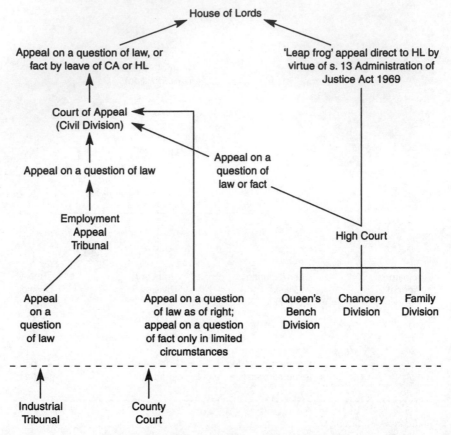

Figure 1.3 The appeal structure in civil cases.

In recent years the House of Lords has more readily applied the *Practice Statement* of 1966. A classic example of this is the decision in *R.* v. *Shivpuri* [1986] 2 All ER 334, in which their Lordships reversed their previous decision in *Anderton* v. *Ryan* [1985] 2 All ER 355 reached not eighteen months previously! This serves to show an increased willingness on the part of their Lordships to recognize the fallibility of their previous decisions. The case of *Murphy* v. *Brentwood DC* [1990] 2 All ER 908, examined in 'the common law in action' section, provides another example of the use of the 1966 *Practice Statement*.

The Court of Appeal

The Court of Appeal is divided into two divisions: the Civil Division and the Criminal Division.

Civil Division. The decisions of this court are binding on all inferior courts trying civil or criminal cases, including divisional courts. The Court of Appeal is bound by decisions of the House of Lords and by its own earlier decisions. *Young* v. *Bristol Aeroplane Co. Ltd* [1944] 2 All ER 293 (CA) affirmed that the Court of Appeal was bound by its previous decisions, save in three exceptional circumstances:

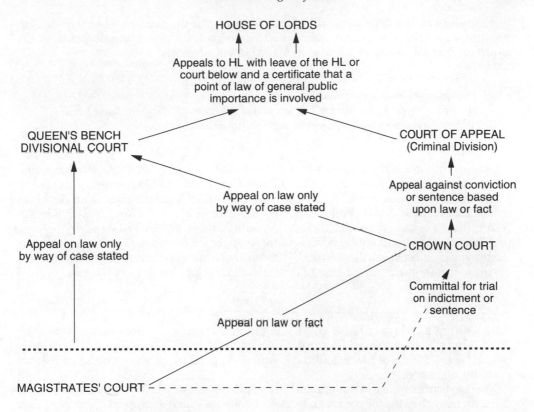

HOUSE OF LORDS

Appeals to HL with leave of the HL or
court below and a certificate that a
point of law of general public
importance is involved

QUEEN'S BENCH
DIVISIONAL COURT

COURT OF APPEAL
(Criminal Division)

Appeal against conviction
or sentence based
upon law or fact

Appeal on law only
by way of case stated

Appeal on law only
by way of case stated

CROWN COURT

Committal for trial
on indictment or
sentence

Appeal on law or fact

MAGISTRATES' COURT

Figure 1.4 The appeal structure in criminal cases.

1   Where there are two conflicting Court of Appeal decisions on a point, the Court
    may choose which it will follow, the decision not followed being deemed to be
    overruled.
2   Where a previous Court of Appeal decision cannot be said to be in line with the
    House of Lords' authority on the same subject.
3   Where the previous Court of Appeal decision was reached *per incuriam*.
The rule in *Young* v. *Bristol Aeroplane Co. Ltd* has not gone unchallenged. Lord
Denning sought to avoid it on a number of occasions, the most notable case being
Davis v. *Johnson* [1978] 2 WLR 182 (CA). In that case Lord Denning argued that the
Court of Appeal should issue guidelines similar to those of the House of Lords in the
1966 *Practice Statement*, thereby enabling the Court of Appeal to depart from its
own previous decision where the decision was wrong; in other circumstances it would
hold itself bound by *Young* v. *Bristol Aeroplane Co. Ltd*. However, the House of
Lords, when hearing the appeal in *Davis* v. *Johnson* [1978] 1 All ER 1132, expressly
affirmed the rule in *Young* v. *Bristol Aeroplane Co. Ltd*, directly criticizing Lord
Denning's proposed departure from the rule.
    Why should the Court of Appeal be bound by its own decisions? The answer to this
question stems from the position of the Court of Appeal in the hierarchy of the courts;
it has an intermediate position. As Scarman LJ observed in *Tiverton Estates Ltd*
v. *Wearwell Ltd* [1974] 1 All ER 209 (CA): 'To a large extent the consistency and

certainty of the law depend on it.' Hence, certainty of the law, an essential requirement in a common-law system, is dependent upon consistency in the decisions of the Court of Appeal. Scarman LJ later in his judgment observes:

> *The appropriate forum for the correction of the Court of Appeal's errors is the House of Lords, where the decision will at least have the merit of being final and binding, subject only to the House's power to review its own decisions.*

Criminal Division. The decisions of the Court of Appeal (Criminal Division) bind courts trying criminal cases, that is the Crown Court and the Magistrates' Court. The Criminal Division also binds the Divisional Court which hears appeals from decisions of the Magistrates' Court. Following from the case of *R.* v. *Taylor* [1950] 2 KB 368 (CA), the Court of Appeal (Criminal Division), whilst generally bound by its own previous decisions, will not be bound where to apply the previous decision of the court would cause injustice to the accused. The rationale for such an approach is that the desire to attain justice in the case overrides the need for certainty in the law.

High Court

When sitting as a first instance court (i.e. the first court to try the case at issue), the High Court binds all inferior courts (i.e. County Court). The High Court itself is bound by the House of Lords and the Court of Appeal, yet it is not bound by its own previous decisions.

The Divisional Court of the Queen's Bench Division, which exercises a supervisory capacity over the inferior courts and sits as a court to which an appeal 'by way of case stated' may be made from the Magistrates' Court, is bound by the House of Lords, the Court of Appeal and its own previous decisions.

The inferior courts

Those courts which do not form part of the Supreme Court of Judicature are collectively known as inferior courts. This group comprises the County Court, the Magistrates' Court and tribunals.

County Court. Bound by the House of Lords, the Court of Appeal (Civil Division) and the High Court, but not by its own previous decisions.

Magistrates' Court. Bound by the House of Lords, the Court of Appeal (Criminal Division) and the Divisional Court of the Queen's Bench Division. The Magistrates' Court is not bound by its own previous decisions.

Industrial tribunal. Perhaps the most important of the tribunals, the industrial tribunal is bound by the House of Lords, the Court of Appeal (Civil Division) and the Employment Appeal Tribunal. The industrial tribunal is not bound by its own previous decisions.

Two courts which strictly are outside the English legal system are of importance.

European Court. The European Court binds all English courts on all matters relating to the Treaties by which the EU was formed and EC legislation. It is only on matters relating to the EU that decisions of the European Court have binding authority.

Judicial Committee of the Privy Council. This is the ultimate judicial body hearing appeals from Commonwealth jurisdictions. Decisions of the Privy Council, whilst they do not bind English courts, are very persuasive. This stems from the fact that members of the House of Lords make up the Judicial Committee of the Privy Council.

The common law in action

An understanding of how the complicated process which we call the common law operates is best achieved by studying the development of a legal concept through decided cases. Of all the twentieth-century cases *Donoghue* v. *Stevenson* [1932] AC 562 (HL) serves to illustrate the process most clearly.

Prior to *Donoghue* v. *Stevenson* the law relating to the tort of negligence had been fragmented. In the House of Lords' decision we see a fundamental principle emerge.

DONOGHUE v. STEVENSON [1932] AC 562 (HL)

The facts. The plaintiff drank a bottle of ginger beer manu-factured by the respondent, which a friend had purchased on her behalf from the retailer. The retailer opened the opaque bottle and poured some of its contents into a glass. The plaintiff drank the ginger beer, and when a second glass was poured for her by her friend a decomposing snail which had been in the bottle floated out. The plaintiff suffered physical illness.

The decision. The House of Lords upheld the plaintiff's claim for damages. It was held that a manufacturer of products, which he sells in such a form as to show that he intends them to reach the ultimate consumer in the form in which they left him, with no reasonable possibility of intermediate examination, and with the knowledge that the absence of reasonable care in the preparation or putting up of the products will result in injury to the consumer's life or property, owes a duty to the consumer to take reasonable care. The House found that the defendant had not fulfilled such a duty to take reasonable care and was thus liable to the plaintiff for the damage caused to her health.

The neighbour principle. The case of *Donoghue* v. *Stevenson* is noted moreover for the general test as to liability in negligence propounded by Lord Atkin where he says: 'You must not injure your neighbour. You must take reasonable care to avoid acts or omissions which you can reasonably foresee would be likely to injure your neighbour. Who, then, in law is my neighbour? The answer seems to be – persons who are so closely and directly affected by my act that I ought reasonably to have them in contemplation as being so affected when I am directing my mind to the acts or omissions which are called into question.' Furthermore, Lord MacMillan observed that 'the categories of negligence are never closed', thus leaving the way open for the broadening of the concept of negligence and its later application to a great number of different situations.

In *Donoghue* v. *Stevenson* we see the synthesis of the previous decisions on the tort of negligence. This case reduces them to a single principle, the 'neighbour principle', which emerges as part of the *ratio decidendi* of the case.

The question arose after *Donoghue* v. *Stevenson* as to how broadly the *ratio decidendi* could be interpreted. The *ratio decidendi* of *Donoghue* v. *Stevenson* is open to two interpretations. The 'narrow *ratio*' of the case may be stated thus:

> *A manufacturer of products, which he sells in such a form as to show that he intends them to reach the ultimate consumer in the form in which they left him, with no reasonable possibility of intermediate examination, and with the knowledge that the absence of reasonable care in the preparation or putting up of the products is likely to result in injury to the consumer's life or property, owes a duty to the consumer to take reasonable care. (per* Lord Atkin).

It is arguable that the *ratio decidendi* of the case is limited solely to this principle, and cannot be extended so as to include the neighbour principle. The 'wide *ratio*' of the case may be stated as being the neighbour principle.

It is important to understand that the *ratio decidendi* of a particular case is not wholly to be found in the case itself; rather one must look to the way in which later courts interpret the case. Will later courts broaden the scope of the *ratio decidendi* when they interpret the case, or will they restrict it and narrow it down, confining it to the particular factual situation of the original case? Which view has been taken by the courts with regard to *Donoghue* v. *Stevenson*? Following from *Donoghue* v. *Stevenson* there have been a number of cases which have sought to apply the neighbour principle to different situations and thus broaden its scope.

HEDLEY BYRNE & CO. LTD v. HELLER & PARTNERS LTD [1964] AC 465 (HL) The plaintiffs, a firm of advertising agents, booked advertising on behalf of E, a customer, on terms that if E defaulted on payment the plaintiffs would have to pay. The plaintiffs obtained a report from the defendants, merchant bankers with whom E had an account, as to E's creditworthiness. The defendants replied in their reports that E was 'trustworthy . . . to the extent of a £100 000 per annum advertising contract'. The defendants' reply incorporated a disclaimer, namely that the report was 'without responsibility on the part of this bank or its officials'. The plaintiffs relied upon the defendants' report and as a result lost some £17 000 in monies owed by E on advertising contracts when E went into liquidation. The House of Lords held that in the present case the defendants' disclaimer was sufficient to exclude the assumption by the defendants of a duty of care towards the plaintiff. However, in the absence of such a disclaimer the circumstances would have given rise to a duty of care. The essential element which gives rise to the duty, in the words of the Lord Morris, was a 'special relationship' between the parties. Lord Morris observed: 'If someone possessed of a special skill undertakes (irrespective of contract) to apply that skill for the assistance of another person who relies on such skill he voluntarily undertakes the responsibility of so acting.'

Although what was said in *Hedley Byrne & Co. Ltd* v *Heller & Partners Ltd* was an *obiter dictum*, later courts interpreted the case as extending the scope of *Donoghue* v. *Stevenson* beyond negligent actions which cause physical damage, to include negligent statements which occasion monetary loss.

This case also identifies a further point, namely that of judicial policy. Lord Pearce in *Hedley Byrne & Co. Ltd* v. *Heller & Partners Ltd* observed:

> *How wide the sphere of the duty of care in negligence is to be laid depends ultimately on the court's assessment of the demands of society for protection from the carelessness of others.*

After *Hedley Byrne & Co. Ltd* v. *Heller & Partners Ltd* there was considerable debate as to how far monetary loss might be recoverable. Was the decision in that case to be limited to those situations where a 'special relationship' existed? Did the decision extend to all negligently caused economic loss or was it confined to economic loss sustained in consequence of physical harm? Lord Denning in *Dutton* v. *Bognor Regis UDC* [1972] 1 QB 375 (CA) highlighted perhaps the most important issue in setting the limits upon the scope of the duty of care in *Donoghue* v. *Stevenson*:

> *It seems to me that it is a question of policy which we, as judges, have to decide. The time has come when, in cases of new import, we should decide them according to the reason of the thing.*

Lord Reid in *Home Office* v. *Dorset Yacht Co. Ltd* [1970] AC 1004 (HL) further explains judicial opinion on this question when he states:

> Donoghue v. Stevenson *may be regarded as a milestone, and the well known passage in Lord Atkin's speech should I think be regarded as a statement of principle. It is not to be treated as if it were a statutory definition. It will require qualification in new circumstances But I think that the time has come when we can and should say that it ought to apply unless there is some justification or valid explanation for its exclusion.*

How has the law developed regarding the neighbour principle in *Donoghue* v. *Stevenson*? In *Anns* v. *London Borough of Merton* [1977] 2 All ER 492 (HL), Lord Wilberforce in a now well-known passage, attempted to articulate a general principle in seeking to determine the existence of a duty of care when he stated:

> *Through the trilogy of cases in this house*, Donoghue v. Stevenson, Hedley Byrne & Co. Ltd v. Heller & Partners Ltd *and* Home Office v. Dorset Yacht Co. Ltd, *the position has now been reached that in order to establish that a duty of care arises in a particular situation, it is not necessary to bring the facts of that situation within those of previous situations in which a duty of care has been held to exist. Rather the question has to be approached in two stages. First one has to ask whether as between the alleged wrongdoer and the person who has suffered damage there is a sufficient relationship of proximity or neighbourhood such that, in the reasonable contemplation of the former, carelessness on his part may be likely to cause damage to the latter, in which case a prima facie duty of care arises. Secondly if the first question is answered affirmatively, it is necessary to consider whether there are any considerations which ought to negative, or to reduce or limit the scope of duty or the class of person to whom it is owed or the damages to which a breach of it may give rise.*

Whilst this provided an approach adopted in subsequent cases, the limitations of such a general principle have, more recently, been recognized in judgments of the House of Lords and Privy Council: see, for example, *Governors of Peabody Donation Fund* v. *Sir Lindsay Parkinson & Co. Ltd* [1985] AC 210; *Yuen Kun-yeu* v. *AG of Hong*

Kong [1987] 2 All ER 705; *Hill* v. *Chief Constable of West Yorkshire* [1989] AC 53; *Caparo Industries* v. *Dickman* [1990] 1 All ER 568. In *Caparo*, a case concerning the duty owed by accountants, as auditors of a company report, to potential and individual shareholders, Lord Bridge recognized that concepts such as 'proximity'

> *are not susceptible of any ... precise definition as would be necessary to give them utility as practical tests, but amount to the features of different specific situations which, on a detailed examination of all the circumstances, the law recognises pragmatically as giving rise to a duty of care of a given scope.*

Note should also be made in this context of the case of *Murphy* v. *Brentwood DC* [1990] 2 All ER 908, discussed below.

What then has happened with regard to cases of economic loss? In *Spartan Steel & Alloys Ltd* v. *Martin & Co. (Contractors) Ltd* [1972] 3 All ER 557 (CA) the question arose whether profits lost in consequence of physical damage were alone recoverable, or whether profits lost which were not related to physical damage were also recoverable. The Court of Appeal decided that only the former and not the latter were recoverable. Lord Denning in his judgment took the following view:

> *At bottom I think the question of recovering economic loss is one of policy. Whenever the courts draw a line to mark out the bounds of duty they do it as a matter of policy so as to limit the responsibility of the defendant. Whenever the courts set bounds to the damages recoverable – saying that they are, or are not, too remote – they do it as a matter of policy so as to limit the liability of the defendant.*

Referring specifically to the decisions on economic loss, Lord Denning later in his judgment observes:

> *The more I think about these cases, the more difficult I find it to put each into its proper pigeon-hole. Sometimes I say 'There was no duty'. In others I say: 'The damage was too remote'. So much so that I think the time has come to discard those tests which have proved so elusive. It seems to me better to consider the particular relationship in hand, and see whether or not, as a matter of policy economic loss should be recoverable.*

Edmund Davies LJ dissents from the views of Lord Denning MR and Lord Justice Lawton. He regards both economic loss which is occasioned by physical damage and 'pure economic loss' regardless of physical damage to be recoverable. He states in *Spartan Steel & Alloys Ltd* v. *Martin & Co. (Contractors) Ltd*:

> *Having considered the intrinsic nature of the problem presented in this appeal, and having consulted the relevant authorities, my conclusion ... is that an action lies in negligence for damages in respect of purely economic loss, provided that it was a*

reasonably foreseeable and direct consequence of failure in a duty of care. The application of such a rule can undoubtedly give rise to difficulties in certain sets of circumstances, but so can the suggested rule that economic loss may be recovered provided it is directly consequential on physical damage.

The Court of Appeal was clearly divided as to the approach which should be taken with regard to economic loss. The question was later considered by the House of Lords in *Junior Books Ltd* v. *Veitchi & Co. Ltd* [1982] 3 WLR 477 (HL). Lord Roskill took the view that:

There was no reason why 'damage to the pocket' simpliciter should be disallowed when damage to the pocket coupled with physical damage has always been allowed. No untoward consequences would result.

Lords Fraser and Russell agreed with this opinion. Obviously this meant that the majority view of Lords Denning and Lawton in *Spartan Steel & Alloys Ltd* v. *Martin & Co. (Contractors) Ltd* was considered 'old law' and to be incorrect, and the dissenting view of Lord Edmund Davies appeared to be vindicated. Lord Keith in *Junior Books Ltd* v. *Veitchi & Co. Ltd* opines:

The Donoghue v. Stevenson duty of care had been extended to situations where pure economic loss was recoverable.

Lord Keith cites *Hedley Byrne & Co. Ltd* v. *Heller & Partners Ltd* and *Anns* v. *London Borough of Merton* as the authorities which give rise to this proposition. He does rather qualify his view where he later considers that the present case is not 'an appropriate case for seeking to advance the frontiers of the law of negligence', and he seeks to confine the decision to its own particular facts. Lord Brandon, who dissents from the majority viewpoint, considers that only economic loss which is consequential upon the existence of actual or threatened physical injury is recoverable, as within the scope of *Donoghue* v. *Stevenson*.

In one respect the Atkinian neighbour principle and Lord Wilberforce's opinion in *Anns* are similar; they both extend the boundaries of tortious liability in negligence to new areas, the former to product liability, the latter to a failure to inspect a defective building. However, the approach taken to each case in subsequent decisions has been entirely different. The neighbour principle did not attain ready acceptance for some years after 1932, whereas Lord Wilberforce's statement in *Anns* became broadly accepted at once. After the courts' acceptance of the neighbour principle, there was an increasing tendency to apply it to new areas, heralding a major advance in the recovery of damages for economic loss (e.g. *Hedley Byrne & Co. Ltd* v. *Heller & Partners Ltd*). With respect to the *Anns* test, there has been a growing reluctance to apply it, and, as noted above, recent cases have cast doubt on its validity. In *Peabody Donation Fund Governors* v. *Sir Lindsay Parkinson & Co. Ltd* [1985] AC 210, it was held that a property developer, as opposed to a building owner, was not owed a duty of care by a local authority.

In *Murphy* v. *Brentwood DC* [1990] 2 All ER 908, the House of Lords has put an end to what it described as the 'uncertainty' created by Lord Wilberforce's wide principle by using the 1966 *Practice Statement* to overrule *Anns*. The effect is consequently a reversion to the pre-*Anns* position of developing new categories of duty incrementally by analogy with established categories rather than by a wide *prima facie* duty constrained only by undefined 'considerations which ought to negate, or to reduce or limit the scope of the duty or the class of persons to whom it is owed'.

Junior Books has raised more questions than it has answered and has wide-ranging implications for the nature of obligations arising in both contract and tort. The tenor of Lord Roskill's speech in *Junior Books* suggests that he intended to develop a principle of general application to cases of pure economic loss caused by negligent acts. In subsequent cases, however, the decision has been described as limited to its own facts, e.g. *Candlewood Navigation Ltd* v. *Mitsui OSK Lines Ltd* [1986] AC I (PC) and *Muirhead* v. *Industrial Tank Specialists Ltd* [1986] QB 507 (CA). In *D & F Estates Ltd* v. *Church Commissioners for England and Wales* [1988] 2 All ER 992 (HL), the House of Lords distinguished *Junior Books* v. *Veitchi* as being peculiar to its own facts. It is therefore unsafe to rely on *Junior Books* as establishing any general principle of liability, a view which accords with the decision of the House of Lords in *Caparo Industries plc* v. *Dickman* [1990] 2 AC 605. This case was decided on a preliminary issue when the House of Lords held that an auditor owed no duty of care to an individual shareholder in the company who wished to buy more shares. The House of Lords considered that, in making a statement, a duty of care is owed only where there is a relationship of sufficient proximity between the maker of the statement and the person relying on it. This will arise in particular situations where the maker of the statement knows that his statement will be communicated to the person relying on it specifically in connection with a particular transaction, and that person will rely on it for the purposes of deciding whether or not to enter into that particular transaction.

It would appear, following *Caparo*, that the House of Lords have decided that it is impossible to use a single general principle of liability.

As to *Junior Books*, this case can be regarded as the furthest extent to which a duty not to cause pure economic loss has been recognized by the courts. In a number of cases after *Junior Books*, the courts have sought to limit its application and to restrict the extent to which there exists a duty not to cause economic loss. However, the House of Lords in *White* v. *Jones* [1995] 1 All ER 691 recognized the existence of a duty, owed by a solicitor, to a person with whom he was not in contract, (a disappointed beneficiary) in circumstances where the only loss sustained by that person was economic loss.

Forms of precedent which are not binding

There are certain forms of precedent which are not binding.
1 Persuasive precedent.
   (a) *obiter dicta*:
   (b) decisions of those courts not within the hierarchy of the English legal system.
      i.e the Judicial Committee of the Privy Council.
2 Precedents which have been overruled by later decisions at a higher level.
3 Precedents which have been distinguished and confined to their own particular facts.

4   Statements of law made *per incuriam* (i.e. without considering relevant
     authorities). In *Young* v. *Bristol Aeroplane Co. Ltd* [1944] 2 All ER 293 (CA) the
     Court of Appeal decided that it was not bound by a previous decision of that
     court, if satisfied that the decision in question was reached *per incuriam*. In effect
     this covers cases where some relevant statutory provision or precedent which
     would have affected the decision was not brought to the attention of the court.

1.4 GOING TO LAW

Whilst we may learn about the legal principles which regulate our daily lives, both at
work and at home, the actual process of 'going to law' and bringing an action before
the courts is not necessarily as simple as one may imagine. Specialist advice should
be sought before embarking upon litigation. Normally one consults a solicitor. A
solicitor is a trained legal professional who has usually obtained a law degree and will
have studied for the Legal Practice Course in order to practise in the profession.
Solicitors undertake a two-year training contract in a firm of solicitors or a legal
department of a company or public sector body. During the training contract they
complete the Professional Skills Course, and if they pass this course they are effectively Admitted and their name entered on the Roll of Solicitors on completion of their
training contract.

In certain areas law centres, staffed by professional lawyers and advisers, offer a
good free legal advice service. Equally citizens' advice bureaux may be able to assist
with advice and information which may further your case.

If more specialized expertise is required, the solicitor whom you have instructed to
act on your behalf may consult, i.e. 'brief', a barrister. Solicitors therefore take counsel's
opinion on difficult or technical questions of law or procedure. A barrister may appear
in any court, whereas a solicitor's rights of audience are currently limited to the inferior
courts. Barristers may not be approached directly by most clients: they may only be
briefed by solicitors. The English legal profession, therefore, is in effect split into two
halves offering a complementary service. There is some doubt about whether such
a system is the most effective. Some people, both in academic circles and within the
profession, think that a single profession, i.e. that of an advocate who could both be
consulted directly and have rights of audience in all courts, might be preferable. One
may on the other hand consider that the ancient traditions and methods of training for
the Bar are worthy of preservation. The Courts and Legal Services Act 1990 increased
solicitors' rights of audience and is to some extent reforming the profession.

Barristers normally take a law degree, after which they join an Inn of Court and
read for Bar finals. They then complete twelve months of unpaid work, known as
pupillage, for a practising barrister at that person's chambers.

The courts of first instance

A court of first instance is one in which an action is commenced. A civil claim is
commenced in either the High Court or the County Court according to the nature and
size of the claim. If the claim is one which relates to employment matters it will
normally be within the jurisdiction of the industrial tribunal. Criminal prosecutions are

commenced either in the Magistrates' Court if the matter is to be tried summarily or, following a committal before a Magistrates' Court, in the Crown Court if the matter is to be tried upon an indictment. Indictable offences are the most serious and are tried before a judge and jury. The Magistrates' Court therefore has a dual function: to try minor cases (summary offences) and to consider whether on indictable offences there is sufficient evidence for a Crown Court trial; this process is known as committal proceedings.

Caterers, hoteliers, innkeepers and restaurateurs may have recourse to any one of a number of courts for a multiplicity of reasons; the following are those which they are most likely to use.

The civil courts

High Court. The High Court is a court of first instance which has unlimited jurisdiction. Recently the respective jurisdictions of the High Court and County Court have been redefined. The High Court is now taking a more specialist role and its jurisdiction is primarily concerned with high-value claims, over £25 000. One may appear in person before the court, but solicitors now have a right of audience; however, a solicitor will normally instruct a barrister to appear before the court on the litigant's behalf – see the provisions of the Courts and Legal Services Act 1990 (ss. 27–33) discussed above. Legal aid is available for most High Court actions. Procedure in the High Court remains complex and cases take a considerable time to come to trial, e.g. 3–5 years.

The County Court. The County Court is an inferior court, in that its jurisdiction is limited. The High Court and County Courts Jurisdiction Order 1991 sets out the parameters of the County Courts' jurisdiction. It is normal to commence proceedings in the local County Court – e.g. for the recovery of a debt. The limitation which used to apply was with regard to the value of the action. A small claim, under the small claims procedure, is up to a maximum of £3000. The High Court and County Courts Jurisdiction Order 1991 provides that cases to a value of £25 000 must be heard in the County Court. Disputes of between £25 000 and £50 000 may be heard in either the County Court or the High Court. Any claim for an amount exceeding £50 000 shall be commenced in the High Court. A case can be transferred from the County Court to the High Court or vice versa if it is for a claim between £25 000 and £50 000 at the determination of the court after the court has considered (a) the financial substance of the case, (b) the importance of the case, (c) the complexity of the legal issues, and (d) the speed of trial.

Two further points should be noted. Firstly, all personal injury claims, e.g. arising from an accident at the work place, for up to £50 000 in damages must be heard in the County Court. Secondly, Default Actions (i.e. debt recovery claims) are no longer subject to geographical limitation or jurisdiction, but proceedings should be commenced in the County Court where the trial is likely to take place.

The County Court is particularly useful in that it operates a small claims procedure. This procedure applies to actions brought for the recovery of a sum, in either contract or tort, not exceeding £3000. The matter is dealt with in an informal way before the Registrar of the County Court, and costs are not incurred by the use of this form of action (i.e. costs cannot be awarded against a party). If the matter is not resolved by the small claims procedure it may go forward to a full hearing before a County Court judge in the normal way. Legal aid is available in the County Court.

Industrial tribunal. Like other tribunals, the industrial tribunal is an inferior court, having jurisdiction in limited matters only, in this case employment. Legal aid is not available for industrial tribunals, and many litigants appear without legal representation.

Procedure before the industrial tribunal is relatively simple, being designed to make applications easy to process without legal advice, and the rules of evidence are not strictly applied by the tribunal. The main work of the industrial tribunal is concerned with individuals' contracts of employment. Hence unfair dismissal and redundancy are considered by the tribunal, as are cases of discrimination on the grounds of race, sex or trade union activities.

Caterers are most likely to come into contact with industrial tribunals if one of their past or present employees refers a matter to the tribunal with regard to his or her contract of employment. Unlike the courts previously considered, which are presided over by a sole judge, the industrial tribunal is presided over by a legally qualified chairperson and two lay persons ('wing men'). The 'wing men' comprise one person nominated by trade unions and employees' federations and one person nominated by the CBI and various employers' federations.

The Magistrates' Court. The primary function of the Magistrates' Court is to try criminal cases. However, a very important civil part (especially for the caterer) of the Magistrates' Court's jurisdiction is the granting of licences. This covers the granting of liquor licences, gaming licences, etc.

The Magistrates' Court consists of a bench of three lay magistrates, or in metropolitan areas a single stipendiary magistrate who is legally qualified. The clerk to the magistrates advises lay magistrates on points of law, practice and evidence. The magistrates' decision may be either unanimous or by a majority of the bench who heard the case.

On an application for a licence, the applicant will normally attend the court. Although applicants are entitled to legal representation, they are not always legally represented, the proceedings being simple and involving little or no legal principle. Legal aid is not available. The Magistrates' Court is an inferior court and solicitors as well as barristers have a right of audience.

The criminal courts

The Magistrates' Court. The Magistrates' Court, when hearing a criminal case, is constituted in the same way as for licensing applications. The Magistrates' Court is limited in its jurisdiction. It may impose a fine of up to £2000 (unless the Statute creating the offence provides otherwise) and a maximum term of six months' imprisonment on any one charge (and a maximum of twelve months where the person is charged with more than one offence triable 'either way', e.g. theft).

With regard to criminal matters the magistrates have a twofold jurisdiction: (a) to try people summarily; and (b) to commit people for trial to the Crown Court before a judge and jury. Summary trial covers the less serious offences and is commenced by the laying of information and a summons. Caterers may come into contact with the Magistrates' Court in this way if they commit one of a number of offences relating to their profession, for example licensing offences, or offences under the Food Safety Act 1990, or possibly offences under the Trade Descriptions Act 1968. Legal aid is available for summary trial. However, because of the nature of the cases concerned in summary trial, it is not often given. Since the Magistrates' Court is an inferior court, the party need not be represented by a barrister; solicitors can provide representation if any is required.

The Crown Court. This court was set up in 1971 by the Courts Act. Unlike the Magistrates' Court, the Crown Court's jurisdiction is not limited to a given area. The Crown Court is presided over by a judge or a recorder and it hears the more serious criminal cases. The mode of trial in a Crown Court is known as trial on indictment. The indictment is the document which charges the defendant with the offence. The trial is before a jury of twelve. The function of the jury is to determine all questions of fact in the case, whilst the function of the judge is to determine the admissibility of evidence and all questions of law raised by the case. It is worthy of note that in the Magistrates' Court the separate functions of the judge and jury are both performed by the magistrates. Caterers may come into contact with the Crown Court either on appeal from a conviction before the Magistrates' Court or when they are tried for serious criminal offences. Since the Crown Court is a superior court, its power to punish is limited only by the maximum penalty set for the offence by an Act of Parliament. Currently a solicitor does not have a right of audience; only members of the Bar may appear before the court, although, again, reference should be made to the provisions of the Courts and Legal Services Act 1990. Legal aid is available for cases in the Crown Court.

1.5 ARBITRATION

When disputes arise in the course of business, or between a business and its customers, the parties to the dispute have to decide how best to resolve it. The main choices, other than one of the parties conceding, are:
*   reporting the matter to the local trading standards office who may institute a criminal prosecution. If the defendant is found guilty the magistrates may order compensation, or
*   litigation, i.e. taking the case to a civil court, or
*   arbitration.

Arbitration in this context refers to a method of dispute resolution which lies outside the court system and is to be distinguished from 'County Court arbitration' or the small claims court.

Arbitration is a means of settling disputes, by which the parties agree to be bound by the decision of an arbitrator. The arbitrator's decision is generally final and legally binding, although there are some forms of arbitration where the process and the decision may not be recognized in law. Arbitration is normally conducted according to the Arbitration Acts 1950–79 as amended.

Any person, company or corporation who can enter into legally binding contracts can go to arbitration, subject to all the parties to the dispute agreeing. Almost any dispute which can be subject to litigation in a court can be settled by arbitration. Arbitration is used commonly for the resolution of disputes in building, rent reviews in commercial leases, insurance, computer applications.

One of the better known arbitration schemes is the Association of British Travel Agents (ABTA) scheme. This allows for disputes between travel companies and their customers to be referred to arbitration, to which ABTA members have to agree.

There are schemes for disputes between many professionals such as lawyers and architects for resolving disputes between themselves and their clients. There are even arbitration schemes for resolving disputes between members of some religions.

Arbitration has certain benefits over litigation. Arbitration can be private i.e. no publicity can be given to the hearing and any subsequent awards. Normally the procedure is informal and it can be organized at the convenience of the parties rather than that of the court. Furthermore the parties may agree to appoint an expert in their field as the arbitrator. Costs can be much less as the hearing may be a lot shorter and fewer professional advisers, such as solicitors and barristers, may be needed. Costs will normally be apportioned after the hearing by the arbitrator.

The Chartered Institute of Arbitrators is recognized as the professional body for arbitrators and appoints arbitrators to many of the independent arbitration schemes. There is no scheme specific to the hospitality industry.

TWO

The catering enterprise

In this chapter we shall examine the various factors which may influence the entrepreneur when deciding on the form the business will take, and consider the legal framework within which the business will operate.

When establishing the catering enterprise the entrepreneur will have to make a number of vital decisions about the form the business will take. These decisions will be based on a range of different factors. Figure 2.1 is a flow chart which covers some of the major decisions which have to be made as part of the formation of a catering enterprise.

2.1 CHOOSING THE FORM OF BUSINESS ENTERPRISE

This decision is of vital importance, and of course it must be made before trading can commence. It is this decision which will affect the size, scope and financing of the enterprise, and determine other operational criteria. According to the type of enterprise chosen, certain formalities may or may not have to be carried out, those participating in the finance of the company may or may not be protected by limited liability, and the potential growth and financial resources of the enterprise may also be determined.

What factors are of influence in the making of this fundamental decision?

Limited liability

Limited liability means that the financial liability of each person responsible as a member of the business is fixed from the outset and limited to a fixed amount. In other

30

words, the people investing money in the enterprise from the beginning know the
extent of their potential financial loss should the enterprise fail. The knowledge that
the failure of the business will not mean inevitable personal disaster has motivated
many business people to seek shelter behind the screen of limited liability. Limited
liability is available in either of two business forms, as follows.

The limited company

This is a distinct and separate legal entity from the people who own it which provides
limited liability for shareholders. Shareholders are liable only to the extent of the
value of their paid-up shares. In other words, they can lose only the value of their
shares in the company. Since most shares issued are 'fully paid up', shareholders may
hide behind the corporate veil, assured that their liability with respect to the company
does not extend beyond the value of their shares. Therefore a shareholder's shares
become valueless; this is the extent of his or her loss. Neither partnership nor sole
trading has this advantage; the owners of these forms of enterprise are fully liable for
all debts incurred by the business. This stems from the fact that neither form has the
advantage of being a separate legal entity; thus the debts of the business are the debts
of the people who own that business.

Limited partnership

This is a specialized form provided for by the Limited Partnership Act 1907. Limited
partnership is not, however, a well-used or popular form of business enterprise.

A limited partnership comprises both limited and full partners. Only limited partners
may claim limited liability. Hence, full partners, of which there must be at least one, are
liable to the full extent of their personal assets, as with other forms of partnership. The
limited partner(s) contribute a fixed amount of money when joining the partnership,
and this money must remain in the partnership. The limited partner must not participate in the management of the partnership. Any interference by limited partners in
the running of the enterprise will render them personally liable for all debts, as with
full partners. Limited partners do, however, have a right to advise full partners, though
it is a matter for the full partners whether or not they follow such advice. Limited
partners, provided they fulfil the above investment criteria and do not participate in the
management of the partnership, may claim limited liability.

Limited liability is such a useful asset to the person in business that one may wonder
why partnership and sole trading still flourish. They flourish in part because the benefit
of limited liability must be weighed against the need for legal formalities in the
formation, running and closure of companies, amongst other burdens which operating
as a company brings (e.g. filing annual returns).

Limited liability is today of reduced significance, since many major creditors, such as
banks, leasing companies, etc., require personal guarantees from directors of a limited
liability company. Such personal guarantees become effective if and when the company
itself cannot meet its financial obligations. Hence a director of a company may stand
to lose financially even though the company has limited liability. Trade creditors,
however, do not normally require personal guarantees; therefore the 'corporate veil' is
effective in guarding against the personal liability of a director for such debts.

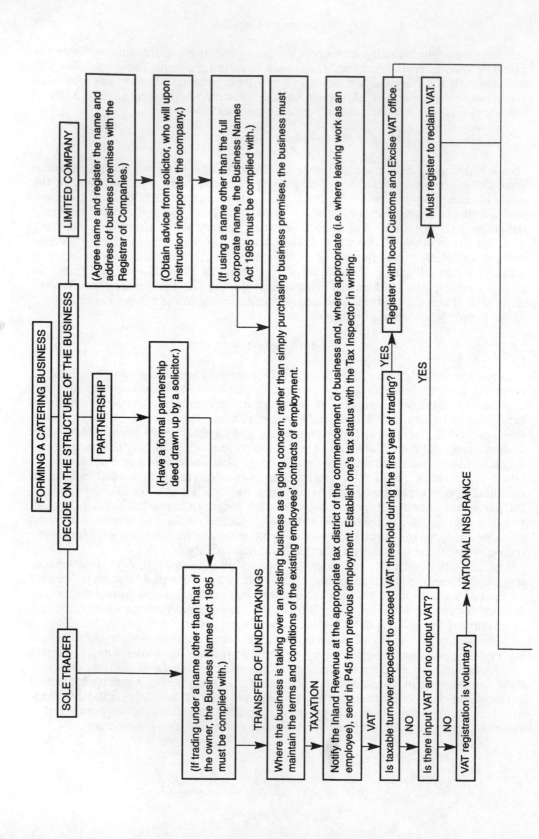

FORMING A CATERING BUSINESS

DECIDE ON THE STRUCTURE OF THE BUSINESS

SOLE TRADER

(If trading under a name other than that of the owner, the Business Names Act 1985 must be complied with.)

PARTNERSHIP

(Have a formal partnership deed drawn up by a solicitor.)

LIMITED COMPANY

(Agree name and register the name and address of business premises with the Registrar of Companies.)

(Obtain advice from solicitor, who will upon instruction incorporate the company.)

(If using a name other than the full corporate name, the Business Names Act 1985 must be complied with.)

TRANSFER OF UNDERTAKINGS

Where the business is taking over an existing business as a going concern, rather than simply purchasing business premises, the business must maintain the terms and conditions of the existing employees' contracts of employment.

TAXATION

Notify the Inland Revenue at the appropriate tax district of the commencement of business and, where appropriate (i.e. where leaving work as an employee), send in P45 from previous employment. Establish one's tax status with the Tax Inspector in writing.

VAT

Is taxable turnover expected to exceed VAT threshold during the first year of trading? — YES — Register with local Customs and Excise VAT office.

NO

Is there input VAT and no output VAT? — YES — Must register to reclaim VAT.

NO

VAT registration is voluntary

NATIONAL INSURANCE

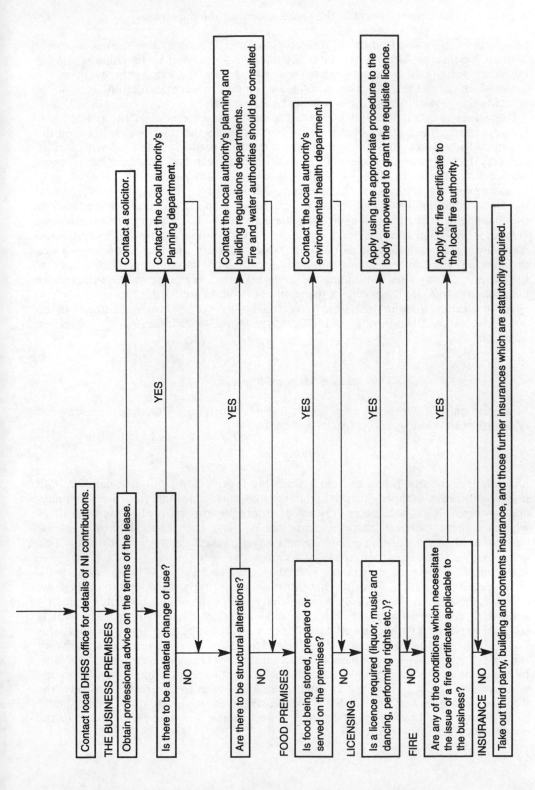

Contact local DHSS office for details of NI contributions.

THE BUSINESS PREMISES

Obtain professional advice on the terms of the lease.

Is there to be a material change of use? — YES → Contact the local authority's Planning department.
NO

Are there to be structural alterations? — YES → Contact the local authority's planning and building regulations departments. Fire and water authorities should be consulted.
NO

FOOD PREMISES

Is food being stored, prepared or served on the premises? — YES → Contact the local authority's environmental health department.
NO

LICENSING

Is a licence required (liquor, music and dancing, performing rights etc.)? — YES → Apply using the appropriate procedure to the body empowered to grant the requisite licence.
NO

FIRE

Are any of the conditions which necessitate the issue of a fire certificate applicable to the business? — YES → Apply for fire certificate to the local fire authority.
NO

INSURANCE

Take out third party, building and contents insurance, and those further insurances which are statutorily required.

Contact a solicitor.

Figure 2.1 The formation of a catering enterprise.

Involvement in the management of the enterprise

Sole traders, otherwise known as proprietors, have total control over the management of their businesses. The proprietor is accountable to no one in the running of the business, for it is the proprietor alone who will sustain the loss in the event of the financial failure of the enterprise. It is the autonomous nature of sole trading which is an attractive feature of this form of business enterprise.

A partner is entitled to full participation in the management of the partnership. However, since the essence of this form of enterprise is the relationship between the partners, to be successful business decisions must be made with the consensus of all partners. Hence autonomy is lost and some form of agreement with the other partners is necessary in order to make worthwhile business decisions.

A company, being a separate legal entity, makes decisions through its annual general meeting of shareholders and its board of directors. Normally, any decision made about the management of the company requires a consensus of a majority of shareholders. A further limitation upon the actions of those managing the company is imposed by the company's memorandum of association, which sets out the bounds within which the company must operate. Only those actions which are within the 'objects clause' of the memorandum of association may be undertaken, otherwise actions are deemed to be *ultra vires* (outside the power of the company) and do not bind it.

An entrepreneur who wishes to have full control over the management of an enterprise may well opt for sole trading as the only form which offers sufficient freedom of action.

Financial considerations

There are many different financial considerations which may affect the decision as to which form of business enterprise to undertake.

Raising capital

Since neither the sole trader nor the partnership is protected by limited liability, both may find difficulty in raising sufficient money to commence trading from a secure financial position. This is because both forms of enterprise are identical to the individuals who own them; their creditworthiness is that of those individuals. Hence, someone wishing to finance a catering enterprise may have to guarantee the loan by using their own personal assets, e.g. their house, as security.

A company, however, may create a 'floating charge', a device which provides sufficient security for a loan. Few financial institutions are prepared to lend to proprietors and partnerships on this basis. A floating charge gives the lender continuing security against all company assets, e.g. stock in trade, plant, machinery. The company may still, of course, deal with these assets as if they were not subject to a floating charge. A floating charge is therefore a most effective and flexible security; it provides security for the lender and allows the company to trade with its assets unencumbered. A company, by virtue of the floating charge, has a distinct advantage over other forms of trading when raising capital. However, if small companies wish to borrow extensively, the directors may be asked to provide personal guarantees for the company's loan; hence their own personal assets may be called upon to repay the loan in the event of the company's financial collapse.

Expense of formation

Neither a sole trader nor a partnership is inhibited by legal formalities when commencing trading. For a company, sizeable fees may be payable because of the need for legal formalities to be followed. A solicitor may be instructed to draft the company's memorandum and articles of association, and a registration fee is payable. Considerable expense is incurred because of the requirement for the annual publication of audited accounts. Furthermore, the duly audited accounts must be filed with the Registrar of Companies, at a fee. Companies make statutory returns to Companies House; their annual accounts must by law be fuller and more complicated than those of a sole trader or a partnership and must be laid out in a statutory format. Minutes of board meetings must be kept and an annual general meeting must be held. The administrative costs of running a business as a company are therefore greater.

Income tax

The sole trader or partner pays income tax under Schedule D (subject to allowances) on all profits, even if they have been reinvested in the enterprise. In a company, directors pay income tax on their salaries under Schedule E. Excess profits can be kept within the company, in which case they are subject to corporation tax. Therefore it may be advantageous to sole traders or partners whose incomes from the business mean that they are taxed under Schedule D at a higher rate to convert the business into a company to minimize the amount of tax to be paid out of the profits made. Whilst this is a clear tax advantage to be considered when forming a company, there are tax advantages to sole trading or trading as a partnership.

1   The national insurance contributions for Schedule D earners (partners and sole traders) are less than the combined contributions of the company and the directors.

2   Schedule D income tax, as paid by partners and sole traders, is paid on a preceding year basis. This is most useful, since it promotes cash flow through the business in the first and early years of trading. The director of a company paying Schedule E income tax does so on a current year basis under the PAYE system.

3   A partner or sole trader paying Schedule D income tax is able to claim more by way of expenses and allowances against income than a Schedule E person earning the same amount.

4   If a partner or sole trader has more than one business enterprise (e.g. two or three small cafés), and one is successful whilst another runs at a loss, the loss incurred by one enterprise may be offset against the tax liability for the successful enterprise. By balancing profits and loss in this way, total tax liability may be reduced. However, if each enterprise is a different company, each company being in itself a separate and distinct legal entity and thus taxed separately, the balancing of profit and loss between the enterprises so as to minimize overall tax liability cannot be achieved. It may be considered advisable with small units which form a chain of enterprises to expand trading by means of partnership or sole trading so that initial losses made in new units may be offset against profit obtained through trading at established units. Balanced against this view one might consider the limited liability offered through trading as a company so advantageous in the event of the business failing that a company is the preferred form of trading.

5   In a family business (such as a tea-room, café, small guest-house or hotel) where
     those working for the business are simply the husband and wife, if the enterprise
     is run on a sole trader basis, the husband, as the proprietor, may claim that his
     wife works in the business as an employee and so she may make use of her
     married woman's earned income allowance against any income she may earn.
     If the business is run as a partnership between the husband and some person
     other than his wife (e.g. his son), the same proposition holds true; the partners
     may employ their wives and take advantage of this form of tax allowance.

Value added tax

VAT is a dirty word among small businesses, mainly because this tax places considerable
administrative burdens upon business people, who often consider themselves to be
unpaid tax collectors. As far as consumers are concerned, they pay VAT when they
make a purchase. As far as business people are concerned, they pay VAT when they buy
goods from other businesses and charge VAT when selling their goods or services.

VAT is charged on what are known as taxable supplies. Not all goods supplied to
a business are taxable; some are exempt, i.e. VAT is not charged on them. Thus
where a business sells another business something which is a taxable supply, the VAT
which that business charges on it is known as output tax. The business to which the
goods are sold (if it is registered for VAT), when it makes its return to Customs
and Excise, claims back the VAT which it has paid on the goods, which is known as
the input tax.

Who must register for VAT? It is the person, not the business, who is registered
for VAT. Each registration covers all the business activities of the registered person.
For VAT purposes, a company is treated as a person. A business is required to register
for VAT if at the end of any month its turnover in the past twelve months exceeds the
VAT threshold.

A business can apply to register for VAT purposes even if the value of its taxable
supplies is below the limit. The Customs and Excise must be satisfied that there is a good
reason for registration, and that the income derived from taxable supplies contributes
substantially to the livelihood of the business.

The practice of 'business splitting' is called 'disaggregation'. The Customs and Excise
have the power to direct that where two or more people purport to trade separately to
avoid registration for VAT, but are really part of a single business, they shall be treated
as a single business for VAT purposes.

What are taxable supplies and what are exempt? Where a business supplies goods and
services these will normally be taxable supplies unless they fall within the category of
being exempt from VAT.

If all the goods and services which the business supplies are exempt, then the business
cannot register for VAT purposes. This also means that the business cannot claim back
VAT on the purchases which it makes. If a business is composed of some taxable and
some exempt supplies, the business will still have to comply with the registration
requirements.

The rate of tax. For taxable supplies there are at present two rates of tax:
(a) the standard rate, which is currently 17.5 per cent; and
(b) the zero rate.

The standard rate is charged unless the government specifies otherwise. Supplies relevant to the hotel and catering industry which are zero rated are food and drink which are *not*:
(a) supplied for catering;
(b) non-essential items, e.g. chocolate and crisps:
(c) hot food to be taken away.

Working out VAT. A business charges VAT on the taxable sales which it makes; this is 'output tax'. The amount of VAT is worked out on the price of the goods supplied by the business.

A business claims back VAT on the goods and services used by the business. VAT *cannot* be reclaimed on certain expenses, e.g. cars or business entertainment expenses.

Registration for VAT requires the business to maintain additional records for VAT purposes which must be kept for six years. These are:
(a) the tax invoice;
(b) a VAT account showing the results for each tax period;
(c) the returns made to Customs and Excise showing the VAT payable or repayable.
If the business fails to keep proper records it may be charged a financial penalty. VAT inspectors will visit registered businesses periodically to ensure that accurate records have been maintained and proper returns made.

Paying VAT. Any VAT which is due to Customs and Excise is payable within one month of the end of the quarterly accounting period. This is so whether or not the business has actually received from its customers the money on which the VAT is due. Late payment of VAT will give rise to severe consequences, in the form of punitive interest charges.

Using the enterprise's money

The restrictions upon the extent to which a person may withdraw money from his or her business vary according to the form of business operated. Clearly, proprietors or sole traders may withdraw as much money from their business funds as they wish; the funds of the business are the same funds as their own. Being sole traders, they are answerable to no one else within the business. Partners may withdraw such funds as they may have agreed with their fellow partners to withdraw. If partners withdraw money from the partnership dishonestly, so as to deprive the partnership permanently of its use, they may, of course, be criminally liable and be prosecuted for theft; see *R. v. Bonner* [1970] 2 All ER 97 (CA). A company director or shareholder is in a more constrained position: the Companies Act forbids loans from the company to directors and reductions in the company's capital.

The size of the enterprise

Sole traders may find that their businesses are retarded in their development by the fact of their being sole traders. They may not be able to raise sufficient capital to fund effective expansion. Hence they are faced with a dilemma: the business may continue to operate at the same level, but without the prospect of expansion, or they may alter the form of business enterprise to a partnership or a company. A company is the most flexible form of business enterprise as far as expansion is concerned. A company may of course have only one director. A company may expand by increasing the share capital and the number of directors.

The nature of the enterprise

If the proposed catering enterprise is novel and the market for the service is uncertain (e.g. the launching of a new type of fast-food outlet), a limited liability company may be the most suitable form of business, since if the venture fails the liability of those concerned with financing the business will be protected. Equally, the catering enterprise may need to be established quickly to take advantage of market trends. If time is of the essence, sole trading or partnership may be the preferred forms, since they require few formalities to commence trading. If trading is likely to be temporary or of uncertain duration (e.g. for one summer season only), sole trading is perhaps the best choice.

It may be that the nature of the enterprise requires substantial investment in capital, equipment or premises. In this instance the size of the venture will determine the form of enterprise. Substantial capital may usually be raised by means of trading as a company.

2.2 THE PROPRIETOR OR SOLE TRADER

Only a 'legal person' can have rights and be subject to duties and obligations under the law. The relevant law recognizes a 'legal person' in either of two forms. An individual is a 'legal person' in the sense that an ordinary man or woman is subject to the laws of the land. Equally, the law recognizes that a company is a discrete and separate legal entity from those individuals who have a financial interest in it. Hence a company has its own legal capacity and is able to contract, etc. in its own right. A sole trader is the proprietor of the business. The business as such is equal to the 'legal person' of the proprietor; he or she is the business. Hence the business debts, and of course the profits, are the proprietor's alone.

Since sole trading is where an individual carries on his or her own business, it is very simple to establish. It is identical to the individual, and the ability of such an enterprise to enter contracts or to be bound by duties or obligations is the same as that of an individual. The only formality required of a person who wishes to commence trading in this way concerns the naming of the business.

Naming the sole trader's business

If one were starting a fast-food outlet aimed at selling sausages of various sorts and sizes prepared in different ways, it is unlikely that one would wish to open one's new premises under the name of the proprietor; 'Alan Pannett's Sausage Café', for instance, hardly has an impressive ring about it for marketing and promotion of this new product and business venture. If one were to choose to operate the enterprise under one's own name there would be no need for any formalities to be observed. If, on the other hand, one wishes to name the fast-food outlet 'The Saucy Sausage', then certain formalities must be observed.

1   Section 4 of the Business Names Act 1985 requires that sole traders who operate their business in any name other than their own must display their own name clearly on all business letters, invoices, receipts, written orders for goods, etc. to be supplied to the business, and written demands for payment of debts owing to the business.

2   On all business letters, etc. there must be included an address within Great Britain where, in the event of legal proceedings being brought against the proprietor, documents may be served. If a proprietor were to trade as 'The Saucy Sausage' and failed to comply with either of the above requirements, then he or she would be liable to criminal prosecution for such a failure.

3   At the business premises, the name and address of the proprietor must be clearly displayed. Such a notice must be displayed at any premises where the business is carried on and to which customers and suppliers have access.

4   The name and address of the proprietor must be supplied to any person who enters into business transactions with the enterprise, or who has entered into discussions with a view to a business transaction. This requirement arises only where such a person demands to know the name and address of the proprietor and not otherwise. Failure to comply with this requirement is also a criminal offence.

Although criminal liability is imposed to ensure compliance with the provisions of s. 4 of the Business Names Act 1985, there is a further sanction, and in practical terms this may be more effective. Section 5 of the Business Names Act 1985 provides that where a person fails to comply with the requirement set out in s. 5 and thereafter seeks to enforce a business contract with a party in default by means of a court action, (a) if the person in default can establish that he or she has a claim against the proprietor, which due to the proprietor's failure to comply with s. 5 he or she has been unable to pursue, or (b) if a breach by the proprietor of s. 5 has caused the person in default some financial loss, the proprietor's claim shall be dismissed, unless it is 'just and equitable' that the proprietor should be allowed to continue the action.

The effect of s. 5, therefore, is to render unenforceable business contracts entered into by the proprietor, where he or she is in breach of the requirements of s. 5 and this breach has caused some 'loss' to the other party. It is clearly a most effective sanction, if proprietors are aware that failure to comply with the requirements under s. 5 may render them unable to enforce what would otherwise normally be enforceable contracts.

2.3 PURCHASING A BUSINESS

It is worth considering the potential legal problems which can arise where a business seeks to expand by purchasing another business.

Illustrative of such problems is the case of *East and Another* v. *Maurer and Another* [1991] 2 All ER 733 (CA). In that case the first defendant owned and managed two successful hair salons in the same town and built up a considerable local reputation as a hair stylist. In 1979 the plaintiffs bought one of the salon businesses for £20 000, being induced to do so in part by a representation made by the first defendant that he

Principles of Hospitality Law

Table 2.1 Some of the advantages and disadvantages of the different forms of business entity.

	Advantages	**Disadvantages**
Sole trader	easy to set up	all personal assets at risk
	accounts are not open to public scrutiny	tends to be seen by other businesses and customers as a small business
	more generous tax treatment than for limited companies	all decisions rest on the individual owner
	tax due may be paid later than in the case of limited companies	tax at the top level is higher than that applying to limited companies
Partnership	as for sole trader	
	risks and decisions can be shared but	risk of partners incurring liabilities which the other partners are liable to meet
	easier to raise finance than in the case of the sole trader and often, in the case of limited companies	
Limited Companies	technically the risk is limited to the amount of share capital invested but	lenders will ask for personal guarantees where the company itself cannot provide sufficient security for any loan – very often the case in a start-up
	creates the impression that the company may be larger than it really is	more legal formalities than is the case for sole traders and partnerships, e.g. to produce memorandum and articles of association and to make annual returns to Companies House
		stricter audit requirements
		responsibilities of company directors are greater than those of sole traders and partners

had no intention of working in the other salon except in emergencies and that he intended to open a salon abroad. In fact the first defendant continued to work full-time at the other salon with such an adverse effect on the plaintiffs' business that it was never profitable and they were forced to sell it in 1989 for £7500. The plaintiffs brought an action for damages against the first defendant and the company through which he traded, alleging breach of contract and fraudulent misrepresentation. The judge found that the representations made by the first defendant were false and awarded the plaintiffs damages of £33 328 consisting of separate awards for the loss incurred on the sale of the business, fees and expenses incurred in buying and selling the business and making improvements, trading losses incurred by the plaintiffs, and disappointment and inconvenience, and an award of £15 000 for loss of profits based on the profits which the first defendant would have made from the salon if he had not sold it, less a 25 per cent deduction for the plaintiffs' lesser experience. The defendants appealed against the award for loss of profits, contending that damages for loss of profits were not recoverable in an action for deceit because such damages were confined to a breach of a contractual warranty of profits and even if they were recoverable the judge had assessed the damages on the wrong basis.

The Court of Appeal held that loss of profits could be recovered in an action for deceit as being actual damage directly flowing from the fraudulent representation. However, they were to be assessed on the basis of compensating the plaintiff for all the loss he had suffered and not, as in breach of contract, on the basis of putting the plaintiff in as good a position as if the statement had been true. Accordingly, the damages for loss of profits were to be assessed on the basis that the first defendant had represented that he would not continue to work as a hair stylist in the immediate area rather than on the basis that he had warranted to the plaintiffs that all the customers with whom he had a professional rapport would remain customers of the plaintiffs' salon. The judge had therefore been right to award damages for loss of profits, but he had assessed those damages on the wrong basis since the proper approach was to assess the profit the plaintiffs might have made if the false representation had not been made, i.e. the profit they might have expected to make in another hair-dressing business bought for a similar sum. On that basis the appropriate measure of damages for loss of profits was £10 000, not £15 000, and to that extent the appeal was allowed.

Although this case deals with an extreme circumstance it is always important to exercise due caution and act only when one has received appropriate legal advice. There are many pitfalls to be considered when purchasing a business such as a public house or a restaurant.

2.4 PARTNERSHIP

A partnership is not a distinct legal person; rather it is a group of individuals who have entered into business with a common aim – profit. The law relating to partnerships is regulated by the Partnership Act 1890. Section 1 of the Partnership Act defines partnership in this way:

> *Partnership is the relationship which subsists between persons carrying on a business in common with a view of profit.*

The intention of the parties entering upon a partnership is seen to be of paramount importance. Section 2 of the Partnership Act 1890 provides that where certain circumstances exist the law presumes that the persons concerned intend to create a partnership. However, where a given circumstance provided for in section 2 exists, this will not of itself affirmatively establish that a partnership exists; it is a matter of fact in each case whether or not there is sufficient evidence to support a presumption of the existence of a partnership. The definition of a partnership provided by s. 1 may be subdivided into three elements.

1   For a partnership to exist there must be a 'business'. Business is defined for the
     purpose of s. 45 of the Partnership Act 1890 as including 'every trade,
     occupation or profession'. Hence the Act is really talking in terms of a
     commercial venture. A single transaction will be sufficient to satisfy s. 45.
2   The business must trade. Section 1 talks in terms of 'carrying on' a business.
     Common sense tells us that this requires some form of trading activity, and
     although this will cover such things as the purchase of raw materials, capital
     equipment, etc., it should be noted that if such actions were merely preparatory
     to the later formation of a company then these cannot be considered as the
     actions of a partnership 'carrying on a business'.

KEITH SPICER LTD v.   X and the defendant agreed to create a limited company in
MANSELL [1970] 1 All   order to run the defendant's restaurant. In pursuance of this
ER 462 (CA)   wish goods were purchased. Later, when they had not been
                             paid for by the defendant, the plaintiff brought an action for
                             payment of the sum due against the defendant. The plaintiff's
contention was that a partnership had existed between the defendant and X at the time the
goods were purchased, prior to the formation of the company, and since the defendant was a
partner, he was fully liable to pay the debt. The Court of Appeal held, however, that there was
no partnership in existence, since no business was being carried on by the defendant and X; on
the contrary, the goods had been ordered in preparation for the formation of a company, and
such transactions could not be considered as 'carrying on a business'.

MARSON (INSPECTOR   It was held that a one-off purchase, and sale three months
OF TAXES) v. MORTON   later, of land that gave rise to a profit was not trade assessable
[1986] 1 WLR 1343   for Schedule D income tax.

3   There must be an intention on the part of the partners to make a profit. If a
     number of people for purely social or philanthropic reasons agreed upon a joint
     plan of action, the purpose of which was not to make a profit, this would not be
     a partnership.

How can we identify a partnership?

A partnership may be entered into either formally, by means of a partnership deed, or informally, simply by verbal agreement or otherwise between partners. We can identify a formal partnership by the partnership deed. With regard to informal partnerships, s. 2 Partnership Act 1890 provides a number of rules whereby we can ascertain the nature of the enterprise and identify whether or not it is a partnership within the scope of the 1890 Act. The rules contained in s. 2 of the 1890 Act may be paraphrased thus:

1   Common or joint ownership of property: s. 2(1) provides that common
     ownership of property is not sufficient in itself to create a partnership. This is so

even if both the joint owners share in the profits made from the property. Section 2(2) provides in like terms for a share in the gross returns from a business or property.

2   Taking a share of the profits: Prior to s. 2(3) of the Partnership Act 1890, the courts had decided that if a person took any share in the profits of a business this made that person a partner. Section 2(3) provides:

> *The receipt by a person of a share of the profits of a business is prima facie evidence that he is a partner in the business but the receipt of such a share, or of a payment contingent on or varying with the profits of a business, does not of itself make him a partner in the business.*

Section 2(3) further provides five particular situations which do not *per se* render the persons involved partners. In each of the five situations the court will consider all the circumstances and decide whether the parties in fact intended that a partnership be brought about.

The formal partnership

There is no legal requirement that a partnership be commenced by a formal written agreement between partners. It is, however, in the best interests of the partners if the partnership is commenced in this way, since the document agreed upon by the partners will make provision for most eventualities which may affect the partnership. Such a document is known as a 'partnership deed' (otherwise known as the 'articles of partnership'). This document indicates the acceptance by each of the partners of the terms and conditions set out in the document. It is these terms and conditions in conjunction with the Partnership Act which will regulate the running of the enterprise. It is the partnership deed which regulates the various legal rights and duties of the partners as between themselves.

The partnership deed

A properly drafted partnership deed should contain articles which seek to regulate the following matters:

(a) the name of the business for the purposes of trading;
(b) management of the business;
(c) financing the partnership;
(d) profits and remuneration of partners;
(e) accountancy procedures and the financial year;
(f) the business premises;
(g) rights and duties of the partners;
(h) termination of the partnership;
(i) disputes between partners.

Rights, duties and liabilities of partners

The partners' rights

The relationship between partners should normally be made clear in the partnership deed. The articles of the partnership deed should clearly state the rights of partners with regard to one another, and the duties which each partner owes to the other members of the partnership. Since not all partnerships are created formally by means of a partnership deed, s. 24 of the Partnership Act 1890 provides for certain rights of partners. Section 24 applies to all partnerships irrespective of the provisions of a given partnership deed.

Partnership property. An individual is not required to contribute either property or capital in order to be a partner. However, once property or capital has been brought into the partnership, the partner as an individual ceases to have any right over the property. Where there is no specific agreement in the partnership deed, all partners, whatever their contribution, are entitled to share equally in the property and capital of the business.

Management. All partners have the right to participate in the management of the firm.

Profits. Each partner is entitled to share in the profits of the business. The proportions in which partners are to share in the profits of the business will normally be set out in the partnership deed. In the absence of an express provision, the profits are to be shared equally.

Remuneration. No partner is entitled, as of right, to a salary for work done for the partnership. Some partnership deeds do, however, expressly provide for the payment of a salary in addition to a share of the firm's profits.

Indemnity. Each partner is entitled to an indemnity for all bona fide expenses incurred on behalf of the partnership.

Accounts. The accounts, records, etc. of the partnership must be kept at the principal place of business, and be held available for inspection by any of the partners.

Membership of the partnership. Any partner may prevent a new partner from being taken into the partnership. Equally, a partner cannot be expelled by the other partners unless there is an express agreement to this effect in the partnership contract.

The partners' duties

A vital component of a partnership is the mutual trust between partners. This is otherwise known as a fiduciary relationship. Since the partners are, in law, agents for the partnership, they may therefore by their actions bind the partnership to a particular course of conduct. The law therefore places duties upon partners which they owe towards the other members of the partnership. These duties seek to regulate the conduct of partners and promote good faith between them.

Disclosure. Partners are under a duty, by s. 28 of the Partnership Act 1890, to disclose to other partners all matters relating to the partnership which are within that partner's knowledge. This duty is of particular importance with regard to money spent by a partner on behalf of the partnership, and funds received by a partner on account of the partnership.

Duty to account. Each partner must deal in partnership affairs with the utmost good faith. Hence partners must inform the other partners of all personal profits which have accrued to them by virtue of their being partners. This is provided for by s. 29 of the Partnership Act 1890.

Competition. Partners must not engage in any form of enterprise which is in competition with the partnership. To do so would be a breach of their fiduciary relationship with the other partners, and contrary to s. 30 of the Partnership Act 1890. A partner who does make a profit through such competition may be required to forfeit such profit and pay the profit over to the partnership.

Care and diligence. There is an implied duty upon partners to exercise reasonable care in the performance of their duties under the agreement. Should partners neglect to do their work or fail to 'pull their weight' through absence, etc,, the other partners are entitled to compensation.

Liabilities of partners

Here we are concerned with the relationship between partners and persons outside the partnership. A partner may be personally bound by legal relations with persons outside the partnership. However, he or she may also render all the partners collectively liable.

Debt. All partners are jointly liable for the partnership's debts. A creditor of the partnership may therefore sue any partner for the full amount of the debt. This may include a partner's tax liability arising from his share of partnership profit.

Prior to the passing of s. 3 of the Civil Liability (Contribution) Act 1978 it was the law that judgment against one partner was a barrier to further proceedings brought against other partners for the recovery of the same partnership debt. However, this barrier was removed by s. 3 of the 1978 Act, the effect of which has been to enable a party to bring an action against any *one* partner for the recovery of the partnership debt irrespective of the liability of other partners.

Where a partner's actions bind the partnership. The partnership will be collectively bound by the actions of a single partner in the following circumstances:
(a) the sale or purchase of goods, being goods either usually employed by the firm for its own business, or in which the firm deals, or goods belonging to the firm;
(b) the settlement and receipt of payment for debts owed to the partnership;
(c) the hiring and dismissal of employees;
(d) the borrowing of money for the partnership's business, or the pledging of partnership property as security for a loan;
(e) the drawing, issuing, receiving and endorsing of negotiable instruments on behalf of the partnership;
(f) engaging the services of a solicitor to defend a legal action brought against the partnership.

Where a partner's actions do not bind the partnership. A partnership will not be bound by the actions of a partner where the partner's actions fall within the following situations:
(a) The execution of a deed on behalf of the firm. Therefore, without express authority by deed, a partner is unable to buy or sell land, or execute a legal mortgage on behalf of the partnership.
(b) A partner may not submit a dispute to arbitration on his or her own authority.
(c) A partner may not by guarantee undertake to pay a debt incurred by another person, on behalf of the partnership.

Closing down the partnership

A partnership may come to an end in any one of a number of different ways, as follows.

Time. A partnership will end with the passing of the fixed period of time set out in the Partnership Deed (s. 32(a) Partnership Act 1890).

Notice. A partnership will end by notice given by a partner of intention to leave the partnership (s. 32(c) Partnership Act 1890).

Bankruptcy. A partnership will cease upon the bankruptcy of any one partner (s. 33(1) Partnership Act 1890).
   An interesting case on bankruptcy of a partnership is *Re Citro (Domenico) A Bankrupt) and Re Citro (Carmine) (A Bankrupt)* [1990] 3 WLR 880 (CA).

In 1985 two brothers, D and C, were adjudicated bankrupt. Their only assets were their half shares of the beneficial interests in their matrimonial homes. D was judicially separated from his wife and she lived in their house together with their three children, the youngest of whom was twelve. C lived in his home with his wife and their three children, the youngest of whom was ten. The debts owing by each of the bankrupts exceeded the values of their interests in the homes. The trustee in bankruptcy of their joint and separate estates applied to the court by notices of motion for declarations as to the beneficial interests in the two properties and for orders under s. 30 of the Law of Property Act 1925 for possession and sale of them. Hoffmann J. declared that in each case the beneficial interest in the property was owned by the bankrupt and his wife in equal shares and he made orders for possession and sale but, after considering the circumstances of the two wives and their children and, in particular, that the half shares to which they would be entitled would be insufficient for them to acquire other accommodation in the area and the educational problems of the children, imposed a provision for postponement until the youngest child in each case attained the age of sixteen.
   On appeal by the trustee in bankruptcy:

Held, allowing the appeal and substituting a period of postponement not to exceed six months (Sir George Waller dissenting), that for the purposes of making an order for sale in favour of a trustee in bankruptcy under s. 30 of the Law of Property Act 1925 no distinction was to be made between a case where a property was being enjoyed as the matrimonial home and one where it had ceased to be so used; that where a spouse, having a beneficial interest in such property, had become bankrupt, the interests of the creditors would usually prevail over the interests of the other spouse and a sale of the property ordered within a short period; that only in exceptional circumstances, more than the ordinary consequences of debt and improvidence, could the interests of the other spouse prevail so as to enable an order for sale to be postponed for a substantial period; and that, accordingly, since the circumstances of the wives and their children, albeit distressing, were not exceptional, the order sought by the trustee should be made.

Death. Any partner's death will bring the partnership to an end.

By court order. Section 35 of the Partnership Act 1890 enables any partner to apply to the court seeking an order that the partnership be dissolved in the following circumstances:
(a) when a partner is, or has become, of unsound mind;
(b) when a partner has become incapable of performing his or her duties;
(c) when a partner has been guilty of misconduct likely to be harmful to the firm's business;
(d) when a partner is guilty of wilful or persistent breach of the partnership deed;
(e) when the business of the partnership can be carried on only at a loss;
(f) whenever the court is of the opinion that in the circumstances it would be just and equitable to dissolve the partnership.

Illegality. Where an event has occurred (e.g. the passing of legislation by Parliament) which renders the business carried on by the partnership unlawful, s. 34 of the 1890 Act provides for the ending of the partnership.

When partners leave the partnership they remain personally liable for all debts incurred during the period of their membership.

Realization and distribution of partnership assets will occur after the dissolution has been brought into effect and all outstanding debts have been settled. The dissolution, taking an account of the distribution of assets, should normally be provided for in the partnership deed.

Section 44 of the Partnership Act makes clear the procedure to be followed for the distribution of assets; s. 44(a) provides:

> *Losses, including losses and deficiences of capital shall be paid first out of the profits, next out of capital and lastly, if necessary, by the partners individually in the proportion in which they were entitled to share profits.*

Section 44(a) deals with cases where the partnership's assets are insufficient to meet its liabilities. In the happier situation where the assets are sufficient, s. 44(b) provides that debts and liabilities to persons outside the partnership are to be settled first: partners' loans should then be repaid; thereafter, partners' capital contributions and finally any surplus assets should be distributed among the partners in the same proportions as they are entitled to take a share in the profits.

Limited partnerships

The essence of limited partnership as a form of business enterprise has been explained on p. 31 in the section on choosing the form of business enterprise. That which sets a limited partnership apart from an ordinary partnership is the fact that provided certain requirements are met 'limited partners' may escape full liability for partnership debts; thus their liability is limited to the extent of their investment in the partnership.

The partnership's name

It is normal for a partnership to trade under the names of the partners. If, however, the partnership trades under a separate name, e.g. 'La Bonne Maison', the provisions in the Business Names Act 1985 will apply. We have discussed these provisions in relation to sole traders in the section on naming a sole trader's business.

2.5 COMPANIES

A company is a distinct and separate 'legal person'. The formation of a company therefore involves the creation of a new legal entity which is able to trade and be responsible for its own actions.

The law relating to companies is regulated by the Companies Acts 1985 and 1989 and other specific legislation, e.g. the Business Names Act 1985, the Insolvency Act 1986.

The various types of companies

We are primarily concerned in the hotel and catering industry with registered companies incorporated and registered under the Companies Act 1985. Registered companies fall into two main categories: public limited companies (PLCs) and private companies. Private companies may be divided into limited and unlimited companies, and private limited companies can be further subdivided into those limited by shares and those limited by guarantee.

Public companies

A public company is one owned by its members; it is not public in the sense that it is nationalized. However, to fall within the category of a public company the company must satisfy the following criteria:
1   The company must have a nominal issued share capital of £50 000.
2   The second clause of the company's memorandum of association must state that the company is a public limited company.
3   The name of the company must include the words 'public limited company' or 'PLC'.
4   There must be a minimum of two members of the company.
5   The company must register (or, where the company is already established, re-register) under the Companies Act 1985.
A public company has a major advantage over a private company in that only public companies are able to offer shares to the public at large, and where possible to be quoted on the Stock Exchange. However, not all public companies are quoted on the Stock Exchange. By virtue of s. 81 of the Companies Act 1985 it is a criminal offence for a private company to offer its shares for sale to the public.

Large hotel and catering organizations, as well as breweries and other large enterprises, fall into the category of public limited companies.

Private companies

Private companies trade on a smaller scale than public companies, although many private companies operate a considerable business organization, e.g. major hotels. The private company was the favoured form of enterprise where the membership of the company was to remain small, and there was a wish to restrict the transferability of share, e.g. within a family business. However, the class of private companies is very broad; a private company under the Companies Act 1985 is any company which is not a public company and which consists of at least two members. Previous restrictions on the transfer of shares in private companies and the limit on the number of members of a private company have been removed. However, by virtue of s. 89 of the Companies Act 1985 both private and public companies which wish to allocate shares for cash must offer these shares for purchase by existing members before offering them outside the company.

A public company, unlike a private company, must be limited by shares. A private company may, however, be limited by shares or limited by guarantee. Alternatively, a private company need not be limited at all, and can trade as an unlimited company.

Limited companies

A fundamental reason for the formation of a company as a form of business enterprise is the protection of limited liability which it affords to members. (For an explanation of limited liability refer to section 2.1.) A limited company is one which provides limited liability for its members. Limited liability may be provided in either of two ways: by shares or by guarantee.

Liability limited by shares. A member's liability is limited to the amount, if any, which remains unpaid upon the member's shares. Since normal practice is for a member to be issued with paid-up shares, the member's liability is limited to the extent that the shares which he or she has in the company are rendered valueless.

Liability limited by guarantee. Where a company is limited by guarantee, the extent of the member's liability is the amount which he or she has pledged to guarantee the company in the event of liquidation. A limited liability company therefore allows its members the privilege of being shielded by the 'corporate veil' from unlimited liability for company debts. An often cited example of how this protection works is as follows.

SALOMON v. SALOMON & CO. [1897] AC 22 (HL)　　Salomon carried on a business as a sole trader. In 1892 he formed a limited liability company to take over his business. The memorandum of association of the new company was signed by Salomon, his wife and his five children, each signatory being issued with one share. The company paid approximately £39 000 to Salomon for the business. The method of payment comprised £10 000 in debentures (secured by a floating charge), 20 000 £1 shares and the remainder in cash. The company later ceased to trade and a liquidator was appointed. The debts owed to unsecured creditors by the company were approximately £8000, whilst the total of the company's assets was only £6000. The unsecured creditors therefore sued Salomon personally for the debts which were owed by the company to them, alleging that the company merely acted as an agent or a 'front' for Salomon himself.

Held:
1　The company incorporated by the memorandum of association was a separate legal entity from Salomon himself.

2   Salomon was not himself fully liable for the company's debts; his liability was limited to the extent of his shares.
3   Salomon, himself a secured creditor of the company, was therefore entitled to the remaining £6000 in company assets as part payment of his secured debentures.

We can see by reference to the *Salomon* case the great advantage of limited liability. Imagine the result if Mr Salomon had continued to trade as a sole proprietor; he would have been personally liable to the full extent for all business debts incurred.

Unlimited companies

If a company is formed without limited liability it will enjoy the benefits of being a corporate personality. Amongst other things:
(a) the company holds its own property;
(b) the company does not die with its membership;
(c) the company can sue or be sued in its own name.
However, the members will be personally liable to the company to the full extent for the debts of the company. Hence the fundamental advantage of incorporation is missing. Imagine what the result would have been in *Salomon*'s case if the company created was one of unlimited liability: all the members would have been personally liable for the debts owned by the company to the creditors.

Starting the company

The formalities required before a company can commence trading are relatively straightforward. However, they are more onerous than the simple formalities involved in undertaking partnership.

Registration

By ss. 10 and 12 of the Companies Act 1985 the memorandum of association, together with the articles of association, are to be delivered to the Registrar of Companies, who retains and registers them. The full list of documents which must be delivered for registration are:
(a) the memorandum (s. 10);
(b) the articles, if any (s. 10);
(c) a statement signed by the subscribers to the memorandum
   (i)   containing the names and particulars of the directors and secretary and a consent signed by each of them to act in the relevant capacity; and
   (ii) specifying the intended situation of the company's registered office (s. 10 and the 1st Schedule);
(d) a statement of capital (s. 47(3) Finance Act 1973);
(e) a statutory declaration of compliance signed by a solicitor engaged in the formation of the company, or a person named as director or secretary in the statement delivered under s. 10 (s. 12(3)).

Once the required documents have been delivered, the registrar, under s. 12(1), must be satisfied that all the requirements of the Act in respect of registration have been complied with. He or she then, in accordance with s. 13(1), issues a certificate of incorporation and, under s. 705, allocates to the company its registered number.

Section 13(3) provides that from the date of incorporation, stated in the certificate, the subscribers to the memorandum become a body corporate with the name contained in the memorandum.

Section 13(7) states that the certificate, once issued, is conclusive evidence that the company has been duly registered. If the certificate contains a statement to the effect that the company is a public company it is conclusive evidence of this fact. The Registrar of Companies must publish notice of the issue of the certificate of incorporation in the *Gazette* (see s. 711). The company is now formed and trading can commence.

Obviously the formalities required to create a company incur costs:
(a) registration fee;
(b) stamp duty of 1 per cent of the actual value of assets of any kind contributed by the members, less any liabilities assumed by the company as consideration for them.

Perhaps the lion's share of the costs of formation is the professional fees of the solicitors and accountants involved in a formation. Where the company to be formed is of a kind which can be purchased 'off the peg' from an agency specializing in company formation, this is a cost-effective way to proceed.

The process of registration enables a private company to commence trading immediately. However, a public company must obtain in addition a trading certificate from the Registrar before it may commence trading.

The memorandum of association

The memorandum of association is of crucial importance to the company, for it is this document which lays down the boundaries of the company's activities. A useful approach is to think of this document as the company's constitution, giving the company power to act in certain ways and limiting its powers in others. Since this document sets out the framework of the company and the purposes for which the company has been established, it is a public document available for inspection at Companies House, where companies are registered.

The contents of the memorandum of association are statutorily laid down by s. 2 of the Companies Act 1985. The document must contain:
(a) The name of the company. If the company is a public company, s. 25(1) requires its name to end with the words 'public limited company', and by s. 1(3) the memorandum must state that the company is to be a public company. If the company is a private company, the last word of its name must be 'limited' (s. 25(2)).
(b) The domicile of the company, i.e. whether the registered office is to be in England and Wales, Scotland or Wales.
(c) The objects of the company.
(d) The limitation of the liability of the members, if the company is limited by shares or guarantee.
(e) Unless the company is an unlimited company, the amount of share capital, divided into shares of a fixed amount.

By s. 2(6) the memorandum must be signed by each subscriber in the presence of at least one witness. Each subscriber must take at least one share, and against his or her name must be shown the number of shares taken (see s. 2(5)). Model forms of memorandum for different types of companies can be found in the Companies (Tables A–F)

Regulations 1985. Table B contains the model form for a private company limited by shares. Section 3(1) requires that the models be followed as closely as circumstances permit.

The company's name. A limited company may register any name it chooses, provided that the word 'limited' appears at the end of it. The Registrar may refuse to register an undesirable name. A public company must use the words 'public limited company' or 'PLC' in its name, and the company's memorandum of association must also state that the company is a public limited company. Public companies are also subject to the provisions of the Business Names Act 1985 if they are trading under a name other than the fully registered name of the company. The reason for the inclusion of the word 'limited' in the title of limited companies is to enable those trading with the company to know that the liability of members of the company with which they are trading is limited.

It is a criminal offence for a company to use a misleading name (s. 33 Companies Act 1985). Equally, it is an offence for a private company to pass itself off as being a public company and vice versa.

As to the choice of name, s. 26 of the Companies Act 1985 prohibits the registration of certain names:

(a) names which include the words 'limited', 'unlimited' or 'public limited company' (or abbreviations thereof) anywhere except at the end of the name;
(b) any name which is the same as a name appearing in the index of names kept by the Registrar of Companies (s. 714);
(c) any name the use of which would in the opinion of the Secretary of State constitute a criminal offence or be offensive.

Once a company has chosen its name it must comply with ss. 348–50 Companies Act 1985 regarding publication. These sections make it compulsory to have the company's name painted on or affixed to the business premises and mentioned on all business documents and negotiable instruments. Non-compliance is punishable by way of a fine.

The registered office. Every company must have a registered office. The fact that the registered office is located in England, Wales or Scotland must be stated in the memo-randum of association, and the full address must be filed with the Registrar of Companies. The importance of the registered office is that it is the address where writs may be served on the company and where communications may be sent. It is also the address at which the following registers and documents must normally be kept:

(a) the register of members;
(b) the register of debenture-holders;
(c) the register of directors and secretaries;
(d) the register of directors' interests in shares and debentures;
(e) the register of charges;
(f) copies of instruments creating the charges;
(g) minute books of general meetings;
(h) the register of interests in shares.

The objects for which the company was formed. The objects clause of the memorandum of association is the most important, since it sets out the purposes for which the company was formed. The general rule was that a company could lawfully do only that which fell within the scope of the objects clause. Should the company do a thing which was outside the scope of the clause it was said to be beyond the company's powers and *ultra vires*. At common law an *ultra vires* act was unlawful and without binding effect and a shareholder could restrain the company from undertaking *ultra vires* activities. A clear example of the *ultra vires* rule is set out in the following case.

ASHBURY RAILWAY CARRIAGE & IRON CO. v. RICHE [1875] LR 7 HL 653

The memorandum of association of the Ashbury Railway Company stated the company's objects to be: 'to make or sell or lend on hire railway carriages, wagons and all kinds of railway plant, fittings, machinery and rolling stock; to carry on the business of mechanical engineers and general contractors, to purchase and sell as merchants timber, coal, metal and other materials, and to buy and sell such materials on commission or as agents'. The directors, on behalf of the company, bought the right to build and run a railway in Belgium. They contracted Riche to do the construction work. Later, when the Ashbury Railway Company ran into financial problems, they declared that they no longer wished to be bound by their contract with Riche. Riche brought an action against the company seeking to enforce the contract.

Held: The House of Lords held that the contract between the Ashbury Railway Company and Riche was outside the scope of the objects clause of the company's memorandum of association. The company's actions in entering into a contract with Riche were *ultra vires*, and therefore the contract between the company and Riche was void and not binding upon either party. Riche could not enforce the contract since the objects clause did not provide for the construction and running of railway systems, only for the manufacture of railway equipment.

Many companies currently in existence have 'objects clauses' in their memoranda of association which run to several pages in an attempt to ensure that the company will have the power to do anything the directors feel it needs to do. The Companies Act 1989 attempts to remove the need for these lengthy clauses by providing that a company's objects may be stated in any manner.

Section 108 of the Companies Act 1989 has amended the *ultra vires* rule previously set out in s. 35 of the Companies Act 1985 by inserting new provisions (ss. 35A, 35B) into that Act. The effect of these changes may be summarized as follows:

- The validity of an act done by a company cannot be questioned on the ground of lack of capacity by reason that the act is beyond the company's objects. This does not prevent members from seeking an injunction to restrain the act from being done, nor does it affect the liability of the directors for such an act (s. 35(1)–(3)CA).
- In favour of a person dealing with a company in good faith, the power of the board of directors to bind the company or to authorize others to do so is deemed to be free from any limitations under the company's constitution (i.e. memorandum of association). This applies only where the person dealing with the company does not know that the action is beyond the powers of the company's directors under its constitution (s. 35A(1)–(3)CA).
- Where the board of directors exceed any limitation on their powers resulting from the 'objects of the company', their actions may be ratified by a special resolution passed by a general meeting of members. Such a resolution does not release the directors or any other person from liability to the company (s. 35A(3)CA).
- A party to a transaction with a company is not bound to enquire whether it is within company's objects or as to any limitation on the powers of its board of directors to bind the company or to authorize others to do so (CA s. 35B). It may arise that the *ultra vires* transaction entered into by the company is one in

which a director or some other person connected with the company has an interest. Section 322A of the Companies Act 1985 now provides that such a transaction is voidable (i.e. can be set aside) by the company unless it is ratified by the company by a special resolution of its members. However, such a transaction is valid as between the company and the other party to it, and the court may on the application of the company or the other party to the transaction, affirm, sever, or set aside the transaction on such terms as the court sees fit (s. 322A(7)CA).

The objects clause of a memorandum of association will normally be drafted in broad terms to enable the directors to have scope to manage the company as they see fit. Two further points arise from s. 110 of the Companies Act 1989 which relate to the breadth of the objects clause:

- A statement in its memorandum of association that the company's object shall be to carry on business as a general commercial company shall mean that its object is to carry on any trade or business whatsoever, and in such a case the company has power to do all such things as are incidental or conducive to the carrying on of any trade or business by it.
- A company may by a special resolution of its members alter its memorandum with respect to the statements of its objects, subject to the power of the court to cancel the alteration.

Liability clause. This simply states, in the case of a limited company, that the liability of members is limited. In the normal trading company, as we have seen, the members' liability will be limited to the amount, if any, unpaid on their shares, but in a company limited by guarantee, it will be limited to the amount which the members have agreed to contribute to the assets in the event of liquidation. This amount will be the sum specified in the capital clause.

Capital clause. This clause must state the company's nominal capital, and how the capital is divided into shares. The figure given in the capital clause of the memorandum is the *nominal* or *authorized* capital of the company. The Act does not state any *minimum figure* for share capital in the case of a private company. This can, in theory, be of any amount, provided the subscribers to the memorandum take at least one share each. The minimum capital for a private company is one penny. In the case of a public company, however, s. 11 requires the capital clause of the memorandum to state a figure which is *not less than the authorized minimum*.

The shares must have a fixed value, which can be any amount. This fixed value is called the nominal value of the shares.

The compulsory clauses of the memorandum are only part of it. The memorandum may have other clauses covering a range of different matters.

The articles of association

The articles of a company are the regulations for its internal management. Sections 3 and 8 of the Companies Act 1985 authorize the Secretary of State to make regulations specifying forms of memorandum and articles for the different categories of registered companies. These regulations are the Companies (Tables A–F) Regulations 1985. The forms of memorandum of association and articles of association are to be found in the Schedule to these regulations.

Section 8 of the 1985 Act deals with the forms of articles. Table A in the Schedule to the Act specifies articles of association for both private and public companies limited by shares. The articles of association as specified in Table A relate to the following aspects of the management of the company:

(a) share (share capital, share certificates, lien on shares, calls on shares and forfeiture, transfer of shares, alteration of share capital, purchase by company of its on shares);
(b) meetings (general meetings, notice of general meetings, proceedings at general meetings, votes of members);
(c) directors (number of directors, alternate directors, powers of directors, delegation of directors' powers, appointment and retirement of directors, disqualification and removal of directors, remuneration and expenses of directors, directors' appointments and interests, directors' gratuities and pensions, proceedings of directors' meetings (including board meetings));
(d) company secretary;
(e) minutes;
(f) company seal;
(g) financial matters (dividends, accounts, capitalization of profits);
(h) notices;
(i) winding up;
(j) indemnity.

A company limited by shares, by s. 7(1) of the 1985 Act, *may* register articles if it so wishes. A company limited by guarantee *must* register. Articles of association must, by virtue of s. 7(3), be signed by the subscribers to the memorandum.

The duties of the subscribers

The duties of the subscribers must at some stage be noted, and since we have already come across three of them, they can now conveniently be listed in full:

1   They must sign the memorandum.
2   They must sign the articles.
3   They must take at least one share each.
4   They normally appoint the first directors.
5   They must sign the statement required by s. 10 on the registration of the company.

The legal effects of the articles

Section 14(1) states that the memorandum and articles of association bind the company and the members as though signed and sealed by each member, and as if they contained covenants by each member to observe their provisions. The effects of the articles of association are:

1   The company is bound to the members *in their capacity as members.*
2   The members *in their capacity as members* are bound to the company.
3   The members are contractually bound to *each other.*
4   The company is *not bound to any person*, except to members in their capacity as members.

Summary

It is appropriate at this stage, having considered the formation and structure of both a partnership and a company, to compare and contrast these two business structures.

1   A limited company is an *artificial legal person*. A partnership is not. It is an association of two or more legal persons, in the same way as a company, but the *association itself* has no legal personality and outsiders deal directly with the members.
2   In a limited company the *liability* of the members is *limited* to the amount unpaid on their shares. In a partnership, the *liability* of the partners is *unlimited* except in the case of a limited partnership, and even then there must be at least one general partner with unlimited liability.
3   A limited company must be *formed by the process of registration*. A partnership may be formed quite *informally*, e.g. orally, or even by conduct, though it is wise to have a written agreement or articles, often called the deed of partnership.
4   In a *public* limited company the *shares* are usually *freely* transferable. In a partnership no partner may transfer his or her share without the *consent* of the others.
5   In a limited company the members are *not ipso facto agents* of the company. In a partnership each partner is an *agent* of the others, and each therefore is also a principal. A partnership is thus a collection of principals and agents.
6   In a limited company the *death or bankruptcy* of a member (or even of all the members) has *no effect* on the existence of the company. In a partnership death or bankruptcy of a partner causes *dissolution* unless the articles provide otherwise.
7   A limited company is subject to many *special rules of law* both statutory and otherwise. The *ultra vires* doctrine is one instance of this. In a partnership the partners are *free* to make any arrangement they like which would be lawful between private persons.

Running the company

There are many complex legal aspects of the running of a company which the nature of this text does not allow time to consider. We shall confine ourselves here to the statutory requirements which must be observed.

Membership

The usual method of investing in a company is by taking shares in it. By taking shares a person becomes a member of the company with voting rights and rights to a dividend. A shareholder is therefore involved in the running of the company, and shares in the profits and losses of the company. If, on the other hand, a person decides to invest in a company by taking debentures (a loan made by the investor to the company which is normally 'secured') that person is not a member of the company and has no involvement in the running of the company.

The rights of members of a company are set out in the articles of association. A principal right of a member is the right to vote on company resolutions. In addition to this right, minority shareholders are afforded further statutory rights by the Companies Act 1985, to ensure that their position is respected by majority shareholders.

Directors

Who is a director? Section 74(1) of the 1985 Act defines a director as 'any person occupying the position of director, by whatever name called'. This defines a director with reference to the functions which he or she performs. A director is an officer of the company and implicitly an agent of the company. A director is *not* an employee of the company and is not entitled to preferential payment when the company goes into liquidation.

How many directors are required? By s. 282 of the 1985 Act every public company must have at least two directors. A private company need have only one. A company which has a sole director is required by s. 283 to have another person as its company secretary. The normal practice is to appoint two or more directors, one of whom is the company secretary.

The appointment of directors. Section 13(5) provides that the persons named in the statement (required by s. 10 upon registration of the company) shall, upon incorporation, be treated as appointed to be the company's directors. By s. 288(1) of the 1985 Act every company must keep a register of its directors at its registered office, giving details of each director – name, address, nationality, business occupation, etc.

The disqualification of a director. The provisions of the Company Directors Disqualification Act 1986 apply here. A disqualification order is an order made by the court forbidding a person from being:
(a) a director of a company; *or*
(b) a liquidator or administrator of a company; *or*
(c) a receiver or manager of a company's property; *or*
(d) in any way, directly or indirectly, concerned in the promotion, formation or management of a company.

DISQUALIFICATION FOR MISCONDUCT. By s. 2 of the 1986 Act the court may make a disqualification order where a person is convicted of an indictable offence in connection with the promotion, formation, management or liquidation of a company. The order may last for a maximum period of 15 years.

By s. 3 of the 1986 Act the court may make a disqualification order where it appears that the person has been persistently in default in delivering returns, accounts or other documents to the Registrar of Companies.

By s. 4 of the 1986 Act a disqualification order may be made by the court in the course of winding up a company, if it appears that the person:
(a) has been guilty of fraudulent trading contrary to s. 458 of the Companies Act 1985;
(b) has been guilty of any fraud in relation to the company while an officer, etc., of the company.
The maximum period of disqualification is 15 years.

Section 5 covers convictions for minor offences, e.g. a failure to deliver a return, account or document to the Registrar of Companies, and may lead to disqualification for a maximum period of five years.

DISQUALIFICATION FOR UNFITNESS. By s. 6 of the 1986 Act the court is required to make a disqualification order against a director when satisfied:

(a) that he or she is or has been a director of a company which has at any time become insolvent (whether while he or she was a director or subsequently); and
(b) that his or her conduct as a director makes him or her unfit to be concerned in the management of a company.

A company becomes insolvent for the purposes of this section if:
(a) the company goes into liquidation at a time when its assets are insufficient for the payment of its debts and other liabilities and the expenses of the winding up; *or*
(b) an administration order is made in relation to the company; *or*
(c) an administrative receiver of the company is appointed.

The minimum period of disqualification is two years and the maximum period is 15 years.

DISQUALIFICATION FOR OTHER REASONS. Section 10 of the Company Directors Disqualification Act 1986 and s. 213 of the Insolvency Act 1986 together provide that if in the course of winding up it appears that any business of the company has been carried on with intent to defraud creditors of the company or other persons, or for any fraudulent purpose, the liquidator may apply to the court for a declaration that any persons who were knowingly parties to such fraudulent trading are liable to make such contributions to the company's assets as the court thinks proper. By s. 10 of the Company Directors Disqualification Act 1986 the court has the power to make a disqualification order against the person concerned, up to a maximum period of 15 years.

Section 18 of the Company Directors Disqualification Act 1986 requires officers of courts to give particulars of cases where a disqualification order is made. The Secretary of State must maintain a register of such orders which is open to inspection.

Removal of directors. Section 303 of the Companies Act 1985 provides that a company may by ordinary resolution remove a director before the expiration of his or her period of office and despite anything in the company's articles or in any agreement between the company and the director. There is one exception for certain directors of private companies.

The intention of the section is clear: the shareholders must have power to remove the board. However, the director so removed is not without remedy. Section 303(5) provides that the section does not deprive the director of the right to sue for damages for breach of contract, if in fact he or she has one.

The legal position of a director. Certain legal rights and duties arise from undertaking the post of director of a company:
1   A company cannot make a loan to a director of the company (see s. 330).
2   A director is an agent of the company and is therefore under a duty not to make a secret profit from the company.
3   A director owes a fiduciary duty to the company; there is nothing which a director can do in his or her capacity as a director which is not required to be done in good faith for the benefit of the company.
4   A director owes a duty to take reasonable care in the discharge of his or her duties as a director.

The role of managing director. The articles of association will usually authorize the appointment of a managing director. The MD will normally be an executive director, with a contract setting out his or her powers and duties, and terms of employment; thus the MD has a dual role – that of director and that of an employee.

The company secretary. The company secretary is an officer of the company, one which every company is required to have by s. 283 of the 1985 Act. The secretary is the chief administrative officer of the company. The status of this role is recognized by s. 286 of the 1985 Act, which in effect requires the secretary of a public company to be a qualified individual.

Meetings

Ultimate control in a company rests in its members; they make up the company. Directors, although often members themselves, are answerable to the majority of shareholders for their actions. Control of company actions is provided for by a general meeting of shareholders. The arrangements for such a meeting are normally set out in the articles of association of the company.

An annual general meeting (AGM) of shareholders must be held in each calendar year, and not more than 15 months may elapse since the previous AGM (s. 366 Companies Act 1985). The AGM will be convened by the company secretary, who must give at least 21 days' notice. A certain number of members must be present before a meeting is said to be quorate and can proceed.

The Companies Act 1985 does not specify in detail the business to be transacted at an AGM but it will normally include:
(a) annual report presented by the chair;
(b) declaration of a dividend, if any;
(c) adoption of the auditor's annual account;
(d) election of directors and auditor.
A complete record of the business transacted at the AGM must be filed with the Registrar of Companies.

An extraordinary general meeting (EGM) may be convened by the directors if some business of special importance has arisen that warrants a meeting of members, or upon the request of members holding 10 per cent of the voting power of a general meeting.

Accounts and company records

The Companies Act 1989 requires a company to keep accounting records which give a true and fair view of the financial position of the company. In Parts I and II of that Act provision is made for a new form of 'annual returns'. A company must also keep the following 'statutory books':
(a) register of members;
(b) register of debenture holders;
(c) register of charges;
(d) minute books;
(e) register of directors' interest;
(f) register of directors' service contracts;
(g) register of substantial individual interests.
These records must be kept at the company's registered office.

Abolition of requirement for company seal

The requirement for a company in England and Wales to have a common seal was abolished on 31 July 1990.

Although a common seal may still be used to execute a document, a document signed by a director and the secretary, or by two directors, and expressed (in whatever form of words) to be executed by the company will have the same effect as if executed under the common seal of the company. The change is effected by the bringing into effect of s. 130 of the Companies Act 1989, which substitutes a new s. 36, and inserts a new s. 36A, into the Companies Act 1985.

Section 1 of the Law of Property (Miscellaneous Provisions) Act 1989 came into effect at the same time. This abolished the need for individuals to seal deeds. A deed is signed and that the signature is witnessed and attested. For both companies and individuals a new requirement is introduced for deeds: that the instrument must make it clear 'on its face' that it is intended to be a deed.

Private versus public companies

In the hotel and catering industry small businesses formed as private companies can easily grow, through successful management, to form very sizeable businesses. The company is then faced with the prospect of stepping from private ownership to public ownership to ensure future prosperity.

A private company differs from a public company in a considerable number of ways. Following from the Companies Acts of 1980 and 1981, it is much more advantageous to register as a private company. Thus a private company may not always consider it advantageous to 'go public'.

Closing down the company

Because a company is a distinct legal person, created by a legal procedure, it can be brought to an end only by further legal processes. A company may be brought to an end by one of the methods of dissolution. These methods include, but are not limited to, winding up, otherwise known as liquidation (see p. 63).

The Insolvency Act 1986 covers the procedures to be followed when closing a company. It should be noted that, while many companies which go into liquidation are insolvent (i.e. cannot pay their debts in full), insolvency is not an essential ingredient of liquidation. All the provisions relating to winding up are contained in the Insolvency Act, regardless of whether or not the company is actually insolvent.

There are two methods of winding up (s. 73(1) Insolvency Act 1986):
1   Voluntary winding up;
    (a)   a members' voluntary winding up;
    (b)   a creditors' voluntary winding up.
2   Compulsory liquidation, i.e. winding up by the court.
The major legislative provisions on insolvency are contained in Part IV of the Insolvency Act 1986 and the Insolvency Rules made pursuant to s. 411 of the Act. These provisions cover:
(a) court procedure;
(b) notices;

(c) the liquidator and his or her functions;
(d) proof of debts;
(e) distribution of company assets;
(f) financial matters, e.g. liquidator's fees;
(g) criminal offences for non-compliance.

Liquidation is not the only option available to a company. Two others exist:
(a) company voluntary arrangements;
(b) administration order.

These are provided for in Part I of the Insolvency Act 1986.

Voluntary arrangements

Sections 1–7 of the Insolvency Act 1986 relate to a procedure whereby a company which is nearly or actually insolvent may resolve its financial difficulties to the satisfaction of its creditors without incurring the expense and adhering to the formalities otherwise involved under the Act.

Administration orders

An administration order is designed to help a company which is likely to become or actually is insolvent to survive as a going concern, or if this is not possible to ensure an advantageous realization of the company's assets. The provisions regarding administration orders are contained in ss. 8–27 of the Insolvency Act 1986.

What is an administration order? It is an order of the court directing that, for the duration of the order, the affairs, business and property of the company shall be managed by an administrator appointed by the court.

When can an administration order be made? The court may make an administration order if:
1 it is satisfied that the company is or is likely to become unable to pay its debts; and
2 it considers that the making of an order would be likely to achieve one or more of the following purposes
   (a) the survival of the company, or part thereof, as a going concern;
   (b) the approval of a voluntary arrangement;
   (c) the sanctioning of a compromise or arrangement between the company and its creditors or members under s. 425 of the Companies Act 1985;
   (d) a more advantageous realization of the company's assets than would be achieved by winding up.

An administration order cannot be made in relation to a company which has gone into liquidation (s. 8(4) Insolvency Act 1986).

How is an administration order obtained? The application for an administration order is made under s. 9 of the Insolvency Act 1986, by a petition presented to the court by the company, its directors, or a creditor (or creditors). Even if the court is satisfied that there is a real prospect that one or more of the purposes (set out above) can be satisfied, it still retains a discretion as to whether or not to make an administration order.

The effects of an administration order. As the purpose of an administration order is to give the company the necessary breathing space to achieve one or more of the purposes for which the order was made, the Act contains provisions designed to preserve the status quo and protect the property of the company against claims by creditors while the administrator attempts to achieve the purpose of the administration order. By s. 10 of the Act, during the period beginning with the presentation of the administration petition and the making of the order or dismissal of the petition:

(a) no resolution may be passed or order made for the winding up of the company;
(b) no steps may be taken to enforce any security over the company's property, or to repossess goods in the company's possession under any hire purchase agreement (defined widely and including conditional sale agreements, chattel leasing and retention of title agreements), except with the leave of the court and subject to such terms as the court may impose;
(c) no other proceedings, or execution or other legal process may be commenced or continued, and no distress may be levied against the company or its property except with the leave of the court and subject to such terms as the court may impose. The question whether a landlord can peaceably re-enter is not clear; it would be prudent to apply for leave.

The moratorium created by presentation of the petition does not prevent:

(a) the presentation of a winding up petition – it has, however, been held that a winding up petition cannot be advertised during this period;
(b) an administrative receiver may be appointed by a floating charge holder. If this happens, the court *must* then dismiss the administration petition unless either:
    (i)   the party that appointed the administrative receiver consents to the making of the administration order (something which is not likely to happen); or
    (ii) the security under which the administrative receiver was appointed was void or released.

The consequences of an administration order being made are as follows:

(a) any outstanding petition for the winding up of the company is dismissed;
(b) any administrative receiver of the company automatically ceases to be the receiver and must vacate office;
(c) any receiver of part of the company's property (e.g. a Law of Property Act 1925 receiver appointed to collect rent) must vacate office if the administrator requires him to do so;
(d) no resolution can be passed or order made for the winding up of the company;
(e) no administrative receiver, Law of Property or any other kind of receiver can thereafter be appointed;
(f) no other step may be taken to enforce any security over the company's property or to repossess goods in the company's possession under any hire purchase agreement, except with the consent of the administrator or the leave of the court and subject (where the court gives leave) to such terms as the court may impose;
(g) no other proceedings, and no execution or other legal process may be commenced or continued, and no distress may be levied against the company or its property except with the consent of the administrator or the leave of the court and subject (where the court gives leave) to such terms as the court imposes;
(h) an application to register a charge out of time over assets of the company will normally be refused.

The administrator is given extremely wide powers under the Act. In general, he may:
(a) do all such things as may be necessary for the management of the affairs, business and property of the company;
(b) remove any director of the company and appoint any person to be a director of it (to fill a vacancy or otherwise);
(c) call any meeting of the shareholders or creditors of the company; and finally
(d) consent to secured or unsecured creditors enforcing their rights.

Voluntary winding up

A voluntary winding up will occur in any of four situations:
(a) where the specific period for which the company was incorporated has expired;
(b) on the occurrence of a specified event which the articles of association determine will bring the company to an end;
(c) where a special resolution has been passed by members to wind up the company;
(d) where there has been an extraordinary resolution to the effect that the company cannot meet its liabilities and should therefore be wound up.

A voluntary winding up may be a members' winding up or a creditors' winding up. The financial circumstances of the company will determine which it is to be; a creditors' winding up will normally occur where the directors fail to register a declaration of solvency and the majority of creditors agree to petition the court for a dissolution of the company.

The consequences of a voluntary winding up. The following consequences arise from a voluntary winding up:

1   The company ceases to carry on business.
2   The powers of the directors cease on the appointment of a liquidator.
3   Where the liquidation arises from insolvency, the company's employees will be dismissed. If they are retained by the liquidator, this will be under a new contract of employment.
4   The liquidator or a creditor of the company is able to apply to the court to decide upon any question arising in the winding up and to exercise those powers which the court might exercise in a winding up by the court.

Winding up by the court

Section 122(1) of the Insolvency Act 1986 provides that a company may be wound up by the court if:
(a) the company has passed a special resolution to that effect;
(b) the company does not commence business within one year from incorporation or suspends business for a whole year;
(c) the number of members is reduced below two;
(d) the company is unable to pay its debts;
(e) the court is of the opinion that it is just and equitable that the company should be wound up.

The most common ground for a winding up by the court is a company's inability to pay its debts.

When is a company considered unable to pay its debts? A company is deemed unable to pay its debts, by s. 123 of the Insolvency Act 1986, where:

(a) a creditor for more than £750 has served on the company a demand for the sum due, and the company has for three weeks failed to pay the debt;
(b) a creditor has judgment for a debt, execution of which is unsatisfied;
(c) the court is satisfied that the company is unable to pay its debts as they fall due;
(d) the court is satisfied that the value of the company's assets is less than the amount of its liabilities.

The procedure for winding up by the court. Section 124 of the Insolvency Act provides that a winding up petition may be presented to the court by:
(a) the company itself, where a special resolution has been passed;
(b) the directors of the company;
(c) a creditor.
The court, when hearing the petition, may dismiss the petition, adjourn the hearing, or make any order which it thinks fit.

The consequences of a winding up order. Where a winding up order is granted the following are the consequences of granting the order:
1   Any disposal of company property or transfer of shares, etc., is void.
2   Any execution of judgment against company property is void.
3   A copy of the winding up order must be sent to the Registrar of Companies immediately, and he or she is required to publish it.
4   Any legal actions against the company are stayed.
5   The official receiver becomes the liquidator of the company.
6   The directors cease to have power.
7   The company's employees are dismissed.

The official receiver

Official receivers, appointed by the Secretary of State for Trade and Industry, are attached to courts. By s. 136 of the Insolvency Act 1986 the official receiver automatically becomes the liquidator of the company upon the granting of the winding up order. Following s. 131 of the Act a statement of affairs, in the prescribed form, must be submitted to the official receiver by the officers of the company.

As liquidator, the official receiver's function is to ensure that the company's assets are got in, sold and distributed to the creditors and other persons properly entitled. By s. 144 of the Insolvency Act 1986 the liquidator obtains custody and control of the company's property. He or she does not obtain ownership, unless this is given by a court order.

The full powers of the liquidator are to be found in s. 167 of the 1986 Act.

Payment of debts

In order to have a claim for payment a creditor must prove the debt owed to him or her by the company. There are detailed rules setting out how proof is to be established. It is important to note that the law gives preference to certain debts owed by the company before non-preferred debts are paid off. Section 175(1) of the Insolvency Act 1986 states that the preferential debts must be paid in priority to all other debts. The expenses of the winding up must always be met first; thereafter all preferred debts rank equally if sufficient funds are available to meet them, otherwise the following 'pecking order' is observed:

(a) debts owed to the Inland Revenue;
(b) debts due to HM Customs & Excise, invariably VAT;
(c) social security contributions;
(d) monies owed by the company as contributions to pension schemes;
(e) wages and salaries payable to employees for the preceding four months.
Interest payable up to the date of winding up is included as part of the debt.

Notifying the public

Section 188(1) of the Insolvency Act 1986 requires that where a company is in liquidation, every business document on which the name of the company appears must state that the company is being wound up.

Company fraud, etc.

To discourage and prevent unjust and criminal practices, and to make provision for the punishment of those who indulge in them, ss. 206–11 of the Insolvency Act 1986 make stringent provisions for company fraud and deception. These offences are ones of which a past or present officer of a company in liquidation can be found guilty.

Section 212 makes provision for the court to compel past and present officers of the company to restore monies or property misapplied, or to contribute such a sum as the court thinks just by way of compensation.

The court may impose personal liability for a company's debts on:
1   Persons who have knowingly been parties to the carrying on of the company's business to defraud creditors. This is known as fraudulent trading.
2   Directors who ought to have realized that insolvent liquidation was inevitable, but who failed to take the necessary step to minimize the potential loss to creditors. This is known as wrongful trading.

The franchise

The franchise is a form of business which has grown up in recent years and offers the would-be entrepreneur what may at first sight appear to be an easy way to start up in business. The perceived advantages of a franchise are:
1   The business format has been tried and tested; thus the problems normally encountered in starting up a business have been overcome.
2   The risk of business failure is reduced in a franchise.
3   The franchisee receives ongoing advice and support from the franchisor.
4   The business will have a recognized brand name to sell, one which is supported by marketing activity for all franchisees.
5   Training is offered by the franchisor; thus the entrepreneur has a helping hand to assist in the early stages and thereafter.
6   Because of the scale of the business, a franchisor has considerable negotiating power with suppliers. The benefits of these cost savings can be passed on to the franchisee.

Operating as a franchise may, however, have a number of disadvantages:
1   An initial fee is payable to the franchisor, as well as a percentage of the annual profits.
2   The franchisor controls and therefore limits the scope of the franchise and the methods of business operated.

3   The franchisor is the supplier of stock to the business, which limits the scope of
    the franchisee to find more competitive suppliers.
4   Sale of the franchise may not always be easy.

Starting a franchise

The initial cost of a catering franchise in the fast-food industry may be extremely high,
depending on the product and its profile within the market. Initial costs can be
between £¼ and £½ million. Usually the initial fee payable to the franchisor is between
5 per cent and 10 per cent of the total investment.

The fees payable by a franchisee to the franchisor include an initial fee which gives
the franchisee the right to use the brand name within the specified territory, product
training and advice on starting up the business. A service fee is payable on sales made
by the franchisee. This varies according to the franchise. but averages between 10 and
12 per cent.

Advertising is a major cost in any business; with a franchise the franchisee hopes to
make the most effective use of the franchisor's resources to raise the profile of the
franchise and the product it sells. The media coverage available to a large franchise
operation is vastly different from that available to a small restaurant or hotel. It is
normal for the franchisor to charge the franchisee an advertising levy for promoting
the product and the franchise.

Under the franchise agreement the franchisor grants the franchisee the right to sell
the product in a particular territory. If the premises are a fast-food outlet, the territory
is delimited by limiting or excluding other outlets within a certain distance of those
premises.

Training and product support are an essential part of a franchise agreement. The
'helping hand' offered by the franchisor is often perceived as a key reason for the
franchisee entering a franchise agreement.

The franchise agreement

The franchise agreement contains clauses covering the following aspects of the business:
(a) the business name and the use to which the name can be put;
(b) the territory within which the franchisee can operate;
(c) the period of time for which the franchise is granted;
(d) the initial fee to be paid by the franchisee for the franchise, the service fee and
     the advertising levy;
(e) the limitations on the scope of the business, including the franchisee's right to
     sell or transfer the franchise;
(f) terms which put the agreement into effect, including sales targets, the purchase
     of supplies from the franchisor, quality control, training and franchise support,
     and management and advisory services.

CASE STUDY

The Blue Parrot is a well-known café in Walford. All its business is carried out under
that name.

1   How should it be possible to find the name(s) of the owner(s) of the Blue Parrot?
2   Discovery of the ownership of the Blue Parrot will enable a person to know the form of business organization which is behind it. What might this be?
3   In the event of the Blue Parrot closing down through lack of business, what, if any, is the significance to its creditors of the form of business organization by which the café was run?
4   If you were considering (either by yourself or with others) taking over the Blue Parrot, what factors would influence you in deciding which form of business organization to select?

Key points

1   How should it be possible to find the name(s) of the owner(s) of the Blue Parrot?
The Business Names Act 1985 makes provision for the declaration of the names of the owners of a business (see p. 39).
   If the Blue Parrot is a company the names of the directors of the company are registered with the Registrar of Companies (ss. 10–13 Companies Act 1985) (see p. 50).
2   Discovery of the ownership of the Blue Parrot will enable a person to know the form of business organization which is behind it. What might this be?
The possible forms of business organization behind the 'Blue Parrot' are:
(a) sole trader (see p. 38);
(b) partnership (see p. 41);
(c) limited liability company (see p. 49).
The Blue Parrot may be operated in any of these forms. It may also be a franchise of a large company which is operated as a limited liability company (see p. 65).
3   In the event of the Blue Parrot closing down through lack of business, what, if any, is the significance to its creditors of the form of business organization by which the café was run?
The significance to the creditors of the form of business organization rests on the issue of limited liability (see p. 30). If a sole trader or a partnership goes bankrupt the sole trader or partners respectively are fully liable for the debts of the business. With a limited liability company the liability of the directors for the debts of the company is limited. Where a company is insolvent, the Insolvency Act 1986 applies (see pp. 60–65).
4   If you were considering (either by yourself or with others) taking over the Blue Parrot, what factors would influence you in deciding which form of business organization to select?
The factors which would influence you in deciding on the form of business include:
(a) financing the business;
(b) grants and government assistance;
(c) taxation and VAT;
(d) formalities when starting the business;
(e) risk and limitation of liability.
These factors are fully explained on pp. 30–50.

THREE

Hotel and catering premises

The decision to embark upon a hotel or catering enterprise and the form that business will take are closely linked with the acquisition of suitable premises. Indeed the type of enterprise envisaged will normally determine the kind of premises required. Catering entrepreneurs will have three choices: first, to take over an existing catering establishment as a going concern and adapt the premises as they see fit; secondly, to convert already existing premises to be used as a catering establishment, such premises being derelict or presently used for some other purpose; and thirdly, to have purpose-built premises designed by an architect and built to their specifications. In any of these circumstances the entrepreneur is advised to seek expert advice from a solicitor. The acquisition of premises and their conversion to a specific use may on occasions raise complex legal issues; the acquisition of an establishment as a going concern may involve different, though equally perplexing issues including Value Added Tax and employment concerns. The points set out below are not intended to be a full explanation of the intricacies of the acquisition of premises and their use as a catering enterprise; they are designed to illustrate some of the legal issues involved.

3.1 ACQUISITION OF PREMISES

A fundamental question to be considered when embarking on any form of business is whether to buy or rent the business premises. Since the passing of the Law of Property Act 1925 there are only two legal estates in land:
(a) freehold, the proper name for this being 'the fee simple absolute in possession';

(b) leasehold, the proper name for this being 'a term of years absolute'.

Hence one may have freehold possession (i.e. ownership) or leasehold possession (i.e. tenancy). Ownership connotes outright purchase. A tenancy connotes the payment of rent. The right to occupy premises may also arise under a contractual licence where a periodic fee akin to rent will be paid. Such licence arrangements will not usually, however, involve sufficient security of tenure to justify embarking upon a long-term business venture from the premises.

Freehold possession

Freehold possession (ownership) describes the situation where the freeholder or owner has more control over the premises than any other person or organization. Ownership does not give the owner absolute rights over the property in question, since in some cases others may also have rights over the property; e.g. Lord Bogside may be the freeholder of Wychwood Manor, including five acres of parkland, yet the owner of the neighbouring property, Wormwood Cottage, may have a right of way to cross over Lord Bogside's land.

The owner of land must have due regard for others who occupy adjoining property. Whilst one of the rights of owners is to use the land which they own as they please, there are restrictions on their use of land due to the rights of others. A person has a right of use and enjoyment of his or her property. Therefore, if the owner of the Wayward Inn, by using the premises as a hostelry, unlawfully interferes with another's use or enjoyment of his or her land, or some right over or in connection with that land, the other will have a right of action under the tort of private nuisance against the owner of the Wayward Inn. Only a person entitled to the quiet enjoyment of land may bring an action for private nuisance, so the occupant of the property affected by the nuisance is the person who should bring the action. It is sufficient for that person to establish that he or she has been prevented to an appreciable extent from enjoying the ordinary comforts of life; there is no need to establish direct injury to health. The types of annoyance to the quiet enjoyment of an occupier are infinite. It may be argued that the use of premises as a disco or late-night entertainment venue, especially if such premises are in a residential area, may amount to a nuisance to adjoining occupiers.

We have considered the tort of private nuisance; public nuisance should also be mentioned. This is some unlawful action or omission endangering or interfering with the lives, comfort, property or common rights of the public. An example might be obstruction of the highway, as in *A-G* v. *Gastonia Coaches* (*The Times*, 12 November 1976). Hence if a wine bar in a residential area attracted such patronage that the patrons of the wine bar blocked access to residents' driveways by parking their cars, this is a potential public nuisance. Public nuisance is a crime as well as a tort. Either criminal or civil proceedings may be brought by the Attorney General. Any private individual who has suffered particular damage as a result of the nuisance (i.e. damage over and above that suffered by the public as a whole) may bring a civil action in tort to seek the abatement of the nuisance and recover damages for loss already sustained.

Aside from issues of private and public nuisance, the right, conferred by ownership of a freehold estate may be diluted by the existence of third party rights of another kind and also by statutory restraints. These are matters which need to be investigated by a solicitor before a freehold purchase is made. Such third party rights principally consist either of easements over the land or the benefit of restrictive covenants affecting the land.

Easements

These amount to the rights of others over the owner's land. Easements include not only rights in the nature of access and drainage but also the right to light. Hence if the construction of the building which is to be the catering premises shuts out light to the adjoining premises it thereby infringes the rights of the neighbours and gives rise to a cause of action for contravention of their easement of light. Easements may cover such things as the erection of advertising hoardings, etc., on the premises of the owner. Interference with an easement may result in a claim for damages or injunctive relief.

Covenants

Restrictive covenants amount to a restriction on the use of the owner's land for the benefit of an owner of other land. Covenants also appear in leases where the person letting the property includes terms in the lease which restrict the person renting the property as to the use he or she can make of the property, e.g. the premises are to be used only for storage, not for retailing goods. A breach of covenant may again result in the third party seeking an award of damages or an injunction.

Statutory restraints

There are various statutory restraints on the manner in which freeholders may use their premises. The local authorities have in recent times been empowered to control both the use to which property is put and the maintenance of premises. Under the Public Health Acts building regulations have been imposed which cover the quality of materials and procedures to be followed during construction. Furthermore, by means of various statutes, e.g. the Fire Safety and Places of Sport Act 1987, etc., Parliament has placed in the hands of local authorities the power to control the condition and usage of business premises. Permission to 'develop' land must now be obtained from the local planning authority prior to building work or any material change in the use of a building. Hence, building, converting or redeveloping premises (or simply changing the use to which premises are put) requires permission (see the section on planning permission on p. 74).

We can see that, whilst freeholders have substantial rights over the property which they own, these rights are by no means absolute. Even the primary right of freedom to dispose of the property as the owner wishes is not absolute. Can owners be forced to sell? Indeed they can. Public bodies may apply for a compulsory purchase order in respect of certain property. The Secretary of State must be convinced before confirming such an order that the granting of the order is in the public interest. The purpose of making such orders is to enable public bodies to carry out their function, e.g. the building of highways, etc. Hence if the Roundabout Motel were to find itself traversed by the proposed M15 bypassing Seachester, it may be compulsorily purchased after the holding of the requisite public inquiry and the approval of the M15 route.

Leasehold possession

This form of possession describes the situation where a tenant (otherwise known as a lessee) occupies the property of another, the landlord (or lessor). Landlords are usually the freehold owners of the property (or they may themselves be the tenants of the freehold owners). The landlords are therefore entitled to all those rights of ownership other than those which they grant to the tenants under the lease, and those which they are prevented from exercising due to statutory restrictions imposed by the Rent Acts, etc. The lease granted by the landlord to the tenant gives the tenant exclusive possession of the premises for a fixed period of time, at the end of which (subject to any statute which provides otherwise) the property reverts to the landlord. The tenants will normally be answerable to the landlord for the use they make of the property, and certain restrictions are normally agreed upon and are contained in the covenants in the lease. The tenant is, of course, subject in the same way as the freeholder to statutory restrictions imposed upon the use of the premises, e.g. Fire Precautions Act 1971. The respective rights and duties of the landlord and tenant, e.g. the duty to maintain and repair, are set out in covenants in the lease. The landlord, being in the stronger bargaining position (even in the commercial setting), may be able to impose onerous requirements upon the tenant by means of covenants in the lease. The normal forms of express covenant contained in a lease include amongst others a covenant to repair by the tenant, and a covenant that the tenant will not sublet the premises. Covenants, though not expressly stated in the lease, may be implied from the fact of a lease being entered into. Such implied covenants include:
(a) a covenant to pay rent;
(b) a covenant not to repudiate the landlord's title or ownership.
Implied covenants are of little significance with regard to business tenancies, since business leases are usually comprehensive and expressly deal with many points which would otherwise be implied.

The aspects of fundamental importance to an entrepreneur when seeking to establish a business in leasehold premises are the amount of rent payable for the premises, the length of the lease and security of tenure. Obviously entrepreneurs will seek to pay the cheapest possible rent in order to minimize costs; moreover, they will seek to establish a fixed rent for the duration of the lease, so that the money paid in rent can easily be forecast when planning the business. In times when there is moderate inflation a fixed rent means that the real cost of the lease decreases over the period of the lease. However, most leases incorporate a rent review clause which provides for the periodic raising of the rent. The question of the Rent Acts' regulation of tenancies is in the main irrelevant, since this legislation applies primarily to domestic tenancies, and business tenancies are outside the scope of the Rent Acts.

Security of tenure is, however, provided by legislation, namely Part II of the Landlord and Tenant Act 1954 as amended by the Law of Property Act 1969. Business tenants within the scope of the 1954 Act are entitled (save in certain circumstances) to a new tenancy at the end of the old one. This is so even if the landlord is otherwise unwilling to grant a new tenancy. Hence if, when the lease of The Country Tearooms comes to an end, the tenant, Ms Prim, wishes to renew the tenancy and the landlord is unwilling to do so, Ms Prim may apply to the local county court for a new tenancy based upon the terms of the tenancy which has just expired. The protection afforded by the 1954 Act applies to the majority of business tenants, even where the tenant is a company rather than an individual.

An exception to the protection of the 1954 Act was licensed premises where the primary purpose was to sell alcohol. However, hotels, restaurants and other places of entertainment where the substantial proportion of the business consisted of transactions other than the sale of intoxicating liquor came within the 1954 Act. The Landlord and Tenant (Licensed Premises) Act 1990 repeals s. 43(1)(d) of the 1954 Act, which provided the above exemption, so licensed premises will no longer be excluded from the 1954 Act. The 1954 Act now applies to any tenancy of licensed premises granted after 11 July 1989, and to any tenancy granted before that date which still subsisted on 11 July 1992.

The landlord may, of course, resist the granting of a new tenancy to the existing tenant on the basis of certain grounds provided for by the Act:

(a) where the tenant has failed to comply with repairing obligations under the existing tenancy;
(b) where the tenant has persistently delayed in paying rent which has fallen due;
(c) where the tenant has substantially breached obligations under the current tenancy;
(d) where the tenant has been offered suitable alternative premises by the landlord;
(e) where the tenant occupies only part of premises, and therefore the landlord is suffering financially by not being able to let the property as a whole;
(f) where the landlord requires the premises for demolition or reconstruction;
(g) where the landlord personally intends to occupy the premises for business or residence, and has been the landlord for five years or more.

Compensation for disturbance may be payable if the tenant is precluded from obtaining a new tenancy on ground (e), (f) or (g).

Where the County Court grants a new lease to the tenant it may not impose a lease for a period exceeding 14 years. The parties may, however, agree upon a longer period and generally agree some or all of their own terms. In the majority of cases the Court does not have to set the terms and where it does it is usually in respect only of matters where there is an outstanding disagreement between the parties. The terms will normally mirror those in the original lease, except that the County Court has the power to increase the rent payable. The court does not, however, have the power to create a more extensive lease than the original expired lease. If the landlord succeeds in opposing the granting of a new tenancy, compensation may in certain circumstances be payable to the tenant (see above).

When tenants take on a lease they may make extensive alterations to the premises in order to make them better suited to the type of catering enterprise they intend to undertake. Obviously, tenants will be unwilling to invest what may be considerable sums in refurbishing premises if at the end of the lease they will not be paid anything in recognition of the improvements to the premises which they have made. Outgoing tenants may, under the 1954 Act, claim compensation from the landlord for any alterations or improvements which they have made to the premises where these have increased the letting value of the premises. Prior to the making of such alterations the tenants should obtain the consent of the landlord to the proposed alterations. The entitlement to such compensation is governed by the Landlord and Tenant Act 1927 and hinges upon the tenant following a strict procedure laid down by that Act. Notice is given to the landlord in writing. If three months thereafter the landlord has not replied in writing to the tenant objecting to the proposed alterations, the tenant is entitled to presume that the landlord consents to the alterations. The tenant may then undertake the alterations, in full knowledge that he or she will be able to claim compensation for the improvements made when the tenancy ends. If, during the three-month period after notice has been given by the tenant, the landlord lodges an objection to the proposed alterations, the tenant may apply to the County Court or High Court, depending on the value of the property, for a certificate authorizing the alterations. A certificate will be issued by the court only if the improvements are ones which are reasonable and suitable and which will add to the value of the premises and do not detract from the value of any other property belonging to the landlord. If the County Court issues a certificate authorizing the alterations, the tenant may claim compensation for the improvements made when the tenancy ends, although the landlord had not actually consented to the alterations.

Compensation in such cases must be claimed within three months of the landlord serving a notice to quit upon the premises, or from three to six months from the date of the expiry of the lease. The County Court rules cover the rules of procedure to be followed when claiming compensation. What does the compensation cover? Obviously the compensation covers improvements to the premises. In addition it may also cover the goodwill of the business. Can a landlord exclude liability to pay compensation by means of an express term in the lease? No, he cannot.

Covenants

We are concerned with two forms of covenant: restrictive covenants, which may affect the use to which freeholders may put their land; and covenants contained in a lease, which restrict the position of tenants.

Restrictive covenants

A restrictive covenant is essentially a contract between two landowners whereby one agrees to restrict the use of his or her land for the benefit of the other. However, this presents a difficulty: what if Lord Sloane, the owner of Ramsden Manor, agrees with Lord Wellworthy, the owner of the Stately Mansion Hotel (a nearby country retreat for 'yuppies'), not to use Ramsden Manor as a hotel, and Lord Sloane thereafter sells Ramsden Manor to Mr Sly, an entrepreneur who wishes to use the premises as a country club? Can Lord Wellworthy enforce the covenant made with Lord Sloane against Mr Sly and prevent Mr Sly's intended use of Ramsden Manor as a country club? The common law does not allow Lord Wellworthy to enforce the covenant against Mr Sly due to the doctrine of privity of contract. Only those who are party to an agreement are bound by the agreement. However, equity does allow the enforcement of the covenant provided three preconditions are satisfied:
1   The covenant must be negative in its terms.
2   The covenant must benefit the land and not be merely for the personal benefit of the person claiming the benefit of the covenant.
3   The person claiming the benefit must retain the land which can benefit from the covenant.
In the example, clearly the covenant is framed in negative terms; however, is it for Lord Wellworthy's personal benefit (i.e. business interests)? Could it be said that it benefits the land (i.e. it seeks to keep the residential character of the area)? Lord Wellworthy can enforce the covenant only whilst he retains the legal estate in the Stately Mansion Hotel.

Restrictive covenants are sometimes used in relation to the future use of licensed premises. If, for example, the Gnat's Water Brewery, which operates three inns in a small country village, wishes to close and sell off one of these inns so as to improve the profitability of its remaining inns, it may insert a restrictive covenant into the conditions of sale of the inn in question, whereby the purchaser of the inn covenants not to use the premises as licensed premises. If the inn is later sold to another person who wishes to reopen as licensed premises or the first purchaser wishes to open the inn once more as licensed premises, the Gnat's Water Brewery will seek to rely upon the covenant to restrain such trading. However, the wording of such covenants is by no means simple.

Covenants in leases

These are usually express, i.e. stated in the terms of the lease, though covenants may also be implied. Covenants in a lease are enforceable as part of the contract between the landlord and tenant. Such covenants are to be found in leases between breweries and their tenants. Two examples are:

1   The tenant undertakes to obtain all his or her liquor from the brewery.
2   The tenant undertakes to do nothing which would put in jeopardy the
     continuation of the licence in respect of the premises.

Certain covenants are explicit, like the above, whereas others are very broad in their scope. In *Egerton* v. *Esplanade Hotels London Ltd* [1947] 2 All ER 88, the tenants covenanted not to do, or allow to be done, on the premises anything which might annoy their landlords or other tenants. In fact the tenants allowed the hotel rented under the lease to be used as a brothel. The landlords were able to enforce the somewhat broadly worded covenant and after due notice evict the tenants for breach of covenant.

An important distinction now arises in the case of leases granted after 1 January 1996 ('new tenancies'). This flows from the passing of the Landlord and Tenant (Covenants) Act 1995. In the case of old tenancies, while after an assignment it may not be possible for the landlord to enforce every single covenant in the lease against the incoming tenant, the doctrine of privity of contract makes the outgoing tenant liable still for the performance of the covenants where his successor fails to comply. (The obvious – and often worst – example is non-payment of rent.) With the passing of the 1995 Act this makes it preferable for someone commencing a new business, who is not in a position to buy freehold premises, to try to arrange matters so that a new tenancy is granted rather than an old tenancy assigned.

Where a new tenancy is granted, the outgoing tenant on an assignment is in a much more beneficial position. In certain circumstances he may be required by his landlord to give a guarantee that the incoming tenant will perform his obligations but that guarantee can only operate for so long as the incoming tenant himself retains the lease.

Planning permission

Since the acquisition of premises (other than where the entrepreneur purchases the premises as a going concern and merely takes over an existing catering enterprise) normally involves at least a change of use and often the development of the premises, planning permission is required. The Town and Country Planning Act 1990 imposes control over the use to which land and property are put. Control is vested in local planning authorities, who are under a duty to ensure that all land and property within their area is used for the best possible purposes in view of the shortage of land and the needs of the community. The Act relates to the development of land, which encompasses building, etc., or any material change in the use of land or buildings. Developments of this sort cannot be carried out without planning permission granted by local planning authority.

For what kind of building work is planning permission required? If, for instance, Ms Intrepid acquires a small café and wishes to convert it to high-class tearooms and this necessitates minor internal building works and extensive redecoration, planning permission may well not be required, since the alterations are purely internal and do not alter the use to which the buildings are put, nor do they materially affect the external appearance of the property. However, any alterations which are external, or any which are internal and arise from an alteration of use, probably will require planning permission. Hence, if Mr Keen purchases a freehold shop which was previously an undertaker's and wishes to open Ghosts, a wine bar, on the premises, although the building work he undertakes may be wholly internal, a change of use is involved and therefore planning permission is required. In the many instances of old warehouses, barns, etc. being converted to catering premises, even though external work may not be undertaken, planning permission is required owing to the change of use, and similarly with large private residences being converted into small country hotels. Where a change of use occurs the local planning authority is concerned with the intended use to which the property is to be put in order that the character of the locality may be maintained in accordance with other development schemes. Before planning permission is required the change of use must be a 'material' change. This is ultimately a question of fact.

In the case of *Forkhurst* v. *Secretary of State* [1982] 46 P & CR 89, Hodgson J gave a clear indication of the way in which the judiciary approach the issue of 'use' and 'change of use' from one class of use to another:

- arrive at an accurate description of the actual use,
- see, as a matter of description, whether that description fits into a use class,
- see whether the description includes activities that fit into more than one class,
- decide, when there are activities that fit into more than one class, whether the one is ordinarily incidental to the other,
- one can have a use that does not come within any of the specified classes but the activity either comes within the use specified or it does not and there is no scope for the management of the problem in terms of facts and degree.

Clearly if a wine bar were to find that the catering side of the business brought more trade and wished to convert part of the bar area into a restaurant, this would not be a material change and would not require planning permission. However, if a pub wished to expand its business by the creation of a restaurant and moreover by offering accommodation, this would amount to a material change and planning permission would be required to convert the premises for such use. 'Use classes' are set out in the Town and Country Planning (Use Classes) Order 1987. A change within each class does not require planning permission, whereas a change from one class of use to another normally does require planning permission. However, even a change from one class of use to another will require planning permission only if the change is deemed to be a 'material' change: if, for instance, an entrepreneur wishes to convert a shop, which falls into the class of buildings used primarily for the sale of goods by retail, into a restaurant see *Westminster City Council* v. *McDonald's Hamburgers* (1986) 7 CL 325 (b). Restaurants, cafés and public houses are outside the ambit of that class of use and planning permission is therefore required. Guest houses and hotels constitute a class of use; hence if premises such as a large farm-house are to be converted to use as a small country hotel or guest house, planning permission is required. However, if a farmer decides to let out, in return for money, some of the rooms in the farmhouse to friends, relatives and associates during the summer months, this may not be a material change of use and planning permission is not required: *Blackpool Borough Council* v. *Secretary of State for the Environment* [1980] 40 P & CR 104 (QBD).

Use classes – some illustrative examples

A1   Shops
A2   Financial and professional services
A3   Food and drink – restaurants, snack bars, wine bars, cafés, public houses, fast-food outlets/take-aways.
B1   Business
B2   General industrial
C1   Hotels and guest houses
C2   Residential – care homes
C3   Dwelling houses
D2   Assembly and leisure – cinema, dance hall, swimming pool, leisure centre

It should be noted that from time to time changes are made to the Use Classes Order. Prior to 1994, Class C1 also included hostels. An amendment was made with prospective effect only. The Government was concerned that hostel use, attracting large numbers of benefit claimants, would pose a threat to amenities in what might be described as traditional hotel areas.

Hostel use is now an example of what is known as a *sui generis* use, literally 'of its own kind' and so not falling within a specified class.

Is planning permission required where the logical expansion of the catering enterprise requires part of the premises to be put to a different use? If Mr Bulger, the proprietor of the Seagull Hotel, Loathesome-on-Sea, wishes to open a non-residents' bar at the hotel to attract passing trade, whereas at present the hotel bar is open to residents only, does Mr Bulger require planning permission? In *Emma Hotels* v. *Secretary of State for the Environment* [1980] 258 EG 64 (QBD), it was held in identical circumstances that the operation of a non-residents' bar was not a material change of use and did not require planning permission. This was due to the fact that the opening of the bar to the public was merely incidental to the existing use of the premises as a hotel. It should not be forgotten that where structural alterations are made to licensed premises the approval of the licensing justices is required in addition to planning permission.

The benefit of planning permission to carry on a business from premises is normally lost by a subsequent change of use of those premises. Hence fresh permission would be required before the original business use could be resumed, as the Court of Appeal held in *Cynon Valley Borough Council* v. *Secretary of State for Wales and Another* [1986] JPL 760.

A further example would be where the proprietor of a country hotel wishes to expand her business by adding a heated swimming pool, sauna, solarium, etc. to the premises and advertising the establishment as a health club open to non-resident members as well as guests at the hotel. Such a proposal transcends three classes of use: first the existing use as a hotel; secondly the use of the premises as a non-residential club; and thirdly use as a swimming pool. Clearly in such circumstances there appears to be a material change of use. However, if the swimming pool, sauna, etc. exist and the 'change of use' is merely to increase their use and attract outside custom to the premises, is such a change merely incidental to the present use of the hotel premises, as in the *Emma Hotels* case above?

Where planning permission is required an architect will need to be instructed to draw up complete plans of the proposed work which are thereafter submitted to the local planning office. There may be an inspection during the course of the work by local authority officials to check that the work is being executed according to the plans submitted. If the developer has not sought planning permission prior to the commencement of work and has started work which requires planning permission, he or she may be served by the local planning authority with an enforcement notice. This notice will require the developer to return the property to its original condition. If planning permission is refused, or an enforcement notice served, the developer has a right of appeal to the Secretary of State for the Environment.

Where the premises include listed buildings, or where they are situated in a conservation area, separate systems of control are imposed by the Planning (Listed Buildings and Conservation Areas) Act 1990. Again it is essential to seek advice from a solicitor before any works of alteration or demolition are commenced.

3.2 THE HOTELIER'S LIABILITY AS AN OCCUPIER OF PREMISES

Occupiers of premises, for example hoteliers, caterers, managers of licensed premises etc. owe a statutory duty of care to all their lawful visitors under the Occupiers' Liability Act 1957. This duty is owed only to lawful visitors and is a statutory form of negligence derived from the 'neighbour principle' in *Donoghue* v. *Stevenson* [1932] AC 562 (HL).

The duty owed to lawful visitors

The extent and nature of the duty owed to lawful visitors are set out in s. 2(1) and s. 2(2) OLA 1957. Section 2(1) states:

> *An occupier of premises owes the same duty, the 'common duty of care', to all his visitors, except insofar as he is free to and does extend, restrict, modify or exclude his duty to any visitor or visitors by agreement or otherwise.*

We shall see later that the power of the occupiers to exclude or restrict their liability towards visitors has to a considerable extent been eroded by s. 2 Unfair Contract Terms Act 1977. Section 2(2) OLA 1957 defines the duty owed:

> *The common duty of care is a duty to take such care as in all the circumstances of the case is reasonable to see that the visitor will be reasonably safe in using*

*the premises for the purposes for which he is invited or permitted by the occupier to
be there.*

In order to understand how the Occupiers' Liability Act 1957 operates we must
consider who may be an occupier and who constitute lawful visitors.

Who is an occupier?

An occupier of premises for the purposes of the OLA 1957 is a person who has control
over the premises. It is important to distinguish control from ownership. Whilst X may
be the owner of a hotel managed by Y, Y has control of the premises and Y will be
the occupier of the premises. However, the point is not clear-cut, since occupancy may
in fact be shared by the owner and the person managing the premises on behalf of the
owner (see *Wheat* v. *E. Lacon & Co. Ltd*). Furthermore, by the doctrine of vicarious
liability, if Y is employed by X, X will be vicariously liable for the actions of Y. The
essence of occupancy therefore is 'occupational control'.

WHEAT v. E. LACON &
CO. LTD [1966] 1 All ER
582 (HL)

The manager of a public house was permitted by the owners,
E. Lacon & Co., to take paying guests into the 'private' rooms
of the manager's living accommodation for his private profit.
The plaintiff and her husband were such guests. The plaintiff's
husband was killed after falling down a staircase in the private
part of the pub. In an action brought by the plaintiff against E. Lacon & Co. under the OLA
1957, E. Lacon & Co. denied liability on the grounds that they were not occupiers of the private
part of the premises.

Held: The defendants, E. Lacon & Co., retained occupation and control of the staircase together
with the manager. Hence the plaintiff's husband was a visitor to whom both E. Lacon & Co. and
the manager owed a duty of care under s. 2(1) OLA 1957. However, on the facts the plaintiff
failed to establish a breach of such duty to take care and E. Lacon & Co. were held not to be
liable to the plaintiff. Lord Denning observed: 'In the OLA 1957 the word occupier is used [as]
. . . a convenient word to denote a person who had a sufficient degree of control over premises to
put him under a duty of care towards those who came lawfully on to the premises.'

Two points should therefore be noted. First, differing parts of the same premises may
be covered by different 'occupiers' who have control over them, and secondly, certain
parts may be jointly occupied. In a hotel a guest may indeed be the 'occupier' of his
or her bedroom for the purposes of the Act. So if a guest invites a friend back to the
room, and the friend is injured in that room, the guest and not the hotel has occupational control and may be liable to the friend. Alternatively, the court may hold that
occupancy was shared between the guest and the hotel. Equally, certain places such as
public rooms or staircases remain in the occupancy of the hotel throughout.

Who is a lawful visitor?

Since the duty under s.2 (1) OLA 1957 is owed only to lawful visitors it is crucial
determine in any given case whether the person in question is a lawful visitor. A lawful
visitor is a person who has the permission of the occupier to enter the premises. In
other words, the visitor has been either expressly or implicitly invited to the premises.
It will be a question of fact in each case whether the person is a lawful visitor and has

been invited to the premises. Since s. 2(2) OLA 1957 requires the occupier to take such care as is reasonable to see that visitors will be reasonably safe in using the premises for the purposes for which they are invited or permitted by the occupier to be there, lawful visitors will be owed a duty only in so far as they remain within the scope of their invitation or permission to be on the premises. Hence people who enter the premises as lawful visitors may not remain so if they step outside of their invitation or permission to be on the premises. Guests will be lawful visitors to those parts of the hotel to which they have been invited, i.e. all public rooms (lounge, reception, restaurant), their bedrooms, conveniences, etc. provided for guests' use. However, guests will cease to be lawful visitors if they enter parts of the premises, such as the kitchen, offices, laundry, etc., which they do not have permission to enter or if they enter parts of the premises where no one would reasonably expect them to go. These principles are clearly illustrated in the following case.

CAMBELL v. SHELBOURNE HOTEL LTD [1939] 2 KB 534 (CA)

The plaintiff was a guest at the defendants' hotel in London. He had previously stayed at the hotel on twelve or thirteen occasions, but had never before occupied a room on the ground floor. At about 11.20 on the night in question he arrived back in his room and wanted to use the lavatory. He had ascertained during daylight that the lavatory was diagonally across the passage from his room door, and, as the passage was now unlit and he was unable to find the light switch, he crossed the passage in the dark and, by feeling his way, came to a door which he believed to be that of the lavatory, but which was in fact a door leading to the basement. On opening the door and passing through the doorway the plaintiff immediately fell down a flight of steps and sustained injury.

Held: The defendants owed to the plaintiff, as a guest, a duty to take all reasonable care to see that the premises were safe, and their failure to light the passage in a London hotel at 11.20 p.m., when guests might reasonably be expected to be using the passage was a breach of that duty which had resulted in injury to the plaintiff. As the plaintiff had not been shown to be guilty of contributory negligence, he was entitled to recover damages, on the grounds of negligence.

If, for instance, guests used a swimming pool at a hotel after dark, it is clear that they have by so doing stepped outside the scope of their invitation or permission to use that part of the premises, and a duty is not owed to them. In *Hillen and Pettigrew v. ICI (Alkali) Ltd* [1936] AC 69 (HL), Lord Atkin observed:

> The duty to a lawful visitor only extends so long as, and so far as the lawful visitor is making what can reasonably be contemplated as an ordinary and reasonable use of the premises by the lawful visitor for the purposes for which he has been invited.

Another aspect of this problem is that the permission of the occupier may be extended to the visitor for a fixed period of time and thereafter the visitor becomes a trespasser, and is outside the scope of the OLA 1957.

STONE v. TAFFE [1974] 3 All ER 1016 (CA)

Mr Stone was a committee member of a society which regularly met at a public house owned by a brewery and managed by their employee, Taffe. Taffe agreed to allow the society, of which he was also a member, to use an upstairs room at the public house for a social occasion. Drinks were served to members of the club by Taffe until the early hours of the morning, without any extension having been granted b the licensing magistrates. Mr Stone, when leaving the premises by a narrow, unlit staircase at approximately 1.00 a.m. fell and was killed. The widow of Mr Stone sued both Taffe and the brewery for damages *inter alia* under s. 2 OLA 1957.

The trial judge held that the brewery, through their employee, Taffe, were the occupiers of the staircase. However, since the presence of the deceased on the premises was in direct contravention of an express instruction issued by the brewery to their manager, the brewery were not liable; his permission to remain on the premises had ceased at closing time, 10.30 p.m.

Held: Upon an appeal by Mr Stone's widow it was held that an occupier who intended to permit another person to enter and use the premises for a limited period of time had to give a clear indication to the other that the permission was subject to a time limit. Accordingly, at the time of the accident the deceased was a lawful visitor on the premises, since the brewery had not given the deceased any indication that the permission they had given him to be on the premises expired at 10.30 p.m. It followed therefore that at the time of the accident the brewery still owed him a duty of care under s. 2 OLA 1957.

Although we have discussed the duty of an occupier to lawful visitors in relation to guests and customers, the duty is also owed to employees and other people such as tradespeople who have a legitimate purpose, and thus an implied permission to be on the premises. In *Stenner* v. *Taff-Ely Borough Council* (*The Independent*, 25 May 1987), the Court of Appeal held that a local authority which employed a gymnastics coach at its leisure centre was not liable to the plaintiff (a friend of the coach), whom the coach had permitted to use the gym at a time when the leisure centre was closed to the public.

Restrictions on the OLA 1957 duty

Exclusion clauses

The duty set out in s. 2(1) OLA 1957 applies 'except insofar as he (the occupier) is free to and does extend, restrict, modify or exclude his duty to any visitor or visitors by agreement or otherwise'. A hotelier may 'so far as he is free to' exclude or restrict his liability under the OLA 1957 by means of a notice (or a clause in the contract of booking *vis-à-vis* guests). The clause must be sufficiently brought to the attention of visitors to the premises and must clearly cover the breach of duty which it seeks to exclude. However, s. 2(1) UCTA 1977 operates to limit the effect of such notices and clauses. Section 2(1) UCTA 1977 states:

> *A person cannot by reference to any contract terms or to a notice given to persons generally or to particular persons exclude or restrict his liability for death or personal injury resulting from negligence.*

Hence a hotelier may **not**, in a case which has resulted in the death of or personal injury to a lawful visitor due to the hotelier's breach of duty under the OLA 1957, rely upon a notice or clause which purports to exclude liability for such injury.

Warning notices

Warning notices may in certain circumstances absolve the occupier of liability for the visitor's injuries. Section 2(4) a OLA 1957 states:

> *Where damage is caused to a visitor by a danger of which he had been warned by the occupier, the warning is not to be treated without more as absolving the occupier from liability, unless in all the circumstances it was enough to enable the visitor to be reasonably safe.*

It will not be all warnings therefore which provide a defence, only such warnings which enable the visitor to be reasonably safe. An example would be if on a door to a storeroom which contained high-voltage electrical equipment involved in the supply of electricity to the hotel there was a notice which said 'Danger: Keep Out: High Voltage'. This might not be sufficient if the guest who strayed into the storeroom and was injured could not read English. A warning notice must be readily understandable and clear symbols explaining the danger are required.

Liability to children

Not all guests at a hotel will be adults. Is a higher duty owed under the OLA 1957 to children? Section 2(3)a OLA 1957 states that in determining the degree of care ordinarily required, 'an occupier must be prepared for children to be less careful than adults'. Thus a higher duty is imposed (i.e. more is required of the occupier).

Liability towards employees and specialist subcontractors

Section 2(3)b OLA 1957 provides:

> *An occupier may expect that a person, in the exercise of his calling, will appreciate and guard against any special risks ordinarily incident to it, so far as the occupier leaves him free to do so.*

If, for example, a hotelier contracts for a window cleaner to clean all the outside windows of the hotel and, while undertaking this job, the person contracted falls and is injured, although the hotelier owes the window cleaner a duty of care under s. 2(1) OLA 1957, the extent of this duty is modified by the fact that window cleaners will themselves guard against the ordinary risks of carrying out the job and thus the hotelier may not be liable for their injuries.

Volenti non fit injuria

This amounts to the voluntary assumption of the risk of injury. Section 2(5) OLA 1957 provides:

> *The common duty of care does not impose on an occupier any obligation to a visitor*
> *in respect of risks willingly accepted as his by the visitor . . .*

It will be a question of fact in each case whether the visitor has voluntarily or willingly accepted the risk as his or her own. Reference here should also be made to s. 2(3) UCTA 1977, which provides in relation to exclusion clauses:

> *Where a contract term or notice purports to exclude or restrict liability for negligence*
> *a person's agreement to or awareness of it is not of itself to be taken as indicating his*
> *voluntary acceptance of any risk.*

Contributory negligence

Where visitors have contributed to the injuries they have sustained due to the defendant's breach of duty under the OLA 1957, then the damages to which they are entitled may be reduced. Section 1(1) of the Law Reform (Contributory Negligence) Act 1945 states:

> *Where any person suffers damage as the result partly of his own fault and partly of the*
> *fault of any other person or persons, a claim in respect of damage shall not be defeated*
> *by reason of the fault of the person suffering the damage, but the damages recoverable in*
> *respect thereof shall be reduced to such an extent as the court thinks just and equitable*
> *having regard to the claimant's share in the responsibility for the damage . . .*

In *Stone* v. *Taffe* (above) a 50 per cent reduction was made owing to the claimant's contributory negligence. See also *Sayers* v. *Harlow UDC* [1958] 2 All ER 342 (CA), and *Adams* v. *Southern Electricity Board* [1993] *The Times*, 21 October.

Liability for work of independent contractors

If, for example, a hotelier contracts with a lift company to repair the lift of the hotel, and thereafter the lift malfunctions and causes injury to a guest, will the hotel or the lift company be liable to the guest? Section 2(4)b OLA 1957 states:

> *Where damage is caused to a visitor by a danger due to the faulty execution of any*
> *work of construction, maintenance or repair by an independent contractor employed*
> *by the occupier, the occupier is not to be treated without more as answerable for the*
> *danger if in all the circumstances he had acted reasonably in entrusting the work to*
> *an independent contractor and had taken such steps (if any) as he reasonably ought*
> *in order to satisfy himself that the contractor was competent and that the work had*
> *been properly done.*

Hence, provided the independent contractor was one who could reasonably be entrusted with such work and the hotelier did what he could to ensure that the work was done properly, the lift company as independent contractors will alone be liable.

Liability to trespassers

The liability of an occupier towards a trespasser is now covered by the Occupiers' Liability Act 1984. At common law an occupier did not owe a duty of care towards a trespasser under the rule in *R. Addie & Son (Collieries) Ltd* v. *Dumbreck* [1929] AC 358 (HL) where the following was said:

> *Towards the trespasser the occupier has no duty to take reasonable care for his protection or even to protect him from concealed danger. The trespasser comes on to the premises at his own risk. An occupier is in such a case liable only where the injury is due to some wilful act involving something more than the absence of reasonable care. There must be some act done with the deliberate intention of doing harm to the trespasser, or at least some act done with reckless disregard of the presence of the trespasser.*

However, this decision was subsequently overruled by the House of Lords.

BRITISH RAILWAYS BOARD v. HERRINGTON [1972] 1 All ER 749

An electrified railway line owned by BRB ran through property open to the public. The fences on either side of the track were in poor repair and in April 1965 children were seen on the line. A particular place in the fence has been used as a route to cross the railway. In June 1965 the plaintiff, a child of six, was severely injured when he stepped on the line, having passed through the broken fence. The plaintiff claimed damages for negligence on the part of BRB due to the disrepair of the fence through which he had passed.

Held: While occupiers do not owe the same duty to trespassers which they owe to lawful visitors, they owe trespassers a duty to take such steps as common sense or common humanity would dictate to avert the danger, or warn persons coming onto the premises of its presence.

Lord Pearson observed: 'In my opinion. the occupier of premises does not owe any such duty to a trespasser: he does not owe to the trespasser a duty to take such care as in all the circumstances of the case is reasonable to see that the trespasser will be reasonably safe in using the premises for the purposes for which he is trespassing. That seems to me to be the fundamental distinction, and should be fully preserved. It does not follow that the occupier never owes any duty to the trespasser. If the presence of the trespasser is known to or reasonably to be anticipated by the occupier, then the occupier has a duty to the trespasser, but it is a lower and less onerous duty than the one which the occupier owes to a lawful visitor. Very broadly stated, it is a duty to treat the trespasser with ordinary humanity . . . the occupier is not at fault if he has done as much as is required of him, if he has taken reasonable steps to deter the trespasser from entering or remaining on the premises, or part of the premises, in which he will encounter a dangerous situation. In simple language, it is normally sufficient for the occupier to make reasonable endeavours to keep out or chase off the potential or actual intruder who is likely to be or is in a dangerous situation. The erection and maintenance of suitable notice boards or fencing or both, or the giving of suitable oral warning . . . will usually constitute reasonable endeavours for this purpose.'

The Occupiers' Liability Act 1984 outlines where an occupier owes a duty to a trespasser in respect of any risk of that person suffering injury on the premises, by reason of any damage due to the state of the premises or to things done or not done on the premises. The Act further outlines the scope of the duty owed.

A point of difference between the 1984 and the 1957 Acts is that liability for loss or damage to the property of the non-visitor is *not* covered by the 1984 Act, whereas loss or damage to the property of a visitor is covered by the 1957 Act.

An occupier owes a duty to non-visitors, including trespassers, by s. 1(1)(a) of the 1984 Act.

When does the duty exist?

The Occupiers' Liability Act 1984 creates separate tests for *the existence of the duty* owed to the non-visitor and *the content of the duty*, if it is found to exist. Section 1(3) states that an occupier owes the statutory duty if:

  (a) *he is aware of the danger or has reasonable grounds to believe that it exists:*
  (b) *he knows or has reasonable grounds to believe that the (non-visitor) is in the vicinity of the danger concerned or that he may come into the vicinity of the danger (in either case, whether the (non-visitor) has lawful authority for being in that vicinity or not); and*
  (c) *the risk is one against which, in all circumstances of the case he may reasonably be expected to offer the (non-visitor) some protection.*

Where the section states 'he knows or has reasonable grounds to believe' this applies to the situation where the occupier knows or is aware of the primary facts but fails to draw the reasonable inference that the premises are dangerous or that the non-visitor's presence is likely.

Whether the risk is one against which the occupier may reasonably be expected to offer some protection will depend upon factors which are more usually taken into account when assessing the standard of care, e.g. the nature and extent of the risk, practicability of precautions and, possibly, the type of entrant.

Where s. 1(3) is satisfied one must then consider the content of the occupier's duty.

The content of the duty

Under s. 1(4), the duty is to take such care as is reasonable in all the circumstances of the case to see that the non-visitor does not suffer injury on the premises by reason of the danger concerned. This is an objective test which does not depend upon either the skill or the resources of the particular occupier. However, what constitutes 'reasonable care' will vary considerably taking account of 'all circumstances of the case'.

Factors to be considered when applying, s. 1(4) OLA 1984 are:

(a) the gravity and likelihood of the probable injury – high risk merits greater precautions;
(b) the nature of the premises.
(c) the foreseeability of the presence of the entrant – the more likely the presence of the non-visitor the greater the precautions required.

Warning notices

Not in all cases, but in 'appropriate cases', an occupier may discharge his or her duty by taking reasonable steps to warn of the danger, or taking steps to discourage people from incurring the risk (see s. 1(5) OLA 1984). Where the non-visitor is a child a warning will be inadequate to discharge the duty; further steps should be taken to discourage the person from taking the risk, e.g. the erection of fencing. With adult non-visitors a warning notice will be sufficient.

Volenti non fit injuria

Section 1(6) OLA 1984 preserves this defence in relation to non-visitors. The defendant must establish not only that the plaintiff consented to the risk but also that he or she agreed that if he or she was injured the loss should be his or hers and not the defendant's. The plaintiff should also appreciate both the nature and extent of the risk, not simply the fact there is some risk.

Excluding liability

The OLA 1984 makes no reference to the question of whether an occupier can exclude or restrict his or her potential liability under the Act. The omission of such a reference suggests that this cannot be a defence under the Act.

Negligence liability outside the OLA 1957

Whilst the OLA 1957 embodies a statutory duty of care towards lawful visitors, liability under the tort of negligence still exists outside the OLA 1957 with regard to visitors to the hotelier's or caterer's premises. The OLA 1957 abolished the previous common-law distinction between invitees and licensees and substitutes a single duty of care. However, there are two further points to be considered, as follows.

Contractual entrants. (See *Maclenan* v. *Segar* [1917] 2 KB 325 (KB) below.) There may be an implied term of contract, namely that the occupier will take reasonable care regarding the safety of the party entering the premises under the contract.

Duty at common law. It is arguable that the 'activity duty', namely a duty owed by people carrying out an activity on their premises (e.g. hotel or catering business) to take reasonable care for the safety of people who may be injured by their activity has survived the OLA 1957. In other words, there may be a common-law duty to ensure that the hotel and catering premises are reasonably safe, apart from the duty owed as an occupier under the OLA 1957.

Duty to ensure that premises are reasonably safe

Whilst it may be argued that this is merely an illustration of the duty owed under the OLA 1957, it may also be said that this exists as a form of liability under the tort of negligence but outside the scope of the 1957 Act.

MACLENAN v. SEGAR   A guest, upon arrival at the hotel, was taken directly to her
[1917] 2 KB 325 (KB)   room by lift. During her night's stay a fire broke out in the

hotel and the guest, in a panic, attempted to leave her second- floor room through her window by means of a 'rope' made from bed linen. She fell through a glass roof and sustained injuries.

Held: The fire was caused by the negligence of the hotel management and, furthermore, the premises were not reasonably safe. The trial judge, in finding for the plaintiff, elucidated two grounds for the decision.

1   'Where the occupier of premises agrees for reward that a person shall have the right to enter and use them for a mutually contemplated purpose, the contract between the parties (unless it provides to the contrary) contains an implied warranty that the premises are as safe for that purpose as reasonable care and skill on the part of anyone can make them.'

2   'The defendant had been personally negligent in that he had failed to take such steps and make such inquiries as would have revealed to him the defects in his structure and the risks of fire thereby occasioned.'

The first ground for the decision appears to be derived from the contract of booking. In other words, there is an implied term of the contract that the premises are reasonably safe. What if the plaintiff in this case had been a tradesperson (i.e a lawful visitor to the premises, but one who was not in a contractual relationship with the hotel) who was injured whilst trying to escape from the fire? It would, of course, not be possible to argue along the lines of an 'implied term' of contract, since no contract exists. However, the tradesperson would surely be a 'neighbour' under the neighbour principle in *Donoghue* v. *Stevenson* and be owed a duty of care in line with that principle. It may, however, be argued that such a duty is identical with the statutory duty set out in s. 2 OLA 1957.

The second ground appears to be straightforward negligence liability regarding defective premises. The case is of course silent as to the neighbour principle since it predates *Donoghue* v. *Stevenson*, but there is no reason to doubt that the facts of the case, if they were to occur again, could be dealt with as a straightforward application of the neighbour principle.

SALMON v. SEAFARER
RESTAURANTS LTD
[1983] 3 All ER 729 (HC)

The plaintiff, a fireman, was injured by an explosion on premises occupied by the defendants, a fish and chip shop, when a fire in the premises melted a seal on a gas meter, thus allowing gas to escape. The fire was caused by an employee of the defendants negligently forgetting to extinguish a gas flame under a chip fryer before leaving the premises for the night, with the result that the oil in the chip fryer continued to heat up until it caught fire. The plaintiff brought an action in negligence against the defendants, contending that, because the fire had been started negligently and because he had been injured as a result, he was entitled to recover damages from the defendants. The defendants denied liability, contending that an occupier's duty of care to firemen attending his premises in the course of their work was limited to protecting the firemen from any special or exceptional risks over and above the ordinary risks necessarily incidental to a fireman's job, and did not extend to protecting firemen from such ordinary risks which, on the facts, included an explosion of the kind which had taken place on the defendants' premises. At the trial of the action the plaintiff conceded that the defendants could not have foreseen the precise chain of events which led to the explosion.

Held: An occupier of premises owed the same duty of care to a fireman attending the premises to extinguish the fire as he or she owed to other visitors under s. 2 of the OLA 1957. In determining whether the occupier was in breach of that duty, it was expected that the plaintiff fireman would exercise those skills expected to be shown by firemen. Since the fire at the premises of the defendants was caused by their employee's negligence, and since it was reasonably foreseeable that firemen would be required to attend the fire and that an explosion of the kind which occurred might result from the fire, the defendants were liable to the plaintiff.

The House of Lords decided a similar case in *Ogwo* v. *Taylor* [1987] 3 All ER 961 (HL):

OGWO v. TAYLOR The defendant negligently started a fire by using a blowlamp
[1987] 3 All ER 961 (HL) to burn off the paint on the fascia board under the guttering
 of the roof of his house, thereby causing the timbers to catch
 fire. The plaintiff, a fireman, went into the roof space to tackle
the fire and sustained serious injuries caused by steam generated by water poured onto the fire, notwithstanding the fact that he was wearing standard protective clothing. There was no suggestion that the contents of the roof space were unusually combustible or that there was any special danger from such a hidden cause. The plaintiff brought an action in negligence against the defendant, contending that because the fire had been started negligently and because he had been injured as a result, he was entitled to recover damages from the defendant.

Held: A person who negligently starts a fire is liable for injuries suffered by a fireman while attempting to put out the fire, regardless of whether the particular injuries suffered by the fireman were reasonably foreseeable or whether the injuries were suffered as the result of exceptional or merely ordinary risks undertaken by the fireman.

There is a clear point of distinction between the two cases. *Salmon*'s case is based on the Occupiers' Liability Act, in that it was key to the decision that the defendant was the occupier. In the *Ogwo* case, the decision is based solely upon the neighbour principle, the issue before the court being whether the injuries sustained by the plaintiff were foreseeable.

The extent of the duty

The duty to ensure that the premises are reasonably safe, either under the OLA 1957 or at common law, only requires the occupier to do that which is reasonably practicable to ensure the safety of visitors to the premises. It is not an absolute duty requiring the closing down of the premises; it is sufficient if the defendant has done that which was reasonably practicable in the circumstances.

LATIMER v. AEC LTD A violent rainstorm flooded the defendants' factory. They put
[1953] 2 All ER 449 (HL) down sawdust but had insufficient to deal with the flooding to
 all areas of the factory. The plaintiff slipped and injured him-
 self on an area of floor to which sawdust had not been applied.
The plaintiff alleged negligence on the part of the defendants, arguing that they should have closed the factory to remove any risk to employees and visitors to the premises.

Held: The risk of injury did not justify the closing of the factory. In the circumstances the defendants had done that which was reasonably practicable and had thereby satisfied the duty of care imposed upon them. Lord Tucker observed: 'I do not question that such a drastic step [closure of the factory] ... may be required on the part of a reasonably prudent employer if the peril to his employees is sufficiently grave, and to this extent it must always be a question of degree, but, in my view, there was no evidence in the present case which could justify a finding of negligence for failure on the part of the respondents to take this step.'

ROBERTSON v. RIDLEY [1989] 2 All ER 474 — The liability of club officials for injuries sustained by club members on the club's premises was considered by the Court of Appeal. The plaintiff, a member of an unincorporated member's club (the Conservative Club at Sale), rode his motorcycle out of the club grounds. In doing so, he failed to see a pothole in the driveway, fell off and was injured. He brought an action against the chairman and secretary of the club, as officers of the club, claiming that they were liable for the injuries he had sustained by reason of the condition of the club's premises. He brought his action on the basis that the rules of the club provided that the chairman and secretary 'were responsible in Law ... for the conduct of the Club' and that by reason of this they were under a duty to maintain the premises in a reasonable state of safety and repair. At first instance the trial judge dismissed the claim. On an appeal by the plaintiff the Court of Appeal held (dismissing the appeal) that in so far as the rules of the club provided that two of its officers were to be responsible in law for the conduct of the club then (in the absence of an express provision that the officers were responsible for the condition of the club premises) the rules did not give rise to a duty of care towards individual members to maintain the club premises in a reasonable state of safety and repair.

This case is illustrative of the general common-law rule that there is no liability between an unincorporated club or its members on the one hand and individual members on the other.

Vicarious liability

While the person who is actually responsible for the tort which caused damage to the plaintiff is always liable, in certain circumstances another person will also be liable. These circumstances relate to the situation where the other person is the employer of the person whose actions caused injury to the plaintiff, and the person causing the injury did so in the course of his or her employment. The respective positions of the employer and employee are discussed more fully in Chapter 9. It must always be proven so as to render the employers vicariously liable for the torts of their employees that the employees were acting in the course of their employment. This has been given a fairly broad meaning, and covers the situation where employees were furthering the employer's business although they were acting in a way unauthorized (or even prohibited) by the employer:

ROSE v. PLENTY [1976] 1 All ER 97 (CA) — Rose was a youth helping Plenty, a milkman, to deliver milk. Plenty's employer, the local Co-op, expressly forbade him from using the services of children to assist in the delivery of milk to clients. Plenty had employed Rose to help him with his milk round. On an occasion when Rose was assisting Plenty with the milk round Rose sustained injury due to an accident caused by Plenty. Rose brought an action for damages against Plenty and his employer, the Co-op. The Co-op defended the action by contesting that Plenty had acted outside the scope of his employment, and thus he alone was liable in damages, and that the Co-op was not vicariously liable for his negligent driving.

Held: The Co-op was vicariously liable for the actions of Plenty, who had been acting in the course of his employment. Lawton LJ dissented from this view. Lord Denning MR observed: 'In considering whether a prohibited act was within the course of the employment it depends very much on the purpose for which it is done. If it is done for his employer's business, it is usually done in the course of his employment, even though it is a prohibited act.'

Hence, even actions prohibited by the employer will still be within the scope of an employee's employment if they are done to further the employer's business. There does appear to be a further limitation upon this principle, namely where the plaintiff is aware at the time that the employee's actions are prohibited by the employer. In *Stone* v. *Taffe* [1974] 3 All ER 1016 (CA) it was held:

> *A prohibition by an employer of what his servant might or might not do was not by itself conclusive of the scope of his employment against third parties injured by the servant, but the injured person could not make the employer liable where he himself knew of the prohibition and had had the opportunity to avoid the danger of injury from the prohibited act before he exposed himself to the danger, or where the employer could prove that the prohibition was likely to be known to the injured person.*

On the facts in *Stone* v. *Taffe*, the manager (who was an employee of the brewery) had failed to provide adequate lighting on the stairway. The brewery was vicariously liable for this failure on the part of the manager, who was acting within the scope of his employment. The fact that the party injured was present at the licensed premises in direct contravention of a company rule forbidding entertainment and service of alcoholic drinks to customers outside licensing hours did not render the manager beyond the scope of his employment. This prohibition contained in the company rules was not one which the plaintiff had knowledge of. Had the plaintiff connived with the manager in the breach of either the licensing laws or the manager's contractual obligations with the brewery, the brewery would not have been liable to him in negligence. (The brewery's liability was, however, reduced by 50 per cent as a result of the plaintiff's contributory negligence.)

Another interesting decision of the Court of Appeal, reported in *The Independent*, 'Case Summaries', on 25 May 1987 is *Skenner* v. *Taff-Ely Borough Council*. A local authority which allowed the gymnastics coach employed by them at their leisure centre to bring friends and children into the gymnasium to coach them at a time when the centre was closed to the public and when he was not working, was not vicariously liable for the employee's negligence which resulted in one of his friends, the plaintiff, being seriously injured while using the equipment because although the employee was doing acts which he was employed to do, he was not acting in the course of his employment but was engaged in a private venture.

SMITH v. STAGES [1989]
1 All ER 833 (HL)

In this case, which provides a recent case example of liability of wrongful acts of employees, the employers were held liable for damages in respect of injuries sustained by one of their employees in an accident which occurred while he was being driven home on a rest day by another employee after working away from their base. The negligent fellow-employee was 'going about his employer's business' when driving home in the employer's time. The critical point appears to be that the employee was 'on duty' (*per* Lord Lowry) or 'employed to make the journey' (*per* Lord Goff), because a normal working day was set aside for the purpose of moving base, for which he received a day's pay as well as travel and lodgings allowance. Lord Lowry made the following useful distinction: 'one must not confuse the duty to turn up for work with the concept of already being "on duty" while travelling to it'. In the former situation the employee is not acting within the course of his employment; in the latter he or she is.

Res ipsa loquitur

This is a rule of evidence which has the effect of reversing the burden of proof in negligence cases. The principle was first established in the following case.

SCOTT v. LONDON & ST KATHERINE DOCKS CO. [1861–73] All ER Rep. 246

The plaintiff was passing under a loading bay to a warehouse when six heavy sacks of sugar fell from the loading bay on the upper floor of the warehouse onto the plaintiff, who sustained injuries. There was no clear explanation as to how this had come about.

Held: Allowing the plaintiff's claim: 'There must .be reasonable evidence of negligence, but, where the thing is shown to be under the management of the defendant, or his servants, and the accident is such as in the ordinary course of things does not happen if those who have the management of machinery use proper care, it affords reasonable evidence in the absence of an explanation by the defendant, that the accident arose from want of care.'

The principle has more recently been expressed by Lord Justice Megaw in *Lloyde* v. *W. Midland Gas Board* [1971] 2 All ER 1249 (CA).

> *It means that a plaintiff* prima facie *establishes negligence where: (i) it not possible for him to prove precisely what was the relevant act or omission which set in train the events leading to the accident; but, (ii) on the evidence as it stands at the relevant time it is more likely than not that the effective cause of the accident was some act or omission of the defendant or of someone for whom the defendant is responsible, which act or omission constitutes a failure to take proper care of the plaintiff's safety.*

Where *res ipsa loquitur* operates it shifts the burden to the defendant to disprove negligence. A modern illustration of how the principle works is as follows.

WARD v. TESCO STORES LTD [1976] 1 WLR 810 (CA)

Yogurt was spilt on the floor of the defendants' store. The plaintiff sustained injury, having slipped on the yogurt, which had been left on the floor and not mopped up by the defendants' staff. There was no explanation of how the yogurt came to be on the floor of the shop.

Held: *Res ipsa loquitur* applied and, since the defendants were unable to discharge the evidential burden placed upon them by the operation of that rule, and thereby show that the accident did not occur as a result of want of care on their part, the defendants were liable in negligence to the plaintiff.

Licensees' duty to their customers

Does a licensee owe a special duty of care to customers whom he or she has served with intoxicating liquor to see the customer safely off the premises?

MUNRO v. PORTHKERRY HOLIDAY ESTATES LTD [1984] 81 LS Gaz. 2450 (HC)

It was held that a licensee's duty towards a customer extends to a duty to guard that person against the dangers arising from the customer's inability to look after himself or herself because of excessive alcohol consumption. However, upon the facts of the case, where the defendants, who were proprietors of a cliff-top holiday complex, served drink to a customer who as so drunk that when he left the defendant's bar he fell over the cliff to his death, selling large quantities of intoxicating liquor could not of itself impose a duty to take care of customers. Only if the licensee knew that the customer was so drunk as to be incapable of looking after himself or herself might such a duty arise.

3.3 PUBLIC HEALTH

Public health and hygiene are important factors in the conduct of a hotel or catering enterprise. The hygiene of the premises is vital to safe and lawful food preparation and service; this is dealt with in Chapter 6. Public health covers two important areas: control over new buildings and control over the conditions in existing premises. It is important to note here the Environmental Protection Act 1990, which makes wide-ranging provision to regulate waste disposal, accumulation of waste on premises and pollution control.

Public health and new buildings

A local authority has power under the Buildings Act 1984 where a new building is built (or existing premises are being altered so as to change their use) to request that the plans for the building or alteration to be lodged with the local authority. This power of inspection is to ensure that the proposed building or alterations comply with the Building Regulations. Building Regulations are distinct from planning permission; they set out the standards to be adopted in the completion of building work. However, planning permission will not be given unless the work is to be executed in accordance with the standards set out in the Building Regulations. The Building Regulations deal with such matters as the materials to be used, lighting, ventilation, provision of an adequate water supply, sanitation and toilet facilities. Non-compliance with the Building Regulations may ultimately lead to the pulling down of the building under official instruction.

Matters which should concern the prospective hotelier include the dimensions of rooms and adequate sanitation and toilet facilities within the building. Moreover, the local authority will be concerned that there is adequate provision of fire escapes. A hotel or guest house should have a fire escape for each storey more than 20 feet above ground level. Equally, large-scale restaurants, discos and public houses should be concerned to ensure sufficient means of escape in the event of fire. Further consideration will be given to fire precautions later.

Public health and existing premises

Local Authority Officers have a power of entry to investigate statutory nuisance – Environmental Protection Act 1990. Such statutory nuisances include excessive refuse, occurrence of loud and unnecessary noise, strong odours and the like. The officer will serve a prohibition notice on the person creating the nuisance, i.e. the proprietor of the catering establishment, which, if not complied with, will lead to summary prosecution in the Magistrates' Court. As to toilet facilities and sanitation, local authorities have the same power over existing premises as they have over buildings under construction. The local authority also has a duty to ensure that a wholesome supply of water is available to premises, and that refuse is removed from the premises. Whereas with an ordinary domestic household the refuse amassed is likely to be limited, the refuse generated by a restaurant, licensed premises or a hotel may be considerable. Therefore the local authority may charge a fee for the removal of such refuse. Hence publicans will be entitled to the free collection of refuse generated by their households, i.e. domestic rubbish, whereas they may be asked to pay for the removal of refuse generated by the public house, i.e. trade rubbish. If the local authority does not take the rubbish from the pub, and the landlord fails to make other arrangements or remove it, this may lead to a statutory nuisance being created and in the final event to criminal prosecution.

Health and safety at catering premises

As well as being a place where food is served, catering premises are in addition places where people are employed. In Chapter 10 we consider in detail the working conditions to be observed in accordance with the law. The HSWA applies to all places where people are employed, and makes provision for the health and safety of those employees (see Chapter 10). However, the scope of the Act incorporates a duty towards persons who are not employees, e.g. customers. Section 3(1) states:

> *It shall be the duty of every employer to conduct his undertaking in such a way as to ensure, so far as is reasonably practicable, that persons not in his employment who may be affected thereby are not thereby exposed to risks to their health or safety.*

Where does s. 3(1) apply? Section 3 is designed to give protection to the general public, to ensure that they are not put at risk from the hazards of another's workplace. If a guest at a hotel was injured, whilst sitting at breakfast, by an explosion in the kitchen which blew debris into the dining room, this situation would be covered by s. 3. The hotel proprietor would be criminally liable for a breach of s. 3 HSWA 1974. Visitors who come to the premises (e.g. guests. tradespeople delivering, etc.) and sub-contractors (e.g. cabaret artistes, window cleaners, etc.) who come to work at the premises may be affected by the way the undertaking is carried on and are thus covered by s. 4(1) HSWA 1974, which states:

> *This section has effect for imposing on persons duties in relation to those who*
> *(a) are not their employees; but*
> *(b) use non-domestic premises made available to them as a place of work or a place where they may use plant or substances provided for their use there and applies to premises made so available and other non-domestic premises used in connection with them.*

How does this provision affect the hotelier or caterer? Section 4(1) clearly covers visiting subcontractors, e.g. window cleaners, personnel servicing equipment at the premises, cabaret singers. Moreover, it covers persons who visit the premises to use 'plant or substances provided for their use'. For example, if a holiday-camp proprietor allows guests to use a coin-operated launderette on the premises and a camper using the machine is injured, s. 4(1) encompasses such a situation. Arguably, it would also cover a coin-operated service area where food and drink are dispensed by vending machines. The duty imposed is set out in s. 4(2):

> *It shall be the duty of each person who has, to any extent, control of the premises to which this section applies or of the means of access thereto or egress therefrom or of any plant or substance in such premises to take such measures as it is reasonable for a person in his position to take to ensure, so far as is reasonably practicable, that the premises, all means of access thereto or egress therefrom available for use by persons using the premises, and any plant or substance in the premises or, as the case may be, provided for use there, is or are safe and without risk to health.*

Section 4 HSWA 1974 is in effect the criminal counterpart of the civil liability contained in the Occupiers' Liability Act 1957.

Section 5(1) provides:

> *It shall be the duty of the person having control of . . . premises . . . to use the best practicable means for preventing the emission into the atmosphere from the premises of noxious or offensive substances, and for rendering harmless and inoffensive such substances as may be emitted.*

This provision could cover the emission from catering premises of strong odours and the like arising from the preparation of food, e.g. curry. However, it would be hard to argue that strong cooking smells were *per se* noxious or offensive.

First aid

In a working environment such as a commercial kitchen there is a risk that personnel could sustain minor injury in the course of their work, e.g. a cut or a burn to a hand. The Health and Safety (First Aid) Regulations 1981 provide for occurrences of this sort. The Regulations lay down two separate general requirements. First, employers shall provide such equipment and facilities as are adequate and appropriate in the circumstances for enabling first aid to be rendered to their employees who are injured or become ill at work. Secondly, employers shall provide such number of suitably trained personnel as is adequate and appropriate in the circumstances for rendering first aid to their employees if they are injured or become ill at work. The Approved Code of Practice sets out the facilities and equipment and the training, etc., of personnel to administer first aid. The reporting of accidents and dangerous occurrences at the workplace is considered in Chapter 10.

3.4 FIRE SAFETY

Fire, should it occur in a place where a substantial number of people congregate, such as a discotheque, public house or hotel, can have tragic consequences. The Fire Precautions Act 1971 was passed in order to improve fire safety standards in premises which are frequented by the general public. Section 1 of the Fire Precautions Act 1971 empowers the Secretary of State to designate certain premises in respect of which a fire certificate is required. Such premises include, *inter alia*:

(a) all premises used for providing, in the course of carrying on the business of a hotelier or boarding-house keeper, sleeping accommodation for staff, or bedroom, dining room, drawing room, ballroom or other accommodation for guests;

(b) any premises which are used as a place of work (s. 78(2) HSWA 1974);

(c) any shop premises in which persons are employed to work (Fire Precautions (Factories, Offices, Shops and Railway Premises) Order 1976).

Section 1 of the Fire Safety and Safety of Places of Sport Act 1987 makes provision for a fire authority to exempt certain premises from the need for a fire certificate. It does so by inserting a new provision, s. 5A, into the principal Act. Section 5A provides:

> (1) *A fire authority may, if they think fit as regards any premises which appear to them to be premises qualifying for exemption under this section as respects any particular use, grant exemption from the requirement to have a fire certificate covering that use.*
>
> (2) *Exemption under this section for any premises as respects any use of them may be granted by the fire authority, with or without the making of an application for the purpose –*
>   (a) *on the making of an application for a fire certificate with respect to the premises covering that use; or*
>   (b) *at any time during the currency of a fire certificate with respect to the premises which covers that use.*
>
> (3) *In deciding whether or not to grant exemption under this section for any premises the fire authority shall have regard to all the circumstances of the case and in particular to the degree of seriousness of the risk in case of fire to persons in the premises.*
>
> (4) *For the purpose of making that decision the fire authority may –*
>   (a) *require the applicant or, as the case may be, the occupier of the premises to give such information as they require about the premises and any matter connected with them and;*
>   (b) *cause to be carried out an inspection of the relevant building.*
>
> (5) *The fire authority shall not grant exemption under this section for any premises without causing an inspection to be carried out under subsection (4) above unless they have caused the premises to be inspected (under that or any other power) within the preceding twelve months.*
>
> (6) *The effect of the grant of exemption under this section as respects any particular use of premises is that, during the currency of the exemption, no fire certificate in respect of the premises is required to cover that use and accordingly –*
>   (a) *where the grant is made on an application for a fire certificate, the grant disposes of the application or of so much of it as relates to that use; and*

    (b) where the grant is made during the currency of a fire certificate, the certificate shall wholly or as respects that use cease to have effect.

(7) *On granting an exemption under this section, the fire authority shall, by notice to the applicant for the fire certificate or the occupier of the premises, as the case may be, inform him that they have granted exemption as respects the particular use or uses of the premises specified in the notice and of the effect of the grant.*

(8) *A notice of the grant of exemption for any premises as respects a particular use of them may include a statement specifying the greatest number of persons of a description specified in the statement for the purposes of that use who, in the opinion of the fire authority, can safely be in the premises at any one time.*

(9) *Where a notice of the grant of exemption for any premises includes a statement under subsection (8) above, the fire authority may, by notice served on the occupier of the premises, direct that, as from a date specified in the notice, the statement –*
    (a) is cancelled; or
    (b) is to have effect as varied by the notice; and, on such a variation the statement shall be treated, so long as the variation remains in force, as if the variation were specified in it.

By s. 5B a fire authority who have granted an exemption under s. 5A from the requirement to have a fire certificate covering any particular use of premises may, if they think fit, at any time withdraw the exemption provided they follow the procedures set out in s. 5B(2)–(4).

Certain premises do not require fire certificates, namely, factory, office, shop and railway premises in which either not more than 20 people are employed to work at any one time, or no more than ten people are so employed to work other than on the ground floor. If the premises are so excluded, they are *non-certificated premises* to which s. 12 of the Fire Precautions Act applies. Section 12 requires, amongst other things, that in all shop premises the following precautions must be observed:

1   The doors through which workers might have to pass in order to get out of the premises must not be so locked or fastened that they cannot easily and immediately be opened by them on their way out.

2   The contents of any workroom shall be so arranged as to afford a free passageway to a means of escape in case of fire.

3   There shall be provided and maintained appropriate means of fighting fire, so placed as to be readily available for use.

It can be seen that non-certificated premises, although outside the more rigorous requirements for certificated premises, must still undertake certain elementary precautions.

Fire certificates

An application for a fire certificate is made on the prescribed form to the local fire authority. The application sets out particulars as to the use to which the premises are to be put, giving information about the structure and specification of the building. The fire authority will thereafter carry out an inspection of the building, and will issue a fire certificate provided the following are such may be reasonable in the circumstances in connection with that use of the premises:
(a) the means of escape in case of fire with which the premises are provided;
(b) the means with which the relevant building is provided for securing that the

means of escape with which the premises are provided can be safely and
effectively used at all material times;
(c) the means of fighting fire (whether in the premises or affecting the means of
escape) with which the relevant building is provided for use by the persons in
the building;
(d) the means with which the relevant building is provided for giving warnings to
persons in the premises.
To summarize the requirements to be met for the granting of a fire certificate one can
say that the premises must be reasonably equipped with means of escape, means of
fire fighting and means for giving fire warnings.

Section 4 of the Fire Safety and Safety of Places of Sport Act 1987 (amending s. 5
of the 1971 Act) defines escape as follows:

> ... 'escape', in relation to premises, means escape from them to some place of safety
> beyond the building which constitutes or comprises the premises and any area
> enclosed by it or enclosed with it; and accordingly, for the purposes of any provision
> of this Act relating to means of escape, consideration may be given to, and conditions
> or requirements imposed as respects, any place or thing by means of which a person
> escapes from premises to a place of safety.

The 1987 Act further creates, in s. 5 (amending s. 9 of the 1971 Act), a general duty
to provide a means of escape and means for fire fighting:

> (1) All premises to which this section applies shall be provided with: –
>   (a) such means of escape in case of fire, and
>   (b) such means for fighting fire,
> as may reasonably be required in the circumstances of the case.

This section applies to certificated premises and to those where the fire authority have
granted an exemption under the Act. In the event of an occupier contravening this
provision, he or she will be guilty of a criminal offence.

By s. 6 of the 1987 Act (amending s. 9 of the 1971 Act), the Secretary of State may
prepare and issue codes of practice for the purpose of providing practical guidance on
how to comply with the duty. A failure on the part of any person to observe any
provision of a code of practice will not itself render that person liable for any criminal
offence, nor will it necessarily incur civil liability. However, where it is alleged that
there is a breach of duty under it to provide means of escape or means for fire fighting,
a failure to observe a provision of a code of practice may be relied on as tending
to establish liability. Compliance with such a code may also be relied on as tending to
negative liability.

Where a fire authority are of the opinion that the duty to provide means of escape
and means of fire fighting has been contravened in respect of premises to which the
provision applies, the fire authority may serve on the occupier of those premises an
improvement notice. Improvement notices are provided for by s. 7 of the 1987 Act
(amending s. 9 of the 1971 Act). An improvement notice states three things:
(a) that the fire authority are of the opinion that the occupier of the premises is in

breach of the duty to provide a sufficient means of escape and adequate
fire-fighting equipment;
(b) by reference to the code of practice, the steps which the occupier should take
and which are necessary to remedy the contravention;
(c) that the fire authority require the occupier to take steps to remedy the
contravention within a specified period (minimum 21 days).

An occupier may, within 21 days, appeal to the Magistrates' Court against the issue of
an improvement notice. On appeal the magistrates may either cancel or affirm the
notice and, if they affirm it, they may do so either in its original form or with such
modifications as the court may in the circumstances think fit. The bringing of an appeal
has the effect of suspending the operation of the improvement notice until the appeal
is disposed of.

It is a criminal offence for any person to contravene any requirement imposed by an
improvement notice. Upon conviction for such an offence tried before the magistrates
a person may be fined; where tried upon indictment in the Crown Court the maximum
penalty is two years' imprisonment.

Section 6 of the Fire Precautions Act 1971 sets out the contents of every fire certificate. Every fire certificate will specify (and may do so by reference to a plan):
(a) the particular use or uses of the premises;
(b) the means of escape with which the premises are provided;
(c) the means with which the building is provided for securing that the means of
escape with which the premises are provided can be safely and effectively used
at all times;
(d) the type, number and location of the means of fighting fire with which the
relevant building is provided for use by persons in the building;
(e) the type, number and location of the means with which the relevant building is
provided for giving persons in the premises warning in case of fire.

The fire certificate may also impose such requirements as the fire authority considers
appropriate in the circumstances for, amongst other things:
(a) securing that the means of escape in case of fire with which the premises are
provided are properly maintained and kept free from obstruction;
(b) ensuring that people employed to work in the premises receive appropriate
instruction and training in what to do in the event of fire;
(c) limiting the number of people who may be in the premises at any one time.

Of these requirements perhaps (c) is the most relevant to catering and hotel premises.
Public rooms in a hotel, e.g. hotel discotheque or function room, may be limited to a
maximum number of people allowed to be present in the room at one time. Moreover,
in view of the fact that guests secure sleeping accommodation in hotels and guest
houses, hotel fire certificates normally require that self-closing and in some case fire-
resistant doors be fitted to bedrooms, and that an automatic alarm system be installed
in the hotel to give 'advance warning'.

Section 7 of the Fire Precautions Act 1971 provides for the criminal prosecution of
those failing to comply with provisions of the Act. If any premises are put to use as a
place of work, being premises in respect of which a fire certificate is required, and one
is not in force, then the occupier of the premises will be guilty of an offence. However,
an offence will not be committed where an application for a fire certificate has been
made and it has not yet been granted or refused. If a fire certificate imposes a requirement (e.g. a limitation on the number of people at the premises at any one time) which
is contravened by reason of something either being done or not done to any part of the
relevant building by the occupier or some other person, and the fire authority consider

it to be appropriate in the circumstances, *the person responsible for the contravention* will be guilty of an offence.

If a person is convicted in the Magistrates' Court of either of the above offences a fine may be imposed. If on the other hand the person is convicted in the Crown Court before a judge and jury, the maximum penalty is two years' imprisonment.

A copy of the fire certificate shall be kept at the premises; failure to fulfil this obligation is an offence punishable in the Magistrates' Court by a fine.

After a fire certificate has been issued the fire authority may inspect the building at any reasonable time to ascertain whether there has been a change of conditions at the premises which render the fire precautions taken inadequate in relation to the use being made of the premises. If the fire authority are satisfied that there has been such a change, a notice may be served on the occupier informing him or her of the fact that there has been such a change and outlining the steps to be taken in order to make the fire precautions adequate in relation to the building and the use to which it is put. The fire certificate will then be cancelled. Once the steps have been taken a new certificate will be issued by the fire authority in relation to the building.

If the proprietor of the hotel or catering premises to which a fire certificate applies wishes to make structural alterations, extend the premises or refurbish the building in some way, he or she must, before such alterations are carried out, give notice to the fire authority of the proposed alterations. Failure to do so amounts to an offence. If on the receipt of such a notice the fire authority are satisfied that the proposed alterations would render the means of escape, the fire-fighting equipment, or the warning system inadequate, then within two months they will serve on the occupier a notice stating the steps to be taken in order to make adequate provision for the above. The fire authority may give such directions as they think fit that the proposed alterations shall not be made until the steps specified in the notice have been complied with. A failure on the part of the hotelier or caterer to comply with the notice amounts to a criminal offence.

Section 9 of the Fire Precautions Act 1971 provides for an appeal to the Magistrates' Court against a decision made by the fire authority in relation to a fire certificate on various grounds, and an appeal thereafter to the Crown Court.

Section 9 of the 1987 Act (amending s. 10 of the 1971 Act) makes detailed provision for premises where it is necessary to restrict the use to which the premises are put until excessive risk to persons in case of fire is reduced. The section makes provision for the issuing of a prohibition notice.

A prohibition notice states:
(a) that the fire authority are of the opinion that the use of the premises involves or will involve a risk to persons on the premises in case of fire which is so serious that the use of the premises ought to be prohibited or restricted;
(b) the matters which in the opinion of the fire authority give rise to, or may give rise to, such a risk;
(c) that the use to which the prohibition notice relates is prohibited or restricted to the extent specified in the notice.
The prohibition notice will usually set out the steps which the fire authority consider necessary to remedy the matters specified in the notice.

Where the fire authority are of the opinion (and so state in the notice) that the risk of serious personal injury is imminent, the notice will take immediate effect. In other cases the notice will specify the period of time before the notice comes into effect.

The occupier of the premises to which the prohibition notice applies has a right of appeal to the Magistrates' Court within 21 days of the issue of the notice.

It is a criminal offence for any person to contravene any prohibition or restriction imposed by a prohibition notice. Where convicted before the magistrates he or she may be fined; where convicted upon a trial on indictment in the Crown Court a maximum of two years' imprisonment may be imposed.

Safety of sports grounds

The Fire Safety and Safety of Places of Sport Act 1987 arose from the Popplewell Inquiry into the fire disaster at Bradford City FC's stadium and concern over crowd safety. Part II of the Act makes detailed provisions as to the safety of sports grounds. These include:
(a) extension of existing provisions under the Safety of Sports Grounds Act 1975 to all sports grounds;
(b) designation of spectator capacity;
(c) safety certificates;
(d) prohibition of use where the use of the sports ground involves serious risk of injury to spectators;
(e) inspection procedures.
Part III of the 1987 Act provides for the requirement for safety certificates for stands at sports grounds.

Although these provisions may not directly affect the caterer, many 'event caterers' and caterers at sporting events would be adversely affected by the closure of the venue(s) or the limitation of spectators at the venue(s) where they provide catering services, so it is important that they are aware of these new safety provisions.

3.5 LOST PROPERTY

One of the minor irritations of running an establishment which is open to the public is the amount of lost property left at the premises. Of course the proper course of action is to try to trace the owner, e.g. where valuables are left in a guest's room. Furthermore, it is the proper practice to hand over lost articles to the police. If, however, a guest finds a valuable article in a public room of a hotel and hands it over to the proprietor, and the proprietor uses his or her best endeavours to locate the true owner but these fail and the article is kept by the hotelier, who is entitled to the article if the true owners cannot be found: the guest who found it or the hotelier?

PARKER v. BRITISH AIRWAYS BOARD [1982] QB 1004 (CA)   A passenger in a lounge of an airport found a valuable bracelet which he handed to a British Airways official, BA being the occupiers of the lounge area. He gave the official a note of his address and asked that the article be returned if it was not claimed by the true owner. The official handed the article to the lost property department. The owner never claimed it and BA sold the article and kept the proceeds, £850. The passenger sought compensation for the failure on the part of BA to return the article to him.

Held: If something was found, whether by an employee of an occupier of premises or by a stranger, the presumption was that the possession of that thing was in the occupier. However, the occupier had a better claim than the finder, not being an employee, only if the occupier had possession of the article immediately before it was found and he or she was able to show that the intention to exercise control was manifest. It was impossible to go further and to hold that the mere right of an occupier to exercise such control was sufficient to give him or her rights in relation to lost property on his or her premises.

The passenger was successful in his claim for compensation, the Court of Appeal taking the view that the occupier, BA, had wrongfully interfered with the goods. The passenger's claim to the goods as a finder took precedence over the claim of BA as the occupier of the premises on which the goods were found.

BRAITHWAITE v.
THOMAS COOK
TRAVELLERS CHEQUES
LTD [1989] 3 WLR 212

Lost traveller's cheques have recently caused considerable consternation to the courts. The plaintiff wished to bring money from his bank in Jersey to London. At 4 a.m., he got up and went to Heathrow Airport, from where he flew to Jersey. At his bank in Jersey, he purchased 400 traveller's cheques issued by the defendants to the value of £50 000. It was a condition of the purchase agreement that the defendants would replace or refund the value of the traveller's cheques lost or stolen provided that the purchaser had 'properly safeguarded each cheque against loss or theft'. He was permitted to leave the bank without signing the cheques. He proceeded to sign the cheques at the airport, on the flight to London and at other public places. All the cheques were signed by about 6 p.m. He carried the cheques in a brown paper envelope with a carton of 200 cigarettes in a clear plastic bag. On the evening of his return the plaintiff spent the time with friends drinking in public houses before returning home on the London Underground. During the journey he fell asleep and, on awakening and leaving the train at his destination, he found he no longer had the plastic bag. The plaintiff claimed reimbursement of the value of the cheques from the defendants, who refused to pay.

On the plaintiff's action to recover the value of the cheques it was held that the burden of showing that the cheques had been properly safeguarded and, if there had been a period of carelessness, that there was no causal link between the lack of care and the occurrence of the loss or theft was on the plaintiff; that, although the fact that the plaintiff signed the cheques in public had not contributed to their loss, his conduct in carrying the cheques in a clear plastic bag on the Underground when he was in no state to keep awake during the journey was a failure properly to safeguard the cheques and was the case of their loss; and that, accordingly, the plaintiff was not entitled to recover in respect of the cheques presented for payment and paid. It was also held that apart from contract, a purchaser is not entitled to any refund of the face value of traveller's cheques which he has lost or which have been stolen from him.

In the subsequent case of *El Awadi* v. *Bank of Credit and Commerce International SA Ltd* [1989] 3 WLR 221, *Braithwaite*'s case was not followed and the plaintiff was able to secure reimbursement of £40 700 worth of traveller's cheques stolen from his car.

3.6 STAFF ACCOMMODATION

Many of the staff who work for a hotelier or innkeeper 'live in'. Where staff 'live in' they occupy their staff accommodation by virtue of a contractual licence. It is clear that staff are not the tenants of the hotelier. The contract of employment between the member of staff and the hotelier normally sets out the basis on which the accommodation is to be occupied. Normally, the contract of employment specifies that the employee is given permission to occupy the accommodation for such time as the employee remains in the employment of the hotel. Hence, upon termination of the contract of employment by either party, the accommodation becomes vacant and the member of staff is no longer entitled to occupation. The situation may become acute where the hotelier and the employee are in dispute over the termination of the employee's contract of employment. This is particularly so where the employee concerned is a club steward (his wife may also be employed by the club) and, with his wife, he occupies a staff flat at the club. Not only may this become embarrassing *vis-à-vis* the membership of the club, but it may also deter prospective new club stewards from taking up the post when the accommodation offered is in dispute. In such a situation the proper course of action is to obtain a possession order from the High Court requiring the ex-steward to vacate the staff flat. Another issue that arises is the Uniform Business Rate and Council Tax. Which is applicable to staff accommodation? Who is responsible for payment?

3.7 SECURITY

We are all increasingly aware of the need for security not only in our place of work, where large sums of money may be kept, but in our homes. Security raises a number of differing issues, and most major companies have a security policy which management are required to follow. Such a policy should cover:
1   Handling money:
    (a)   handling and banking cash, retaining cash on the premises;
    (b)   the use of the safe;
    (c)   the use of tills;
    (d)   wages for manual staff.
2   Keys:
    (a)   retention of keys of premises;
    (b)   responsibilities of key-holders.
3   Securing the premises:
    (a)   closing-down procedure;
    (b)   safety checks (water, gas, electricity);
    (c)   safety of premises;
    (d)   fire exits, etc.
4   Maintenance of equipment.
5   Fire-fighting appliances – maintenance and inspection.
6   Safety of premises:
    (a)   areas open to public;
    (b)   work areas;
    (c)   storage of waste, etc.;
    (d)   toilets;
    (e)   first-aid equipment.
7   Burglary/theft/fraud:
    (a)   informing management;

    (b)   informing the police;
    (c)   securing the premises;
    (d)   stocktaking and cash reconciliation;
    (e)   written reports;
    (f)   theft, etc. by staff;
    (g)   searching staff and customers.

Managers and staff need to be aware of the procedures to be followed if they wish to detain an individual and make an arrest. The police are in a completely different position from individual citizens when making an arrest. It is essential that a member of the management team or a member of staff does not make an arrest themselves unless they are aware of the relevant law and problems which may arise if they wrongfully arrest an individual. In essence an employee may be liable in civil law for assault, and/or false imprisonment of the person whom they 'arrest'.

In taking the steps which they took, they may also render their employer vicariously liable for their actions. Assault involves the doing of something which induces in another reasonable fear and apprehension of immediate violence.

Assault does not need to involve any physical touching – whether or not an assault is committed depends on the emotions which are aroused in the other party. Battery involves the unlawful application of force to the person of another – handling them whether or not one does it in a rough way is technically a battery.

False imprisonment consists of wrongful deprivation of personal liberty, and not necessarily by force or incarceration. In the case of *Warner* v. *Riddiford* (1858) the defendant after dismissing the plaintiff as manager of a beer house, prevented him from going upstairs to collect his possessions. It was held that this amounted to false imprisonment. However, it will not be false imprisonment if the plaintiff has a reasonable means of leaving. Consider the situation where a member of the security staff employed by the management of a leisure facility, night club etc. detains a person for some reason (e.g. suspicion of theft from the premises or another member of the public) and that suspicion is unfounded, the person who has been detained against his will, whether by force or not, may have a claim against the security guard and the guard's employer.

There are two defences which are relevant. The first is self-defence, a person may use reasonable (i.e. necessary and proportionate) force to defend himself or any other person against unlawful violence. This protects the member of staff who restrains a threatening or violent person, provided the force used is 'reasonable'. The second is the preservation of public peace.

What would otherwise be a trespass to the person may be justified if done to support the law or maintain the peace. The onus is on the defendant to prove that he acted for those reasons.

Force may be justified if used to effect a lawful arrest. Any person can arrest another person for a breach of the peace committed in his presence – this will amount to a defence if a member of the security staff arrests a customer who is threatening another customer or member of staff with violence. Any person may arrest with reasonable force for an arrestable offence or to preserve life. It is important to note that the onus is on the arrester to show reasonable and probable cause – i.e. that the arrestable offence was committed. This means that a private citizen's liability for false imprisonment depends on proof that the offence was committed. A police constable need only establish that he/she had a reasonable suspicion of an offence having been committed, even where one had not in fact been committed.

In short, undertaking a 'citizen's arrest' is a risky step to take for any public-spirited person, and for a person who is employed in a situation where she or he may take steps which amount to an arrest, she/he is no better protected by the law than any other person.

3.8 CAR PARKS

Many organizations have a policy of clamping vehicles which are left on their premises without permission. This clamping may be sub-contracted to a security company or undertaken by its manager and his/her staff.

The law relating to the clamping of vehicles is a legal minefield. The criminal law in England is unclear. In Scotland, in the case of *Black and Another* v. *Carmichael* [1992] SLT 897 it was held that the clamping on private land amounted to extortion and theft under Scottish law – private clamping is therefore illegal in Scotland. Depriving a driver of his vehicle by detaining it against his will is theft.

In England and Wales it is difficult to see how the English courts could hold that detaining a car is theft of the vehicle – there is no intention to *permanently deprive* the motorist of his vehicle, which is a crucial element of the offence of theft under S.1 Theft Act 1968. In *Lloyd* v. *DPP* [1992] RTR 215 a clamper brought criminal proceedings for criminal damage against the owner of a vehicle after the owner had removed the clamp placed on it by him by cutting through two padlocks. The question was whether or not the owner of the vehicle had a lawful excuse for the damage which he had caused to the wheel clamp. The court took the view that if a motorist parked his car without permission on another person's property knowing that he ran the risk of being clamped, he had no right to damage or destroy the clamp, in order to release his vehicle.

An important issue of civil law arises from this activity, namely: Can the clamping itself amount to the tort of interference with goods (whether or not damage is caused to the vehicle by the clamping)? See Section 1 of the Torts (Interference with Goods) Act 1977. Such an action can be brought by the person in possession of the vehicle at the time of the tort.

One defence for the defendant to such an action is to show that the interference was lawful. However, does this cover where a car is clamped and the clamper is seeking to detain the vehicle until the appropriate fee is paid for storage of the vehicle? Another defence is to show that the tort was committed in order to avert immediate danger to persons or property – it will need to be shown that the danger was both real and imminent, and that he had acted reasonably in the circumstances. In the recent case of *Arthur and Another* v. *Anker, The Times*, 1 December 1995 the Court of Appeal expressly rejected such a 'self help' remedy by stating that the application of the remedy to the facts in such cases was remote from anything that could have been contemplated by those who developed it.

One of the rare cases to come before the courts is an unreported decision of the Oxford County Court, *Total Car Park Management Ltd.* v. *Dr Colin Fink* (1994). In that case Dr F.'s car had been clamped while visiting a hospital where unknown to him a pay and display car park had been introduced – previously it had been free of charge. Dr F. had signed a form in order to have his car released stating that he would pay a £25 penalty plus a £13 administration fee. The plaintiff sued on that agreement when

Dr F later refused to pay. Dr F. alleged that he had signed the form under duress and counterclaimed unlawful interference with goods. The court had to directly decide whether plaintiff was entitled to clamp Dr F.'s car. The court held that the clamping of Dr F.'s car – without him having caused damage as a trespasser to the car park – could not be justified. The case was based on the breach of the agreement to pay the penalty and the administration fee – breach of contract.

The decision in Dr F.'s case might well have been different had the trial judge found as an issue of fact that the clamping had been undertaken to secure an actual lost benefit – lost car parking revenue. The release fee payable would have to reflect the likely lost car-parking charges and could not amount to a fine on the person who had parked the car. In most cases the release fee is set at a level which is far higher than the car park fee as a deterrent to those who might park without paying.

A further defence is that of consent or *volenti non fit injuria*: 'one who has invited or assented to an act being done towards him cannot, when he suffers from it, complain of it as a wrong' (Lord Herschell, *Smith* v. *Baker and sons* (1891)).

This defence was central in the *Anker* case. Mr Anchor ran a security firm offering land owners a service whereby he clamped illegally parked cars and collected a fee for their release. No charge was made to the land owner for this service. Mr Anker's car had been clamped by Mr Arthur after it had been parked without authority on private land.

Mr Arthur accepted that he had seen a sign erected by Mr Anker warning that vehicles parked without authority would be wheel clamped and released only on payment of a £40 fee and that the fee was reasonable. Mr Arthur removed the clamp and refused to pay the fee. Mr Anker successfully sued for the fee in the County Court. Mr Arthur unsuccessfully appealed to the Court of Appeal. The Court held that by voluntarily accepting the risk that his car might be clamped Mr Arthur had also accepted the risk that the car would remain clamped until the fine was paid – he consented to both otherwise tortious acts of clamping and detaining the vehicle.

In the lead judgment, Sir Thomas Bingham, Master of the Rolls, did not however accept that a clamper could exact an unreasonable or exorbitant charge for releasing the car – a court being slow to find implied acceptance of such a charge.

The same would be true if the warning was not of clamping but of conduct likely to cause damage to the vehicle. In addition, a clamper would be unable to justify detaining a vehicle where the owner had indicated a willingness to comply with the condition for release.

There appears to be no right for a land owner or a management company acting on behalf of a landowner to clamp cars – fitting the clamp to the vehicle amounts to a trespass and is actionable against the person who fitted it. However, the defence of *volenti non fit inuria* will assist the landowner or management company if an action for trespass is brought against them. This defence will be a complete answer to the claim, if, but only if, the landowner or management company can clearly show that the person parking the vehicle clearly knew of the risks he was taking when he parked the car. In *Total Car Park Management Ltd.* v. *Dr Colin Fink* it was found as a matter of fact that Dr F. did not know as he had not read the signs in the car park.

In order to levy a fee for the removal of the clamp and the release of the vehicle there must have been an appropriate notice setting out that vehicles are liable to be clamped and the fee chargeable for releasing them.

There are a number of simple precautions which the landowner or management company can appropriately take:

- Large, clear signs warning persons parking their vehicles that clamping is in operation.
- The release fee should be a reasonable reflection of the loss to the landowner or management company and not an excessive fine/penalty for parking.
- When cars are clamped, place a clear notice on the vehicle of who to contact and how to do so in order to facilitate the release of the vehicle.
- If practicable the release service should operate throughout 24 hours of the day.
- If the landowner, e.g. hotel, golf club, leisure facility etc. sub-contracts the work to a management company, fully investigate the company, its background and operational strategy to ensure that through the proper procedures they do not render you liable for the actions which they have taken by clamping vehicles on your property.

CASE STUDY

Bert is the manager of the Lazy Dog public house. Bert is also Chief Walrus of the Walrus Club, a philanthropic organization which meets at the Lazy Dog in a clubroom at the rear of the premises on the first floor, each Monday evening.

Reginald, the Treasurer of the Walrus Club, with other members, remains on the licensed premises of the Lazy Dog until 12 midnight, the bars having closed at 11.00 p.m. at the end of licensing hours. Reginald leaves the clubroom via an unlit emergency staircase in search of the lavatory, which he knows to be outside in the car park.

Reginald slips down the unlit iron staircase, severely injuring his spine.

Advise Bert and the Gnat's Water Brewery Co., owners of the Lazy Dog, as to their liability for Reginald's injuries.

Key points

The first matter which is to be determined is who is the occupier of that part of the premises where Reginald was injured – Bert or the Gnat's Water Brewery (see p. 78, *Wheat* v. *Lacon*). It should be noted that shared occupation is possible. Note also *Stone* v. *Taffe* (p. 79).

The next issue is whether at the material time Reginald was a lawful visitor (see *Campbell* v. *Shelbourne Hotel Ltd*, *Stone* v. *Taffe* and *Senner* v. *Taff-Ely Borough Council*). If Reginald was a lawful visitor then the Occupiers' Liability Act 1957 applies. The duty owed by an occupier to a lawful visitor is set out in s. 2(1) and s. 2(2) (see p. 79). Both the brewery and Bert may seek to show that Reginald is not owed a duty by each of them under the Act, or alternatively that the defence of *volenti non fit injuria* applies (see s. 2(5) OLA 1957). More clearly, a defence of contributory negligence is applicable (see s. 1(1) Law Reform (Contributory Negligence) Act 1945 and *Stone* v. *Taffe*).

If Reginald was *not* a lawful visitor then the Occupiers' Liability Act 1984 is applicable. Full details of this are given on pp. 82–85. Note that the occupier here owes a lesser duty of care, and that the potential defences of *volenti non fit injuria* and contributory negligence are applicable.

Reginald may also seek to establish that he was owed the common duty of care under *Donoghue* v. *Stevenson*. This has been the basis for recent actions in *Salmon* v. *Seafarer Restaurants Ltd* and *Ogwo* v. *Taylor*. Again, the same defences apply.

FOUR

The hotelier and the guest I

The relationship between hoteliers and their guests is central to the hotel and catering industry. This relationship gives rise to a number of different legal problems. It raises questions of both civil and criminal law. Legal duties are imposed upon an innkeeper under the Hotel Proprietors Act 1956 which apply only to *inns* as defined by s. 1(3) of the Act. Innkeepers covered by the Innkeepers Act 1878 are able to benefit from certain rights over their guests' property which only they may exercise.

The discussion of the relationship between the hotelier or innkeeper and the guest is divided in this text between two chapters. This chapter deals primarily with the contract of booking between the guest and the hotel and Chapter 5 considers the duties and liabilities of an innkeeper regarding guests.

4.1 THE CONTRACT OF BOOKING

A contract of booking between the hotelier and the guest may be defined as a legally binding agreement between them for the provision of food and drink and, if so required, accommodation or some other service, such as the provision of conference or banqueting facilities.

In Chapter 5 we shall consider the legal definition of 'an inn' (s. 1(3) Hotel Proprietors Act 1956), but for the purposes of discussing contracts of booking the term will not be given its strict legal meaning under the Hotel Proprietors Act 1956. The term 'hotel' will be used to describe not only inns covered by the Act but also other establishments such as guest houses and the like where the same legal principles apply.

The contract of booking is primarily a civil matter. A booking contract is subject to the same civil legal principles as any other contract. However, certain statutorily imposed regulations relate to the formation of a booking contract, i.e. requirements as to the registration of guests. Similarly, people booking under such a contract are consumers and they are afforded some protection by the Trade Descriptions Act 1968. The Trade Descriptions Act imposes criminal sanctions for the breach of obligations imposed under the Act; hence the hotelier may be prosecuted and punished for a breach of the Trade Descriptions Act.

Essentials of a contract

The essential elements of any contract are:
* Offer
* Acceptance
* Consideration
* Capacity
* Intention to create legal relations
* Legality of purpose.

It is important to distinguish a pre-contractual stage – which may include an invitation to treat (e.g. advertisements) and pre-contractual negotiations. These are preliminary but do not themselves form part of the contract which follows from them.

Negotiations prior to contract

Not all contracts will involve a period of pre-contractual negotiation during which the parties negotiate on the terms of the agreement between them. Indeed, many hotels and tour operators deal mainly on a 'standard form' of contract, this being a document including the terms on which a party is willing to contract. If the other party is not willing to contract on those terms then no agreement, and hence no contract, can be reached. Standard form contracts are very common in large commercial organizations in the hotel and catering industry. Some large companies and tour operators use a standard form contract for booking contracts, which is usually to be found appended to the brochure as part of the booking form. We shall in the course of this chapter examine some of the terms included in such standard form contracts to analyse both their effect and the purpose for which they are included by the hotelier.

When does a booking contract come into being? It is vital to be able to identify the point in time when the contract comes into being, for after that point in time the terms of the contract are fixed and the respective duties and liabilities of each party set. It is important from the outset to understand the elements which are necessary to form a contract. These elements may be listed as follows:

(a) an offer made by the offeror to the offeree;
(b) an acceptance of the terms of the offer by the offeree;
(c) some recognized form of consideration given by the offeree in return for what is promised by the offeror;
(d) an intention on the part of both the offeror and the offeree to create a legal relationship between them.

The descriptions 'offeror' and 'offeree' are simply a lawyer's way of describing the parties. The offeror is the party making the offer to contract, and the offeree is simply the person to whom that offer is addressed. Our primary concern is to recognize when an offer to contract has been made and when there has been sufficient acceptance of it, and thus a binding contract has arisen.

How do we identify an offer to contract? Prior to the point in time when the offeror makes an offer to contract there may be a number of pre-contractual stages which, whilst they may be steps on the way towards the making of an offer, are not in themselves an offer to contract.

Advertisements

The first step which many hotels and catering organizations take towards the formation of a booking contract is to advertise their accommodation, restaurant and other services in a newspaper or magazine. Does this advert form part of the contract of booking? The answer is generally no. Advertisements fall short of amounting to an offer and are known as an invitation to treat. In the case of *Partridge* v. *Crittenden* [1968] 1 WLR 1204 (QBD) it was held that a classified advertisement in a magazine did not amount to an offer to contract. The reasoning for this is quite clear: there is not sufficient in an advertisement to amount to an offer. An advertisement is usually silent on matters which are vital to the contract, e.g. the availability of the product or service advertised. In *Grainger & Son* v. *Gough* [1896] AC 325 (HL), where the advertisement described wines for sale by a merchant, Lord Herschell observed:

> *The transmission of such a price list does not amount to an offer to supply an unlimited quantity of the wine described at the price named, so that as soon as an order is given there is a binding contract to supply that quantity. If it were so, the merchant might find himself involved in any number of contractual obligations to supply wine of a particular description which he would be quite unable to carry out, his stock of wine of that description being necessarily limited.*

This proposition can be applied directly to an advertisement of hotel accommodation. Such an advertisement is subject to the same limitation of availability; the maximum number of rooms available at a hotel is fixed by the capacity of the establishment, hence such an advert cannot be construed as an offer to contract. Can an advertisement be sufficiently certain to amount to an offer to contract? In the case of *Carlill* v. *Carbolic Smoke Ball Co.* [1893] 1 QB 256 (CA) an advertisement purporting to offer a reward to any person who used the medication advertised in the prescribed manner and thereafter caught influenza was held to be an offer to contract. The proposition derived from the case, namely that an advertisement may amount to an offer to contract upon the terms stated in the advertisement, is said to be limited to those advertisements offering a reward or prize in return for some act (e.g. use of the advertiser's product) done by the person to whom the advert is addressed. What is clear from the case is that an offer to contract need not be directed to an individual but may be directed to the public at large, any one of whom may respond to the terms of the offer and accept them.

The brochure

Often when prospective customers reply to advertisements put out by hoteliers they will be forwarded a brochure explaining in further detail the accommodation or services offered by the hoteliers. Does this brochure amount to an offer to contract? Again the question is posed of whether there is sufficient certainty in the details of the brochure to amount to an offer. Usually the brochure is silent about the availability of the accommodation. Hence, for the same reasons as discussed above, the brochure will not normally be considered an offer to contract. Normally appended to the brochure is a booking form to be completed by the customer. It is this document which will form the first stage in the contractual process. At the end of the booking form there are a number of conditions which outline the basis on which the hotelier is willing to contract. The customer may fill in the booking form and return it to the hotelier. The form upon receipt by the hotelier, amounts to an offer to contract, made by the customer to the hotelier.

Telephone bookings

It may be that a prospective customer telephones a hotel to inquire about the services or accommodation provided at the establishment. Can such a telephone conversation form the basis of a contract? Yes, a contract may be created by spoken words as well as in writing. However, oral contracts are often exceptionally difficult to prove before a court of law. In addition, the words relied upon as forming the contract must be sufficiently clear and must establish an offer made by one party to the conversation and an acceptance of it by the other party. It is therefore normal booking practice to require some written confirmation of booking, which will take the form of a letter from the inquirer to the hotel requesting accommodation or facilities on a given day or dates. This letter will amount to an offer to contract and the hotelier's reply will be the acceptance of it. If, however, this approach is not adopted, it is perfectly possible for an oral contract of booking to be made over the telephone. One must look to the actual words used to decide whether or not there is sufficient in them to amount to an offer to contract and acceptance of it. An example where the courts considered a purported oral contract made by telephone is as follows.

LEVISON v. PATENT STEAM CARPET CLEANING CO. LTD [1977] 3 All ER 498 (CA)

The plaintiff owned a carpet valued at £900. On 5 July 1972 she telephoned the defendants and requested them to collect and clean the carpet. On 17 July the defendants' driver called to collect the carpet. The driver requested the plaintiff to sign an order form. The order form contained the terms upon which the defendants were prepared to contract. The plaintiff signed the order form without reading it. The order form contained a term limiting the defendants' liability to £40 and providing 'all merchandise is expressly accepted at the owner's risk'. The carpet disappeared whilst in the care of the defendant company. The plaintiff brought an action claiming damages to the full value of the carpet. The High Court gave judgment to the plaintiff. On appeal the Court of Appeal held:
1   The only contract made between the parties was the written contract made on 17 July which incorporated the printed terms and conditions. The arrangements made on the telephone on 5 July did not constitute a contract.
2   The wording of the clause exempting and limiting the defendants' liability was not sufficient to cover the defendants' breach in losing the carpet.

Facsimile

The fax machine is used in many instances as an alternative to the post. Often, however, persons using a fax for business communication will also post the document that is faxed to the recipient as a matter of record or confirmation. Faxed communications can be equated with either telephone calls (instantaneous communication) or post.

Obviously, the postal rules are difficult to apply in this instance, and specific issues of 'despatch' and 'receipt' could be raised in litigation. Electronic Mail (e-mail) using the Internet falls into the category of instantaneous communication, and the postal rules do not apply.

Chance call bookings

Chance call booking describes the situation where a prospective customer pays a casual call at the hotel looking for accommodation. The reception manager will normally check the daily room availability chart and inform customers whether or not they can be accommodated. This amounts to an offer to contract. When customers respond by telling the reception manager that they will take the rooms, this amounts to acceptance, and the contract is formed. Certain formalities of registration must then be undertaken.

Any attempt to include further terms in the contract by means of a notice displayed in the guest's room will be of no effect:

OLLEY v.
MARLBOROUGH COURT
LTD [1949] 1 KB 532

A married couple arrived at a hotel as guests; they paid for the accommodation. The couple then went to their room, where on a wall was displayed the notice 'The proprietors will not hold themselves responsible for articles lost or stolen unless handed to the manageress for safe custody.' The wife closed the door, which locked, and took the key to reception. A third party took the key and stole some of the wife's property from the bedroom. The plaintiff sued the hotel for damages with regard to the stolen property . The defendant hotel tried to rely on the notice in the room as a term of the booking contract exempting them from liability.

Held: The contract was completed at the reception desk and no subsequent notice could affect the plaintiff's rights. The notice was not sufficient to incorporate the exclusion clause into the booking contract. A chance booking is made at the time when the guest books in at the reception desk. The proprietor, to include a term in the contract, must do so then and there, either by informing the guest verbally or by displaying a notice at the reception desk.

Booking by an exchange of correspondence

A prospective guest may enter into correspondence with a hotel in order to find out information about both the hotel and its locality. It may be that the guest has a special need, e.g. a vegetarian diet, or requires special arrangements owing to infirmity or disability. If the correspondence becomes lengthy and complex it may not be clear whether a contract of booking has been entered into with the guest. The approach to be taken to ascertain when a contract has been entered into by means of an exchange of letters was set out in the speech of Lord Diplock in *Gibson* v. *Manchester City Council* [1979] 1 All ER 972 (HL), where he observes:

> *there may be certain types of contract, though I think they are exceptional, which do not fit easily into the normal analysis of a contract as being constituted by offer and acceptance; but a contract alleged to have been made by an exchange of correspondence between the parties in which successive communications other than the first are in reply to one another is not one of these. I can see no reason ... for departing from the conventional approach of looking at the handful of documents relied on as*

constituting the contract . . . and seeing whether on their true construction there is to be found in them a contractual offer by [the offeror] . . . and an acceptance of that offer by the [offeree] . . .

Offer and acceptance in booking contracts

Professor Treitel, in his text *The Law of Contract*, defines an offer to contract as:

An expression of willingness to contract on certain terms, with the intention that it shall become binding as soon as it is accepted by the person to whom it is addressed.

To constitute an offer the words used, whether oral or written, must be sufficiently clear and certain. Furthermore, an offer is effective only when communicated by the offeror (or a reliable third party) to the offeree. Acceptance is a final expression of assent by the offeree to the terms set out in the offer. The offeree must clearly accept the terms of the offer and communicate this to the offeror before the acceptance is said to be effective and the contract formed. It is important therefore to identify when there has been an acceptance sufficient to establish a contract between the parties.

Written acceptance

The general proposition as to acceptance of an offer, whether or not the acceptance is in writing or oral, is that the acceptance must be communicated to the offeror. However, there are important exceptions to this rule which affect the booking contract. The postal rule is perhaps the most relevant exception. Where an offeree replies to the offeror's offer in writing and posts a reply to the offeror, at the point in time when the reply (acceptance) is posted it is effective and the contract is formed:

HOUSEHOLD FIRE INSURANCE CO. LTD v. GRANT (1879) 4 Ex. D 216

K was the agent of a company. The defendant handed to K an application in writing for shares in the company which K represented. The application stated that the defendant had paid to the company's bankers five pounds, being a deposit of one shilling per share, and requested an allocation of one hundred shares, agreeing to pay a further nineteen shillings per share within twelve months of the date of allocation. K forwarded the application to the plaintiffs, and the secretary of the plaintiff company made out a letter allocating to the defendant one hundred shares and posted it, addressed to the defendant. The letter never arrived. The defendant's name was entered in the register of shareholders and he was later credited with two dividends. The defendant did not pay the money outstanding on the shares prior to going into liquidation. In an action brought by the plaintiffs claiming the money outstanding in payment for the shares, the defendant claimed that since he had not received the letter of allocation he was not bound by the contract.

The High Court held the defendant to be bound; he appealed. In the Court of Appeal it was held, dismissing the defendant's appeal, that the plaintiff's letter of allocation amounted to an acceptance of the defendant's offer to purchase shares. The acceptance was effective when posted by the plaintiff to the defendant and thus a binding contract for the purchase of shares had been made. It did not matter that the fact of acceptance was not communicated to the defendant.

Example. Freda writes to Basil requesting information about the cost and availability of accommodation for the week commencing 13 July. Basil, in answering her inquiry, states that accommodation is available for that week at a cost of £150, and that if Freda responds with a deposit of £15 within seven days the room will be allocated to her. This letter from Basil to Freda is an offer to contract. Freda responds to Basil's letter by writing a letter accepting the terms and enclosing a £15 postal order. When is Freda's acceptance valid and the contract complete? Is it when she posts the letter to Basil, or not until Basil receives it? What if the letter of acceptance is lost in the post? The approach taken by the law as explained in *Household Fire Insurance Co. Ltd* v. *Grant* is that the letter of acceptance is valid when posted and the contract is then binding, provided:

(a) it was reasonable for the offeree to use the post as a means of communicating acceptance of the offer; and

(b) the letter of acceptance was properly addressed and postage had been paid.

It is always open to the offeror when making the offer to the offeree to exclude the operation of the postal rules by use of a term in the offer. The postal rule will not operate where, if applied, it would lead to manifest inconvenience and absurdity (*Holwell Securities Ltd* v. *Hughes* [1974] 1 WLR 155 (CA)).

Instantaneous communications

An acceptance which is made verbally or by some instantaneous mode of communication, such as telex, must actually be communicated to the offeror in order to be effective and form a binding contract – *Entores Ltd* v. *Miles Far East Corporation* [1955] 2 All ER 493 (CA).

In *Brinkiban Ltd* v. *Stahag Stahl und Stahlwarenhandelsgesellschaft GmbH* [1983] 2 AC 34 (HL), Lord Wilberforce remarked:

> Since 1955 the use of telex communications has been greatly expanded, and there are many variants on it. The senders and recipients may not be the principals to the contemplated contract. They may be servants or agents with limited authority. The message may not reach, or be intended to reach, the designated recipient immediately: messages may be sent out of office hours, or at night, with the intention, or on the assumption, that they will be read at a later time. There may be some error or fault at the recipients' end which prevents receipt at the time contemplated and believed in by the sender. The message may have been sent and/or received through machines operated by third persons. And many other variations may occur. No universal rule can cover all such cases; they must be resolved by reference to the intuitions of the parties, by sound business practice and in some cases by a judgement where the risks should lie.

In this case the House of Lords applied *Entores Ltd* v. *Miles Far East Corporation*, holding that instantaneous communication through telex meant that the contract was made when acceptance of the offer was received.

In recent years the advent of the fax and e-mail has meant further scope for complication of the law on communication of acceptance. The instantaneous nature of communication by computers and fax machines puts them clearly outside the rule on postal acceptance. These forms of communication fall most naturally within the rules on telephone communications.

Of equal importance (whether the contract is in writing or oral) is to consider whether there is anything in the supposed acceptance which contradicts the terms of the offer. This is known as a 'counter offer'. If the offeree's acceptance is qualified in some way, or seeks to amend the terms of the offer, this will amount to a rejection of the offer, being a counter offer, and no contract will arise. It is important to note that at any time up until the moment when the offeree's acceptance is effective, the offeror can withdraw the offer to contract.

Privity of contract and agency bookings

The doctrine of privity of contract works hand in hand with the principle of consideration. The doctrine of privity means that a contract cannot, as a general rule, confer rights or impose obligations arising under it upon any person other than the parties to it. This doctrine may be clearly seen in the following case.

DUNLOP PNEUMATIC TYRE CO. LTD v. SELFRIDGE & CO. LTD [1915] AC 847 (HL) The appellants manufactured tyres; the respondents were retailers of the appellants' products. The appellants sold to the retail trade through wholesalers. In a contract between the appellants and a wholesaler, Dew and Co., there was a price maintenance clause which required the wholesaler to sell the tyres at a fixed price, and required the wholesaler to include a similar clause in his contract with any retailer, thereby guaranteeing the retail of the tyres at a set price. The consideration for the inclusion of this clause in the contract between the appellants and the wholesaler was a discount of ten per cent to the wholesaler. The appellants sold goods to the wholesaler, who thereafter sold the goods to a retailer by a contract which included the price maintenance clause. Thereafter the retailer sold the goods at a price less than that required by the price maintenance clause. The question arose whether the appellant manufacturers could enforce the price maintenance clause in the contract between the wholesaler and the retailer.

The House of Lords held that the clause was unenforceable by the appellants, since they were not a party to the contract between the wholesaler and the retailer, and furthermore they had given no consideration to the retailer for the inclusion of the price maintenance clause. It was, of course, perfectly open to the wholesaler to sue the retailer for breach of the price maintenance clause.

It would seem, therefore, that where a person is not a party to the contract, that person cannot sue upon the contract. But can such a person derive any benefit from the contract despite the fact that he or she is not party to it? The answer, according to the principles stated above, is no. However, as far as booking contracts are concerned there would appear to be a wholly anomalous situation.

Example. Mr Peg books a holiday for himself, his wife and their two children with Palm Springs Hotel. In breach of the terms of the booking contract the hotel fails to provide Mr Peg and his family with facilities contracted for. Mr Peg and his wife and children all suffer disappointment and loss of enjoyment because of the absence of the facilities contracted for. Damages for disappointment are a recognized form of damages which are recoverable through the courts (see below). Can Mr Peg recover only for his own disappointment, or may he recover damages for the disappointment sustained by his wife and children, although they are not parties to the contract of booking with the hotel? The answer would appear to be that Mr Peg can recover damages not only for his own disappointment but also for that of his wife and children.

JACKSON v. HORIZON
HOLIDAYS [1975] 3 All
ER 92 (CA)

The plaintiff booked a holiday for himself, his wife and their two children in Ceylon. The total cost of the holiday, including air fares, was £1200. The holiday provided failed to meet the description given in the defendant's brochure in a number of vital respects. The plaintiff brought an action claiming damages, including a claim for his own personal disappointment and that of his wife and children due to the failure of the holiday to meet the description given by the defendant company. The trial judge allowed, when assessing the damages payable by the defendants (£1100), for the disappointment of the plaintiff alone, and not for the disappointment of his wife and family. The defendants appealed against the quantum of damages.

Held: The Court of Appeal, dismissing the defendant's appeal, held that the quantum of damages, whilst high when considering the disappointment and distress suffered by the plaintiff alone, was appropriate if the distress and disappointment of his wife and family were to be considered. Whilst his wife and family themselves could not sue upon the booking contract, since they were not a party to it, the contract was made in part for their benefit. Since the contract was to benefit the wife and family, the plaintiff could receive damages for the loss of benefit sustained by them due to the defendant's breach of the contract.

The exception stated in *Jackson* v. *Horizon Holidays* appears to be limited solely to booking contracts made by one party for his or her benefit and the benefit of others. It does not seem to extend beyond this limited area (*Woodar* v. *Wimpey Construction Ltd* [1980] 1 WLR 277 (HL)). However, two points remain undecided:
1   Suppose that Mr Bloggs books ten single rooms for old age pensioners who belong to a local club. If the hotel breaches the terms of its contract with Mr Bloggs, thereby causing disappointment to himself and the old age pensioners for whom he has booked, will the hotel be liable to all the OAPs and Mr Bloggs for the disappointment?
2   Does the principle embodied in *Jackson*'s case apply to contracts of booking other than for accommodation? If Jane books a reception and buffet with the Hotel Splendide for her twenty-first birthday and the arrangements made by the hotel are inadequate, the food of poor quality and the service dreadful, can Jane recover damages not only for her own disappointment but also for the disappointment of her guests with the reception and buffet provided by the hotel?

Many hotels and catering enterprises arrange the booking of their accommodation and facilities through an agent. The agent is in real terms a third party whose function is to negotiate a contract between the customer and the hotel or catering organization which the agent represents (otherwise known as the agent's principal). The situation can be seen more clearly by means of a diagram (see Figure 4.1).

The role of the agent is to negotiate and bring into effect a contract of booking between the hotelier and the customer. The agent is not a party to this contract; rather the agent is the means by which the contract is made. The agent is normally instructed by hoteliers to act on their behalf. Thus between the hotelier and the agent a contract of agency arises, the terms of which provide for payment of the agent for arranging each contract of booking with the customer, usually on a percentage basis, e.g. 12½ per cent of the contract price.

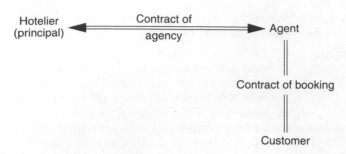

Figure 4.1 The role of an agent.

Agency does not arise only with regard to booking contracts. Many high-street fast-food outlets operate as agents for larger catering operations.

Consideration

A contract is not complete until there has been a sufficient form of consideration. Consideration is given by the offeree and forms part of the terms of the contract. Hence, offer and acceptance alone do not make a contract; the further element of consideration is vital. Consideration may be defined as either some detriment to the offeree (e.g. the payment of a sum of money or the doing of some action) or some benefit to the offeror (e.g. receipt of money) in exchange for the offeror's promise. It is normal in the booking contract for the consideration to be either the actual payment of the contract price at the time of booking by the offeree, or a promise to pay the contract price at some later date agreed between the parties. This latter form of consideration is known as executory consideration, since it has still to be performed, and the former is known as executed consideration, since it has been performed.

The general rule is that the consideration must be sufficient, i.e. recognized as an acceptable form of consideration by the law. The law is not concerned with the fairness of the bargain. Hence, the adequacy of the consideration is not considered: one could contract a holiday for £5 per week per person if one could agree such terms with a hotelier. Since consideration normally takes the form of a money payment in contracts of booking, there are rarely legal problems in that field which relate to the sufficiency of consideration. However, since not all hotels demand payment in advance, some customers may receive the benefit of the hotel's accommodation and services and thereafter default on payment.

The guest's capacity to contract

The capacity of the guest to enter into a booking contract with the hotel is important. If the guest lacks the capacity to contract and defaults on payment of the bill for the services rendered by the hotel, then the hotel cannot recover the money owing by an action in the courts.

The capacity of a minor, that is, a person under the age of 18, to contract is limited in two ways: by the common law, to contracts for necessaries, and by the Minors' Contracts Act 1987. The meaning of 'necessaries' is defined for present purposes by s. 3(3) Sale of Goods Act 1979:

Necessaries means goods suitable to the condition in life of the minor or other person concerned and to his actual requirements at the time of the sale and delivery.

If the goods are deemed necessaries, the minor may be compelled to pay a reasonable price for them, and this is not necessarily the price agreed between the parties; it may be less (s. 3(2) SGA 1979). However, the s. 3 definition relates only to contracts for the sale of goods (see s. 2(1) SGA 1979); a contract of booking is not within that definition but, of course, a restaurant meal may be a contract for the sale of goods (see *Lockett* v. *A. & M. Charles Ltd* [1938] 4 All ER 170). Is a restaurant meal a necessary? The courts would probably take the view that it is not. Illustrations of how the courts have interpreted 'necessaries' can be seen in the following cases.

NASH v. INMAN [1908] 2 KB 1   The plaintiff, a Savile Row tailor, sought to enforce a contract for various items of gentlemen's clothing against a wealthy Cambridge University undergraduate. The clothes totalled £122 in value, and included a number of 'fancy waistcoats'.

The defendant argued that the items of clothing purchased were not necessaries and thus the contract was unenforceable.

Held: Since the defendant already possessed sufficient clothing, these further articles were not 'necessaries'.

ELKINGTON v. AMERY [1936] 2 All ER 86 (CA)   The defendant, a wealthy minor, purchased two items of jewellery and a gold vanity bag. The jewellery comprised two rings, which the Court of Appeal held to be necessaries as an engagement and a wedding ring for his fiancée. The gold vanity bag was held not to be a necessary.

In a contract, other than a contract for the sale of goods, only if the minor contracts for necessaries will he or she be bound by the contract. Necessaries may, of course, cover services, such as legal advice or funeral arrangements. The test as to whether a service is a necessary will depend on the minor's condition in life. It may be argued, therefore, taking a broad approach to necessaries as in *Elkington* v. *Amery*, that a holiday is a necessary if it is for convalescence after an illness, or the minor's condition of life is such that holidays spent in hotels are an inevitable part of it. Whether a contract is a contract for necessaries is a question of fact in each case; hence it will be a question of the trial judge considering the subject matter of the contract and the social condition and position of the minor.

The common-law limitations

Where a minor enters into a contract for necessaries, then as already seen he or she may be compelled to pay a reasonable price for them.

The Minors' Contracts Act 1987

This piece of legislation is based on the recommendations of the Law Commission and deals with the extent to which a minor may be required to repay loans under loan agreements which he or she has entered into.

Section 1 of the Act repeals the Infant Relief Act 1874 and s. 5 of the Betting and Loans (Infants) Act 1892. Thus a loan agreement entered into by a minor during his or her minority is now repayable by the minor.

Section 2 of the Act makes binding any guarantee by an adult to support a loan or an advance of credit to a minor. Parents guaranteeing the loans of their children during their minority may now be required to honour the guarantee.

Section 3 of the Act provides a general remedy for an adult plaintiff who has entered into an unenforceable contract with a minor. Where the court considers it just and equitable to do so, it may require the minor to transfer to the plaintiff any property acquired by the minor under the contract (or any property 'representing it').

Although the provisions of the 1987 Act are not directly referable to the supply of a service to a minor, they are particularly important in relation to the supply of goods on credit.

The terms of a booking contract

The terms of a particular booking contract will, in the main, be express terms, i.e. terms stated as between the parties. However, since the passing of the Supply of Goods and Services Act 1982, statutorily implied terms are now imposed in 'contracts for the supply of a service'.

Express terms of the contract

The terms contained in any given contract of booking will vary according to the needs of the hotel with which the contract is made. Since contracts of booking cover contracts for both the provision of accommodation and the booking of other facilities, e.g. conferences, banquets, etc., the terms of the contract may vary according to the service to be provided. The terms of a booking contract are likely to relate to the following points:
(a) payment and confirmation of booking;
(b) alteration and cancellation by the client;
(c) alteration by the hotel;
(d) liability of the hotel;
(e) arbitration;
(f) *force majeure* and frustration;
(g) law to be applied.
It is important to understand the effect of the various terms which form the contract. A distinction can be drawn between the various sorts of terms which make up the booking contract, as shown below.

Conditions. The hotelier can make any term a condition of the contract. A condition is an important term, one which goes to the root of the contract, i.e. it is vital to the very existence of the contract.

Warranty. A warranty is a term of the contract of lesser importance not vital to the contract; its purpose is to make the contract work. It is a peripheral term, i.e. one which relates to a matter of lesser importance within the contract, such as the provision of a games room in a hotel.

The importance of this distinction relates to the effect of breach of the term. Breach of a condition gives the victim of the breach the right to treat the contract as at an end and sue for damages. However, a breach of warranty does not allow the victim of the breach to treat the contract as at an end. The victim's only claim is for damages.

Mid-terms. There is a class of terms between conditions and warranties. Breach of a mid-term may give rise to the same result as a breach of condition where breach of a mid-term would substantially deprive the victim of what he had contracted for; this proposition was set out in the case of *Hong Kong Fir Shipping Co. Ltd* v. *Kawasaki Kisen Kaisha Ltd* [1962 1 All ER 474 (CA).

Implied terms of the contract

Implied terms fall into two categories: implied terms of fact and implied terms of law.

Implied terms of fact. An implied term of fact in a contract arises from the circumstances in which the contract was made. Such a term in a contract for the booking of hotel accommodation is that the hotel will exercise reasonable care and skill in providing the service for which they have contracted with a client.

Recent case law on implied terms of fact has centred on the provision of medical services. In *Eyre* v. *Measday* [1986] 1 All ER 488 (CA), the plaintiff underwent a sterilization operation, and later became pregnant. She sued the gynaecologist who performed the operation for breach of contract, on the basis that an implied term of the contract was that the operation would render her permanently sterile. The Court of Appeal held that the gynaecologist had merely agreed to perform the procedure; a term that the procedure would be successful could not be implied into the contract. The Court of Appeal, however, were prepared to imply a term that the gynaecologist would perform the operation with reasonable care and skill. On the facts there was no evidence of lack of such care.

In *Thake* v. *Maurice* [1986] 1 All ER 497 (CA), Maurice performed a vasectomy on Thake which proved to be unsuccessful, and Thake's wife subsequently became pregnant. Thake had not been warned of the inherent risk of resumed fertility. Thake brought an action against Maurice based on breach of contract. The Court of Appeal held that Maurice had not given any implied guarantee that Thake would be permanently sterile.

It is interesting to note that the second ground on which Thake based his case was negligence. The Court of Appeal on this ground found in Thake's favour, holding Maurice to have been negligent in failing to warn Thake and Mrs Thake of the risk of resumed fertility.

These cases show, in the context of a contract for the provision of medical services, that the circumstances must be most exceptional before the court will regard the provider of a service as guaranteeing its success. In the context of the hotel and catering industry, given that there is a recognized form of damages known as 'damages for disappointment', one wonders whether the courts would imply a term into a contract of booking that the holiday is to be a reasonably enjoyable experience?

Implied terms of law. These arise from statutes, the main purpose of which is to protect consumers. Implied terms of law relate to contracts for the sale of goods and consumer credit, the most recent example being the Sale and Supply of Goods Act 1994 (see p. 176 below). However, since the passing of the Supply of Goods and Services Act 1982 (SGSA), certain terms are implied into 'a contract for the supply of a service'. A booking contract is clearly such a contract, the definition of which is to be found in s. 12(1) SGSA 1982:

> *A contract for the supply of a service means ... a contract under which a person (the supplier) agrees to carry out a service.*

The hotelier, in agreeing to accommodate a guest or to provide banqueting or conference facilities, is clearly a supplier of a service within the Act. In a contract for the supply of a service, s. 13 SGSA 1982 implies a term as to the care and skill with which the service is to be provided. Section 13 of the Act states:

> *In a contract for the supply of a service where the supplier is acting in the course of a business, there is an implied term that the supplier will carry out the service with reasonable care and skill.*

This implied condition gives rise to the right of the client to terminate the contract, treat it as at an end, and sue for damages, where the hotelier in providing the accommodation or other types of facility has not exercised reasonable care and skill. An example may be that the accommodation is poorly cleaned and is unfit for occupation.

The care and skill required of the hotelier are those which would be exercised by a directly comparable establishment.

Exemption clauses and booking contracts

It is important to consider the exact words used in the contract to determine the rights, duties and liabilities of the contracting parties. This is particularly important in relation to exclusion clauses and clauses which seek to limit the liability of one of the contracting parties. It is normal commercial practice for hotels and other business organizations to seek to limit their liability towards their clients. However, business enterprises, such as hotels, are not completely free to limit or exclude certain forms of liability with regard to 'consumers' with whom they trade. This is due to the provisions of the Unfair Contract Terms Act 1977, and the EC Directive on Unfair Contract Terms (93/13 EEC OJ 95) implemented in the UK by the Unfair Terms in Contracts Regulations 1994.

Incorporation of exclusion clauses

It is normal practice for exclusion and other clauses which seek to limit hotels' liability towards their clients to be incorporated into the booking contract by means of a written term. An exclusion clause may be incorporated into the booking contract by means of a notice. Such a notice must be brought to the attention of the client either before or at the time of making the contract, and must be sufficiently clear. If the hotelier seeks to incorporate an exclusion clause by a notice after the contract has been made, the notice will be of no effect and the term will not form part of the booking contract (*Olley* v. *Marlborough Court Ltd* [1949] 1 KB 532) (see p. 111).

The case of *Thornton* v. *Shoe Lane Parking Ltd* [1971] 1 All ER 686 (CA) emphasizes the fact that even if the notice is displayed either before or at the time when the contract is made, it must be sufficiently brought to the party's attention. The wider the scope of the exemption contained in the clause, the bolder and more explicit the notice must be. In *Interfoto Picture Library Ltd* v. *Stiletto Visual Programmes Ltd* [1988] 1 All ER 348 the Court of Appeal had to consider whether an onerous clause regarding the payment of 'compensation' for non-return of photo transparencies within fourteen days was incorporated within the contract between the parties. The CA held that it was, although it had not been emphatically drawn to the attention of the person hiring the trans-parencies, e.g. by bold type or by 'red ink'. However, the CA took the view that whilst the clause may have been properly incorporated into the contract it could still have been challenged on other grounds; i.e. it amounted to a 'penalty' as the sums claimed for retention of the transparencies exceeded a genuine pre-estimate of the loss caused to the plaintiff's photographic library.

Where the booking is made through an agent, such as a travel agent, it is vital that when the booking is made at the agency all the terms which the hotel wishes to be incorporated into the booking contract are brought to the notice of the client.

HOLLINGWORTH v. SOUTHERN FERRIES LTD [1977] Lloyd's Rep. 70   A contract of booking for the carriage of a passenger upon a ferry was concluded by acceptance by the travel agent on behalf of the ferry company. Hence any terms and conditions contained in a ticket later sent to the client were not incorpor-ated into the contract. Such terms were outside the scope of the contract since they were not brought to the attention of the passenger before or at the time the contract was made.

We may summarize the above cases by stating that if a clause seeking to exclude or limit liability of a party is not properly incorporated into the contract it does not form part of the agreement between the parties and is not effective in excluding or limiting the liability of the party seeking to rely on it.

Construction of the clause. It is important to consider the actual words of the exclusion clause to see whether or not they actually cover the breach which has occurred. The court will interpret the words of the clause strictly as against the person who seeks to rely on them. If the clause on its true construction actually covers the breach which has taken place the clause will be given effect (*Photo Production Ltd* v. *Securicor Transport Ltd* [1980] 1 All ER 556 (HL)).

Unfair Contract Terms Act 1977

Not all exclusion and limitation clauses which have been incorporated into the contract will be given full effect. Parliament, in passing the Unfair Contract Terms Act 1977 (UCTA), sought to limit the effect of exclusion clauses imposed by businesses when contracting with consumers. This Act also limits the extent to which the business may exclude liability towards another business arising under a contract where the first business which is seeking to rely upon the clause has imposed its written standard terms of contract upon the other.

The Unfair Contract Terms Act 1977 prevents certain exclusion clauses from having any effect whatsoever. Section 2(1) of the Act states:

> *A person cannot by any reference to any contract term or to a notice given to persons generally or to particular persons exclude or restrict his liability for death, or personal injury resulting from negligence.*

Hoteliers cannot, therefore, either in the terms of the booking contract or otherwise, limit their liability for death or personal injury caused to guests which results from the negligence of the hoteliers, their employees or their agents. 'Negligence' for the purposes of UCTA is defined in s. 1(1) of the Act as follows:

> *'Negligence' means the breach:*
> *(a) of any obligation, arising from the express or implied terms of a contract to take reasonable care or exercise reasonable skill in the performance of a contract;*
> *(b) of any common law duty to take reasonable care or exercise reasonable skill;*
> *(c) of the common duty of care imposed by the Occupiers' Liability Act 1957.*

Hence where hoteliers are in breach either of an express term to take reasonable care or of an implied term (see s. 13 SGSA 1982), they cannot exclude their liability if this breach results in death or personal injury to the guest. Similarly, if in breach of the duty of care towards the guest (see *Donoghue* v. *Stevenson*), and such a breach results in the death of, or injury to, the guest, hoteliers cannot exclude or limit their liability by means of an exclusion clause. The same applies with regard to their duty towards a guest under s. 2 of the Occupiers' Liability Act 1957.

Where hoteliers seek to limit their liability for negligent damage caused to the guest's property, or negligence which results otherwise than in the death of or personal injury to the guest, s. 2(2) UCTA applies:

> *In the case of other loss or damage, a person cannot so exclude or restrict his liability for negligence except insofar as the term or notice satisfies the requirement of reasonableness.*

The 'requirement of reasonableness' is defined by s. 11(1) of the 1977 Act:

> *In relation to a contract term the requirement of reasonableness ... is that the term shall have been a fair and reasonable one to be included having regard to the circumstances which were, or ought reasonably to have been, known to or in the contemplation of the parties when the contract was made.*

For a recent illustration of the working of these sections see the joint appeals in *Smith* v. *Eric S. Bush (a firm)* and *Harris* v. *Wye Forest District Council* [1989] 2 All ER 514 (HL).

Where hoteliers seek to limit their liability for any breach of contract which they may have committed towards the client the provisions of s. 3 UCTA apply. If the person with whom the hotelier contracts is a consumer, or that party contracts with the hotelier on the hotelier's written standard terms of contract, s. 3(1) applies:

> *This section applies as between contracting parties where one of them deals as consumer or on the other's written standard terms of business.*

'Dealing as consumer' is defined by s. 12(1) UCTA:

> *A party to a contract 'deals as a consumer' in relation to another party if:*
> (a) *he neither makes the contract in the course of a business nor holds himself out as doing so; and*
> (b) *the other party does make the contract in the course of a business; and*
> (c) *in the case of a contract governed by the law of sale of goods or hire purchase, or by s. 7 of this Act, the goods passing under or in pursuance of the contract are of a type ordinarily supplied for private use or consumption.*

Hence, where a private individual books with a hotel, that client deals as a consumer. A business which books accommodation for its employees, e.g. for a conference, is not dealing as a consumer. However, such a business may obtain the protection afforded by s. 3(2) below if the contract it has made with the hotel is upon the hotel's written standard terms of contract.

> *As against that party the other cannot by reference to any contract term –*
> (a) *when himself in breach of contract, exclude or restrict a liability of his in respect of the breach; or*
> (b) *claim to be entitled –*
> > (i) *to render a contractual performance substantially different from what was reasonably expected of him, or*
> > (ii) *in respect of the whole or any part of his contractual obligation, to render no performance at all,*
> *except insofar as (in any of the cases mentioned above in this sub-section) the contract term satisfies the requirement of reasonableness.*

Section 3(2) operates so as to require that any clause which purports to entitle the party seeking to rely upon it to restrict or exclude any liability for that breach, or to entitle such a party to render either a substantially different contractual performance or no performance at all, must satisfy the requirement of reasonableness in s. 11(1) UCTA.

The Unfair Contract Terms Act 1977 is an effective means of limiting the type of exclusion clauses upon which a hotelier may seek to rely. The purpose of the Act is to protect the client from the inclusion of unjust clauses in consumer contracts, such as booking contracts. Hoteliers purporting in their terms of booking to offer services which in fact they do not offer, or to provide accommodation of a stated quality when the accommodation falls short of the stated standard, cannot rely on any exclusion or limitation clauses to enable them either to provide no service (or accommodation) at all or to offer a substantially different accommodation from that contracted for.

The EC Directive on Unfair Contract Terms

The Unfair Contract Terms Act which covers consumer transactions and contracts entered into on the other's written standard terms of business, is fairly narrow in its scope. It is directed towards clauses which exclude or limit liability. The EC Directive on Unfair Contract Terms implemented in the UK by the Unfair Terms in Contracts Regulations 1994 though confined to contracts between a consumer and a supplier of goods and services covers all types of contractual term – see Article 2. Under the EC Directive unfair terms do not bind the consumer, and the contract shall continue to bind the parties if it is capable of existing without the unfair terms – see Article 6(1). For this purpose a contractual term which has not been individually negotiated is to be regarded as unfair if, contrary to the requirement of good faith, it causes a significant imbalance in the parties' rights and obligations arising under the contract to the detriment of the consumer – see Article 3.

Article 5 of the Directive provides that terms offered to the consumer in writing must always be drafted in plain, intelligible language, and that in the case of doubt as to the meaning of a term the interpretation most favourable to the consumer is to prevail.

Article 7 makes possible representative actions by consumer groups (e.g. the Consumers' Association) and organizations with a legitimate interest to challenge contractual terms drawn up for general use which are considered unfair.

Ending a contract

A contract may come to an end in a number of different ways.

Performance

The normal mode of completion is by performance of the contract. A booking contract is performed by the provision of the stated services and accommodation on the part of the hotel and the payment of the contract price by the client. However, not all contracts come to a successful conclusion. One or other of the parties may cancel the contract or seek to alter the terms upon which it is based. Hence, it is normal practice for booking contracts to make provision for such eventualities. A cancellation by either party will amount to a breach of contract. It is important to consider the time when the cancellation is made. If the cancellation is made on or after the date for the commencement of the holiday or booking then this is known as an actual breach, since it is on or after the date set for the performance of the contract. If the cancellation is made prior to the date of the commencement of the holiday or booking, it is known as an anticipatory breach of contract, since it is made prior to the contractual date for performance, in anticipation of that event.

Where both parties agree to an alteration of the terms of the contract this is known as a variation. The variation brings to an end the original contract and creates a further contract on different terms. A variation will occur where a client wishes to alter the nature of the holiday, e.g. change of accommodation, or from bed, breakfast and evening meal to full board. An alteration by one party only (i.e. the hotelier) of the terms of the contract without the other's consent amounts to a breach of contract. The severity of the breach will depend on the term altered. Hoteliers and holiday companies normally seek to limit liability for alterations made by them in the terms of the contract by means of a limitation clause, particularly where the reason for the alteration is some factor outside the company's control. Such clauses are known as *force majeure* clauses.

Frustration

Frustration is another way in which a contract may come to an end. Where some external event outside the control of either party to the contract occurs which renders performance of the contract impossible, this is known as frustration.

TAYLOR v. CALDWELL [1863] 3 B & S 826

The defendant let to the plaintiff a music hall for the purpose of holding four concerts. Prior to the first concert the music hall was destroyed by fire. The plaintiff sued the defendant for damages for not having the music hall available for his use on the dates booked.

Held: Since the music hall had ceased to be usable owing to fire, the contract was impossible of performance, and the defendant was not liable to pay damages.

For frustration to apply, the impossibility of performing the contract must arise without the fault of either party. Events which will frustrate a booking contract are, for instance, the destruction of the hotel by fire, or the death of the client. It is not clear, however, whether the illness of the client would be sufficient to frustrate a contract of booking.

POUSSARD v. SPIERS & POND [1876] 1 QBD 410

Madame Poussard, an opera singer, entered into a contract to play in an opera. The date of the first night was 28 November 1874. On 23 November Madame Poussard was taken seriously ill and was unable to appear until 4 December. The defendant company hired a substitute to play Madame Poussard's role; however, the substitute would appear only if her contract was for the whole period when Madame Poussard was to appear. On 4 December Madame Poussard went to the defendants' theatre and offered her services for the remaining performances; the defendants refused. Madame Poussard sued for breach of contract.

Held: The failure of Madame Poussard to perform the contract as from the first night due to the serious illness was sufficient to discharge both parties to the contract from their obligations under it. The contract was frustrated.

Hence, a sudden illness of unknown duration which strikes a client down may frustrate a contract of booking between the client and the hotel. However, *Poussard*'s case should be contrasted with the following.

BETTINI v. GYE [1876] 1 QBD 183

The plaintiff was an opera singer, the defendant the director of an opera company. The plaintiff had agreed to sing on a tour of Britain commencing 30 March 1875 and to be in London for rehearsals six days prior to that first engagement. The plaintiff became ill and did not arrive in London until 28 March. The defendant would not accept the plaintiff's services, and treated the contract between them as at an end.

Held: The question raised was whether the plaintiff's late arrival caused by illness was a sufficient course of conduct to entitle the defendant to treat the contract between them as at an end. Since the plaintiff had failed only to appear at rehearsals prior to the commencement of the tour, and this requirement was a warranty rather than a condition of the contract, the plaintiff's failure did not entitle the defendant to treat the contract as at an end. The plaintiff's illness had not frustrated the contract between them. Hence the plaintiff was entitled to damages for the remuneration lost due to the defendant's action. The defendant, however, could counter-claim for any loss sustained due to the plaintiff's late arrival.

The factors which may be used to distinguish between these two cases are the nature and expected duration of the respective illnesses. Illness is, of course, an event which can be provided for, in that many insurance companies and tour operators offer an insurance policy to provide for the event of the client's not being able to take the holiday contracted for due to illness. Such policies also provide for payment of doctor's fees, etc. should the client fall ill whilst on holiday. An event which is foreseeable and one which can be provided for cannot form the basis for frustration of a contract. Hence, where clients telephone the hotel to inform the proprietor that they cannot take up their bookings due to illness this is an anticipatory breach of contract on the part of the client; the contract is not frustrated. It may, however, be argued by clients, if the illness which prevents them from taking up the booking is particularly severe, that following *Poussard*'s case the contract is frustrated.

Separate, though similar, legal problems are raised by the situation where a client books a facility (i.e. a banqueting or conference suite) or accommodation for a particular event, such as a wedding, a twenty-first birthday or some similar celebration, and the event is no longer possible; e.g. the principal guest falls ill or is imprisoned. Is the contract of booking frustrated?

KRELL v. HENRY [1903] 2 KB 740 (CA)

The defendant entered upon an agreement with the plaintiff to use the plaintiff's premises at Pall Mall to view the coronation procession of King Edward VII on 26 and 27 June 1902.

The defendant agreed by letter to pay the plaintiff £75 for the use of the room on those two days and paid £25 in advance. The procession did not in fact take place on 26 and 27 June as planned owing to the serious illness of the King. The defendant refused to pay the remaining £50.

Held: The contract had been frustrated. The cancellation of the procession discharged the parties from their obligations, since the purpose for which the contract was made was no longer capable of being achieved.

This case, however, should be contrasted with the following:

HERNE BAY STEAM BOAT COMPANY v. HUTTON [1903] 2 KB 683 (CA)

In this case the defendant chartered a boat to view the naval review at Spithead on the occasion of Edward VII's coronation. The naval review did not take place, but the navy remained anchored at Spithead on the dates for which Hutton had chartered the launch. Was the contract for the charter of the launch frustrated?

Held: The contract was not frustrated.

The point of distinction between the two cases is simply that in the former case the purpose of the contract was defeated, yet in the latter the purpose of the contract could still be fulfilled (i.e. the navy could still be observed by a trip on the hired launch); only a secondary purpose (to see the King) had been defeated.

Another scenario which may prevent a holidaymaker from taking up his or her booking with the hotel is his or her imprisonment for a criminal offence. This may amount to the frustration of the contract of booking. The only case law on the effect of imprisonment upon continuing contractual relations is with regard to contracts of employment. In *F.C. Shepherd* v. *Jerrom* [1986] 3 All ER 589 (CA) it was held that a sentence of borstal training frustrated a contract of apprenticeship between the plaintiff and his employer. Obviously there are clear points of difference between a contract of booking and a contract of employment, but none of these differences makes the application of the rule in this case unlikely.

Foreseeable events do not amount to frustration; therefore, in *Davis Contractors Ltd v. Fareham UDC* [1956] 2 All ER 145 (HL), where the 'frustrating' events relied upon were a shortage of skilled labour and adequate materials with which to do the work contracted for, the House of Lords held that this did not frustrate the contract, since such eventualities were foreseeable at the time the contract was made. Therefore, by analogy, a hotelier would be unable to rely upon a strike or industrial action being taken by staff as an event which frustrates the contracts of booking with guests.

Where it is clearly established that the event relied upon amounts to a frustrating event then the Law Reform (Frustrated Contracts) Act 1943 operates. This sets out the respective rights and liabilities of the parties to the contract upon frustration of the contract.

1   Money paid before the circumstances which frustrated the contract can be recovered. Money due to be paid under the contract yet not in fact paid at the time of frustration ceases to be payable – s. 1(2).

2   A party who has incurred expenses prior to the time at which the contract was frustrated is able to recover those expenses up to a limit of the sums paid or payable to him or her under the contract. If, however, no monies were paid or became payable prior to the frustrating event, the party will not be able to recover any expenses at all – s. 1(2).

3   A party who has gained a valuable benefit under the contract may be required to pay a just sum for the benefit to the other party – s. 1(3).

4   Where the contract contains a clause which upon the true construction of the contract is intended to cover events which frustrate the contract, that clause shall operate and the provisions of this Act shall have effect only in so far as they are consistent with the clause – s. 2(3).

Breach

Breach of contract may occur in a number of ways. As previously discussed, there may be a breach prior to the contractual date for performance of the contract; this is known as an anticipatory breach. After the contractual date for performance a breach is known as an actual breach. Hoteliers may breach the contract of booking by either declaring prior to the date of performance that they will no longer be bound by its terms (i.e. by cancelling the booking), or failing, after the date of performance, to fulfil one or more of the terms of the booking contract. The effect of this failure on the part of the hoteliers will depend on the type of term breached. If the term is a condition or a mid-term the client may treat the contract as at an end and sue the hotelier for damages. A 'mid-term' is one where the effect of non-performance will depend on the nature and consequence of the breach – see *Bunge Corporation* v. *Tradax SA* [1981] 1 WLR 711 (HL). Hence, if the hotelier failed to provide any accommodation for the client, or provided accommodation which was well below the standard contracted for with the client, this would amount to a breach of condition. If the term breached by the hotelier is merely a warranty, this does not entitle the client to treat the contract as at an end. The client may, however, sue for damages. A warranty may be breached where services, such as use of a sauna or swimming pool, provided for by the booking contract are not in fact available. Whether a breach is one of warranty or mid-term is a question of the significance of the term in the contract – has the guest been deprived of a substantial benefit of the contract?

Damages

Parties who are the victims of breach of contract may sue for damages. The amount they are likely to receive is the amount of money which would put them in the position they would have been in had the contract been performed by the other party. If, for example, a client cancels a booking contract for accommodation, the hotel will sue for the contract price, the money they would have received had the client performed the contract and paid for the holiday. The hotel is claiming the sum which the client had agreed to pay for the holiday. Technically, therefore, it is an action for an agreed sum rather than for damages. However, in all situations the victims of the breach are under a duty to mitigate their loss – *British Westinghouse Electric and Manufacturing Company* v. *Underground Electric Railway Co. of London* [1912] AC 673 (HL). Hence, where clients cancel the contract of booking, the hoteliers are bound by this rule to use their best endeavours to relet the accommodation, thereby minimizing the loss they have suffered. The hotel will also be unable to claim for the cost of any service which it did not provide for the client by reason of the cancellation, e.g. laundry of bed linen, food, etc. The total amount which the hotel is likely to recover is the contract price minus any monies received upon reletting (plus the cost, if any, of advertising the vacancy) or saved by not providing the services for the client.

A further limitation upon liability to pay damages is that the damage must either arise naturally from the breach (i.e. according to the usual course of things) or be such as may reasonably be supposed to have been, in the contemplation of both parties at the time when they made the contract, the probable result of breach of it – *Hadley* v. *Baxendale* (1854) 9 Ex. 341. Hence, where a hotelier is in breach of the booking contract by failing to provide accommodation as contracted for and the client treats the contract as at an end and books in at another hotel for the duration of the time he or she would have been staying at the first hotel, can the client claim the cost of staying at the second hotel as damages? Are such costs within the scope of damages recoverable? The answer would appear to be yes, provided the second hotel was of a comparable standard, and not of a higher standard than the one which breached the contract of booking. If the client chose a hotel of a higher standard this would not be mitigating the loss.

For what are damages recoverable? Damages are recoverable for a number of purposes. When a client books a holiday with a hotel and in breach of that contract the accommodation and holiday provided are not of the standard contracted for, the client may claim the contract price of the holiday as damages, minus an amount for any benefit that the client may have derived from the holiday provided.

In addition to any claim for the contract price the client may claim damages for disappointment incurred by the failure of the accommodation or holiday to meet the standard contracted for. This follows from the case below.

JARVIS v. SWAN'S TOURS
[1973] 1 All ER 71 (CA)

The defendants' travel agents described in glowing terms a holiday in Switzerland. The holiday was to be a house party and clients were promised 'a great time'. The plaintiff booked the holiday with the defendants and paid £63.45. He took the holiday during his annual fortnight's leave. The house party was a failure; during the second week Mr Jarvis was the only guest. The holiday failed to comply with the terms of booking in numerous ways. The plaintiff sued for damages. He was awarded £31.72 in the County Court and appealed to the Court of Appeal.

Held: The plaintiff's appeal was allowed and he was awarded damages of £125. The plaintiff could recover, in addition to those damages normally recoverable, additional damages for the disappointment and distress caused to him by his loss of enjoyment of the holiday.

Following from *Jarvis* v. *Swan's Tours* a client may recover damages for a greater amount than the contract price. This is in recognition of the disappointment, distress, upset and frustration that clients may suffer through loss of their holiday. If, for example, a bridegroom books the honeymoon suite at the Grand Hotel, only to find upon arrival at the hotel that he and his bride have not been allocated the honeymoon suite, but an ordinary double room with twin beds, the bridegroom may sue the Grand Hotel for the disappointment, upset and frustration which has been caused, not only to him but also to his bride. In *Cook* v. *Spanish Holiday Tours Ltd* (*The Times*, 6 February 1960), a honeymoon couple recovered damages for disappointment against a travel agent who broke his contract to provide them with holiday accommodation.

The *Jackson* case raises the question of damages for disappointment where a block booking is made. Lord Denning MR, in his judgment in *Jackson* v. *Horizon Holidays Ltd*, explains:

> In this case it was a husband making a contract for the benefit of himself, his wife and children. Other cases readily come to mind. A host makes a contract with a restaurant for a dinner for himself and his friends. The vicar makes a contract for a coach trip for the choir. In all these cases there is only one person who makes the contract. It is the husband, the host or the vicar, as the case may be. Sometimes he pays the whole price himself. Occasionally he may get a contribution from the others. But in any case it is he who makes the contract. It would be a fiction to say that the contract was made by all the family, or all the guests, or all the choir, and that he was only an agent for them. Take this very case. It would be absurd to say that the twins of three years old were parties to the contract or that the father was making the contract on their behalf as if they were principals. . . . No, the real truth is that in each instance the father, the host or the vicar, was making a contract himself for the benefit of the whole party. In short, a contract by one for the benefit of third persons. What is the position when such a contract is broken? At present the law says that the only one who can sue is the one who made the contract. None of the rest of the party can sue, even though the contract was made for their benefit. But when that one does sue what damages can he recover? Is he limited to his own loss? Or can he recover for the others? Suppose the holiday firm puts the family into an hotel which is only half built and the visitors have to sleep on the floor? Or suppose the restaurant is fully booked and guests have to go away, hungry and angry having spent so much on fares to get there? Or suppose the coach leaves the choir stranded halfway and they have to hire cars to get home? None of them individually can sue. Only the father, the host or the vicar can sue. He can, of course, recover his own damages. But can he not recover for the others? I think he can . . . at any rate so long as the law forbids the third persons themselves to sue for damages. It is the only way in which a just result can be achieved. The guests ought to recover from the restaurant their wasted fares. The choir ought to recover the cost of hiring the taxis home. There is no one to recover for them except the one who made the contract for their benefit. He should be able to recover the expense to which they have been put, and pay it over to them. Once recovered, it will be money had and received to their use. If he can recover for the expense, he should also be able to recover for the discomfort, vexation and upset which the whole party have suffered by reason of the breach of contract, recompensing them accordingly out of what he recovers.

Lord Denning clearly allows people who book 'for the benefit of others' to recover damages not only for their own disappointment but also for those persons for whose benefit the contract was made. An example would be where a bride's father books with a hotel for the wedding breakfast, and the room, food and other facilities provided by the hotel are in breach of the contract made between the parties. The bride's father could recover damages not only for his vexation, disappointment, etc. but also for that of his wife, daughter, son-in-law and other guests. Lord Denning appears also to state that once the money is recovered from the party in breach, the money so received by the person booking on behalf of others shall be distributed by that person to those upon whose behalf the holiday, etc. was booked. This is of limited importance where we are concerned with family groups (e.g. *Jackson* v. *Horizon Holidays*) but is of some significance where the situation is one of a club leader, etc., or the vicar in Lord Denning's example.

These cases all arise from disturbance and disappointment caused to the client by the actions of the defendant. Can a holiday company be held liable for annoyance and disappointment caused to the plaintiff by third parties at the holiday company's hotel?

The case of *Freemantle* v. *Thomas Cook* (*The Times*, 25 February 1984) is of considerable importance to the hotelier. Mr Freemantle booked a package holiday in Greece with the defendant travel company. The hotel in which he and his family stayed was occupied by a large number of students. The conduct of the students was such that the Freemantle family's holiday was ruined; e.g. they booby-trapped the children's pool with broken glass and threw chairs into the pool, and residents were required to eat in the hotel annexe. The hotel's bars were forced to close, along with its restaurants. The Freemantle family left the Rhodos Bay Hotel after only three days. The County Court judge, on hearing the case, held:

1   The defendant company's representative at the Rhodos Bay Hotel had been negligent by fobbing off Mr Freemantle and other tourists, rather than attending to their grievances.
2   That the plaintiff, Mr Freemantle, be awarded £716.73 for the disappointment of himself and his family over the loss of the holiday for which he had contracted.

The case is novel, since it is the first where a travel company has been held liable in circumstances where the advertised facilities were available, but unuseable due to the actions of a third party (i.e. the students). The case is an important step forward in booking contracts from a consumer's point of view.

If *Freemantle*'s case is applied further it will mean that a hotel or travel company can no longer argue that they provided the facilities and that they cannot guarantee the good behaviour of others, thus it is not their responsibility if the facilities are unusable owing to the actions of third parties. It seems, therefore, that following this case the travel company or hotel is under a duty, arising either from the contract (i.e. an implied term) or from the neighbour principle in *Donoghue* v. *Stevenson*, to ensure that guests are able to make reasonable use of the facilities provided.

Example. Mr Snide, the proprietor of the Restful Hotel, Barking, specializes in holidays for the disabled. At the hotel is a special swimming pool and sun lounge. However, because profits in past years have declined, the pool has fallen into disrepair and is no longer open to guests, and the sun lounge has many broken windows and is overgrown with weeds. Mr Snide has not changed his advertising material throughout his ownership of the hotel and the literature sent out to prospective guests states 'a fully equipped swimming pool for the disabled and a pleasant sun lounge are special attractions at this charming hotel'. Mr Weak, a disabled pensioner who is keen on swimming, books at the Restful Hotel in reliance upon the advertising literature. He arrives at the hotel only to find that the pool is unusable, though otherwise the accommodation was as described and satisfactory. Does Mr Weak have a claim for misrepresentation?

WITH v. O'FLANAGAN [1936] Ch. 575

The defendant was a doctor who wished to sell his practice. The plaintiff purchased the practice in May 1934, relying upon the defendant's previous representation in January 1934 that the income from the practice was £2000 per annum. In the period between January and May 1934 the defendant had himself been unwell, and receipts from the practice had fallen dramatically to the equivalent of £300 per annum. The defendant did not inform the plaintiff of this development prior to contract. The plaintiff sought rescission of the contract.

Held: The representation made in January was of a continuing nature and had induced the plaintiff to contract. The plaintiff had a right to be informed of the developments; therefore, the defendant's silence amounted to an actionable misrepresentation. The court allowed rescission of the contract.

In the example cited above Mr Weak might successfully claim rescission of the contract of booking based on Mr Snide's misrepresentation by silence.

Liability for misrepresentation

In cases such as *Jarvis* v. *Swan's Tours*, where the hotelier makes a false statement which forms a term of the contract between the hotelier and the client, the client may sue for breach of contract. Misrepresentation, on the other hand, deals with the situation where the hotelier makes a false statement and, in reliance upon that statement, the client enters upon a contract with the hotelier. The false statement does not form one of the terms of the contract, so the client cannot sue for breach. Misrepresentation therefore covers a separate and distinct area from that of breach of contract.

Liability for misrepresentation may arise in any of a number of different ways. Some of these are based on the common law and arise under the law of torts; other forms of liability for misrepresentation arise under statute, namely the Misrepresentation Act 1967.

Tort of deceit

Where the hotelier knowingly, or without belief in its truth, makes a statement of fact upon which the client relies, and in consequence of which the client suffers loss, the client may sue for fraudulent misrepresentation – *Derry* v. *Peek* (1889) 14 App. Cas. 337.

Negligent misstatement

A 'special relationship' under the rule in *Hedley Byrne & Co. Ltd* v. *Heller & Partners Ltd* [1964] AC 465 (HL) exists between a hotelier (or a travel agent) and the client. A 'special relationship' is one where the client in seeking advice is trusting the hotelier (or travel agent) to exercise such a degree of care as the circumstances require, and it is reasonable for the client to rely on the hotelier's (or travel agent's) representation. Hence, if hoteliers (or travel agents) make a representation which they know or ought to have known that the client would rely upon, the hoteliers (or travel agents) may be liable for negligent misstatement, if the representation is in fact false. This applies only where parties making the representation voluntarily make the statement and thereby take upon themselves the risk in so doing. Since the *Hedley Byrne* case, which was the first case in this area, the principle enunciated there has been refined in two ways:

1 In *Esso Petroleum* v. *Mardon* [1976] 2 All ER 5 (CA), the *Hedley Byrne* principle was held to apply between parties who were negotiating prior to contract. Hence where a hotelier or travel agent makes a representation (i.e. the hotel serves vegetarian meals, or the hotel has special facilities for the disabled) and the client, in reliance upon such a representation, books with the hotel or through the travel agent, then if the representation is false, the client may bring an action founded upon negligent misstatement.

2 In *Junior Books Ltd* v. *Veitchi & Co. Ltd* [1982] 3 WLR 477 (HL), Lord Roskill, who gives the leading speech and with whom Lords Fraser and Russell agreed, takes the following view:

> *There was no reason why 'damage to pocket' simpliciter should be disallowed when the damage to the pocket coupled with physical damage has always been allowed. No untoward consequences would result.*

It used to be argued that this decision removed the need for a 'special relationship' to be established before damages for economic loss may be recovered.

Junior Books is now a case which has been confined to its own particular facts following the House of Lords' decision in *Caparo Industries plc* v. *Dickman* – (see p. 22 above).

Negligent misrepresentation

Unlike either deceit or negligent misstatement, which are both based in the law of torts, negligent misrepresentation arises out of contract law, and is statutorily provided for by s. 2(1) Misrepresentation Act 1967:

> *Where a person has entered into a contract after a misrepresentation has been made to him by another party thereto and as a result thereof he has suffered loss, then, if the person making the misrepresentation would be liable for damages in respect thereof had the misrepresentation been made fraudulently, that person shall be so liable notwithstanding that the misrepresentation was not made fraudulently, unless he proves that he had reasonable ground to believe and did believe up to the time the contract was made that the facts represented were true.*

This section gives rise to a separate course of action. It is easier to succeed under s. 2(1) than under either deceit or negligent misstatement, since with s. 2(1) it is not necessary to prove the fault of the defendant in making the representation. It is for the defendant to justify his or her actions under s. 2(1) rather than for the plaintiff to prove fault. It is worth remembering, however, that s. 2(1) operates only where the person to whom the representation was made thereafter enters into a contract with the party making the representation. In the situation we are considering, i.e. where statements are made prior to a contract of booking and the client enters a contract with the hotelier, both negligent misstatement (as discussed above) and negligent misrepresentation are possible actions which the client may bring against the hotelier. A client would be better advised to commence an action under s. 2(1) Misrepresentation Act 1967 for negligent misrepresentation, since this is easier to establish.

Innocent misrepresentation

If the hotelier is neither fraudulent nor negligent, the client may still have a remedy under s. 2(2) Misrepresentation Act 1967 for innocent misrepresentation. Section 2(2) provides:

> *Where a person has entered into a contract after a misrepresentation has been made to him otherwise than fraudulently, and he would be entitled, by reason of the misrepresentation, to rescind the contract, then, if it is claimed, in any proceedings arising out of the contract, that the contract ought to be or has been rescinded, the court or arbitrator may declare the contract subsisting and award damages in lieu of rescission, if of the opinion that it would be equitable to do so, having regard to the nature of the misrepresentation and the loss that would be caused by it if the contract were upheld, as well as the loss that rescission would cause to the other party.*

This form of action does not give rise to a claim for damages; it gives the client the right to treat the contract as at an end. However, the trial judge has a discretion to award damages instead of allowing the client to exercise the right to terminate the contract. A judge will normally exercise this discretion to award damages where the fact which the party misrepresented is only of minor importance.

What are the remedies available for misrepresentation?

Damages. The measure of damages for misrepresentation will vary according to the form of misrepresentation. Where the misrepresentation is fraudulent the measure of damage is to place clients in a position they would have been in had the statement not been relied upon by them. If the misrepresentation is either one which falls under s. 2(1) Misrepresentation Act 1967 or within the scope of the rule in *Hedley Byrne* v. *Heller* the damages recoverable are those which the client had lost by being induced to enter the contract or in consequence of the defendant's misstatement. Where the misrepresentation is innocent there is no right to damages. However, where judges exercise their discretion and award damages, the measure is normally the same as under s. 2(1) Misrepresentation Act 1967.

Rescission. Fraudulent, negligent and innocent misrepresentations all give rise to the right of the client to rescind the contract, i.e. to treat the contract as at an end. The purpose here is to restore the parties to the position they would have been in had the contract never been made. One important limitation upon this principle is where the client has, after learning of the misrepresentation, affirmed the contract by either expressly or implicitly showing an intention to proceed with the contract.

Can liability for misrepresentation be excluded or limited by a clause in the contract? If by the contract of booking the hotelier seeks to exclude liability for misrepresentation, such a clause is only operative where it satisfies the requirement of reasonableness within s. 11 Unfair Contract Terms Act 1977. This limitation upon the operation of such a clause is provided for by s. 8 Unfair Contract Terms Act 1977 and operates regardless of whether the client was acting as a consumer. Section 8 states:

> *If a contract contains a term which would exclude or restrict –*
> *(a) any liability to which a party to a contract may be subject by reason of any misrepresentation made by him before the contract was made; or*
> *(b) any remedy available to another party to the contract by reason of such a misrepresentation,*
> *that term shall be of no effect except insofar as it satisfies the requirement of reasonableness as stated in s. 11(1) Unfair Contract Terms Act 1977; and it is for those claiming that the term satisfies that requirement to show that it does.*

General tortious liability

A case on damages for disappointment illustrates the availability of a remedy under the general law of negligence where the disappointment arises from illness suffered by the holidaymaker which is clearly attributable to the accommodation etc. provided by the tour operator.

DAVEY v. COSMOS AIR HOLIDAY [1989] 1 CL 327   In March 1984 P booked a two-week package holiday with D to be taken in October 1984 in the Algarve for his family. The whole family succumbed to diarrhoea whilst on holiday. P's wife and son contracted dysentery. The judge found that the illness was due to the appalling lack of hygiene at the resort and in particular that raw sewage was being pumped into the sea 50 yards from the beach. D had resident representatives in the Algarve and at the resort. During the summer of 1984, reports had appeared in British and Portuguese newspapers of problems related to pollution.

Held: That D's representatives had known of the danger and should have reported it to D, who should have warned P before P left England. By an implied term in the contract and by virtue of a common duty of care, D were under a duty to take such steps as were reasonable, taking all the circumstances into account, to avoid exposing their clients to any significant risk of danger or injury to their health. Damages of £1000 were awarded for a ruined holiday; special damages for ruined clothing were awarded; £200 each was awarded to P and his daughter, £250 to his son and £500 to his wife for the pain and suffering of the illness.

Package Travel Directive

The EC Package Directive came into force on 1st January 1993. The Department of Trade and Industry is responsible for implementing the directive in the UK. The DTI produced the Package Travel, Holidays and Package Tours Regulations 1992 which define a package as 'a pre-arranged combination of at least two of the following components, provided the service covers a period of at least 24 hours or involves a night away from home; ... *transport, accommodation, other tourist services not ancillary to transport or accommodation and accounting for a significant proportion of the package'.*

It is this last component which is of significance to hoteliers.

Simply transporting guests to the hotel from the neighbouring station or airport would not normally create a package. Nor does the fact that a hotel has facilities such as tennis courts or swimming pools create a package. However, if an hotel were to promote a tennis-coaching package (implying guaranteed coaching) a package will have been created within the terms of the directive. A test of whether the offering of a component creates a package might be to ask if the component, additional to the hotel accommodation, is the reason for people choosing to buy the package. If the answer is yes, then the hotel has probably created a package and is subject to the requirements of the directive.

Conferences normally do not come within the definition, because in most cases hotels are merely offering the hotel services to the conference organiser (who may well be covered by the terms of the directive).

The brochure. If the 'offering' comes within the scope of the directive then certain information must be put into the package brochure. For UK hotel operators this includes: '. . . *destination, means of transport (if provided), accommodation, meals, programme, amount of deposit required, minimum number of people required for the package to go ahead, cancellation deadlines, arrangements in case of travel delays, arrangements for the security of payments such as deposits'.*

Contract. Before a contract is entered into the customer has to be given certain information, either in writing or verbally. Most of the information concerns overseas packages but for domestic packages customers must be told of the arrangements made for the security of their deposits.

The contract itself has to contain information on any of the following components which a hotel is responsible for providing: '. . *destination, dates, details of transport (if provided), accommodation (location, standard), a statement that appropriate legislation such as Fire Regulations and the Food Safety Act are adhered to, any meals included, minimum number of people required for the package to go ahead, cancellation deadlines, programme of entertainments/activities, name and address of organiser, price, details of possible price revisions and any taxes or fees not included in the prices, payment method including deposit, any special personal requirements (e.g. diet), complaints procedure'.*

In many cases hotel 'packages' already contain much of this information so to meet the additional requirements should not be too difficult.

Telephone booking. Many packages offered by hotels are booked by telephone and obviously it is not possible to give all the required information over the telephone. However, good advice would be to send a brochure and a confirming letter to the customer as part of the confirmation procedure. Where a 'walk-in' customer buys a package then he or she should be given a brochure at least on registering.

Protection against insolvency. An organiser (a hotel) must be able to refund pre-payments in the case of insolvency. This may be by one of three ways.
- Bonding: organisers may buy a bond, from a bonding organisation approved by the DTI. The bond has to be up to the value of any pre-payments held. The bond would be for a maximum period of 18 months and would have to cover 25% of the value of the pre-payments received in a year.

- Organisers may create a trust fund, from which fund can only be drawn with the trustee's approval, after the customer has received what was paid for.
- Organisers may insure against insolvency, which would reimburse customers' deposits in case of insolvency. Obviously, this is the simplest method for most hoteliers being an addition to the normal policy.

Tour operators and their customers. The English common law will still have an important role to play, but the nature of the current law does not lend itself to precision in dealing with disputes between tour operators and customers.

What is clear from the case law is that a number of different approaches have been taken by the courts.

WALL v. SILVER (1981) (Unreported)　　　This case identifies a duty on the part of tour operators to take reasonable care of the safety of holiday-makers. The plaintiffs stayed at a hotel in Tenerife, booked through the defendant tour operator, where a fire broke out. Owing to the inadequacy of the fire escapes they sought to leave the hotel from an upper-storey window by knotting bedlinen to make an escape ladder. They sustained injuries in their escape attempt. The plaintiffs were unsuccessful in their claim. Hodgson J took the view that he 'would find it wholly unreasonable to saddle a tour operator with an obligation to ensure the safety of all the components of the package over none of which he had any control at all'. Thus it was thought that if the tour operator has no control over the activities of the hotel he should not be liable for them unless some fault might be attributed to him.

In *Usher* v. *Intasun* (1987) the same view was taken; here technical problems in a charter airlines plane caused considerable delay to holiday-makers travelling with the tour operator. A tour operator is not therefore liable for the acts of a properly selected sub-contracting airline. A similar point was raised in *Toubi* v. *Intasun* (1988).

In *Kaye* v. *Intasun* (1987), where the plaintiff holiday-makers complained of cockroach infestation in a four-star hotel bedroom, the tour operator was held to have taken all reasonable steps in selecting the hotel.

A tour operator in the main organizes and co-ordinates the provision of services by others. One basis upon which a holiday-maker may base a claim against a tour operator is s. 13 of the Supply of Goods and Services Act 1982 (see p. 120). The holiday-maker might argue that the tour operator is applying his skills in bringing together the elements of the 'package'. The fact that the tour operator does not perform all the obligations himself does not affect his liability, under this provision. Section 13 SGSA 1982 may be an effective tool for holiday-makers seeking redress for disrupted, inadequate or substandard holidays.

The courts have not fought shy of talking above 'strict liability' in the context of a tour operator's obligations to a holiday-maker. In *Jarvis* v. *Swan's Tours* [1973] 1 All ER 71, Lord Justice Edmund Davies took the view that if a tour operator fails to provide a holiday of the quality contracted for he is liable in damages. This approach was endorsed in *Adcock* v. *Blue Sky* (1980) and in *Spencer* v. *Cosmos* (1989). Although in each of these cases the views expressed seem to impose a form of strict liability on the tour operator, there are no supporting arguments for this and in none of these cases was liability directly in issue.

COOK v. SPANISH HOLIDAY TOURS (*The Times*, 6 February 1960)　　　The plaintiffs found on arrival at their hotel that their room had been double-booked. They were offered unhygienic, substandard accommodation in an annexe. The Court of Appeal held that the tour operators had a duty to provide the holiday-maker with a room; this was not discharged merely by booking a room for the holiday-maker. The tour operator must in effect 'deliver' what the client has booked and paid for – the tour operator is liable to provide the components of the package.

In order to comply with the basic requirements of s. 13 SGSA 1982 to exercise reasonable care and skill a tour operator should:
• undertake a reasonable investigation of the hotel/facilities;
• monitor the hotel/facilities effectively;
• take reasonable steps to resolve 'problems' whilst the holiday-maker is using the hotel/facilities;
• take reasonable steps at all times to deal effectively with the holiday-maker's complaints.
It is possible that a tour operator may seek to avoid liability either by contracting as agent for another or by use of exclusion and limition of liability charges.

In *Spencer* v. *Cosmos*, Muskill LJ looked unfavourably upon the contention that the tour operator was the agent of the airline, coach company, hotel, etc. Some operators seek through their brochures to assert that their position is one of agent, not principal. It would be important in determining this issue in any specific case to examine the nature of the contracts between the tour operator and the airline, coach company, hotels, etc. If these contracts are in terms of the tour operator buying the services and accommodation on his own behalf the fiction of agency is entirely destroyed. As to exclusive clauses, the Unfair Contract Terms Act 1977 affords some protection to holiday-makers (see p. 120).

Often, however, the issue is one of whether or not the matter complained of was covered by the terms of the contract, e.g. late or non-arrival of transportation. If the matter complained of is not within the contract, no breach has occurred and no liability can therefore arise – more to the point, construction of the exclusion clause is irrelevant.

Where there is a breach and UCTA does apply the question most usually confronted is that of the reasonableness of the clause purporting to exclude liability. Examples of how exclusion clauses operate in holiday contracts include *Askew* v. *Intasun* (1980), *Usher* v. *Intasun* (1987) and *Spencer* v. *Cosmos*.

4.2 CONSUMER PROTECTION AND BOOKING CONTRACTS

A prospective hotel guest is protected in various ways from possible unfair trade practices on the part of the hotel with which he or she intends to book. This protection is given by s. 14 of the Trade Descriptions Act 1968, the Tourism (Sleeping Accommodation Price Display) Order 1977, and the Consumer Protection Act 1987.

Trade Descriptions Act 1968

The Trade Descriptions Act 1968 is concerned with the prosecution and punishment of criminal offences rather than with providing a civil remedy. The law we have examined so far in this chapter has been the means by which a guest who is dissatisfied with the services provided by a hotel can seek redress and obtain monetary compensation. However, the Trade Descriptions Act 1968 creates certain forms of criminal offence, the purpose of which is to regulate the trading practices of business organizations and to ensure that certain minimum standards are met. Hence, the proprietor of a hotel who acts in breach of the Trade Descriptions Act 1968 may be prosecuted for a criminal offence by the local authority's trading standards office and, if found guilty before the Magistrates' or Crown Court, punished for the offence. Section 14(1) of the Trade Descriptions Act 1968 provides:

It shall be an offence for any person in the course of any trade or business –
(a)   to make a statement which he knows to be false; or
(b)   recklessly to make a statement which is false;
as to any of the following matters, that is to say –
>   *(i)   the provision in the course of any trade or business of any services,*
>   *accommodation or facilities;*
>   *(ii)   the nature of any services, accommodation or facilities provided in the*
>   *course of any trade or business;*
> *(iii)   the time at which, manner in which or persons by whom any services,*
>   *accommodation or facilities are so provided;*
>   *(iv)   the examination, approval or evaluation by any person of any services,*
>   *accommodation or facilities so provided; or*
>   *(v)   the location or amenities of any accommodation so provided.*

Section 14(2) provides:

For the purposes of this section –
(a)   anything (whether or not a statement as to any of the matters specified in
      s. 14(1)) likely to be taken for such a statement as to any of those matters as
      would be false shall be deemed as a false statement as to that matter; and
(b)   a statement made regardless of whether it is true or false shall be deemed to be
      made recklessly, whether or not the person making it had reasons for believing
      that it might be false.

The *mens rea* (guilty mind) to be proven by the prosecution in order to establish the defendant's guilt of the offence is either knowledge that the statement made is false, or that he was reckless as to whether it was true or false. It is essential that the prosecution prove the defendant's knowledge or reckless state of mind at the time when the statement was made; subsequent recklessness will not render criminal an earlier statement.

SUNAIR HOLIDAYS LTD v. DODDS [1970] 1 WLR 1037 (CA)	The defendant's brochure advertised package holidays in Majorca. It described the facilities on offer at the hotel, and stated that double rooms each had 'private bath, shower, WC and terrace'. The defendants had a contract with the hotel under which the hotel was required to supply rooms fitting

the description in the brochure. However, on the occasion in question a double room was provided which had no terrace. The defendants had not checked that its customers were provided with rooms corresponding to the description in their brochure.

Held: At the time when the statement was made in the brochure it was true; accommodation corresponding to the description was being made available. The mere fact that the defendants had subsequently been negligent in failing to check that the correct rooms had been allocated on the occasion in question did not render the initial statement 'false or recklessly made'.

What amounts to recklessness under the Trade Descriptions Act 1968? In *MFI Warehouses Ltd* v. *Nattrass* [1973] 1 All ER 762, the Divisional Court held that an offence could be committed 'recklessly' whether or not there had been any dishonesty on the part of the defendant, provided the defendant does not have sufficient regard to the falsity or otherwise of the statement he or she is making.

In *Yugotours* v. *Wadsley* (*The Guardian*, 3 June 1988), the Divisional Court held that where the statements made in a holiday brochure and accompanying letter were clearly false, and were known to be so by the company, and nothing was done to correct them, there was sufficient evidence for a court to infer that the maker of the statements had been reckless.

Section 14(1) deals, therefore, with false statements applied to services. Examples of how the law operates in this area are to be found in *R.* v. *Thomson Holidays Ltd* and *Wings Ltd* v. *Ellis*.

R. v. THOMSON HOLIDAYS LTD [1974] 1 All ER 823 (CA)

Thomson Holidays Ltd organized and sold package holidays. In August and September 1970 they prepared, published and distributed to travel agencies and the general public two million copies of a brochure giving particulars of the holidays they had to offer for the 1971 season. Mr and Mrs B read the brochure, were attracted by an advertisement in it for a holiday at a hotel in Greece, and booked for that holiday. On arrival at the hotel they found that it did not have certain of the amenities that had been described in the brochure. On their return Mr and Mrs B complained and informations were preferred against Thomson Ltd, charging them with recklessly making a false statement in the course of their trade or business as to an amenity or accommodation provided at the hotel, contrary to s. 14(1)(b) of the Trade Descriptions Act 1968. X, a holiday-maker from Stockport, who had also read a copy of Thomson Ltd's brochure, stayed at the same hotel in Greece as Mr and Mrs B and, having found that some of the amenities that had been described in the brochure were non-existent, he also complained. When the informations relating to X's complaint were heard in July 1972, Thomson Ltd pleaded guilty to the charges made therein under s. 14(1)(b) of the 1968 Act and were fined a total of £450. Thomson Ltd's trial in respect of Mr and Mrs B's complaints started in March 1973. Thomson Ltd there entered a plea of *autrefois convict* (i.e. that Thomson Ltd had been convicted once for the offence already). The judge ruled that in the circumstances the plea was not available to Thomson Ltd and he directed the jury accordingly. Thomson Ltd were convicted, fined a total of £1000 and, under s. l(l)(b) of the Criminal Justice Act 1972, ordered to pay £50 by way of compensation to Mr and Mrs B. Thomson Ltd appealed, contending *inter alia* that only one offence had been committed (i.e. that the false statement had been 'made' within the meaning of s. 14(1)(b) when it was printed or published) and, as they had already been prosecuted in respect of it, the judge should have ruled that their plea of *autrefois convict* was valid and directed the jury accordingly.

Held: The appeal would be dismissed for the following reasons. A false statement was 'made' within the meaning of s. 14(1)(b) when it was communicated to someone and, each time a false statement in a brochure was communicated to a reader, a fresh offence was committed. It followed that Thomson Ltd were not entitled to plead *autrefois convict* at the trial and the judge's direction to the jury had been correct.

WINGS LTD v. ELLIS   Wings Ltd published a travel brochure which contained
[1984] 1 WLR 731 (QBD),   photographs and descriptions of hotels. Unknown to the
[1984] 3 WLR 965 (HL)   defendant company at the time of publication, the brochure
                               falsely described a hotel in Sri Lanka as air-conditioned, and
                               a photograph wrongly purporting to be one of a room at the
hotel indicated that the hotel was air-conditioned. After the brochures had been distributed the
error was found. Wings Ltd sent a memo to travel agents, etc., telling them of the error and
asking them to inform customers of this. All customers who had already booked were informed
by letter. The complainant, who read an unamended brochure and who was not informed of the
error by the travel agent with whom he booked, informed a trading standards officer that the
hotel was not as described in the brochure. Wings Ltd were prosecuted under s. 14(1)(a)(ii) and
s. 14(1)(b)(ii), and were convicted.

On appeal by Wings Ltd to the Divisional Court it was held, allowing the appeal, that in order
to establish the commission of an offence contrary to s. 14(1) the requisite state of mind (namely
knowledge of, or recklessness as to, the falsity of the statement) had to exist at the time the
statement was made. This had not been established on the facts of the case.

The Trading Standards Officer, Mr Ellis, appealed to the House of Lords. The question on
appeal was therefore 'whether a defendant may properly be convicted of an offence under s.
14(1)(a) of the Trade Descriptions Act 1968 where he has no knowledge of the falsity of the
statement at the time of its publication but knew of the falsity when the statement was read by
the complainant'.

The House of Lords held:
1   Knowledge by a defendant of the making of a statement was *not* a necessary ingredient
     of offence under s. 14(1)(a) of the Trade Descriptions Act 1968.
2   A statement could be 'made' for the purpose of s. 14(1) at times other than its
     communication to another person. In the instant case the statement was made when the
     complainant read the brochure.

Lord Scarman in his opinion outlined the elements of the offence: 'The necessary ingredients
of the offence under s. 14(1)(a) were that: (i) a person in the course of a trade or business (ii)
made a statement, (iii) which he knew to be false (iv) as to the provision in the course of trade
or business of any services, accommodation or facilities.'

Lord Scarman went on to say that in order to establish the commission of the offence 'it
sufficed to prove that the statement was made on a person's behalf in the course of his business
and that its content was false to the knowledge of the person carrying on the business'.

Whilst Lord Scarman approved the Court of Appeal's decision in *R. v. Thomson Holidays
Ltd* (above), he considered: 'It was unnecessary for the Court of Appeal in *Thomson* to hold
that communication was of the essence and in that they erred.' In the instant case he held that
the statement was made when the brochure was published.

The appeal was allowed and the certified question answered as follows: 'A statement which
was false was made by the company in the course of its business when it was read by the complainant, an interested member of the public doing business with the company on the basis of
the statement. The offence was committed on that occasion because the company knew that the
statement was false. The fact that it was unaware of the falsity of the statement when it was
published in the brochure was irrelevant.'

What are the situations which s. 14(1) covers?

The statement must be one relating to a present fact. This has led to a number of cases.

R. v. SUNAIR HOLIDAYS
LTD [1973] 1 WLR 1105
(CA)

The defendants published a travel brochure for the forth-coming summer season which referred to a hotel in Spain. The hotel in question was described as having a swimming pool, push-chairs for hire for children, and a special children's menu. A guest who had booked on the strength of such statements arrived to find that the pool was incomplete and unusable and no push-chairs or special children's food were available. It was established that when the defendant travel company had booked the guest's accommodation with the hotel all these facilities were intended to be provided by the time the guests were due to take their holiday.

Held: Since the defendants had only made promises for the future and these were not covered by s. 14(1),the defendants fell to be acquitted. Parker CJ observed: 'we hold that s. 14(1) is limited to statements of fact past or present and does not include assurance about the future'. Only if a future assurance can be construed as an implied statement of present intention, means or belief will it be a statement within s. 14(1). McKenna J observed: 'a promise or forecast may contain by implication a statement of present fact. The person who makes the promise may be implying that his present intention is to keep it or that he has at present the power to perform it. The person who makes the forecast may be implying that he now believes that his prediction will come true or that he has the means of bringing it to pass. Such implied statements of present intention, means or belief, when they are made, may well be within s. 14(1) and therefore punishable if they were false and were made knowingly or recklessly. But if they are punishable, the offence is not the breaking of a promise or the failure to make a prediction come true. It is the making of a false statement of an existing fact, somebody's present state of mind or present means.'

It would appear, following *R. v. Clarksons Holidays Ltd* (1972) 57 Cr. App. R 38, that it is a question of fact for the jury to determine whether or not the defendant's statement was one of present fact or merely a statement of future intention. The principle therefore seems to be that in each case the jury must determine whether the statement was a mere fallible forecast or prediction or whether the statement, although relating to services to be performed in the future, contained a statement as to existing fact – see *British Airways Board* v. *Taylor* [1976] 1 WLR 15 (HL) below.

Overbooking

It is a common practice within the hotel industry for reception staff to overbook the rooms available at the hotel in the expectation that certain of those bookings will be cancelled, and thus the hotel can still be maintained at full occupancy. In *British Airways Board* v. *Taylor* [1976] 1 WLR 15 (HL) it was held that overbooking may come within s. 14(1) Trade Descriptions Act 1968.

BRITISH AIRWAYS
BOARD v. TAYLOR
[1976] 1 WLR 15 (HL)

BOAC (the predecessor to BA) wrote to a passenger, who had paid in advance for a flight, confirming his reservation for a specified flight on a particular day at a particular time. BOAC operated an overbooking policy; passengers were booked on flights in excess of the number of seats available. When BOAC wrote to the passenger confirming his seat, the flight in question was not overbooked. However, when the passenger arrived on the appointed date he could not be carried on the flight on which he was booked. BOAC, which had now been re-formed as BA, were prosecuted for breach of s. 14(1) in that they recklessly made a statement about the provision of services which was false as to the time and manner in which the service was to be provided.

Held: The House of Lords held that BOAC's letter to the passenger and the ticket were a state-ment of fact that the passenger's booking on the flight in question was certain. This statement in view of s. 14(1) was false, since the passenger was exposed to the risk that he might not get a seat upon that particular flight.

Example. Applying the rule in this case, if a hotelier overbooks his accommodation and corresponds with a guest assuring him of room 214 on a given date, and on the date when the statement was made room 214 was booked, and on the date in question the hotel is full and the guest is provided with either no accommodation at all, or substitute accommodation which does not have the facilities described, an offence has been committed under s. 14(1), provided the original statement was made either knowingly or recklessly.

Section 14(1) covers services and facilities (i.e. banquets or conferences) as well as accommodation.

Section 14(1)(b)(iv) covers the accreditation of the accommodation or services. If a hotel falsely describes itself as a three- or four-star RAC or AA accredited hotel a s. 14(1) offence has been committed. Equally, a restaurant which falsely describes itself as Egon Ronay recommended has committed a s. 14(1) offence.

Location and amenities

A hotel which states that it has certain amenities, e.g. swimming pool, child minders, creche, when in fact these services are not available, is within the scope of s. 14(1). Equally, a hotel which claims to be ' 100 yards from the sea front', or to possess 'sea views from the dining room', if such statements are false, is covered by s. 14(1).

Defences

Defences to prosecution under s. 14(1) Trade Descriptions Act 1968. Section 24(1) Trade Descriptions Act 1968 provides for a third-party defence to prosecution. It provides:

> *In any proceeding for an offence under this Act it shall . . . be a defence for the person charged to prove –*
> *(a) that the commission of the offence was due to a mistake or to reliance on in-formation supplied to him or to the act or default of another person, an accident or some other cause beyond his control;*
> *and*
> *(b) that he took all reasonable precautions and exercised all due diligence to avoid the commission of such an offence by himself or any person under his control.*

Section 24(2) requires a defendant who seeks to rely upon the s. 24(1) defence to serve a notice in writing on the prosecutor seven clear days prior to the hearing, identifying the other person whose fault is relied upon as forming the basis for the defendant's defence. It should be noted that both parts s. 24(1) (a) and (b) must be satisfied before the defendant may successfully establish the defence under the section.

The s. 24(1) defence can be used by employers who have been prosecuted for the actions of one of their employees, or principals who have been prosecuted for the default of one of their agents.

BECKETT v. KINGSTON BROS LTD [1970] 1 QB 606	The defendants purchased a quantity of turkeys from Denmark. The turkeys had 'Norfolk King Turkeys' printed on their labels. Branch managers were instructed to remove these labels prior to display. A branch manager did not do this and the defendants were prosecuted under s. I Trade Descriptions Act 1968, and sought to rely on s. 24(1) as providing a defence.

Held: The defendants were entitled to rely on s. 24(1) as affording a defence. The default was that of the branch manager.

However, this case related to s. 1 TDA 1968, which is an offence of strict liability. Section 14, however, requires proof of knowledge of recklessness in order to secure a conviction. Therefore, where an employee acts on his or her own initiative, the employer will have a complete defence without reference to s. 24(1); the defence will be simple lack of knowledge, i.e. the employer neither knew of nor was reckless as to the misdescription by the employee; see *Coupe* v. *Guyett* [1973] 2 All ER 1058 (QBD).

The principle in this case was approved and applied in *Tesco Supermarkets Ltd* v. *Nattrass* [1971] 2 All ER 127 (HL). Hence, if a hotelier is prosecuted under s. 14(1) in an overbooking case, and overbooking is not company policy, i.e. it was due to the actions or default of the receptionist or reception manager, the hotelier would be afforded a s. 24(1) defence, provided that he or she could attribute the overbooking to the receptionist or manager, and provided the hotelier had taken all reasonable precautions and shown due diligence in seeking to prevent the occurrence of over-booking. Section 23 Trade Descriptions Act 1968 provides for the prosecution of the 'other person'. Section 24(1) also provides a defence where the offence occurred by accident or due to circumstances beyond the defendant's control.

Hotel accommodation: pricing

The pricing of hotel accommodation is regulated by the law in two ways: the Tourism (Sleeping Accommodation Price Display) Order 1977 and the Consumer Protection Act 1987.

Part III of the Consumer Protection Act 1987 creates a general criminal offence of giving a misleading price indication. Section 20, which defines the crime, provides:

> ... *a person shall be guilty of an offence if, in the course of any business of his, he gives (by any means whatever) to any consumers an indication which is misleading as to the price at which any goods, services, accommodation or facilities are available (whether generally or from particular persons).*

The scope of s. 20 is analysed in detail in Chapter 6 on p. 215.

Tourism (Sleeping Accommodation Price Display) Order 1977

This order requires the display of overnight accommodation prices in residential establishments with four or more rooms.
1   The prices must be clearly displayed by means of a notice at reception or in the hotel entrance.
2   Both maximum and minimum prices should be displayed.
3   The Order does not apply to youth hostels, members' clubs, rooms in the same occupation for at least 21 consecutive nights and establishments such as holiday camps which provide facilities other than those of a normal hotel as part of the price.
4   The information which must be provided in the notice comprises:
     (a)   price of a single room;
     (b)   price of a double room;
     (c)   price of any other type of bedroom;
     (d)   all prices must be inclusive of service charge, and this must be stated;
     (e)   VAT may be shown separately if desired, but the VAT element in the price must be shown in some form or other;
     (f)   it should be made clear whether the price is inclusive of meals.
5   Enforcement is by the local authority trading standards office. A fine may be imposed upon conviction for breach of the order.

ABTA Tour Operators' Code of Conduct

The Association of British Travel Agents (ABTA) provides a code of practice which is legally binding upon all ABTA travel agents. This code embodies the practices and standard terms of contract to be observed between ABTA travel agents and their customers. The code was revised in 1990 and now contains the following key provisions in relation to package holidays sold by tour operators who are members of ABTA:
1   Since 1990, operators have had to include, as a form of the contract with consumers, acceptance of responsibility should the services they are obliged to provide prove deficient or not of a reasonable standard (e.g. poor-quality accommodation). The test is an objective one: was the holiday of reasonable standard from the consumer's point of view?
2   With regard to death, illness or injury, new rules came into force on 1 November 1990. Tour operators must include in their contracts a term accepting responsibility for the negligent acts or omissions of employees, and also of suppliers and subcontractors. For the first time, therefore, ABTA agents will be liable for, e.g., a salmonella outbreak caused by poor food handling in the hotel restaurant, or injuries caused by the crash of a transfer coach which has bald tyres.
3   Even where death, injury or illness is caused by a misadventure not connected with the package, there is liability placed on the tour operator to give 'advice, guidance and initial financial assistance up to a limit of £5000 per booking form'.
The code consequently goes beyond liability as traditionally imposed by the law, i.e. that the tour operator must choose the supplier with care, monitor its performance reasonably thereafter and alert future customers to any major problems, and therefore adds a great deal to consumers' legal rights.

4.3 THE REGISTRATION OF GUESTS

By the Immigration (Hotel Records) Order 1972, all guests over the age of 16 are required upon arrival at a hotel to register their full name and nationality, or have it registered for them. The hotelier is required to keep a record of such information which is open to inspection by the police for a period of up to twelve months.

British subjects and Commonwealth citizens need not give their address. Each guest must be entered separately in the register. 'Aliens', those who are neither British nor Commonwealth citizens, must give their passport details as well as their name and nationality. In addition they must state the date on which they intend to leave the hotel and their intended destination.

CASE STUDY

In September 1994 Mr Bunce sent details of his hotel in Sandhills to travel agents. He included the following statement: 'The hotel serves splendid meals at special prices to suit children (fish fingers, ice cream, etc.).'

In March 1995 Lily Dale went to a travel agent, Mr Dunn, who read out the details and the statement above about Bunce's hotel. She asked him about rooms with a balcony facing the sea. He phoned Bunce's hotel and booked, at her request, a holiday for £300 for Lily and her two children in two rooms with balconies facing the sea. A week later she received a printed confirmation of booking, and paid half the price in advance, as required.

In July 1995, on holiday at Bunce's hotel, two things particularly disappointed Lily:
1. The special meals for children were set items from the adult menu, often including offal and boiled milk puddings, neither of which Lily's children would eat.
2. On the first night she was told she had to sleep in a back room with the children because Mr Bunce said there had been a misunderstanding with other guests about when their holiday should end. The Dales had to spend all week in the back room because, in fact, Mr Bunce had overbooked.
   (a) Examine the criminal liability of Mr Bunce and Mr Dunn, if any, for their statements and actions.
   (b) Examine any civil remedy Lily may have against Mr Bunce or Mr Dunn. Discuss whether she is entitled to damages for the disappointment that she and her children have suffered with respect to the holiday.

Key points

(a) Examine the criminal liability of Mr Bunce and Mr Dunn, if any, for their statements and actions.

Mr Bunce is the proprietor of the hotel and the publisher of the brochure in which statements about children's meals were contained. He may be charged under s. 14(1)(a)(ii) of the TDA 1968 (see p. 138). Mention should be made of the *mens rea* of this offence and the fact that the statement must be 'made' (see *Wings Ltd* v. *Ellis*).

Mr Dunn, if charged under s. 14(1)(a)(ii) in respect of these facts, would have a complete defence under s. 24(1) TDA 1968 (third party defence) (see p. 142).

Mr Bunce may be charged under s. 14(1)(a) with regard to overbooking the hotel (see *British Airways Board* v. *Taylor*, p. 141).

Mr Dunn, if charged under s. 14(1) in respect of these facts, could again avail himself of a complete defence under s. 24(1) TDA 1968 (see above).

(b) Examine any civil remedy Lily may have against Mr Bunce or Mr Dunn. Discuss whether she is entitled to damages for the disappointment that she and her children have suffered with respect to the holiday.

Mr Bunce, the proprietor of the hotel, is the only person with whom Lily is in a contractual relationship. Mr Dunn is the agent of Mr Bunce and therefore drops out of the picture (see p. 114).

In bringing an action for breach of contract against Mr Bunce, Lily would need to establish the terms which Mr Bunce breached. Clearly, by failing to provide the accommodation for which Lily contracted, Mr Bunce is in breach of an express condition of the contract (see pp. 118–19). Whether or not the fact that the rooms must have a balcony and a sea view is a condition or a warranty is open to debate. It is more likely to be a 'mid-term'.

Reference should be made to implied terms of fact (see p. 119) and to the implied conditions under s. 13 of the Supply of Goods and Services Act 1982.

Lily may claim damages for the disappointment arising from the poor quality of the accommodation offered, not only on her own behalf (*Jarvis* v. *Swan's Tours Ltd*), but also on behalf of her children (*Jackson* v. *Horizon Holidays Ltd*) (see p. 115).

She may also have an action for breach of contract regarding the provision of children's meals. The statement made in the brochure may not be incorporated into the terms and conditions of booking, however, and a clearer form of action would be for misrepresentation (see Misrepresentation Act 1967, p. 131).

Lily's action against Mr Dunn is tortious. The issue here is one of negligent misstatement. If she is to succeed she must establish all the elements of this tort (see p. 131). Damages for disappointment are *not* available in tort.

FIVE

The hotelier and the guest II

In considering the contract of booking and the various legal aspects of it we have not sought to distinguish between the various forms of hotel which offer accommodation, food and drink. The law of England does in fact draw a distinction between inns and other establishments. The term 'inn' is used as a term of art, to describe those hotels which fall within the scope of the Hotel Proprietors Act 1956. 'Inn', therefore, has a specific legal meaning and only those establishments which fall within the definition of an inn are subject to the duties and able to exercise the rights accorded to establishments of that status. Those establishments which fall outside the scope of the definition are not subject to the burdens imposed upon inns nor may they exercise the right of lien to which innkeepers are entitled. So as to avoid confusion, for the purposes of this chapter, establishments which fall within the scope of the Hotel Proprietors Act 1956 will be termed inns, and those which fall outside it will be termed private hotels.

5.1 INNS

What is the definition of an inn? Section 1(1) of the Hotel Proprietors Act 1956 (HPA) states that only hotels within the meaning of the Act shall be deemed to be inns and that the rights and duties of an innkeeper shall apply only to such establishments. The definition of a hotel under the Act is to be found in s. 1(3):

> In this Act the expression 'hotel' means an establishment held out by the proprietor as offering food, drink and, if so required, sleeping accommodation, without special contract, to any traveller presenting himself who appears able and willing to pay a reasonable sum for the services and facilities and who is in a fit state to be received.

147

It is not easy to define in any positive, prescriptive way what a hotel is within the meaning of s. 1(3) HPA 1956. Obviously the larger establishments, such as major hotels like the Hilton, are clearly within the definition, as are more modest hotels, but where is the borderline to be drawn in legal terms?

The hotel must be 'held out' as ready and willing to take travellers 'without special contract'. That is to say, innkeepers will not pick and choose between travellers to whom they will offer their services, provided such travellers are fit to be received and willing to pay a reasonable sum for the services rendered. Therefore, any establishment which advertises that it restricts its clientele is not within the definitions, e.g. 'no children', 'no coaches'. Of course hoteliers are able to restrict their clientele in certain ways, e.g. by having a rule that all men using the lounge bar of a hotel must wear a jacket and tie. Such a restriction may be justifiable on the ground that those men who are not so dressed are not 'in a fit state to be received'. Hoteliers must not, of course, restrict their clientele on the basis of either sex or race; see pp. 156–60 on the restrictions on the right to refuse service.

There may be a presumption that if the words 'inn' or 'hotel' appear in the title of the establishment it is an inn under s. 1(3) HPA 1956. However, many establishments use the world 'hotel' in their name in order to give an impression of grandeur which otherwise they may not give; e.g. the Waterside Hotel sounds more impressive than the Sunny Bank Guest House. The better view is that the title given to the establishment is irrelevant.

Public houses are often assumed to be inns, since the word 'inn' is used colloquially to describe public houses: the contrary would seem to be the law. Only a few public houses offer sleeping accommodation and those which do not are obviously excluded from the operation of s. 1(3). Not all public houses provide food, and this may be a further reason to exclude some pubs from the category of inns. If, however, a public house does offer both food and drink, and has sleeping accommodation which is available without prior booking, it will be afforded the status of an inn. Where s. 1(3) refers to drink, it does not confine the definition of an inn to those establishments which offer alcoholic drink. The fact that an inn does or does not hold a licence for the sale of intoxicating liquor is irrelevant. Therefore temperance establishments are within the Act. The only authority for this is a nineteenth-century case, *Cunningham* v. *Philip* [1896] 12 TCR 352, which was concerned with the common-law definition. The mere holding of a licence is not conclusive proof or even indicative of the fact that the establishment is an inn under the HPA 1956.

There is no law which obliges a hotel to display a notice stating that it is an inn under s. 1(3) HPA 1956. No conclusion should therefore be drawn from the fact that a hotel displays a 'schedule notice' pursuant to s. 2 HPA 1956 (see section 5.3). This is because the terms of such a notice include the sentence: 'This notice does not constitute an admission either that the Act applies to this hotel or that liability thereunder attaches to the proprietor of this hotel in any particular case'.

The keeping of a register of guests does not amount to conclusive evidence that the establishment is an inn (see p. 145 on registration of guests). The Immigration (Hotel Records) Order 1972 applies both to inns and to other establishments such as boarding houses, private hotels, etc.

A restaurant is not an inn, since it does not offer sleeping accommodation. However, if a restaurant forms part of an inn, e.g. the dining room of an inn will be open to non-residents, it is not open to the proprietor of the inn to argue that the restaurant is a distinct and separate entity and therefore patrons of the restaurant are not owed the same duties by the inn as are 'travellers' – *Orchard* v. *Bush* [1898] 2 QBD 284.

The safest course of action is to define an inn by means of negative terms. An inn does not include:

(a) any establishment which offers food and drink but not accommodation, e.g. a public house or restaurant;
(b) any establishment which offers both food and drink and accommodation, but requires that accommodation be booked in advance, e.g. lodging houses;
(c) any establishment where the proprietor makes it known that it reserves the right to pick and choose between those who wish to use the accommodation available;
(d) membership clubs or such institutions where accommodation is available only to club members and their guests;
(e) youth hostels and similar organizations where membership of an organization is required of those seeking accommodation;
(f) establishments which take only long-term guests by prior arrangements, e.g. rest homes.

By way of conclusion it may be observed that unless each element of s. 1(3) is satisfied, the hotel is not an inn under the Act. Hence, many establishments which may have certain but not all of the elements are not covered by the Act, though many of the general public may consider them to be inns. A large guest house or private hotel is outside the scope of the Act, although it may at first sight appear to be covered.

5.2 DUTIES OF THE INNKEEPER

To avoid confusion we shall call the proprietor of a hotel within the HPA 1956 an innkeeper, i.e. the proprietor of an inn. The innkeeper may not be an individual; indeed in many cases the innkeeper will be a company. The innkeeper is the party upon whom the duties arising at common law and under the 1956 Act are placed, and the party who may exercise those rights given by the Innkeepers Act 1878 and such other rights as an innkeeper may exercise. Where the proprietor of an inn is a company, and the business is carried on by means of a manager, the innkeeper is the company and not the manager (*Dixon* v. *Birch* (1873) LR 8 Exch. 135). This is so even if licence for the sale of intoxicating liquor is in the name of the manager. To whom does an innkeeper owe the duties? Section 1(3) HPA 1956 uses the words 'any traveller'; it is important to understand the meaning of the term 'traveller'. A traveller is not necessarily a guest. The term 'guest' is used to describe a traveller who has engaged sleeping accommodation at the inn. Hence a traveller becomes a guest upon taking one night's sleeping accommodation. Who then is a traveller? 'Any traveller' is given a very broad definition: it includes any person *en route* from one place to another who calls at the inn to make use of the services available, i.e. food, drink and accommodation. Whether a person is a traveller is primarily a question of fact.

WILLIAMS v. LINNITT [1951] 1 All ER 278

A farmer on his way home from business in Nuneaton drove to an inn, having passed his own home, in order to meet friends for a drink. It was not his intention to spend the night at the inn. The question arose of whether or not the farmer was a traveller and thus owed (prior to the HPA 1956) the common-law duties afforded to travellers. It was held that if a person came to an inn to use the services there available, he or she would be afforded the protection given to travellers. This was so even if that person was a local resident and did not intend using the sleeping accommodation at the inn. It did not matter that the farmer used the inn only for temporary refreshment. The farmer was a traveller.

Hence, if Mr Bunn were to call at an inn for food or drink whilst on a journey (even a very short one) he would be a traveller – *Orchard* v. *Bush* [1898] 2 QBD 284 and *Williams* v. *Linnitt* (above). Equally, if Farmer Spiers were to call at the local inn for an evening drink, he would be a traveller (even if he had walked only a few yards to get there) in the same way as a visitor to the inn who had travelled from a foreign country.

A negative approach to defining who is a traveller may be adopted. A traveller is not: (a) a friend of the innkeeper making a social call; (b) a repair person or trader calling in the course of his or her work; (c) a representative or salesperson seeking to do business in the inn; (d) a long-term guest at the inn; or (e) a postman or postwoman or person delivering goods to the inn. A traveller includes, however, any person who calls at the inn to use it as a place of refreshment or for the purposes of securing accommodation.

The safest and most sensible course of action for the proprietor of an inn is to assume that all visitors to the premises are travellers. However, people who arrive at the hotel as travellers do not necessarily remain travellers for the duration of their stay.

LAMOND v. RICHARD [1897] I QB 541 (CA)

Mrs Lamond, a woman of good character, arrived at the hotel in November 1895. She paid her bill regularly. In August 1896 she was given verbal notice by the manager to quit her room by the end of that month. She did not leave. On 31 August, whilst she was out taking a walk, her luggage was packed by hotel staff and she was refused re-entry to her room. Mrs Lamond claimed that she had a right to remain at the hotel, since she was a traveller and there were rooms vacant at the hotel.

Held: The action of the management in 'locking out' Mrs Lamond was lawful, since she had ceased to be a traveller. Esher MR stated: 'the question seems to me . . . to be a question of fact, and mere length of residence is not decisive of the matter, because there may be circumstances which show that the length of stay does not prevent the guest being a traveller, as, for instance where it arises from illness; but it is wrong to say that length of time is not one of the circumstances to be taken into account in determining whether the guest has retained his character of traveller'.

Lord Justice Lopes took a slightly different approach: 'In my opinion there is no such rule as suggested, that a person who comes to an inn as a traveller and remains there must remain as a traveller . . . the plaintiff when she was required to leave had ceased to be a traveller, and that, therefore, the innkeeper was fully justified after giving reasonable notice in acting as he did.'

The hotel's case could possibly be argued on another ground. Mrs Lamond had to an extent been disturbing other guests at the hotel; she was under a delusion that her enemies were out to get her. If this was the reason why the hotel sought to exclude her from the premises it might be argued that she had ceased to be a traveller who was 'in a fit state to be received' (see pp. 154–6) on the innkeeper's right to refuse service). In *Rothfield* v. *North British Hotels* (1920) SC 805, a person was asked to leave by the management on the ground that he was an annoyance to other guests. The court held that he had ceased to be in a fit state to be received.

The duty to provide refreshment

The duty to provide refreshment for a traveller is outside the scope of the 1956 Act; it is a duty imposed upon innkeepers by the common law. The duty of the innkeeper is to provide the traveller with that which amounts to reasonable refreshment at any hour of the day or night. However, innkeepers may refuse to provide food and drink if their excuse for doing so is reasonable. We can say, therefore, that the duty is not absolute and innkeepers might lawfully refuse refreshment if they can show reasonable excuse for doing so. Failure may, if it is without reasonable excuse, render the innkeeper liable to criminal prosecution.

What amounts to 'reasonable refreshment'? Clearly this will vary according to the time of day at which the traveller calls at the inn. It would not be reasonable for an innkeeper of a large establishment, which included restaurants, to offer a traveller a mere sandwich to fulfil the innkeeper's duty. However, a traveller calling at an inn in the dead of night cannot expect a full three-course meal, and an innkeeper who offered refreshment such as a sandwich and a cup of coffee would have fulfilled the duty to the traveller. Indeed at an inn which has set meal times when the inn's restaurant is open, a traveller can demand a full cooked meal only at those times. It would be sufficient to discharge the duty if at other times the innkeeper offered cold buffet-type food, a sandwich or similar fare. Equally, travellers can demand alcoholic drinks only during licensing hours if they are not guests. Innkeepers are under a duty to provide only that which they have available; they need not send out for further supplies of food and drink in order to satisfy the demands of a traveller; nor does the proprietor have to place the demands of the traveller above those of guests at the inn. Indeed innkeepers may, if they have only limited supplies of food and drink (e.g. in times of shortage or when stocks at the inn are very low after Christmas and New Year), place the needs of guests above those of the traveller and reserve the limited supplies for the guests.

R. v. HIGGINS [1948] 1 KB 165 (CA)

A family arrived at the defendant's inn at Sunday lunchtime and demanded food and drink. The defendant refused them a full meal, although tables were available in the restaurant, and offered them sandwiches, on the grounds that he had only a limited supply of food and this was required for the evening meal and Monday morning breakfast of existing guests.

Held: There was a duty incumbent upon an innkeeper to supply a traveller with refreshment (and, if so required, accommodation). An innkeeper may lawfully refuse to fulfil the duty where his or her refusal is based on a reasonable excuse. What amounts to a reasonable excuse in any given case is primarily a question of fact to be determined by the jury. However, an innkeeper is not legally bound, if he or she has no food available at the inn, to send out for food or to procure it elsewhere in order to provide refreshment for the traveller. Furthermore, it may be a reasonable excuse for a proprietor to reserve his or her limited supplies of food for existing guests. On the facts in question the defendant innkeeper had reasonable grounds for refusing refreshment to the travellers.

This case raises a number of interesting issues. First, can a poorly planned and managed inn which has, through its own incompetence, run short of food seek to rely on the *Higgins* case as a reason for refusing refreshment to travellers? That is to say, can the innkeeper say, 'I am so incompetent in my food ordering, etc. that I let stocks fall to a ridiculous level and that is why I could not provide for the legitimate requests for refreshment by these travellers'? The purpose of the law is to enforce standards, i.e.

that all inns hold available sufficient means of refreshment for travellers. The above interpretation would clearly defeat the purpose of the law. Obviously, if an inn has had an unexpectedly high demand for refreshment, e.g. on the arrival of a coach or coaches which had not been pre-arranged, and had run out of food, *Higgins*'s case provides an appropriate defence if other travellers should later call and demand refreshment.

Secondly, if an inn operates a system of prior booking in its restaurant and a traveller demands a meal in the restaurant without having booked, when the restaurant is full, has the innkeeper breached the duty to the traveller? No. In *R.* v. *Higgins*, Goddard LCJ expressly deals with this situation. He says that there is no reason why an innkeeper should not operate a system of prior booking. To operate such a system does not breach the innkeeper's duty to provide food and drink 'without prior contract'. It is arguable, however, that the innkeeper should, in order to discharge his or her duty to the traveller, at least offer some form of refreshment in order to fulfil the duty. If in a large inn a traveller were to be refused service in the restaurant because it was fully booked, the traveller should be offered some form of refreshment in, for example, the lounge bar. Many travellers might leave the premises and seek a full restaurant meal elsewhere; others might take the lighter refreshment offered. However, if an innkeeper refuses point-blank to serve the traveller in the restaurant and offers no alternative when one might be made available elsewhere within the inn, the duty may be breached. Most inns which offer formal restaurant fare by prior booking also offer a selection from the menu or a snack menu at the bar, and the above problem is overcome in this way.

Other grounds which will constitute a reasonable excuse justifying the refusal of refreshment are if the traveller is not in a fit state to be received, or if the traveller appears unable to pay a reasonable sum for the refreshment to be provided. By means of these two forms of reasonable excuse innkeepers can legitimately refuse refreshment to vagrants, etc., and other people they consider to be unfit to be received. It also enables the innkeeper to regulate the kind of clientele he or she serves. If, for instance, the innkeeper makes a house rule that no man without a jacket and tie will be served, if required to justify this restriction the innkeeper could argue that those who do not comply with these requirements as to dress are not in a fit state to be received. Hence a young person who was fully prepared and able to pay for the refreshment which he or she sought, but who was outlandishly dressed, could be refused service. The innkeeper could justify refusal on the basis of the 'unfit to be received' rule. This clearly amounts to an injustice to those who may not conform to the standard forms of dress, particularly younger people. The rule does have an overriding advantage to the innkeeper; it enables the innkeeper to regulate the inn and maintain good order and service. However, it may be abused by unscrupulous and unthinking innkeepers. If an innkeeper were to refuse service on the basis that a person was not in a fit state to be received merely because she was female, or of a different colour or ethnic group from the innkeeper, this would not be within the scope of 'reasonable excuse'. Furthermore, it would render the innkeeper liable in the case of sex discrimination under s. 29 Sex Discrimination Act 1975, and in the case of racial discrimination under s. 20 Race Relations Act 1976. An innkeeper may refuse service to a traveller who insists upon bringing into the inn a dog or some other animal. This was justified in *R.* v. *Rymer* [1877] 2 QBD 136 on the basis that the dog in question (a muzzled mastiff) was unhygienic and a potential cause of alarm and annoyance to other guests. Today the point may be put in a slightly different way. The Food Hygiene (General Regulations) 1970 state that 'No person shall expose food to the risk of contamination'; therefore the innkeeper could refuse service to a traveller who insisted on bringing a dog onto the premises on the grounds that to allow the traveller and the dog entry would cause the innkeeper to breach the Food Hygiene Regulations. Manisty J in *R.* v. *Rymer* put the point more forcefully: 'in my opinion, a guest cannot, under any circumstances, insist on bringing a dog into any room or place in an inn where other guests are'. However, not all the members of the court were in agreement on this point.

It would appear that the fact that travellers are at the time of seeking refreshment (or accommodation) unwell does not necessarily mean that they are not in a fit state to be received. The somewhat ancient case of *R.* v. *Luellin* (1701) 12 Mod. Rep. 445 is authority for this principle. However, today it is arguable that the principle should no longer be applied.

The principle that 'reasonable excuse' covers where the traveller appears unable to pay a reasonable sum, and where the traveller is not in a fit state to be received, is derived from the definition of an inn provided by s. 1(3) HPA 1956.

The duty to provide accommodation

An innkeeper is under a duty to provide accommodation at the inn without prior contract to any traveller who seeks accommodation. The duty is not absolute and is qualified to the extent that the traveller must be in a fit state to be received (see *Rothfield* v. *North British Hotels* (1920)) and able to pay a reasonable sum; indeed, payment may be required in advance of the use of the accommodation (see the section on payment). If the inn is full and no rooms are available to be let to the traveller, is the innkeeper under a duty to provide the traveller with some form of shelter? This is of particular importance where the innkeeper has to deal with the 'stranded motorist' situation. An example is where, owing to poor weather conditions or mechanical breakdown, a family cannot continue their car journey, and call at the inn seeking accommodation for the night, and there are no rooms vacant.

BROWNE v. BRANDT   A traveller called at an inn during the night (2.00 a.m.) after
[1902] 1 KB 696   his vehicle had broken down. He asked for refreshment and
                              accommodation. He was provided with refreshment but was
                              refused accommodation because all the rooms at the inn were
occupied. The traveller asked the innkeeper if he could sleep in a public room, but the innkeeper refused.

Held: An innkeeper whose inn was fully occupied was perfectly within his rights to refuse accommodation to a traveller. A traveller is owed no further duty when the inn is full: nor has the traveller any right to demand that he be allowed to pass the night in a public room.

Lord Alverstone LCJ opined: 'I think a person who comes to an inn has no legal right to demand to pass the night in a public sitting-room if the bedrooms are all full, and I think that the landlord has no obligation to receive him.'

We can say therefore that the innkeeper is only bound to provide accommodation so long as the inn is not full. When the inn is full the duty to accommodate travellers is at an end, and an inn can be said to be full if all the bedrooms are occupied. It may well be the case that the innkeeper in an emergency situation, as with the case of a stranded motorist, has some sympathy for the plight of the traveller and affords the traveller shelter; but innkeepers are not bound to do this, nor is their failure to provide shelter a breach of their duty as innkeepers to provide accommodation.

It may be the case that an inn is one of a number owned and run by the innkeeper. Can an innkeeper discharge the duty towards the traveller after refusing to accommodate the traveller at one inn by directing him or her to another inn managed by the innkeeper where he or she will be accommodated? No: the duty is a personal duty, owed by innkeepers in relation to each inn which they manage. Hence the duty owed by inn X cannot be discharged by inn Y on behalf of the common innkeeper of both inns.

| CONSTANTINE v. IMPERIAL LONDON HOTELS LTD [1944] 2 All ER 171 | Learie Constantine, a West Indian cricketer, a person of some standing, was refused accommodation at the Imperial Hotel, London, on the basis that he was black. The Imperial Hotel had vacant rooms at the time Mr Constantine sought accommodation. Mr Constantine was directed to another hotel, namely the Bedford Hotel, owned by the same company. |

Mr Constantine brought an action against the defendants in respect of their refusing him accommodation at the Imperial Hotel. The defendants argued that they had fulfilled their duty as innkeepers towards Mr Constantine by affording him accommodation at the Bedford Hotel.

Held: An innkeeper owes separate duties to travellers at each inn. A duty which the innkeeper has not discharged at one inn cannot be discharged at another inn under the innkeeper's control.

It should be noted that, whilst the point raised by Mr Constantine's case is still valid, the facts of the case would give rise today to a further form of action under s. 20 of the Race Relations Act 1974.

When might an innkeeper legitimately refuse accommodation to a traveller?
(a) when all the bedrooms are full;
(b) when the traveller is not in a fit state to be received;
(c) when the traveller is unable to pay for the accommodation.

A traveller's arrival at a late hour or during the night is not a reasonable excuse for refusing accommodation – *R. v. Ivens* (1835) 7 C & P 213. Travellers' refusal to inform the innkeeper of their identity and address is not *per se* sufficient reason to refuse them accommodation – *R. v. Ivens* (above). This rule has to an extent been superseded by legislation. The Immigration (Hotel Records) Order 1972 places a duty on a proprietor of any premises where sleeping accommodation is provided for reward to require any persons who stay at the premises to sign a statement as to their nationality and, in the case of an alien, to give their name, date of arrival, passport number and address. Hence, if an alien were to refuse to provide such information, this would constitute a reasonable excuse for the innkeeper failing to accommodate the traveller.

If there is no reasonable excuse by reason of which the innkeeper can refuse accommodation, what is the innkeeper bound to provide? An innkeeper is only bound to supply such reasonable and proper accommodation for guests and guests' luggage as the innkeeper in fact possesses. A traveller is not entitled to insist upon a particular room; the allocation of a room to the traveller is solely at the discretion of the innkeeper – *Fell v. Knight* (1841) 8 M & W 269.

The innkeeper's right to refuse service

In considering the duty of the innkeeper to provide refreshment and, if so required, accommodation to travellers, the right to service claimed by the traveller has been emphasized. In point of fact the innkeeper has a right to refuse service to the traveller in certain circumstances. These circumstances are derived from the common law and s. 1(3) HPA, 1956 which defines the meaning of the term 'inn', and thereby sets the parameters of the duty owed to travellers. Section 1(3) HPA 1956 requires that the traveller 'appears able and willing to pay a reasonable sum for the services and facilities provided' and furthermore that the traveller 'is in a fit state to be received'. These restrictions on the classes of traveller to whom the duties to provide refreshment and accommodation are owed amount to a right on the part of the innkeeper to refuse service to certain travellers. This right allows the innkeeper a certain amount of latitude to pick and choose between those requiring service, and so enables the innkeeper to regulate his or her premises.

One should not forget a fundamental principle in English civil law, namely freedom of contract. This is the right of any person to contract (or refuse to contract) with any other person, the terms of the agreement being negotiated between the parties. It can be argued that the innkeeper's duties towards travellers operate as an exception to freedom of contract. This point arises from the fact that, since innkeepers are under a duty to contract with travellers who seek refreshment or accommodation, they do not have freedom of contract, since they cannot refuse the traveller service. The fact that the innkeeper has a right to refuse service to those travellers who do not appear able to pay for the services or who are not in a fit state to be received bolsters the notion that even in this area of the law the innkeeper retains a certain amount of freedom of contract. The innkeeper's freedom of contract is limited in other ways too. Limitation is placed upon the reason which can be given for refusing service. Section 20 of the Race Relations Act 1976 and s. 29 of the Sex Discrimination Act 1975 provide a right of action for persons who have been refused service either on racial grounds or by reasons of their sex, if by so refusing the service to such persons the proprietor has treated them less favourably than he or she would treat others. This restraint applies to inns and other establishments alike.

We have in the course of examining the duties to provide refreshment and accommodation considered cases which illustrate the innkeeper's right to refuse service, e.g. *R.* v. *Rymer* [1877]. A case which clearly illustrates how this right to refuse service is a flexible tool which can be used by the innkeeper to preserve good order at the inn is the following.

ROTHFIELD v. NORTH BRITISH HOTELS (1920) SC 805   Rothfield, a moneylender, who was otherwise of good character and well behaved whilst staying at the hotel, sought business from other guests staying at the hotel. Rothfield was a person not averse to publicity, and his methods of business, coupled with the fact that he was a German in the United Kingdom during and after the First World War, caused much disquiet and annoyance to the guests at the hotel, and British Army officers who frequented the hotel in question objected to his presence. Rothfield was asked to leave the hotel by the management, because of the annoyance which he had caused to other patrons. The court held that the innkeeper was fully justified in having Rothfield removed from the hotel. Lord Dundas opined: 'having regard to the decency, order and repute of their hotel, and to the legitimate interests of those whom they received in it, the conduct and manner of Rothfield rendered him unsuitable to the class of people whom they took into the hotels'.

A number of points are raised by this case. First, the innkeeper's right to refuse service is a flexible tool by which the innkeeper can maintain a proper standard of behaviour at the inn. Secondly, travellers may be perfectly fit to be received upon arrival at the inn yet their conduct whilst at the inn shows them to be unfit to be received. Service may be withdrawn and the travellers asked to leave the premises. In other words, the test as to whether a traveller is in a fit state to be received continues to be applied throughout the traveller's presence at the premises, e.g. a sober man who is fit to be received upon arrival may cease to be received if his subsequent conduct is unsatisfactory or disruptive. Thirdly, the standard of 'fitness' is relative to the inn. The standard maintained at a five-star hotel may be different from that at a small country inn. Whilst wellington boots, no jacket and an open-necked shirt may render a traveller not in a fit state to be received in the former, in the latter such a mode of dress may be perfectly reasonable.

Restrictions upon the right to refuse service

The restrictions imposed by s. 20 of the Race Relations Act 1976 and s. 29 of the Sex Discrimination Act 1975 apply to all establishments and not only to inns. These restrictions, therefore, are of a general nature and do not depend on the establishment being classified as an inn.

Section 20(1) of the Race Relations Act 1976 states:

> *It is unlawful for any person concerned with the provision (for payment or not) of goods, facilities or services to the public or a section of the public to discriminate against a person who seeks to obtain or use those goods, facilities or services –*
> *(a) by refusing or deliberately omitting to provide him with any of them; or*
> *(b) by refusing or deliberately omitting to provide him with goods, facilities or services of the like quality, in the like manner and on the like terms as are normal in the first-mentioned person's case in relation to other members of the public or (where the person so seeking belongs to a section of the public) to other members of that section.*

Section 20(2) of the Race Relations Act 1976 states:

> *The following are examples of the facilities and services mentioned in s. 20(1) –*
> *(a) access to and use of any place which members of the public are permitted to enter;*
> *(b) accommodation in an hotel, boarding house or other similar establishment . . .;*
> *(c) facilities for entertainment, recreation or refreshment.*

Section 29(1) of the Race Relations Act 1976 states:

> *it is unlawful to publish or to cause to be published an advertisement which indicates, or might reasonably be understood as indicating, an intention by a person to do an act of discrimination. . . .*

'Discriminate' is defined by s. 1(1) of the 1976 Act as follows:

> *A person discriminates against another in any circumstances relevant for the*
> *purposes of any provision of this Act if –*
> *(a) on racial grounds he treats that other less favourably than he treats or would*
> *treat other persons; or*
> *(b) he applies to that other a requirement or condition which he applies or would*
> *apply equally to persons not of the same racial group as that other but –*
> > *(i) which is such that the proportion of persons of the same racial group as*
> > *that other who can comply with it is considerably smaller than the propor-*
> > *tion of persons not of that racial group who can comply with it; and*
> > *(ii) which he cannot show to be justifiable irrespective of the colour, race,*
> > *nationality or ethnic or national origins of the person to whom it is applied;*
> > *and*
> > *(iii) which is to the detriment of that other because he cannot comply with it.*

It is essential to establish that the discriminator discriminated against the plaintiff either *on racial grounds* or because of the plaintiff's belonging to a *racial group*; these terms are defined by s. 3(1) of the 1976 Act as follows:

> *'racial grounds' means any of the following grounds namely colour, race, nationality,*
> *or ethnic or national origins;*

> *'racial group' means a group of persons defined by reference to colour, race,*
> *nationality or ethnic or national origins . . .*

Clearly, where the proprietor of an inn or other establishment refuses either refreshment or accommodation to a person because of their colour, race, nationality or national or ethnic origins, and if the person requiring service was not of that colour, etc. the proprietor would serve that person, the proprietor has unlawfully discriminated against that person within the meaning of s. 20(1) of the Race Relations Act 1976. Equally, if the proprietor provides a service, e.g. refreshment, but attaches conditions to the provision of such service that have to do with the colour, race, etc., of the person seeking the service (e.g. no blacks to be served in the lounge bar, only in the public bar), this will also amount to unlawful discrimination under s. 20(1) of the 1976 Act. If the facts of *Constantine* v. *Imperial London Hotels Ltd* [1944] 2 All ER 171 were to occur today, the actions of the innkeeper concerned would amount to unlawful discrimination within s. 20(1). The courts have encountered considerable difficulty in determining who is covered by the 1976 Act. The Act does not cover discrimination on the basis of religion. Therefore, if the proprietor of a private hotel were to refuse accommodation to a traveller because the traveller was a Catholic, this would not be unlawful discrimination on racial grounds. If an innkeeper were to refuse accommodation to a traveller because of his or her religion, this would not constitute unlawful discrimination under the 1976 Act, but it would constitute a breach of duty as an innkeeper to provide accommodation. Although religion is not covered by the 1976 Act, the Act does cover discrimination based on a person's 'ethnic origins'. Certain followers of religious beliefs may also constitute ethnic groups, and to discriminate against a person on the ground that he or she is a member of an ethnic group is unlawful discrimination. This problem has been raised in relation to Jews and Sikhs.

SEIDE v. GILLETTE INDUSTRIES [1980] IRLR 427 (EAT)

Mr Sidney Seide was a member of the Jewish faith and a refugee from the Holocaust. He worked as a toolmaker at the defendants' factory on the night shift. Mr Garcia, a member of the same shift, made a number of anti-semitic remarks and threats over a period of time. Mr Seide was transferred to the day shift by management to avoid further provocation to Mr Seide and to prevent disruption in the toolroom. Mr Seide argued that his transfer to the day shift, with a commensurate loss of shift allowance, amounted to unlawful discrimination on racial grounds by the defendant company. The question arose of whether Jews were a racial group within the 1976 Act, and moreover whether management's transfer of Mr Seide to the day shift was on the ground of his religion or in consequence of his racial or ethnic group.

Held: The fact that the complainant is Jewish brings the complainant within the Race Relations Act 1976. The EAT took the view that ' "Jewish" could mean that one was a member of a race or a particular ethnic origin as well as being a member of a particular religious faith'. Both the industrial tribunal at first instance and the EAT found that what happened was not because Mr Seide was of the Jewish faith, but because he was a member of the Jewish race or of Jewish ethnic origin. Mr Garcia's remarks were on the basis of Mr Seide's race or ethnic origin. However, the decision to transfer Mr Seide to the day shift was based on the need to maintain production and good order.

It would seem, therefore, that to refuse service to a person on account of their being Jewish does not amount to unlawful discrimination under the 1976 Act. In the case of Sikhs the House of Lords has recently considered the issue.

MANDLA v. DOWELL LEE AND OTHERS [1983] 2 WLR 620 (HL)

Mr Mandla was a Sikh who applied to send his son to Park Grove School in Birmingham, of which Mr Dowell Lee was the headmaster. Park Grove School is a private school of high repute, run on a multiracial basis. Mr Dowell Lee refused to admit Mr Mandla's son as a pupil to the school because Mr Mandla would not agree to his son cutting his hair and ceasing to wear a turban to comply with school rules as to uniform, on account of Mr Mandla's religious beliefs. In the High Court and the Court of Appeal [1982] 3 WLR 932, Mr Mandla's claim of unlawful discrimination on racial grounds was rejected, since amongst other things Sikhs were not a racial group, and thus outside, the scope of the Act.

Held: The House of Lords allowed Mr Mandla's appeal, stating that Sikhs were a racial group and thus within the scope of the Race Relations Act 1976. 'Ethnic origins' in s. 3(1) of the 1976 Act means a group identifiable as a segment distinguished from others by a sufficient combination of shared customs, beliefs, traditions and characteristics derived from a common past.

In reaching its decision, the Court identified various characteristics of an ethnic group. Two were held to be 'essential': a long shared history, and a cultural tradition of its own. A further five were held to be 'relevant': common geographical origin or descent from a small number of common ancestors; common language (not necessarily particular to the group); common literature particular to the group; common religion different from that of neighbouring groups or the general surrounding community; finally, being a minority, or being an oppressed or a dominant group within a larger community.

Mandla's case is of paramount importance, since it gives a broad interpretation to the scope of the Race Relations Act 1976. Many groups which, prior to the House of Lords' decision, were not clearly within the ambit of the legislation now are.

In *Commission for Racial Equality* v. *Dutton* [1989] 1 All ER 306, the Court of Appeal held that gypsies were capable of being a separate 'racial group'. In that case, the defendant, who was the licensee of a public house, refused to serve a person who was living in an illegally parked caravan nearby and put up a sign saying 'Sorry, no travellers'. The Commission for Racial Equality sought a declaration that the sign contravened section 29 of the 1976 Act. The action was dismissed at first instance. On appeal, the Court of Appeal, in applying the conditions laid down in *Mandla*'s case, held that gypsies were a separate 'racial group' within s. 3(1) of the 1976 Act. They further held that since the proportion of gypsies who could comply with the condition 'no travellers' was considerably smaller than the proportion of non-gypsies, the action by the defendant in posting the sign amounted to indirect discrimination under the 1976 Act, s. 1(1)b.

In *Dawkins* v. *The Crown Suppliers* (*The Independent*, 3 May 1991) the applicant brought an action claiming both direct discrimination contrary to s. 1(1)a and indirect discrimination contrary to s. 1(1)b of the 1976 Act. The facts of the case were that the applicant applied for a job with the respondents as a van driver. He alleged that he was refused the job because he was a Rastafarian who wore his hair in dreadlocks concealed under a hat and consequently could not comply with a condition that he cut his hair. The applicant's claim rested entirely upon whether or not Rastafarians were capable of being defined as an 'ethnic group' within the 1976 Act. At both industrial tribunal and an appeal to the employment appeal tribunal, the conditions laid down in *Mandla* v. *Dowell Lee* were applied to the given facts to determine whether Rastafarians were a racial group defined by ethnic origin within the meaning of the Race Relations Act 1976. Whilst the industrial tribunal found in favour of Mr Dawkins and held that there had been both direct and indirect discrimination, their decision was reversed on appeal to the Employment Appeal Tribunal. It was held that Rastafarians were a religious sect but not a racial group defined by ethnic origin within the meaning of the 1976 Act because they were not sufficiently distinguishable from the rest of the Afro-Caribbean community and because the movement did not possess a long shared history, being a movement that went back for only 60 years.

An interesting development in the area of refusal of service is the case of *Gurmit Singh* v. *Vaulkhard* (*The Times*, 7 December 1984). This was a case of indirect discrimination brought under the Race Relations Act 1976. The importance of the case lies in the fact that the 'no hats rule' sought to be imposed by the proprietor of the establishment was not itself directly discriminatory, as it was applied universally to everyone seeking entry to the premises. However, the rule was discriminatory in an indirect way, as Sikh customers, who could not comply with the rule, were excluded from the premises. This, the court held, amounted to unlawful indirect discrimination.

As to discrimination on grounds of a person's sex, the Court of Appeal have recently considered the question in relation to the refusal of service in a catering establishment:

GILL AND ANOTHER v. EL VINO CO. LTD [1983] 2 WLR 155 (CA)   El Vino Wine Bar, a well known and much frequented establishment in Fleet Street, London, operated a rule that women were not allowed to stand and drink at the bar. The plaintiffs, both women, entered the El Vino Wine Bar, stood at the bar, and asked for two glasses of wine. In accordance with the management's rule the barman refused to serve them at the bar and told them that if they sat at a table the drinks would be brought to them. There were two tables in the bar and a smoking room to the rear of the premises where a waitress took orders from customers at the tables. This service was also available to male customers. The plaintiffs alleged unlawful discrimination under s. 1(1)a and s. 29(1) of the Sex Discrimination Act 1975.

Section 1(1)a SDA 1975 provides: 'A person discriminates against a woman in any circumstances relevant for the purposes of any provision of this Act if . . . (a) on the ground of her sex he treats her less favourably than he treats or would treat a man . . . '

Section 29 SDA 1975 provides:

> (1) It is unlawful for any person concerned with the provision (for payment or not) of goods, facilities or services to the public or a section of the public to discriminate against a woman who seeks to obtain or use those goods, facilities or services –
>   (a) by refusing or deliberately omitting to provide her with any of them, or
>   (b) by refusing, or deliberately omitting to provide her with goods, facilities, or services of the like quality, in the like manner and on the like terms as are normal in his case in relation to male members of the public or (where she belongs to a section of the public) to male members of that section.
> (2) The following are examples of the facilities and services mentioned in subsection (1) –
>   (a) access to and use of any place which members of the public or a section of the public are permitted to enter;
>   (b) accommodation in an hotel, boarding house or other similar establishment.

Held: The Court of Appeal, applying the simple words of the statute, held that by allowing male customers to stand and drink at the bar if they so wished but not allowing female customers to do likewise, the defendants unlawfully discriminated against women by refusing or deliberately omitting to provide them with facilities which were afforded to men. The defendants' refusal of service was contrary to s. 29(1) of the Sex Discrimination Act 1975, and furthermore, by so acting the defendants had treated the women less favourably than men contrary to s. 1(1)a SDA 1975, since the women had been deprived by the defendants of a facility much prized by male customers and sought by the plaintiffs.

Lord Justice Griffiths in the *El Vino* case put the point succinctly: 'There is no doubt whatever that she is refused facilities that are accorded to men, and the only question that remains is: is she being treated less favourably than men? I think that permits only one answer: of course she is. She is not being allowed to drink where she wants to drink . . . '

5.3 THE INNKEEPER'S DUTY TOWARDS THE PROPERTY OF GUESTS

Innkeepers have a strict duty to care for the property of their guests. This duty, it should be noted, is not owed to travellers, only to guests. A guest is a person who has engaged a minimum of one night's accommodation. The innkeeper is an insurer of the property of guests which is lost or stolen within the *hospitium* of the inn. *Hospitium* covers more than the inn itself; it incorporates the precincts of the inn and those parts of the premises closely related with operation of the inn, e.g. stable buildings, garages, swimming pool, car park. The test as to whether a particular area comes within the *hospitium* of the inn appears to be: 'Is the area in question intended and suitable for use in connection with the innkeeper's business?' This test is derived from the case of *Williams* v. *Linnitt* [1951] 1 All ER 278 (see p. 149). If, for instance, the innkeeper places guests' property or invites guests to leave their property by the entrance to the inn, the innkeeper will still be liable for the property so placed since, although the property is outside the inn itself, it is still within the *hospitium of the inn – Watson* v. *People's Refreshment Association Ltd* [1952] 1 KB 318.

The innkeeper's liability for guests' property is strict. It does not depend on proof of negligence on the part of the innkeeper, or upon contract or bailment. Innkeepers' duty is to keep the goods safe; their liability is not dependent on how the goods are lost or damaged, save to say that loss or damage due to the fault of the guest is not within the scope of innkeepers' liability. This strict liability for the loss of or damage caused to guests' property attaches only to innkeepers; proprietors of establishments outside s. 1(3) HPA 1956 are not subject to such a duty.

The scope of the duty

The scope of the duty owed by an innkeeper in relation to the property of a guest is limited by s. 2 HPA 1956. Section 2(1) HPA 1956 states:

> *Without prejudice to any other liability incurred by him with respect to any property brought to the hotel, the proprietor of an hotel shall not be liable as an innkeeper to make good to any traveller any loss of or damage to such property except where –*
> (a) *at the time of the loss or damage sleeping accommodation at the hotel had been engaged for the traveller; and*
> (b) *the loss or damage occurred during the period commencing with the midnight immediately preceding, and ending with the midnight immediately following, a period for which the traveller was a guest at the hotel and entitled to use the accommodation so engaged.*

Section 2(2) HPA 1956 states:

> *Without prejudice to any other liability or right of his with respect thereto, the proprietor of an hotel shall not as an innkeeper be liable to make good to any guest of his any loss of or damage to, or have any lien on, any vehicle or any property left therein, or any horse or other live animal or its harness or other equipment.*

Section 2(1) sets out the parameters of the duty, and to whom the duty is owed, whilst s. 2(2) restricts the kinds of property to which the duty applies. Section 2(2) modifies the common-law rule as to liability for guests' vehicles (see *Williams* v. *Linnitt* [1951] 1 All ER 278). In order that an innkeeper be strictly liable for the loss or damage to guests' property guests must prove:

(a) that they have been received at the hotel;
(b) that at the time of the loss or damage they were travellers who had engaged
     accommodation at the inn; and
(c) that the goods in question were of a sort covered by the innkeeper's duty.
The goods will be within the scope of the innkeeper's duty if they are goods which
are not of an exceptional character. The nature of goods covered by the duty is
discussed in *Robins* v. *Gray* [1895] 2 QB 501 (CA), where Lord Esher takes the view
that:

> *If a traveller comes to an inn with goods which are his luggage – I do not say his*
> *personal luggage, but his luggage – the innkeeper by the law of the land is bound to*
> *take him and his luggage in.*

Lord Esher goes on to state that if the traveller brought something exceptional which
is not luggage (he cites a tiger or dynamite as examples), the innkeeper might refuse
to take it in. But unless there is some reason to the contrary due to the exceptional
nature of the article in question the innkeeper is duty bound to take in both the
traveller and his or her luggage. The innkeeper is not entitled to be told the nature
of the traveller's luggage, nor to whom the articles of luggage belong. In *Robins*
v. *Gray* the innkeeper sought to enforce his right of lien (see p. 166 on the
innkeeper's right of lien) over luggage which was sewing machines owned not by
the guest but by his employer. The machines were held to constitute part of the
guest's luggage.

Further restraints upon the scope of the innkeeper's duty are imposed by s. 2(3)
HPA 1956.

> *Where the proprietor of an hotel is liable as an innkeeper to make good the loss of*
> *or any damage to property brought to the hotel, his liability to any one guest shall*
> *not exceed fifty pounds in respect of any one article, or one hundred pounds in the*
> *aggregate, except where –*
>
> (a) *the property was stolen, lost or damaged through the default, neglect or wilful*
>   *act of the proprietor or some servant of his; or*
> (b) *the property was deposited by or on behalf of the guest expressly for safe custody*
>   *with the proprietor or some servant of his authorised, or appearing to be author-*
>   *ised, for the purpose, and, if so required by the proprietor or that servant, in a*
>   *container fastened or sealed by the depositor; or*
> (c) *at a time after the guest had arrived at the hotel, either the property in question*
>   *was offered for deposit as aforesaid and the proprietor or his servant refused to*
>   *receive it, or the guest or some other guest acting on his behalf wished so to offer*
>   *the property in question but, through the default of the proprietor or a servant*
>   *of his, was unable to do so:*
>
> *Provided that the proprietor shall not be entitled to the protection of this subsection*
> *unless, at the time when the property in question was brought to the hotel, a copy of*
> *the notice set out in the Schedule to this Act printed in plain type was conspicuously*
> *displayed in a place where it could conveniently be read by his guests at or near the*
> *reception office or desk or, where there is no reception office or desk, at or near the*
> *main entrance to the hotel.*

The situations where an innkeeper will *not* be liable for the loss of a guest's property are as follows:

1   An innkeeper is not liable where the loss or damage is caused by the misconduct or negligence of the guest who suffers the loss. This exception may cover the situation where the guests leave their valuables lying around either in their room or elsewhere and they are stolen, lost or damaged. In *Armistead* v. *Wilde* (1851) 17 QB 261 the innkeeper was found not to be liable where the guest had left money lying around where others could not fail to see it. The guest was said to have caused his own loss. Another instance is *Jones* v. *Jackson* (1873) 29 LT 399, where money was left in the guest's room in an easily discoverable place. A notice was displayed informing guests that the innkeeper was prepared to take charge of valuables and the guest left the room empty from morning until evening, during which time the money was taken. The guest was held to be negligent. See also *Chamier* v. *De Vere Hotels Ltd* (1928) 72 Sol. Jo. 155, where valuables were left in a drawer in a guest's room and the guest was held to be negligent. However, the courts have in many cases held the innkeeper liable and found the guest not to have been negligent. The distinction between such cases appears to be one of fact, and the degree to which the guest has been culpable for the loss or damage.

CARPENTER v. HAYMARKET HOTEL LTD [1931] 1 KB 364 (QBD)	Mr and Mrs Carpenter checked in at the inn. After taking tea they dressed for dinner. Mrs Carpenter placed a diamond ring which she had been wearing in a jewel case and thereafter in an unlocked case which she left in the bedroom and locked the bedroom door. The room key was then deposited with the hotel receptionist. The jewel case and ring were

thereafter stolen. The defendant hotel argued that they owed Mrs Carpenter no duty, since she had acted negligently in leaving the ring and jewel box in the bedroom.

Held: Mrs Carpenter had taken reasonable care of the ring and jewel box; accordingly, the loss was not due to negligence on the part of Mrs Carpenter and the innkeeper was liable.

SHACKLOCK v. ETHORPE LTD [1939] 3 All ER 372 (HL)	Ms Shacklock, being a guest at the defendant's inn, left her jewellery and money (about £600 in value) in her bedroom locked in a jewel box which was itself locked in a large suitcase. However, she left the door to the room open. Ms Shacklock departed to London for the day and upon her

return found that her bag had been broken into and the jewel box and contents removed. They had been stolen by another guest at the hotel.

Held: Since the hotel did not request guests to lock their rooms (indeed they wished guests to leave them open to enable chambermaids to have access to clean, etc.), the hotel had itself been negligent. Ms Shacklock had not been negligent by not locking her room, since she knew of the need for rooms to be left unlocked and was mindful of this.

2   The innkeeper will not be liable where the loss or damage sustained to a guest's property is due to an act of God or the actions of the Queen's enemies.

3   The innkeeper will not be liable for property excluded from the duty by s. 2(2) HPA 1956.

The liability of an innkeeper will be limited to £50 in respect of any one article, or £100 in total where a schedule notice is displayed in compliance with s. 2(3) HPA 1956. The innkeeper is not entitled to the statutory limitation of liability provided for in s. 2(3) unless at the time when the property in question was brought to the hotel a copy of the schedule notice printed in plain type was conspicuously displayed in a place where it could be read with ease by guests at or near the reception desk (if there is no reception desk, at the main entrance). The proper display of the schedule notice is a precondition to the innkeeper being afforded the limitation of liability for guests' property contained in s. 2(3). If the notice exhibited at the inn does not comply with that set out in the Schedule to the HPA 1956, similarly the innkeeper will not be able to claim the limitation upon his liability. Equally, the innkeeper will not be afforded such protection in the following circumstances.

Section 2(3)(a). The property was stolen, lost or damaged owing to the default, neglect or wilful act of the innkeeper or some servant of the innkeeper (see *Behrens* v. *Grenville Hotel (Bude) Ltd* (1925) 69 Sol. Jo. 346). The burden of proving that the loss or damage due to the neglect of the innkeeper rests upon the guest – *Whitehouse* v. *Pickett* [1908] AC 357 (HL).

Section 2(3)(b). The property was deposited by or on behalf of the guest expressly for safe custody with the proprietor or some servant authorized, or appearing to be authorized, for the purpose, and, if so required by the proprietor or that servant, in a container fastened and sealed by the depositor.

Section 2(3)(c). At the time after the guest had arrived at the hotel, either the property in question was offered for deposit as aforesaid and the proprietor or the proprietor's servant refused to receive it, or the guest or some other guest acting on his or her behalf wished so to offer the property in question but, through the default of the proprietor or the proprietor's servant, was unable to do so.
  Goods are deposited expressly for safe custody as under s. 2(3)(b) above only if the guest informs the innkeeper that the deposit is for safe custody. Hence, if a guest leaves a package with extremely valuable contents at the reception desk of the inn this will not be enough to amount to a deposit for safe custody; the guest will have to expressly state that this is the purpose of his leaving the package with the receptionist. Equally, if guests were trying to show the innkeeper to be fully liable under s. 2(3)(c) it would not be enough for them to establish that there was a queue at reception which deterred them from depositing valuables. It must be proven that the innkeeper or the staff refused to take them, or that by their acts or default they made it impossible for the guest to deposit the article for safe keeping.

Insurance. It is possible for innkeepers to insure themselves against the risk of loss or damage to guests' property. Although innkeepers are not the owners of property which belongs to their guests, they do have an insurable interest arising from their potential right of lien over guests' property. Furthermore, insurance relates to potential liability. Since the innkeeper is potentially liable for loss of or damage to guests' property, the innkeeper may obtain liability insurance to cover such potential claims.

5.4 THE ENFORCEMENT OF THE INNKEEPER'S DUTIES

The enforcement process may be divided into the civil remedies of the traveller or guest and the criminal prosecution of the innkeeper.

Civil remedies of the traveller or guest

Where an innkeeper has refused to receive a traveller, that is to say the traveller has been refused refreshment or accommodation, if the traveller can establish that he or she was refused service and the innkeeper can adduce no reasonable excuse for failure to provide the service, the innkeeper will be civilly liable in damages to the traveller. Where the refusal is alleged to be by reason of either sex or race discrimination, additional civil remedies are available under the Sex Discrimination Act 1975 or the Race Relations Act 1976. The remedy of damages is obtainable against an innkeeper for loss or damage to the property of the guest.

Criminal prosecution of the innkeeper

If an innkeeper refuses without lawful excuse to receive a traveller, i.e. the innkeeper refused the traveller either refreshment or accommodation, the innkeeper is liable to criminal prosecution upon indictment in the Crown Court. The offence does not arise under statute (i.e. the HPA 1956); rather it is a common-law offence, certain elements of which, e.g. the definition of an inn, are contained in the HPA 1956.

5.5 THE INNKEEPER'S LIABILITY AS AN OCCUPIER OF PREMISES

An innkeeper is the occupier of the inn, e.g. *Wheat* v. *E. Lacon & Co. Ltd* [1966] 1 All ER 582 (HL), and therefore the duties incumbent upon an occupier under the Occupiers' Liability Act 1957 apply equally to innkeepers. An explanation of the operation of the law is given on pp. 77–90. Specific reference, however, should at this point be made to *Campbell* v. *Shelbourne Hotel Ltd* [1939] 2 KB 534 (CA) and *Stone* v. *Taffe* [1974] 3 All ER 1016 (CA).

5.6 THE RIGHTS OF AN INNKEEPER

Because an innkeeper is subject to certain duties to which other forms of establishment are not, the corollary to this is that the innkeeper has certain rights which other hotels, etc. do not possess. The most important right which an innkeeper has, which other establishments do not possess, is the right of lien.

Contractual rights

The innkeeper is in a similar contractual position to any other hotelier or caterer. The innkeeper's freedom to contract is somewhat curtailed by the duties to provide refreshment and accommodation, but the provisions contained in s. 2 and 3 of the Unfair Contract Terms Act 1977 apply equally to innkeepers and other hotel proprietors and caterers (see pp. 121–4).

Payment

Innkeepers have a right to payment in advance. This arises from the fact that they are only bound to receive travellers who 'appear able and willing to pay a reasonable sum for the services and facilities provided' (s. 1(3) HPA 1956). The innkeeper can require payment in advance to ascertain whether the traveller is able to pay a reasonable sum. If a traveller wishes to insist upon the right to be received at the inn, the traveller must tender a reasonable sum in advance payment. An innkeeper may of course sue a traveller for the price of refreshment afforded to the traveller, and a guest for the price of accommodation provided.

The right to control the inn

Innkeepers have control over the conduct of the inn subject to the duties which they owe to travellers and guests, and other statutory constraints. An innkeeper may enter the room let to the guest at any time. The innkeeper retains control over the guests' rooms during their stay, and may bring their stay to an end (see *Lamond* v. *Richard* [1897] 1 QB 541 (CA)).

The innkeeper's right of lien

The innkeeper may detain, and thereby has a right of lien over, any property (other than that excluded by s. 2(2) HPA 1956) brought by the guest into the *hospitium* of the inn, in respect of the guest's unpaid bill. The innkeeper is not, however, entitled to detain the guest (*Sunbolf* v. *Alford* (1838)). Because of the statutory exclusions an innkeeper is not entitled to detain the guest's vehicle or property left in the vehicle. The innkeeper's lien is over the property of the traveller or guest, until the bill has been met for the refreshment and accommodation afforded to the traveller or guest. The lien extends not only to the property of the travellers; it also includes any property which they bring with them to the inn as their luggage – *Robins* v. *Gray* [1895] 2 QB 501 (CA). This point has again been raised in the recent case of *Berman & Nathans* v. *Weibye* (1981) 6 CL 658. The innkeeper's lien attaches to property as soon as the property is brought within the *hospitium* of the inn by guests on their arrival. However, property which is acquired by guests subsequent to their arrival at the inn may be subject to the innkeeper's lien, if it is brought into the inn by them as guests – *Marsh* v. *Police Commissioner* [1944] 2 All ER 392 (CA). This case raises further important issues, particularly concerning against whom the lien may be claimed. In *Marsh* v. *Police Commissioner* the property over which the innkeeper claimed a lien was a stolen ring proffered by the thief as a surety against the money he owed in payment of his bill. Could the innkeeper claim a lien over the ring to defeat the lawful return of the ring to its true owner? First the police have the right to take the ring from the innkeeper, since the ring will constitute evidence against the thief in later criminal proceedings. The innkeepers may, however, once the trial of the thief has been concluded, reclaim the stolen goods. However, s. 28 Theft Act 1968 empowers the court of trial to order the restitution of the goods to the true owner. The question still remains, who is entitled to the ring, the true owner or the innkeeper? In *Marsh* v. *Police Commissioner* the innkeeper's lien was held to extend to the ring and therefore arguably the innkeeper retains a right to the goods until the bill incurred has been paid. It should be remembered that the innkeeper's lien applies to travellers taking refreshment, as well as guests engaging accommodation. Furthermore, the lien extends to the property of a spouse accompanying a guest at the inn – *Mulliner* v. *Florence* [1878] 3 QBD 484 (CA). An innkeeper owes to the guest whose property the innkeeper is retaining by exercise of lien a duty to take reasonable care of the property in question.

Innkeepers have a power of sale in relation to goods over which they are exercising a lien. The right of lien in itself would be of little value to an innkeeper if it were not accompanied by a right of sale. If innkeepers did not have a right of sale they would be left with property which they could not realize in order to satisfy guests' debts to them. The right of sale is provided for, subject to certain requirements, by s. 1 of the Innkeepers Act 1878.

> *The landlord, proprietor, keeper or manager of any hotel inn or licensed public house shall, in addition to his ordinary lien, have the right absolute to sell and dispose by public auction of any goods chattels carriages horses wares or merchandise which may have been deposited with him or left in the house he keeps, or in the coach-house stable, stable-yard or other premises appurtenant or belonging thereunto, where the person depositing or leaving such goods chattels carriages horses wares or merchandise shall be or become indebted to the said innkeeper either for any board or lodging or for the keep and expenses of any horse or other animals left with or standing at livery in the stables or fields occupied by such innkeeper.*
>
> *Provided, that no such sale shall be made until after the said goods chattels carriages horses wares or merchandise shall have been for the space of six weeks in such charge or custody or in or upon such premises without such debt having been paid or satisfied, and that such innkeeper after having, out of the proceeds of such sale, paid himself the amount of any such debt, together with the costs and expenses of such sale, shall on demand pay to the person depositing or leaving any such goods chattels carriages horses wares or merchandise the surplus (if any) remaining after such sale: Provided further, that the debt for the payment of which a sale is made shall not be any other or greater debt than the debt for which the goods or other articles could have been retained by the innkeeper under his lien.*
>
> *Provided also, that at least one month before any such sale the landlord, proprietor, keeper, or manager shall cause to be inserted in one London newspaper and one country newspaper circulating in the district where such goods chattels carriages horses wares or merchandise, or some of them, shall have been deposited or left, an advertisement containing notice of such intended sale; and giving shortly a description of the goods and chattels intended to be sold, together with the name of the owner or person who deposited or left the same where known.*

This right of sale attaches to any property left at an inn, hotel, etc., and is in addition to and separate from the ordinary right of lien. Out of the proceeds of a sale the innkeeper may retain the amount of the debt due to him, together with the costs and expenses of the sale; the innkeeper must thereafter pay the surplus, if any, to the traveller or guest upon demand.

5.7 THE RIGHTS AND DUTIES OF A HOTELIER

The rights and duties of an innkeeper form a special category; the proprietor of a private hotel does not owe such duties to travellers and guests. No special duties or rights attach to proprietors of establishments other than inns. They are, however, covered by the same law as inns in many areas.

Duties owed by both inns and private hotels

1   The duty owed as an occupier of premises towards lawful visitors (e.g. guests and travellers) to the premises, under the Occupiers' Liability Act 1957.
2   A civil duty to take reasonable care of guests' property brought to the premises under the tort of negligence, or as an implied term of the contract of booking.
3   The duty not to discriminate in the provision of services to the public, on the basis of a person's race or sex – s. 20 Race Relations Act 1974, s. 29 Sex Discrimination Act 1975.

The rights common to both an innkeeper and the proprietor of a private hotel

The right to control the premises and refuse service so as to maintain good order and decency.

The sole rights of the proprietor of a private hotel

1   The right to pick and choose between persons requesting service.
2   The right to refuse service (subject to statutory restraints as to race and sex discrimination) to any person at the will of the proprietor.

The sole rights of the innkeeper

1   The right to demand payment in advance of service.
2   The innkeeper's lien over property.

The sole duties of the innkeeper

1   The duty to provide a traveller with refreshment and, if so required, accommodation.
2   The strict duty of responsibility for the property of guests at the inn.

5.8 NON-PAYMENT BY GUESTS AND TRAVELLERS

Where travellers seeking refreshment are provided with food and drink, and fail to pay before they depart from the premises, they may be charged under s. 3 of the Theft Act 1978. This provision is explained in detail on p. 220. The innkeeper (unlike the proprietor of a private hotel) may demand payment prior to the provision of the service. This right, therefore, affords some protection from defaulters. Where any persons seeking refreshment or accommodation act dishonestly, that is, knowing that they cannot pay for the service to be rendered, they thereafter deceive the innkeeper or proprietor into providing the service, they will be guilty of an offence under s. 1(1) of the Theft Act 1978. Section 1(1) of the Theft Act 1978 states:

> *A person who by any deception dishonestly obtains services from another shall be guilty of an offence.*

Section 1(2) of the Theft Act 1978 states:

> *it shall be an obtaining of services where the other is induced to confer a benefit by*
> *doing some act, or causing or permitting some act to be done, on the understanding*
> *that the benefit has been or will be paid for.*

Where the person is tried and convicted upon indictment the maximum penalty is five
years' imprisonment.

CASE STUDY

On 1 June 1995 Ms Vacant, the receptionist at the Wayside Hotel, which is owned by
Brighton Ltd, received a phone call from Mr Jack Smith seeking to book a single room
for 3 June 1995 for one night. Ms Vacant agreed to reserve accommodation for the
night of 3 June for Mr Smith, although she knew at the time that the hotel was fully
booked for 3 June, the majority of rooms being occupied by National Front members
attending a conference in the town. Ms Vacant informed Mr Smith in the course of
the telephone conversation that the room would be held until 6.00 p.m. on 3 June,
after which it might be relet.

By 6.15 p.m. on 3 June Mr Smith has not arrived, and a further two guests who had
booked with the hotel have not turned up. Mr and Mrs Churchill and their child,
Winston, who are all Nigerian, arrive at the Wayside Hotel at 6.20 p.m. and inquire
whether there are any rooms available that night. Ms Vacant turns the Churchills
away, thinking it tactful to do so. She tells Mr Churchill that they may find vacant
accommodation at the Bogside Hotel, also owned by Brighton Ltd, and within a ten-
minute walk of the Wayside Hotel. At 6.30 p.m. Mr James, a man of rather unkempt
appearance and wearing a Communist Party tie, is turned away by Ms Vacant, having
inquired about accommodation at the hotel. At 7.00 p.m. Ms Vacant books in Mr and
Mrs Wilson and their two sons to the three empty rooms. Whilst Mrs Wilson is at
dinner later that evening her fur coat is stolen from her room, which she had left
unlocked. At 8.15 p.m. Mr Jack Smith finally arrives and demands a room for the
night.

Advise the parties.

The liability of the innkeepers, Brighton Ltd, is the central issue in this case study. Ms
Vacant, as the employee of Brighton Ltd, is acting on behalf of the innkeeper. One
must be certain, before determining the liability of Brighton Ltd, that the Wayside
Hotel comes within the definition of a 'hotel' at law ('inn'), under s. 1(3) of the Hotel
Proprietors Act 1956 (see pp. 147–9).

On the assumption that the Wayside Hotel is within s. 1(3) of the HPA 1956, the
liability of the innkeeper (Brighton Ltd) to each of the visitors to the 'inn' should be
determined.

Mr and Mrs Churchill. At the time when they called at the Wayside Hotel, there had
been three 'no shows', so there were rooms to accommodate the Churchill family. Thus

the innkeeper was in breach of the duty imposed to accommodate travellers (*Browne* v. *Brandt*) (see p. 153). Only if the Churchills were unable to pay a reasonable sum for the accommodation, or were unfit to be received, could the innkeeper turn them away. Race and colour, even in the circumstances where racist people were staying at the inn, do not make a visitor unfit to be received. Moreover, in refusing service the innkeeper is in breach of s. 20 of the Race Relations Act 1976 (see pp. 156–9).

Mr Churchill is informed that suitable alternative accommodation is available at the Bogside Hotel. The innkeeper cannot rely on this as a method of discharging his duty to provide accommodation – *Constantine* v. *Imperial London Hotels Ltd* (see p. 154).

Mr James. In turning away Mr James the innkeeper is again arguably in breach of his duty to accommodate travellers calling at the inn. However, owing to Mr James's unkempt appearance, he may not be in a fit state to be received, and this relieves the innkeeper of the duty to accommodate him – *Rothfield* v. *North British Hotels*, and *R.* v. *Rymer* (see p. 155).

Mr Jack Smith. The innkeeper held open Mr Smith's room until the specified time had passed. The innkeeper is not liable to accommodate Mr Smith when he arrives. The inn is full, and the room has been relet. There is no breach of any contractual obligation to Mr Smith. However, it should be noted that when Ms Vacant took Mr Smith's booking on 1 June, in overbooking the hotel rooms, Ms Vacant committed an offence under s. 14(1) TDA 1968 – see *British Airways Board* v. *Taylor* (pp. 141–2).

Mr and Mrs Wilson. At the time of the theft of the coat the Wilsons were guests at the inn, having contracted for accommodation. An innkeeper owes a duty to guests with respect to the property which they bring within the *hospitium* of the inn – s. 2(1) HPA 1956 (p. 161). However, a duty is not owed where the loss is due to the negligence of the guest – see *Armistead* v. *Wilde, Carpenter* v. *Haymarket Hotel*, and *Shacklock* v. *Ethorpe* (p. 163). The alleged negligence here is in Mrs Wilson's leaving the room unlocked.

SIX

The restaurateur and the customer

The relationship between restaurateurs and their customers is similar in many ways to the relationship between hoteliers and their guests. Both situations involve civil and criminal liability. Both the client at a restaurant and the guest at a hotel enter into a contractual relationship with the restaurateur or hotelier. Equally, both may be owed a duty under the tort of negligence by the restaurateur and hotelier respectively. Both hotelier and restaurateur may be rendered liable for prosecution under the Trade Descriptions Act 1968, the hotelier under s. 14(1) for the false description of accommodation or services available and the restaurateur under s. 1(1) for the false description of goods, e.g. food and drink. Furthermore, in cases relating to the sale of food and drink, specific provision is made by the Food Safety Act 1990 to ensure the quality of food and drink, and breach of such standards will render the person in breach liable for prosecution. Certain specific regulations set food standards, e.g. for food storage, temperature, to which certain food products must comply, e.g. cream, and breach of these is a criminal offence. The criminal law also regulates the standards of hygiene to be observed in establishments where food is produced, prepared for sale, sold or consumed.

The legal aspects with which this chapter deals concern not only restaurants, but also hotels, guest houses and canteens, indeed all catering establishments where food and drink are produced, prepared, sold or consumed.

6.1 DISPLAYING MENUS AND PRICE LISTS

Under the Price Marketing (Food and Drink on Premises) Order 1979, prices of both food and drink (collectively described in the Order as food) must be displayed in a

171

clear and legible way by persons selling food by retail for consumption on the premises. The Order does not apply in the following circumstances:

(a) where the supply is only to members of a *bona fide* club or their guests;

(b) at staff restaurants, works canteens and similar establishments;

(c) at guest houses or hotels where the supply is only to people staying there.

Any food which is not normally available but specially prepared at the request of the customers or food which is provided at a price agreed in advance is excluded from the Order.

The main provisions of the Order are:

(1) Prices must be displayed so as to be seen by an intending customer before he reaches the eating area. Where there is a direct access to a restaurant from the street the price list must be at the entrance so that it can be read from the street. Where the eating area is part only of the premises then the price list must be at the entrance to that part.

(2) In the case of self-service premises the price list must be at the place where the customer chooses his food and also at the entrance if the price list cannot otherwise be seen there.

(3) Prices of at least 30 items (other than the table wine, i.e. wine sold for consumption with food) must be shown and, if the premises sell not more than 30, then all must be included. If the price list is divided into different parts, i.e. starters, main course etc., then the prices of at least five items in each category must be shown, or all if less than five.

(4) If both food and drink are sold the price list must not include food only or drink only.

(5) If a price is given by measurement, e.g. half a pint, and the other prices are directly proportionate, e.g. for a pint, only one price need be given.

(6) In the case of table wines, the price of at least six must be shown. If there are two or more of each of red, rosé or white wine the price of at least two of each type must be shown and, if only one of any type, its price must be included.

(7) The price of any table d'hôte meal must be given.

(8) The prices shown must include any value added tax. If a service or cover charge is made, this must be shown either as an amount or as a percentage.

Under Part III of the Consumer Protection Act 1987 additional charges are discouraged, the recommendation under the Act's code of practice being that if customers are to pay non-optional extra charges (e.g. a service charge) these should be incorporated within fully inclusive prices, where possible. This fact, along with any other charges such as cover charge or a minimum charge should be clearly displayed on menus, both inside and outside. Optional additional sums also are not to be suggested (e.g. service not included) in the menu or on the bill presented to customers.

Metrication

From 1 October 1995 regulations were introduced which brought to an end the legal use, for pre-packed foods, of most imperial measures such as the pound, the ounce, the gallon. Loose food such as vegetables may still be sold by imperial weight until the year 2000.

'Descriptive' weights such as 'quarter pounder' on menus are still permitted. The law does not require the metric measure to be shown, although good practice and increasing understanding of the metric system by the public should, in time, lead most caterers to show the metric weight as well. Such weights are of course subject to the requirements of weights and measures legislation. See chapter 8, Licensing Law, for details of the impact of metrication law on the sale of alcohol.

6.2 CONTRACTS FOR THE SALE OF FOOD AND DRINK: OFFER, ACCEPTANCE AND PRIVITY

When is a contract for the sale of food and drink formed?

A contract for the sale of food and drink is formed in different ways and at various times according to the nature of the establishment providing the service.

Most of the law relates to the potential liability of the restaurateur towards a client who dines at the restaurant and finds the food and/or service unsatisfactory. Increasingly, there has been a tendency for restaurateurs to contemplate bringing proceedings against clients who book with the restaurant but do not thereafter take up the booking and dine at the restaurant. Obviously 'no shows' can lead to a loss of profit; equally, suing customers who do not show up can lead to bad public relations. Also, it may be cost-ineffective to recover the debt.

Formal restaurants

In a formal restaurant where there is waiter service, the menu, whether posted outside as an attraction to passers-by or placed in the customer's hands by the waiter or waitress, is merely an invitation to treat, and of no legal effect.

It is, as it were, a mere preliminary to contract. If the menu were considered to be an offer to contract, capable of acceptance by any person entering the restaurant, it would bind the restaurant to provide any item mentioned therein, since the customer's order would amount to acceptance of the offer made in the menu. The commercial reality of the situation is different. A restaurant may display a full menu, or advertise a certain menu, yet on a given evening be unable to supply all the items stated therein, either because of the demand from earlier customers for certain items or for other reasons, e.g. a breakdown in supply, or the fact that the item is out of season. If the menu constituted an offer then the restaurant would be bound to supply the item. This, however, is not the case; the menu is merely preliminary to contract (an invitation to treat). When the customer selects an item from the menu this amounts to an offer to contract for that item. If the item is available the waiter or waitress will take the order and thereby accept the customer's offer to contract. If the item selected is unavailable the waiter or waitress will apologize for the misunderstanding and thereby reject the customer's offer; no contract is formed and the customer cannot legally demand that particular item from the menu.

Self-service outlets

In a self-service or cafeteria type of catering establishment, where the customer selects pre-packed foods from a display, the display is not an offer but an invitation to treat. The offer is made by the customers when they take the pre-packed meal on the tray to the cash desk. The customer thereby offers to purchase and the cashier accepts by ringing up the price on the till. This can be seen in the case of *Pharmaceutical Society of Great Britain* v. *Boots Cash Chemists (Southern) Ltd* [1953] 1 QB 401 (CA). In this case it was held that the display of articles covered by s. 17 of the Pharmacy and Poisons Act 1953 in a self-service shop where goods were paid for at a cash desk did not amount to an offer to sell those goods. The offer was made by the customers when they placed the goods at the cash desk. Hence, in the example of a self-service restaurant given above, the customers do not offer to purchase the pre-packed food until they place it on the cash desk, and may therefore reject the food and return it to the display up until that time, without breaking any contractual obligation with the restaurant. The situation is different where the customer at the cafeteria bar asks the server to, for example, prepare an omelette, take a portion from a larger dish or slice some meat to order. It is arguable that in these cases, when customers request the server to do something with the food which changes the food's identity (i.e. it ceases to be a part of a larger dish, or joint, or capable of being served in another way), in so doing they offer to purchase it. The server by 'dishing it up' accepts the customer's offer and the contract is complete; the incidence of payment is simply at another place, i.e. the cash desk. Hence, if the customers thereafter change their minds and seek to reject the meal selected they are still contractually bound to the restaurant to purchase it.

Fast-food outlets

The comprehensive price list and menu above the counter in a fish and chip shop, burger bar, etc. is merely an invitation to treat. The customer, in asking for cod and chips or a double cheeseburger, is making an offer to contract. The server may then accept the offer and serve the food selected, or reject the offer, explaining that the item is 'off' that evening and requesting the customer to reselect. When the server makes up a portion of fish and chips or cooks the burger, he or she is performing the contract, and the customer is bound to pay. A wise commercial practice is, once the selection has been agreed upon, to require the customer to pay before or whilst the food is prepared.

The consideration for a contract for the sale of food and drink is the agreed price of the items selected by the customer.

With whom does the restaurant contract?

The question of privity of contract is of vital importance, since it will determine the remedy available to the customer. Where a person eats alone at a restaurant, clearly that person is privy to a contract for the sale of food and drink with the restaurant. Hence, only that person and the restaurant are subject to the liabilities and benefits arising under the contract. Therefore, if in some way the restaurant has breached the contract the client may sue for breach and claim damages.

LOCKETT v. A. & M. CHARLES LTD [1938] 4 ALL ER 170 (KB)	The plaintiffs, husband and wife, called in at a hotel for lunch. They ordered their respective choices from the menu, although it was agreed that the husband would pay the bill.

The wife sustained food poisoning as a result of the lunch she had eaten at the hotel. Both plaintiffs sued the defendant company, who were the proprietors of the hotel, for breach of contract and breach of duty.

Held: There being no evidence that either the husband or the wife was in charge of ordering the food, each of them was, as between them and the proprietor, liable to pay for the food ordered. On the facts there was an implied contract between the wife and the proprietor. The wife was therefore able to recover damages for breach of the implied term of such a contract that the food supplied was fit for human consumption.

Tucker J took the view that 'when persons go into a restaurant and order food, they are making a contract of sale in exactly the same way as they are making a contract of sale when they go into a shop and order any other goods. I think that the inference is that the person who orders the food in a hotel or restaurant *prima facie* makes himself or herself liable to pay for it, and when there are two people whether or not they happen to be husband and wife who go into a hotel and each orders and is supplied with food, then, as between those persons and the proprietor of the hotel, each of them is making himself liable for the food which he orders, whatever may be the arrangement between the two persons who are eating at the hotel.'

Examples

1   A husband takes his wife out for a meal, and the meal which is provided breaches the terms of the contract under which it is supplied. Can the husband alone sue the restaurant for breach of contract? The traditional answer is yes. This view is supported by the case of *Buckley* v. *La Reserve* (1959) CLY 1330. This case is, however, of only limited authority. Only the husband is privy to the contract; the wife cannot be bound to pay for the meal if the husband defaults; hence, she cannot claim damages for breach of the contract by the restaurant. A contrary view was taken in *Lockett* v. *A. & M. Charles Ltd* (above). This is to be preferred. Following *Jackson* v. *Horizon Holidays Ltd* [1975] 3 All ER 92 (CA), if the wife sustains disappointment, she may recover additional damages for her suffering.

2   A group of friends book a table for a meal in a restaurant. Each member of the group orders food separately and each intends to pay for the food plus an equivalent amount for the wine consumed. The table was booked in the name of Roger, one of the group. If Sally, another member of the group, sustains injury from the meal which she has eaten, can she sue the restaurant for breach of contract? Is it only Roger who can sue for breach of contract? At first sight the answer would appear to be that only Roger can sue the restaurant in contract, since it was he alone who booked the table. This view is incorrect. The booking of the table is precontractual, the contract being made by each member of the group when he or she orders a meal. Sally may therefore sue for breach of contract. As we shall see later, regardless of this point Sally has a potential remedy against the restaurant under the principle in *Donoghue* v. *Stevenson*. Even if one concluded that Sally herself did not contract with the restaurant, it is still open to Roger to sue for breach of contract and recover damages for disappointment on her behalf (see *Jackson* v. *Horizon Holidays Ltd*, p. 115).

3   John makes a block booking for ten guests to celebrate his twenty-first birthday. John himself selects a set menu from which the guests may choose. John intends that he alone will pay for the food and wine served. Mavis, John's mother, eats her meal, which is tasteless, and suffers disappointment. Can Mavis claim breach of contract on the part of the restaurant or sue for damages for disappointment? No; only John is in a contractual relationship with the restaurant. He alone is privy to the contract and he alone can sue for breach of it. John may, however, claim damages for disappointment for those persons for whose benefit the contract was made, *per* Denning MR *Jackson* v. *Horizon*

Holidays. Mavis herself does not in this instance have a remedy under the principle in *Donoghue* v. *Stevenson*, since the damage sustained (disappointment) is not recognized as a form of damage recoverable in tort. Had Mavis sustained physical injury or nervous shock in consequence of the meal such damage would be clearly recoverable by an action brought under the *Donoghue* v. *Stevenson* principle provided the damage could be attributed to the 'fault' of the restaurant.

The terms of the contract

As with any other contract, a contract for the sale of food and drink incorporates both express and implied terms. When a customer orders home-made soup as a starter, it is a term of the contract of sale of that item that the soup is made on the premises and not bought-in tins or packets of soup heated by the restaurant. However, a contract for the sale of food and drink falls into a category of contracts known as contracts for the sale of goods. Contracts for the sale of goods are governed by the provisions of the Sale of Goods Act 1979. That Act implies into such contracts certain terms as to the description of the product, the suitability for purpose and the quality of the product. In *Lockett* v. *A. & M. Charles Ltd* [1938] 4 All ER 170 (KB) it was held that a contract to prepare and supply food in a restaurant was a contract for the sale of goods under the Sale of Goods Act 1893, and there is no reason to doubt that this remains so under the 1979 Act. However, Parliament has recently passed the Supply of Goods and Services Act 1982 which implies in 'contracts for the transfer of property in goods' terms as to description, quality and fitness for purpose of those goods. If *Lockett*'s case was not applied, and therefore a contract for the supply of a restaurant meal was outside the scope of the Sale of Goods Act 1979, it would be covered by the Supply of Goods and Services Act 1982. It is important, therefore, to consider the terms implied by both Acts, and the extent to which, if at all, the restaurateur is free to exclude them by means of an exclusion clause stated in the contract of sale with the customer.

The Sale of Goods Act 1979 (SGA)

Section 13 SGA 1979. This section deals with sales by description. Section 13(1) provides:

> Where there is a contract for the sale of goods by description, there is an implied condition that the goods will correspond with that description.

Hence, if a restaurateur sells to a customer a starter described in the menu as smoked salmon and the food is actually a smoked salmon trout, this will constitute a breach of the implied term as to description in s. 13 SGA 1979, and amount to a breach of condition. Therefore the customer may treat the contract as at an end and sue for damages. In the self-service restaurant or cafeteria there may still be a sale by description where the food is displayed and described on a menu or price list above the counter. This follows from the case of *Grant* v. *Australian Knitting Mills Ltd* [1936] AC 85 (PC), where Lord Wright observed:

> there is a sale by description even though the buyer is buying something displayed before him on the counter; a thing is sold by description, though it is specific, so long as it is sold not merely as the specific thing but as a thing corresponding to a description.

Furthermore, s. 13(3) SGA 1979 provides:

> A sale of goods is not prevented from being a sale by description by reason only that, being exposed for sale . . . they are selected by the buyer.

The essence of a sale by description is that, in deciding to purchase, the buyer has placed some reliance upon the description.

Does a sale by description relate in any way to the quality of the goods? If a restaurant sells as smoked salmon an article which is in fact smoked salmon trout it may appear to amount to a question of the product's quality. However, it can be seen from the case of *Ashington Piggeries* v. *Christopher Hill* [1971] 2 WLR 1051 (HL) that s. 13 operates only in relation to the description and not the quality of the goods. If, for example, the restaurant describes an item as home-made apple pie and it is inedible due to the inferior quality of the apples used, s. 13 SGA 1979 does not provide a remedy. The article was in fact home-made apple pie as described, although of an inferior quality, and therefore meets with the description applied. The customer's remedy here comes under s. 14(2) SGA 1979.

Section 14 SGA 1979. Sections 14(2) and 14(3) provide implied terms as to the quality of the goods sold. Section 14(2) SGA 1979 as amended by the Sale and Supply of Goods Act 1994 states:

> Where the seller sells goods in the course of a business, there is an implied condition that the goods supplied under the contract are of satisfactory* quality, except that there is no such condition –
> (a) as regards defects specifically drawn to the buyer's attention before the contract is made; or
> (b) if the buyer examines the goods before the contract is made, as regards defects which that examination ought to reveal.

This condition is implied only if the goods are sold 'in the course of a business', so the restaurateur is clearly covered by the section. Where at a party or a social event organized by a club or at a children's party arranged by a playgroup, for which tickets for food have been purchased by guests, it is not clear whether s. 14(2) implies a term as to satisfactory quality of the food purchased by means of the ticket. The simplest view is to say that it does not, and the ticket purchaser does not have a remedy under s. 14(2) SGA 1979 if the food is inedible. The meaning of 'satisfactory quality' is defined by s. 14(6) SGA 1979 as amended by the SSGA 1994:

*Until the SSGA 1994 the description 'merchantable' was used.

> *Goods of any kind are of satisfactory quality within the meaning of s. 14(2) above if they are fit for the purpose or purposes for which goods of that kind are commonly bought as it is reasonable to expect having regard to any description applied to them, the price (if relevant) and all other relevant circumstances.*

Food will therefore not be of satisfactory quality if it is inedible, i.e. unfit for human consumption. A customer could not, however, return food, wine or other drink and say that it was not to his or her taste. Merely because food is bland does not mean that it is not of satisfactory quality. Steak, for example, will be of satisfactory quality if it is not particularly tender; it will not be of satisfactory quality if it is so tough as to be inedible. However, if an exceptionally high price is asked for a particular cut, say fillet steak, and the steak is tough though edible, the factors of price and the quality of steak which a customer 'might reasonably expect' having regard to the description 'fillet steak' may render such a steak as being not of satisfactory quality.

Section 14(3) SGA 1979 implies a term as to the goods' fitness for purpose.

> *Where the seller sells goods in the course of a business and the buyer, expressly or by implication, makes known ... to the seller ... any particular purpose for which the goods are being bought, there is an implied condition that the goods supplied under the contract are reasonably fit for that purpose, whether or not that is a purpose for which such goods are commonly supplied, except where the circumstances show that the buyer does not rely, or that it is unreasonable for him to rely, on the skill or judgement of the seller.*

Clearly the purpose for which a customer purchases food and drink is for human consumption as food and drink. If, therefore, food or drink supplied by restaurateurs is not fit to be eaten or drunk, then they are in breach of s. 14(3) SGA 1979. This point was considered in *Frost* v. *Aylesbury Dairy Co. Ltd* [1905] 1 KB 608, where it was held, under the equivalent provision as to fitness for purpose in the SGA 1893, that milk which was purchased was intended for human consumption, and was unfit for that purpose by reason of the fact that it was infected by typhoid, and that the defendant retailer was in breach of the implied condition as to fitness for purpose. It would seem that although s. 14(3) requires reliance by the buyer upon the seller's skill and judgement, the courts appear willing to infer reliance from the fact the customer goes to the restaurant in the confidence that the proprietor has selected the stock (food, etc.) with skill and judgement.

Remedies for breach of implied terms. The remedy available for breach of the implied terms under ss. 12, 13 and 14 is that which is available for any other breach of condition in a contract. The party who is the 'victim' of the breach may rescind the contract (treat it as at an end) and sue for damages.

Supply of Goods and Services Act 1982 (SGSA)

This Act was implemented to cover contracts outside the scope of the SGA 1979 under which goods are supplied. The Act implies in 'contracts for the transfer of goods', which are 'contract(s) under which one person transfers or agrees to transfer to another the property in goods' (s. 1(1) SGSA 1982), terms as to description, quality and fitness for purpose of the goods. These provisions, namely s. 3(1) (description), s. 4(2) (satisfactory quality) and s. 4(5) (fitness for purpose), reflect those made by s. 13, s. 14(2) and s. 14(3) SGA 1979.

Whilst it may be said that the preparation and supply of a restaurant meal are either a contract for the sale of goods under the SGA 1979 or a contract for the transfer of goods under the SGSA 1982, it may also be considered to be a 'contract for the supply of a service' under s. 12 SGSA 1982. Section 12(1) provides:

> A 'contract for the supply of a service' means (subject to s. 12 (2)) a contract under which a person (the supplier) agrees to carry out a service.

Clearly the provision of food and drink is a service. The Act itself does not define 'service'. It is unlikely, however, that a court would interpret the supply of food to be outside the scope of s. 12(1). The importance of this statute lies in s. 13, which provides:

> In a contract for the supply of a service where the supplier is acting in the course of a business, there is an implied term that the supplier will carry out the service with reasonable care and skill.

Hence, if the chef, in preparing the food, or even the waiter or waitress who serves it, does not exercise 'reasonable care and skill', then this gives rise to an action for breach of the implied condition in s. 13 SGSA 1982. A distinction needs to be drawn here between the supply of a service and the sale or supply of goods. With the supply of a service we are not so much concerned with the food itself as with the manner of preparation and service. Hence, if a perfectly edible fillet steak is rendered inedible by the method of preparation, e.g. if it is overcooked or dropped on the floor, the proper course of action would be under s. 13 SGSA 1982, since it is the service rather than the product itself which gives rise to the remedy.

It should be remembered that the provisions of the SGSA 1982 apply only where the supplier acts in the course of a business. Hence, if a person supplies a meal to a friend or guest at his or her home and the friend or guest suffers an illness as a result thereof, the guest does not have a right of action under s. 13 SGSA 1982. The guest's remedy lies in the principles set out in *Donoghue* v. *Stevenson* under the tort of negligence.

Who is liable for breach of the implied terms?

In many instances the food which a caterer or restaurateur prepares is bought in from a supplier rather than created by the chef. For example, the Winds Restaurant purchases a pie from Pise Ltd (a manufacturer of meat products), and serves the pie as part of a meal ordered by Mr Smith. If Mr Smith thereafter suffers food poisoning caused by the pie, is it the proprietor of the Winds Restaurant, Mr Guff, or Pise Ltd who is liable, under either the SGA 1979 or the SGSA 1982, to Mr Smith? It is Mr Guff, the proprietor of the restaurant. Pise Ltd is not privy to the contract with Mr Smith and therefore may be liable only under the tort of negligence (*Donoghue* v.

Stevenson). Will Mr Guff be liable although he has no idea about the contents of the pie? Yes: the SGA 1979 and the SGSA 1982 do not require fault as a precondition to liability.

Exclusion of liability for breach of statutorily implied terms

Where a restaurateur or caterer seeks to rely on an exclusion clause incorporated into a contract for the sale of food and drink with a customer the provisions contained in s. 6 of the Unfair Contract Terms Act 1977 (UCTA 1977) and the EC Unfair Contract Terms Directive 93/13 apply. It must always be established, prior to considering the actual wording of any given exclusion clause, that the clause has been incorporated into the contract. This must be done prior to or at the time of the formation of the contract – *Olley* v. *Marlborough Court Ltd* [1949] 1 KB 532 (CA). This will normally be done by means of a sufficiently clear notice. Can a restaurateur use such a clause to exclude liability for breach of an implied condition under the SGA 1979 or the SGSA 1982?

SGA 1979

The exclusion of liability for breach of the implied terms under ss. 13 and 14 SGA 1979 is governed by s. 55(1) SGA 1979 and s. 6 UCTA 1977. Section 55(1) states:

> *Where a right, duty or liability would arise under a contract of sale of goods by implication of law, it may (subject to UCTA 1977) be negatived or varied by express agreement, or by the course of dealing between the parties, or by such usage as binds both parties to the contract.*

Therefore, it may be open to a caterer or restaurateur to seek to rely upon an exclusion clause to exclude or limit liability to a customer for breach of ss. 13 or 14 SGA 1979. However, ss. 6(2) and 6(3) UCTA 1977 and the EC Unfair Contract Terms Directive 93/13 limit the usage of such a clause.

> *As against a person dealing as consumer, liability for breach of the obligations arising from – (a) s. 13, s. 14 or s. 15 (SGA 1979) . . . cannot be excluded or restricted by reference to any contract term.*

Hence, a restaurateur who seeks to exclude liability as to description (s. 13), satisfactory quality (s. 14(2)), or fitness for purpose (s. 14(3)) is unable to do so when the person purchasing the meal is 'dealing as consumer'. When does a customer deal as a consumer? Section 12(1) UCTA 1977 states:

> *A party to a contract 'deals as a consumer' in relation to another party if –*
> *(a) he neither makes the contract in the course of a business nor holds himself out as doing so; and*

(b) the other party does make the contract in the course of a business; and

(c) in the case of a contract governed by the law of sale of goods ... the goods
     passing under or in pursuance of the contract are of a type ordinarily supplied
     for private use or consumption.

Hence, where a restaurateur serves a meal to an individual or a group of individuals,
e.g. a rugby club, those persons 'deal as consumers' and liability cannot be excluded.
Where the diners contract as a business, e.g. a sales or business conference, they do
not 'deal as consumers' and s. 12(1) is inapplicable. The extent to which a restaurateur
can exclude liability for breach of ss. 13 or 14 SGA 1979 is governed by s. 6(3) UCTA
1977.

> As against a person dealing otherwise than as a consumer liability (under s. 13, 14 or
> 15 SGA 1979) ... can be excluded or restricted by reference to a contract term, but
> only so far as the term satisfies the requirement of reasonableness.

The 'requirement of reasonableness' is set out in s. 11(1) UCTA. It would be for the
restaurateur to satisfy the court that the term is a fair and reasonable one, having
regard to the guidelines set out in Schedule 2 to UCTA 1977.

SGSA 1982

Section 11 SGSA 1982 applies the same provisions of UCTA 1977 to contracts for the
transfer of goods under s. 1 SGSA 1982, i.e. s. 6(2) and s. 6(3) UCTA 1977 operate
here. As for contracts for the supply of a service and the possible exclusion of liability
for breach of s. 13 SGSA 1982, s. 16 of the 1982 Act applies. This again applies s. 6(2)
and s. 6(3) UCTA 1977 to such contracts.

Damages for breach of contract

A contract for the sale of food and drink is like any other contract. Hence, the general
rules as to damages for breach of contract apply.

Damages for breach of statutorily implied terms

Where the restaurateur is in breach of the statutorily implied terms under either the
SGA 1979 or the SGSA 1982, this entitles the customer to treat the contract as at an
end and sue for damages. This is because statutorily implied terms are conditions of
the contract.

Damages for disappointment

This form of damages was created by the decision in *Jarvis* v. *Swan's Tours Ltd* [1973]
1 All ER 71 (CA). It has been held to cover not only the person with whom the party
contracts but also such other persons on whose behalf the contract is made – *Jackson*
v. *Horizon Holidays Ltd* [1975] 3 All ER 92 (CA). Whilst damages for disappointment

have not been sought in a case relating to the provision of catering facilities or food and drink, there is no cogent reason why the principle should not apply.

Example. Mr Jones books with the Ivy Leaf Hotel for a wedding breakfast for forty guests. To be provided is a formal buffet, the food for which he and his wife and daughter have selected. On the appointed day the buffet is provided; the food, however, is of poor quality and certain of the dishes selected to form part of the buffet are not provided. The guests, whilst polite, are clearly disappointed by the quality and quantity of the buffet. Applying *Jarvis* v. *Swan's Tours*, Mr Jones may sue the proprietor of the Ivy Leaf Hotel for breach of contract. Where a breach is established Mr Jones may obtain damages to represent the disappointment and anxiety caused to himself. He may also recover damages on behalf of his daughter and son-in-law, his wife and his son-in- law's parents, who have all suffered anxiety and disappointment. Liability for damages for disappointment may even extend to all the guests present. The total amount recoverable in damages will therefore exceed to a degree the contract price of the buffet.

Reliance loss

It would be misguided to believe that it is always the restaurateur or caterer who is in breach of contract. For example, a person books with an outside caterer to provide a marquee and reception for 100 guests on the occasion of his twenty-first birthday. The caterer does not have readily available sufficient equipment, e.g. chairs, silver, plates, to provide for the occasion and therefore, under separate contract, hires them and a marquee. Hence, in reliance upon the contract with the customer, the caterer enters into other arrangements in order to satisfy the customer's contract. What if the customer, a week prior to the event, cancels the contract with the caterer? This will amount to an anticipatory breach of contract, i.e. a breach before the contractual date for performance. The caterer will, of course, require damages to represent the loss sustained due to the customer's breach. The damages sought are reliance damages, i.e. to represent the monies wasted by the caterer in arranging the marquee, hire of silver, etc. This principle can be seen most clearly in the following case.

ANGLIA TELEVISION v. REED [1972] 1 QB 60 (CA)	The plaintiff television company incurred expense in preparation for filming a television play. Subsequently they entered into a contract with the defendant to play the leading role. The defendant broke the contract. The plaintiffs thereafter abandoned the play.

Held: The plaintiffs were entitled to recover the wasted expenditure in full.

Hence the caterer can recover all expenses and monies paid out in reliance upon the customer's contract, provided such monies were within the contemplation of the parties, or ought reasonably to have been within their contemplation. Reliance loss reflects wasted expenditure, damages for loss of bargain cover and loss of profit. It is possible for the caterer to recover both the profit he would have made had the contract been performed and damages reflecting the monies lost in reliance upon the contract. He cannot, however, recover 'double damages', only those which reflect the true loss to the plaintiff.

Liability in tort for the sale of food and drink

Tortious liability exists although there is no privity of contract between the caterer and the party wishing to bring an action.

Example. John buys for Tess a drink which is manufactured by Fizz and Co., from the Hotel Pacific lounge bar. Tess drinks some of the drink and suffers illness, since the drink contained a dead mouse which had been bottled with the drink in the course of manufacture by Fizz and Co.

Tess is not in a contractual relationship with either Fizz and Co. or the Hotel Pacific. John has a contract with the Hotel Pacific and the Hotel Pacific has a contract with Fizz and Co. (see Figure 6.1). Tess may, however, sue either the Hotel Pacific or Fizz and Co. under the tort of negligence and the principles set out in *Donoghue* v. *Stevenson*.

Whom should Tess sue? On what basis is liability determined? Tess will have to establish three things:

1 The proposed defendant owed her a *duty of care*.
2 The proposed defendant acted in *breach of duty*.
3 As a result of the defendant's breach she sustained *damage*.

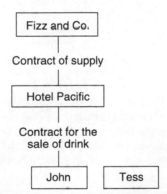

Figure 6.1 Contractual relationships in the example.

Duty of care

This was established in *Donoghue* v. *Stevenson*.

DONOGHUE v. STEVENSON [1932] AC 562 (HL)

A manufacturer of ginger beer had sold a quantity to a retailer. The drink was bottled in opaque glass. The retailer resold it to X, who purchased it and gave it to the plaintiff. The plaintiff drank a quantity of the ginger beer, and when a further glass was poured a decomposing snail emerged from the bottle. The snail had found its way into the bottle at the defendant's factory. The plaintiff sustained illness in consequence of the drink and sued the manufacturer for negligence. There was no contractual relationship between the plaintiff and defendant manufacturer.

Held (*per* Lord Atkin): 'A manufacturer of products, which he sells in such a form as to show that he intends them to reach the ultimate consumer in the form in which they left him, with no reasonable possibility of intermediate examination, and with knowledge that the absence of reasonable care in the preparation or putting up of the products is likely to result in injury to the consumer's life or property, owes a duty to the consumer to take reasonable care.'

This is so even though the parties were not in a contractual relationship.

Applying this to our example, Fizz and Co. clearly owe a duty of care to Tess. Tess may therefore be advised that Fizz and Co. is a possible defendant against whom she may successfully claim, if she can establish breach of the duty of care owed to her by Fizz and Co.

Can Tess sue the Hotel Pacific? A further principle was established in *Donoghue* v. *Stevenson*, namely the neighbour principle. Lord Atkin observed:

> *You must take reasonable care to avoid acts or omissions which you can reasonably foresee would be likely to injure your neighbour. Who, then, in law is my neighbour? The answer seems to be – persons who are so closely and directly affected by my act that I ought reasonably to have them in contemplation as being so affected when I am directing my mind to the acts or omissions which are called into question.*

Clearly Tess is a 'neighbour' of the Hotel Pacific and is owed a duty of care under the neighbour principle.

Breach

It is essential in each case to establish breach of the duty of care owed by the defendant to the plaintiff. What, then, is the standard of care required to fulfil the duty? The standard is that of the reasonable man. What standard of conduct would he have applied if in the same position as the defendant? This is sometimes called the 'average standard'. In *Glasgow Corporation* v. *Muir* [1945] 2 All ER 44 (HL) Lord Macmillan observed:

> *My Lords, the degree of care for the safety of others which the law requires human beings to observe in the conduct of their affairs varies according to the circumstances. There is no absolute standard, but it may be said generally that the degree of care required varies directly with the risk involved. ... Legal liability is limited to those consequences of our acts which a reasonable man of ordinary intelligence and experience so acting would have in contemplation ...*

Hence, the standard of care required of a manufacturer of food products is that which a reasonable food manufacturer would adopt. The courts take the view that if the party has done so much as is reasonably practicable in the circumstances to ensure the safety of the plaintiff, that is sufficient to show that the defendant has discharged the duty of care towards the plaintiff. Hence, in our example, if Fizz and Co. have done that which a reasonable drinks manufacturer would do to ensure the quality of the product and the safety of the bottling process to prevent injury to the ultimate consumer, then Fizz and Co. have done sufficient to discharge their duty of care towards Tess.

Furthermore, in each case it must be established that there is a causal link between the defendant's actions and the plaintiff's damage:

BARNETT v. CHELSEA & KENSINGTON HOSPITAL MANAGEMENT COMMITTEE [1968] 1 All ER 1068 (QB)	The plaintiff's husband drank a quantity of tea which unknown to him had been poisoned with arsenic. After a short while, and following persistent vomiting, he went with two others who had also drunk some of the tea to the defendant's hospital casualty department. The doctor on duty relayed through a nurse that the plaintiff's husband should return home and call his doctor in the morning. The plaintiff's husband did this but

later died from arsenic poisoning. The question arose whether, even if the doctor had himself examined the deceased, he would have been able to treat the condition and save the man's life.

Held: The plaintiff had failed to establish that the doctor's failure to examine the deceased and treat him caused his death. Although the court found the defendant (Hospital Management Committee) to be negligent, since they did not admit the deceased to hospital or treat his condition, this failure did not cause the death and therefore they were not liable to pay damages.

In our example, therefore, it was the omission by the defendant manufacturer which allowed for the presence of the mouse in the bottle and thus caused her injury. If she cannot establish this causal link her action will fail. Clearly, if Tess brought an action against the Hotel Pacific, she would fail to establish any causal link between their actions in serving the drink and the illness she sustained. Her action against them would therefore fail.

Damage

The injury sustained by the plaintiff must be reasonably foreseeable (*The Wagon Mound (No. 2)* [1966] 2 All ER 709 (PC)). Furthermore, the injury must be of a sort which the courts recognize as a form of loss which is recoverable in damages:
(a) physical injury – *Donoghue* v. *Stevenson*;
(b) nervous shock – *Bourhill* v. *Young* [1942] 2 All ER 396 (HL);
(c) monetary loss linked with physical injury – *Spartan Steel & Alloys Ltd* v. *Martin & Co. (Contractors) Ltd* [1972] 3 All ER 557;
(d) economic loss *simpliciter* – *Junior Books Ltd* v. *Veitchi & Co. Ltd* [1982] WLR (HL) – a case very much based on its own facts.
In our example Tess's sickness is a reasonably foreseeable form of injury arising from the negligent manufacture or processing of a food product. Furthermore, such injury is recognized by the law as a head of damages, namely physical injury.

Product liability: the Consumer Protection Act 1987

Product liability was once used as a label to describe the areas of contractual and tortious liability relevant to the sale of goods. The classic case in which this form of 'product liability' can be seen is:

DANIELS v. R. WHITE & SONS LTD & TARBARD [1938] 4 All ER 258 (KB)	A husband and wife sued the manufacturer and retailer of a bottle of lemonade for damages for injuries received by reason of the fact that the bottle of lemonade purchased by the husband contained, in addition, a quantity of carbolic acid. Both husband and wife, in suing the manufacturer,

relied upon *Donoghue* v. *Stevenson* as grounding their action in negligence. The husband, who had purchased the lemonade, sued the retailer for breach of the implied conditions of contract as to merchantable quality and fitness for purpose (s. 14 SGA 1893, now s. 14 SGA 1979).

It was found as a question of fact that the manufacturers, by adopting a foolproof process and by carrying out that process under proper supervision, had taken reasonable care to ensure that there was in the lemonade no defect that would injure the plaintiffs.

Held: The duty owed by the manufacturers to the consumer was not to ensure that the goods were in perfect condition, but merely to take reasonable care to see that no injury was done to the consumer or ultimate purchaser. This duty, upon the facts as found, had been fulfilled. Hence the manufacturers were not liable under the tort of negligence to either husband or wife. However, the vendor (Tarbard) was liable to the husband, with whom he had entered into a contract, for breach of the implied term as to merchantable quality under s. 14 SGA 1893 (now s. 14 SGA 1979), but not to the wife.

Daniels's case illustrates an important point which is not always readily appreciated, namely, that whilst tort-based liability under *Donoghue* v. *Stevenson* requires fault, i.e. breach of duty on the part of the defendant, liability under s. 13 or s. 14 SGA 1979 does not. Sections 13 and 14 impose 'strict' liability in the sense that it is not necessary to show fault on the part of the defendant. However, ss. 13 and 14 SGA 1979 require the plaintiff and defendant to have entered into a contractual relationship, whereas negligence-based liability under *Donoghue* v. *Stevenson* does not.

There are two further aspects to product liability: the role of the criminal law in enforcing standards of commercial behaviour, e.g. the Food Safety Act 1990 and the Trade Descriptions Act 1968; and the Consumer Protection Act 1987. In outline, the Consumer Protection Act 1987 has three main purposes:

(a) to provide consumers with a strict liability remedy against a producer whose defective products cause personal injury or damage to property (bringing UK law into line with the EC's Product Liability Directive (1985));
(b) to create an offence of supplying goods which contravene a new general safety standard – the 'general safety requirement';
(c) to replace s. 11 of the Trade Descriptions Act 1968 and the Price Marking (Bargain Offers) Order 1979 with new offences of giving to consumers a misleading price indication and of failing to correct a price indication which has become misleading.

Part I of the 1987 Act is relevant to our present discussion. Parts II and III will be considered under section 6.3, 'Criminal liability for the sale of food and drink' (pp. 189–219).

Part I of the Act creates a new statutory strict liability tort, one where it is not necessary for the plaintiff to prove fault on the part of the defendant. Section 2(1) provides:

> ... *where any damage is caused wholly or partly by a defect in a product, every person to whom subsection (2) below applies shall be liable for the damage.*

Section 2(2) provides:

> *This section applies to –*
> *(a) the producer of the product;*

(b) any person who, by putting his name on the product or using a trade mark or
   other distinguishing mark in relation to the product has held himself out to be
   the producer of the product;

(c) any person who has imported the product into a member State from a place
   outside the member States in order, in the course of any business of his, to supply
   it to another.

The Act imposes initial liability upon the producer, the proclaimed producer or the
importer of the product. A supplier of the product faces liability only where one or
more of those facing primary liability cannot be identified. The producer therefore has
primary liability for the defective product, whereas the supplier has secondary liability,
based on his or her inability to identify the producer. Where more than one person is
liable to the victim under the Act for damage arising from a defective product, their
liability is to be joint and several, i.e. each person liable may be sued for the full
amount of the victim's loss – s. 2(5).

Whilst the supplier of a defective product is *prima facie* liable under the Act for all
loss or damage caused by the defect, where the loss or damage is caused partly by the
defect and partly due to the actions of a third party, the supplier remains liable for
the entire loss. The supplier, however, may seek a contribution from the third party –
s. 2(5).

Where the loss to the victim is caused in part by the victim's own actions the normal
rules on contributory negligence under the Law Reform (Contributory Negligence)
Act 1945 will apply.

Liability under the 1987 Act arises only where the product supplied by the producer
was supplied in the course of his or her business – s. 4(1).

Section 1(2) defines 'product' for the purposes of the Act. It includes:

(a) *any* goods *or* substance;

(b) *component parts and raw materials.*

'Goods' includes growing crops as well as a broad range of finished products.
'Substance' includes any natural or artificial solid, vaporous or liquid substance –
s. 45(1).

Clearly some foods are within the scope of the 1987 Act, and the provisions in s. 1
and s. 2 apply to the manufacture and supply of these. It should be noted, however,
that the Act does not apply to 'primary agricultural products'; these include products
of the soil, stock farming and fisheries. There are clear reasons why agricultural
products should be included in the legislation, and little effort has been made to
explain their exclusion from the Act. Two points should be considered:

1   Food poisoning arising from harmful food seems no different from any other
   injury caused by a defective product, e.g. *Donoghue* v. *Stevenson* (above).

2   By excluding these products the Act creates an anomaly. A seller of food may
   be sued under the Sale of Goods Act 1979. A manufacturer of food may be sued
   under the tort of negligence, where fault can be established (see *Donoghue* v.
   Stevenson). It would seem anomalous to exclude food from the 1987 Act, which
   is directed at product liability when both of these remedies may be available
   but neither is necessarily effective, contractual liability under the SGA 1979

requiring privity of contract, and tortious liability in negligence requiring proof
of fault.

Where agricultural produce has been 'processed', liability under the Consumer
Protection Act 1987 may arise. A 'processor' of primary agricultural produce is to be
strictly liable not just for the defects which are introduced at the processing stage but
also for defects which existed in the produce when it was supplied to him or her for
processing.

Example. Mr Archer, a farmer, supplies peas to Carrot Crunchers, a food-canning
company, for canning. Mr Archer had, when growing the crop, used a pesticide which
was poisonous. The peas were poisonous when supplied to Carrot Crunchers.

In this example Mr Archer (the farmer) is not liable under the Consumer Protection
Act 1987 when the peas cause food poisoning to Colonel Blunt when he eats them as
part of a pub lunch at the Bull.

Carrot Crunchers (the food-processing company) are liable to Colonel Blunt under
the Consumer Protection Act 1987 (n.b. the food-processing company will probably
sue Mr Archer under s. 14 of the Sale of Goods Act 1979 unless there is an operative
exclusion clause in the contract of supply – see Chapter 7).

The publican at the Bull, who sold the peas as part of a lunch to Colonel Blunt, may
be sued by the Colonel under the Sale of Goods Act 1979 and/or the Supply of Goods
and Services Act 1982 (see pp. 176–85).

Strict liability (that is, liability without proof of fault on the part of the defendant)
arises under the 1987 Act for products which are *defective*. A product is defective for
the purposes of the 1987 Act where it is *unsafe*. It must pose a danger to persons and
to their property – s. 3(1).

The Act is very narrow on this point; thus a product is *not* defective if it is unmerchantable or unfit for the purpose for which it was purchased. It becomes defective
only when it is unsafe. Thus a consumer's remedy where the product which he or she
has purchased is merely unmerchantable or useless, and not unsafe, is under s. 14 SGA
1979 (see pp. 177–79).

For the purposes of the 1987 Act a product is defective if its safety is not such as
people generally are entitled to expect. What constitutes a legitimate expectation of
safety is not made clear in the Act. Section 3(2) does give guidance as to matters to
be considered when determining the issue; these include manufacturing defects, design
defects, defects in components and failure to issue appropriate warnings about use of
the product.

Given that the plaintiff can establish that the defendant is a person within the
definition of those who may be liable for a defective product under the 1987 Act and
that the product was defective, one final matter needs to be established, namely, that
the defect caused the loss (e.g. personal injury or damage to property). The 1987 Act
does *not* require that the plaintiff establish that the loss was foreseeable. It should
be noted that the plaintiff must show that the defect itself caused the loss; merely to
establish the defect and the loss is insufficient of itself. The two must be directly
linked.

The losses which are recoverable under the 1987 Act are limited by s. 3(1) and
s. 5(1) to death, personal injury or damage to the victim's property which is caused by
the defective product. Economic loss is not recoverable under the 1987 Act.

Can liability under Part I of the Consumer Protection Act be excluded? Section 7
provides:

The liability of a person by virtue of this point to a person who has suffered damage caused wholly or partly by a defect in a product, or to a dependant or relative of such a person, shall not be limited or excluded by any contract terms, by any notice or by any other provision.

6.3 CRIMINAL LIABILITY FOR THE SALE OF FOOD AND DRINK

Soon after the passing of the Food Act 1984 the government announced a full-scale review of food law. The existing food law had remained unchanged for some time during a period of considerable technological and social development, e.g. the arrival of 'fast food' and various new methods of food presentation. Food additives and the development of new techniques for growing, processing and packaging food militated toward a thorough review of food law and its enforcement.

In 1989 the government published a White Paper, *Food Safety – Protecting the Consumer*, and announced its intention to introduce new legislation. The Food Safety Act 1990 retains the main structure of offences concerned with food safety contained in the previous law, but seeks to tighten up the perceived gaps and counter difficulties faced by those seeking to enforce the earlier legislation.

In short, the Food Safety Act 1990 is founded upon earlier legislation regulating the standard and quality of food. The Act creates new offences and strengthens the powers of the enforcement agencies.

An outline of the Food Safety Act

This outline serves simply as a checklist of important provisions contained in the Food Safety Act (FSA) 1990:

Provision	*Offence*
Section 7	Offence of rendering food injurious to health.
Section 8	Sale of food which does not comply with food safety requirements, namely it is unfit for human consumption or contaminated.
Section 14	Food not of nature, quality or substance demanded by the purchaser.
Section 15	Falsely describing or presenting food (compliance with EC Food Labelling Directive (79/112/EEC)).

Provision	*Enforcement Process*
Section 9	Power to inspect and seize unsafe food.
Section 10	Service of improvement notices.
Section 11	Prohibition orders to enforce hygiene regulations.
Section 12	Emergency action – emergency prohibition orders.
Section 13	Ministers' power to make an emergency control order.

Many matters of detail will be dealt with by Regulation – see s. 16 and Schedule 1. Regulations will be made to ensure compliance with the European Communities commitments – see s. 17.

Section 19 empowers the minister responsible to make regulations requiring the registration or licensing of premises used for the purposes of food businesses. The minister may also issue Codes of Practice under s. 40 on the execution and enforcement of the Act and regulations made under it.

The Act and the regulations made under it are binding on the Crown (see s. 54), and although the Crown may not be held criminally liable under the Act, the High Court may declare unlawful any act or omission of the Crown which contravenes the Act.

Immunity from criminal liability applies only to the Crown – individuals who are employed by the Crown are subject to the full force of the Act. This means that where an offence under the Act has been committed by an individual who is employed as a servant of the Crown, he or she can be prosecuted under the Act, whilst the Crown is immune from such prosecution.

The Food Safety Act 1990 applies to the whole of Great Britain and repeals the whole of the Food and Drugs Act 1956 and much of the Food Act 1984 (Parts III and V remain in force in amended form).

The responsibility for enforcing the Food Safety Act 1990 is divided between local and central government bodies. Section 5 defines 'Food Authorities'; these bodies, through authorized officers, enforce most of the provisions of the Act. Food Authorities have responsibility for enforcing the main criminal provisions of the Act – notably ss. 7, 8, 14 and 15, and for exercising the enforcement powers contained in ss. 9, 10, 11 and 12. Food authorities enforce all regulations made under the Act. By s. 19 the Food Authorities are responsible for maintaining any register of food premises, and may also provide food hygiene training (see s. 23).

Certain powers remain the province of central government, which in most instances will be the Ministry of Agriculture, Fisheries and Food (MAFF). These powers include that of making regulations under s. 16. Section 13, which provides for the power to issue emergency control orders, is also exercised by the Minister.

The Act extends the range of duties imposed on local authorities as food authorities.

Summary

The main aims and objectives of the Food Safety Act 1990 may be summarized as being:
(a) to revise and improve the main offences in existing law, and to include an umbrella offence of supplying food that fails to comply with 'food safety requirements';
(b) to strengthen the powers of enforcement, including the detention and seizure of food and in-factory enforcement;
(c) to enable detailed legislation to be made adapting the law to new technical developments, and regulating novel foods;
(d) to provide power to require registration of food premises, allow the issue of improvement notices, and enable premises to be closed down more quickly if the public health is at risk;
(e) to allow Ministers to tackle potentially serious problems immediately by the use of emergency control orders;
(f) to strengthen controls over contaminants and residues;
(g) to enable Ministers to require hygiene training for food handlers;
(h) to modernize the system of statutory defences to ensure that all those

responsible for supplying food take appropriate responsibility for ensuring its safety; and
(i) to introduce tougher penalties.

It should be remembered that the 1990 Act applies to every business involved in the food chain, from farmers and grocers, primary food-processing establishments, e.g. dairies, food manufacturers, companies transporting, distributing and storing food, through to retailers, restaurants and cafés. This of course incorporates those organizations and individuals running small catering businesses (often from their own home) and non-profit-making organizations, e.g. WRVS, WI, who may process and sell food at bazaars, fetes, etc.

The government by legislating in this way has set out to:
(a) ensure that all food produced for sale is safe to eat and not misleadingly described;
(b) strengthen the enforcement regime;
(c) conform with EC legislation;
(d) keep in step with technological change in the food production and service industries.

The scope of the Food Safety Act 1990

Many of the substantive provisions of the Act relate to 'food' and the safety of 'food'. It is an offence:
* to render 'food' injurious to health – s. 7;
* to sell 'food' which does not comply with food safety requirements – s. 8;
* to sell 'food' which is not of the nature, substance or quality demanded by the purchaser – s. 14;
* to sell 'food' under a misleading or false description – s. 15

'Food' is defined in positive terms in s. 1(1) of the Act whilst s. 1(2) lists those items which are not 'food' for the purposes of the Act.

Section 1 provides:

> *(1) In this Act 'food' includes –*
> *(a) drink;*
> *(b) articles and substances of no nutritional value which are used for human consumption;*
> *(c) chewing gum and other products of a like nature and use; and*
> *(d) articles and substances used as ingredients in the preparation of food or anything falling within this subsection.*
> *(2) In this Act 'food' does not include –*
> *(a) live animals or birds, or live fish which are not used for human consumption while they are alive;*
> *(b) fodder or feeding stuffs for animals, birds or fish;*
> *(c) controlled drugs within the meaning of the Misuse of Drugs Act 1971; or*
> *(d) subject to such exceptions as may be specified in an order made by the Ministers –*
> > *(i) medicinal products within the meaning of the Medicines Act 1968 in respect of which product licences within the meaning of that Act are for the time being in force; or*

> (ii) *other articles or substances in respect of which such licences are for the time being in force in pursuance of orders under section 104 or 105 of that Act (application of Act to other articles and substances).*

Food clearly covers drink – including bottled mineral water. However, tap water is outside the scope of the 1990 Act (it is covered by the Water Act 1989). Not all the provisions of the 1990 Act are concerned with 'food' as defined in s. 1 - e.g. s. 13. Equally, regulations made under s. 16 in respect of food, 'food sources' (see s. 1(3)) and 'contact materials' cover aspects broader than 'food' itself.

'Food source' is defined in s. 1(3) as 'any growing crop or live animal, bird or fish from which food is intended to be derived (whether by harvesting, slaughtering, milking, collecting eggs or otherwise)'. This position broadens the scope of the legislation to incorporate within the regulatory regime aspects of the 'food chain' not previously covered, e.g. live cattle infected with BSE. The extension of the legislation to incorporate 'contact materials' brings the UK into line with EC legislation on materials and articles which come into contact with food (EC Directive 76/893/EEC) .

The Act applies to food businesses. A food business is defined by s. 1(3) of the Act:

> *'food business' means any business in the course of which commercial operations with respect to food or food sources are carried out.*

In this context s. 1(3) further provides that

> *'business' includes the undertaking of a canteen, club, school, hospital or institution, whether carried on for profit or not, and any undertaking or activity carried on by a public or local authority;*
> *'commercial operation', in relation to any food or contact material, means any of the following, namely –*
> (a) *selling, possessing for sale and offering, exposing or advertising for sale;*
> (b) *consigning, delivering or serving by way of sale;*
> (c) *preparing for sale or presenting, labelling or wrapping for the purpose of sale;*
> (d) *storing or transporting for the purpose of sale;*
> (e) *importing and exporting;*
> *and, in relation to any food source, means deriving food from it for the purpose of sale or for purposes connected with sale.*

It would appear that the broad-based definitions used in s. 1(3) bring within the scope of the Act any type of business, profit making or otherwise, involved at any stage of the food chain.

Many of the offences created by the 1990 Act are committed when food is sold for human consumption; these include:
*   selling food which fails to comply with the safety requirements – s. 8;
*   selling food not of the nature, quality or substance demanded by the purchaser – s. 14;
*   selling food with a false or misleading description – s. 15.

In addition, the statutory powers of inspection, seizure and condemnation of food (see s. 9) arise where food is sold. However, an offence may also be committed by the doing of specified actions preparatory to selling the food:

- offering or exposing the food for sale – see ss. 8, 9 and 15;
- advertising the food for sale – see s. 8;
- possessing the food for the purposes of sale – see ss. 8, 9 and 15;
- possessing food for preparation for sale – see ss. 8 and 9;
- consigning the food or depositing it with another person for the purposes of sale – see ss. 8 and 9

Section 2 of the Act sets out the extended meaning of 'sale' for the purposes of the Act:

> (1) For the purposes of this Act –
>   (a) the supply of food, otherwise than on sale, in the course of a business; and
>   (b) any other thing which is done with respect to food and is specified in an order made by the Ministers,
>   shall be deemed to be a sale of the food, and references to purchasers and purchasing shall be construed accordingly.
> (2) This Act shall apply –
>   (a) in relation to any food which is offered as a prize or reward or given away in connection with any entertainment to which the public are admitted, whether on payment of money or not, as if the food were, or had been, exposed for sale by each person concerned in the organisation of the entertainment;
>   (b) in relation to any food which, for the purpose of advertisement or in furtherance of any trade or business, is offered as a prize or reward or given away, as if the food were, or had been, exposed for sale by the person offering or giving away the food; and
>   (c) in relation to any food which is exposed or deposited in any premises for the purpose of being so offered or given away as mentioned in paragraph (a) or (b) above, as if the food were, or had been, exposed for sale by the occupier of the premises;
>   and in this subsection 'entertainment' includes any social gathering, amusement, exhibition, performance, game, sport or trial of skill.

Sale is given a very broad meaning by the Act. When the definition of 'business' (see s. 1(3)) is considered alongside 'sale', the supply of a meal to a patient in a hospital, a child at a school or a worker at a canteen are all brought within the Act, even where the circumstances may not at first appear to be a sale of food.

Where the Act creates offences or enforcement powers in the event of a sale or some act preparatory to the sale of food, the sale in question must generally be a sale for human consumption. Section 3 of the Act creates a presumption that food which is commonly used for human consumption is sold, or prepared for sale, for human consumption.

Section 3 provides:

> (1) The following provisions shall apply for the purposes of this Act.
> (2) Any food commonly used for human consumption shall, if sold or offered, exposed or kept for sale, be presumed, until the contrary is proved, to have been

> sold or, as the case may be, to have been or to be intended for sale for human
> consumption.
>
> (3) The following, namely –
>   (a) any food commonly used for human consumption which is found on
>   premises used for the preparation, storage, or sale of that food; and
>   (b) any article or substance commonly used in the manufacture of food for
>   human consumption which is found on premises used for the preparation,
>   storage or sale of that food,
>   shall be presumed, until the contrary is proved, to be intended for sale, or for
>   manufacturing food for sale, for human consumption.
>
> (4) Any article or substance capable of being used in the composition or preparation
>   of any food commonly used for human consumption which is found on premises
>   on which that food is prepared shall, until the contrary is proved, be presumed to
>   be intended for such use.

The presumption created by s. 3 can be rebutted by evidence, but it will be for the
defendant who is charged with the offence to call evidence to satisfy the court and
thereby displace the presumption.

Food safety

The main provisions of the Act concerned with food safety are to be found in ss. 7–13
as well as in the Regulations made under ss. 16 and 26. Section 7 makes it an offence to
render food injurious to health; s. 8 creates a series of offences which apply to the sale
of food which fails to comply with a 'food safety requirement'. Sections 9–13 contain
administrative and enforcement powers to be exercised by food authority enforcement
officers. Section 9 provides a power for enforcement officers to inspect and seize food
which fails to comply with safety requirements. Sections 10 and 11 provide powers
for enforcement officers to serve improvement notices and to apply to the court for prohibition orders where certain regulations have been breached. Section 12 provides for
emergency prohibition notices and the process of application for emergency prohibition
orders. The minister is given power by s. 13 to make emergency control orders in respect
of any commercial operations involving imminent risk of injury to health.

The issue of 'injury to health' is central to the food safety provisions contained in
ss. 7–13 and the regulations made under ss. 16 and 26. It is fundamental to the offence
set out in ss. 7 and 8 that the food is injurious to health and therefore fails to comply
with the food safety requirements, which in turn triggers the enforcement powers set
out in ss. 9–13 of the Act. 'Injury to health' is defined in s. 7(3) as 'any impairment,
whether permanent or temporary'.

Section 7(2) provides:

> In determining for the purposes of this section and section 8(2) below whether any
> food is injurious to health, regard shall be had –
> (a) not only to the probable effect of that food on health of a person consuming it;
>   but
> (b) also to the probable cumulative effect of food of substantially the same
>   composition on the health of a person consuming it in ordinary quantities.

This definition focuses attention not only on the immediate effects of the food but also on the long-term effect of consuming similar food. It reflects existing case law and covers illnesses such as food allergies, heart disease and dental deterioration referrable to 'food' consumed by the sufferer.

Section 7 creates a specific offence of rendering food injurious to health. Section 7(1) provides:

> (1) *Any person who renders any food injurious to health by means of any of the following operations, namely –*
>
> (a) *adding any article or substance to the food;*
> (b) *using any article or substance as an ingredient in the preparation of the food;*
> (c) *abstracting any constituent from the food; and*
> (d) *subjecting the food to any other process or treatment,*
>
> *with intent that it shall be sold for human consumption, shall be guilty of an offence.*

This offence addresses concerns about the processes and treatments through which food is put as part of the cycle of production. Examples include the use of chemicals to treat and preserve fruit and vegetables. Where food producers are prosecuted under s. 7(1) they may of course seek to rely on the 'due diligence' defence to avoid liability – see s. 21 (p. 212). Section 7(1) creates an offence of 'strict liability' in so far as it may be committed in circumstances where the defendant had no intention to render the food injurious to health, nor was he or she reckless as to whether his or her actions rendered the food injurious to health. In the illustration given above, where a food producer adds chemicals to fruit in order to preserve them, the offence under s. 7(1) is committed even where the chemicals used by the food producer were not known by the food producer to be injurious to health; again, reliance may be placed on the due diligence defence to seek to escape liability.

Section 7(1) appears to have one major gap: whilst an offence is committed by adding or subtracting things from food and by subjecting the food to a treatment or process, an offence cannot be committed by omission, i.e. by failing to subject the food to a necessary process or treatment. A failure to treat a 'food' effectively cannot give rise to liability under s. 7(1). The sale of food which does not comply with the food safety requirements is an offence under s. 8 and may be committed where the failure to treat the 'food' gives rise to a breach of the food safety requirements. A person convicted on indictment of an offence under s. 7 may be sentenced to up to two years' imprisonment and/or an unlimited fine. Where he or she is convicted summarily in the Magistrates' Court the maximum penalty is a £20 000 fine and/or a period of up to six months' imprisonment – see s. 35.

The sale of food which does not comply with the food safety requirements

Section 8 establishes a food safety requirement and creates a series of offences concerning the sale of food which fails to meet those requirements. It is important to understand that the Act does not impose a general safety standard for all food; it does, however, create a number of offences.

Sections 8(1), (2) and (3) provide:

(1) Any person who –
   (a) sells for human consumption, or offers, exposes or advertises for sale for such consumption or has in his possession for the purpose of such sale or of preparation for such sale; or
   (b) deposits with, or consigns to, any other person for the purpose of such sale or of preparation for such sale,
   any food which fails to comply with food safety requirements shall be guilty of an offence.

(2) For the purposes of this Part food fails to comply with food safety requirements if –
   (a) it has been rendered injurious to health by means of any of the operations mentioned in section 7(1) above;
   (b) it is unfit for human consumption; or
   (c) it is so contaminated (whether by extraneous matter or otherwise) that it would no be reasonable to expect it to be used for human consumption in that state;
   and references to such requirements or to food complying with such requirements shall be construed accordingly.

(3) Where any food which fails to comply with food safety requirements is part of a batch, lot or consignment of food of the same class or description, it shall be presumed for the purposes of this section and section 9 below, until the contrary is proved, that all of the food in that batch, lot or consignment, fails to comply with those requirements.

The presumption set out in section 3, that food commonly used for human consumption is intended for sale for human consumption, applies to offences created by section 8.

The offence of selling food unfit for human consumption is an absolute offence. This has been established for many years under previous legislation. The leading case is *Hobbs* v. *Winchester Corporation*.

HOBBS v. WINCHESTER CORPORATION [1910] 2 KB 471

Hobbs, a butcher, had meat confiscated under a previous Act which contained a provision similar to s. 8 FSA 1990. The meat was analysed and found to be unfit for human consumption, although Hobbs did not know that it was unfit nor would he have been able to find out by the means available to him. Hobbs sought compensation for the confiscated meat, arguing that since he had not known of the defect in the meat and since he could not have found it out, he was innocent of an offence and the meat improperly confiscated.

Held: Hobbs was found to be guilty as charged, albeit that the impurity was unknown to him and could not have been found out by him. Compensation was not payable.

Hobbs's case establishes an important principle, namely that persons may be criminally liable if, without knowledge of its condition, they sell food which is in fact unfit for human consumption. Section 8 therefore requires neither intention nor knowledge on the part of the defendant. Section 8 may therefore be described as an 'absolute offence', requiring only the most limited mental element, if any. Why does the law impose such liability? The policy behind the courts' thinking may be seen in Kennedy LJ's statement in *Hobbs*'s case:

if a man chooses for profit to engage in a business which involves the offering for sale of that which may be deadly or injurious to health he must take that risk; it is not a sufficient defence for anyone who chooses to embark on such a business to say 'I could not have discovered the disease unless I had an analyst on the premises.' He has chosen to engage in that which on the face of it may be a dangerous business and he must do so at his own risk.

The courts therefore impose absolute liability to ensure, so far as is possible, that people in the business of food processing and sale comply with the requisite standards.

An offence may be committed under s. 8 even though the item sold is not food at all, provided that the item was sold as food.

MEAH v. ROBERTS
[1978] 1 All ER 97 (QBD)

L was employed as a fitter by a firm which installed draught beer and lager equipment in licensed premises. L visited an Indian restaurant and cleaned the pipes of the equipment using caustic soda. L tried to explain the cleaning process to a waiter at the restaurant (who understood very little English). L placed the remaining caustic soda in an empty lemonade bottle, wrote 'cleaner' on the bottle and placed it under the bar counter. Bottles of lemonade for service to customers were also stored under the bar. L did not tell any member of the restaurant staff that he had placed the caustic soda under the bar; nor did he explain the cleaning procedure to M, the restaurant manager.

S, a customer, ordered food and drink at the restaurant, including glasses of lemonade for his children. By mistake the drinks served to the children were caustic soda from the lemonade bottle marked 'cleaner'. The children became ill as a result of drinking the caustic soda. M was charged under s. 2 and s. 8 FDA 1955. He invoked the 'third party defence' under s. 113(1) FDA 1955, namely that the offence had occurred through the act or default of L. M and L were both convicted of offences under s. 2 and s. 8 FDA 1955. They appealed to the Queen's Bench Divisional Court, contending that there had been no sale of 'food' within s. 2(1) or s. 8(1)(a), since caustic soda was not a food.

Held: The appeals were dismissed. The expression 'sells . . . any food' in ss. 2(1) and 8(1)(a) of the 1955 Act meant the supply, under an agreement to sell food, or something purporting to be the food demanded by the purchaser. The fact that the article supplied was wholly different from the article demanded did not prevent there being a sale of the article demanded for the purposes of ss. 2 and 8 FDA 1955. Therefore the sale to S of caustic soda in pursuance of the sale of lemonade to him amounted to a sale of food within the scope of ss. 2(1) and 8(1) FDA 195.

The 'food safety requirement' which forms the essence of the s. 8 offence is set out in s. 8(2) (see above), and the failure to satisfy the food safety requirement activates the powers of inspection and seizure contained in s. 9. Section 8(3) (see above) is also of practical importance to the operation of the powers of inspection and seizure.

The scope of the s. 8 offence is broader than provisions under the 1955 and 1984 Acts in that it now covers the possession of food for the purposes of preparation for sale and depositing food with or consigning food to another. The offence of sale, possession, deposit or consignment of contaminated food under s. 8 of the 1990 Act is a completely new offence.

For s. 8 liability to be established it must be proven by the prosecution that the food has been rendered injurious to health by one of the means contained in s. 7.

The concept of food being 'unfit for human consumption' is derived from previous legislation and decided cases. The question of whether or not food is unfit for human consumption is primarily a question of fact. The question to a large extent is not capable of prescriptive definition and turns on the facts of each particular case. When an article of food is mouldy, *prima facie* it is 'unfit'; however, the matter is one of degree.

DAVID GREIG LTD v. GOLDFINCH [1961] 59 LGR 304 (QBD)	A pork pie was purchased on a Saturday from the defendants' store. The pie had been baked by the defendants four days previously. The purchaser cut into the pie later on Saturday and found mould under the pie crust. A small amount of mould had been present at the time the pie was purchased.

Held: 'Unfit' means something more than unsuitable for consumption. The prosecution should normally adduce evidence that the food would be injurious or dangerous to health. However, the word 'unfit' should be looked at in a broad sense; therefore it is a question of degree in each case whether the food is 'unfit'. Moreover, 'unfit' should not be confined to the situation where the food would cause injury to health.

On the facts of the case the Divisional Court accepted that such a mould would not normally cause illness. However, it found the pie to be unfit for human consumption.

R. v. SOUTHAMPTON JUSTICES *Ex Parte* BARROW LINE & BALLARD LTD (*The Times*, 22 July 1983 (QBD))	Southampton justices ordered the destruction of 46 000 kg of dates shipped to the port from Iraq. The dates were to be used in the manufacture of brown sauce. The sample of dates analysed by the port health authority were found to contain insect extracts, dead larvae, etc., and had undergone infestation to such an extent that they were clearly unwholesome for human consumption. However, on the evidence, the dates were perfectly usable for the manufacture of brown sauce.

Woolf J took the view that where food has more than one normal use and normally underwent different processes according to the intended use, it may be regarded as unwholesome and be destroyed by the authorized body if it was unwholesome for one of its normal uses.

Although this case relates to importation controls placed upon food cargoes it is an illustration of the standards applied before food can be considered unfit for human consumption. The dates in this case were fit, although they were not wholesome. In other words, a prosecution under s. 8 FDA 1955 (new s. 8 FA 1984) would not be possible if the dates were thereafter consigned for sale for human consumption.

Where extraneous matter is present in a food product this may render a seller liable under s. 14 FSA 1990 for selling food not of the quality demanded by the purchaser. Equally, a seller may be liable under section 8 if the presence of extraneous matter renders the food unfit for human consumption. This will not be so in every case, since extraneous matter does not necessarily render the food unfit. In *J. Miller Ltd* v. *Battersea Borough Council* [1956] 1 QB 43 the presence of a small piece of metal in a cake rendered the defendant company liable under s. 2(1) of what was then the FDA 1955 (equivalent to s. 14 FSA 1990) though not for an offence of selling food unfit for human consumption.

In *Barton* v. *Unigate Dairies Ltd* [1987] Crim. LR 121 (QBD), the Divisional Court considered *Miller*'s case to be limited to its own particular facts. In this case the respondents were charged with two offences contrary to what was s. 8(1)b FA 1984 in that they had failed to ensure that bottles of milk were fit for human consumption. One bottle contained a dead mouse and the other a piece of glass. Before the magistrates it was contested by the respondents that there was no case to answer; the informations should have alleged an offence under what was s. 2(1) FA 1984. The magistrates upheld the submission. The prosecutor appealed to the Divisional Court.

The Divisional Court, allowing the prosecutor's appeal, took the view that *Miller*'s case was confined to the particular circumstances where there was no evidence to show that the product was unfit for human consumption. It was not authority for the proposition that, if unfitness for human consumption was proved but was caused by the presence of some added substance as opposed to the natural processes of decay or putrefaction, the prosecution must proceed under s. 2.

A further form of failure to satisfy the food safety requirements is where the food is contaminated. This is a completely new provision. It would of course cover situations such as that which occurred in *Miller* v. *Battersea Borough Council* (above). The section is more broadly based than the facts disclosed by that decision, and seeks to cover all forms of contamination, not just through the pressure of extraneous matter.

A person charged with an offence under s. 8 may rely on the 'due diligence' defence – see s. 21, which is explained on p. 212. The same penalties apply to this section as those which pertain to s. 7 above.

Inspection and seizure

By virtue of s. 9 the authorized officer of the enforcement authority has power to inspect food and, if it is unsafe, either to serve a notice preventing its sale for human consumption or removal, or to take the food immediately before a magistrate in order to obtain an order for its destruction. Where a notice is served, the enforcement officer effectively buys time in order to decide if the food in question does satisfy food safety requirements or if it is necessary to seek a destruction order. Section 9 provides:

> *(1) An authorised officer of a food authority may at all reasonable times inspect any food intended for human consumption which –*
>   *(a) has been sold or is offered or exposed for sale; or*
>   *(b) is in the possession of, or has been deposited with or consigned to, any person for the purpose of sale or of preparation for sale;*
>   *and subsections (3) to (9) below shall apply where, on such an inspection, it appears to the authorised officer that any food fails to comply with food safety requirements.*
>
> *(2) The following provisions shall also apply where, otherwise than on such an inspection, it appears to an authorised officer of a food authority that any food is likely to cause food poisoning or any disease communicable to human beings.*
>
> *(3) The authorised officer may either –*
>   *(a) give notice to the person in charge of the food that, until the notice is withdrawn, the food or any specified portion of it –*
>   *(i) is not to be used for human consumption; and*
>   *(ii) either is not to be removed or is not to be removed except to some place specified in the notice; or*
>   *(b) seize the food and remove it in order to have it dealt with by a justice of the peace;*
>   *and any person who knowingly contravenes the requirements of a notice under paragraph (a) above shall be guilty of an offence.*

(4) *Where the authorised officer exercises the powers conferred by subsection (3)(a) above, he shall, as soon as is reasonably practicable and in any event within 21 days, determine whether or not he is satisfied that the food complies with food safety requirements and –*

    (a) *if he is so satisfied, shall forthwith withdraw the notice;*

    (b) *if he is not so satisfied, shall seize the food and remove it in order to have it dealt with by a justice of the peace.*

(5) *Where an authorised officer exercises the powers conferred by subsection (3)(b) or (4)(b) above, he shall inform the person in charge of the food of his intention to have it dealt with by a justice of the peace and –*

    (a) *any person who under section 7 or 8 above might be liable to a prosecution in respect of the food shall, if he attends before the justice of the peace by whom the food falls to be dealt with, be entitled to be heard and to call witnesses; and*

    (b) *that justice of the peace may, but need not, be a member of the court before which any person is charged with an offence under that section in relation to that food.*

(6) *If it appears to a justice of the peace, on the basis of such evidence as he considers appropriate in the circumstances, that any food falling to be dealt with by him under this section fails to comply with food safety requirements, he shall condemn the food and order –*

    (a) *the food to be destroyed or to be so disposed of as to prevent it from being used for human consumption; and*

    (b) *any expenses reasonably incurred in connection with the destruction or disposal to be defrayed by the owner of the food.*

(7) *If a notice under subsection (3)(a) above is withdrawn, or the justice of the peace by whom any food falls to be dealt with under this section refuses to condemn it, the food authority shall compensate the owner of the food for any depreciation in its value resulting from the action taken by the authorised officer.*

(8) *Any disputed question as to the right to or the amount of any compensation payable under subsection (7) above shall be determined by arbitration.*

The enforcement officer may inspect any food intended for human consumption which is sold, offered or exposed for sale or possessed by, deposited with or consigned to any person for the purpose of sale or preparation for sale. This power of inspection may be exercised at any reasonable time. Section 9 does not provide a power to inspect premises nor any process undertaken on the premises.

If on inspection the food appears to the enforcement officer not to satisfy the food safety requirements set out in s. 8 the officer may utilize the powers to serve a notice or seize the food. For the purposes of s. 9, food fails to satisfy the food safety requirements if it fails to comply with regulations made pursuant to Part II of the Act – see s. 26(1)b.

Section 9(2) may cause difficulties since the power to serve notices and seize food arises under this section where 'it appears ... that any food is likely to cause food poisoning'. There is a lack of definition of what amounts to 'food poisoning', which can be construed in a strict technical sense or more broadly as food-borne infection.

Section 9 gives the enforcement officer the power either to serve a notice restricting the movement or sale of food or to seize it immediately. It is an offence under s. 35(2) knowingly to contravene the requirements of a notice made under s. 9(3).

The service of a notice under s. 9 gives the enforcement officer time to determine whether the food satisfies food safety requirements; if satisfied that the food does comply with food safety requirements, the officer must withdraw the notice (s. 9(4)(a)); compensation is then payable in respect of any depreciation in the value of the food (s. 9(7)). If the officer is not satisfied that the food complies with food safety requirements, the officer may seize the food in order to have it dealt with by a magistrate. The officer must make a decision as soon as is reasonably practicable and in any event within 21 days. During that time the food is likely to be subjected to analysis and tests using the powers under ss. 29–30.

Where food is seized:

(a) following inspection – see s. 9(1);

(b) where it appears likely to cause food poisoning, etc. – see s. 9(2);

(c) following service of a notice – see s. 9(4);

the officer must notify the person in charge of the food of his or her intention to have it dealt with by a magistrate. Any person who might be liable to prosecution for an offence under ss. 7 or 8 of the Act in respect of that food may then appear before the magistrate, and be heard and call witnesses (s. 9(5)); at such a hearing he or she might explain that it was intended that the food should undergo further processing to make it safe. The magistrate may hear 'such evidence as he considers appropriate in the circumstances'. If the magistrate decides that the food fails to comply with food safety requirements, the magistrate must condemn the food and order it to be disposed of so as to prevent its use for human consumption; in that case the magistrate must order that any expenses reasonably incurred in connection with the destruction of the food be met by the owner of the food (s. 9(6)). Where food which fails to comply with food safety requirements forms part of a lot, batch or consignment, the presumption in s. 8(3) applies, and the whole of the relevant lot, batch or consignment is presumed not to comply. Thus a destruction order could apply to the whole lot, batch or consignment. However, if the magistrate refuses to condemn the food, compensation is payable to the owner in respect of any depreciation in its value (s. 9(7)).

Section 9 contains powers exercisable only with regard to unsafe food. Sections 10, 11 and 12 contain powers of enforcement available in a broader range of circumstances.

Section 10 facilitates enforcement officers ensuring compliance with regulations made with regard to food safety and hygiene pursuant to s. 16. Section 10 provides:

(1) If an authorised officer of an enforcement authority has reasonable grounds for believing that the proprietor of a food business is failing to comply with any regulations to which this section applies, he may, by a notice served on that proprietor (in this Act referred to as an 'improvement notice') –

(a) state the officer's grounds for believing that the proprietor is failing to comply with the regulations;

(b) specify the matters which constitute the proprietor's failure so to comply;

(c) specify the measures which, in the officer's opinion, the proprietor must take in order to secure compliance; and

(d) require the proprietor to take those measures, or measures which are at least equivalent to them, within such period (not being less than 14 days) as may be specified in the notice.

(2) Any person who fails to comply with an improvement notice shall be guilty of an offence.

(3) *This section and section 11 below apply to any regulations under this Part which make provision –*
    (a) *for requiring, prohibiting or regulating the use of any process or treatment in the preparation of food; or*
    (b) *for securing the observance of hygienic conditions and practices in connection with the carrying out of commercial operations with respect to food or food sources.*

Section 11 contains additional powers available in the event of contravention of food process or hygiene regulations. By virtue of this section, where a proprietor of a food business is convicted of an offence under the above regulations, the court has the power in certain circumstances to make orders prohibiting the use of a specified process or treatment, or of premises or equipment, for the purposes of a food business, and to prohibit the involvement of the convicted person in the management of a food business. These are more far-reaching and effective powers than contained in previous legislation.

Section 11 provides:

(1) *If –*
    (a) *the proprietor of a food business is convicted of an offence under any regulations to which this section applies; and*
    (b) *the court by or before which he is so convicted is satisfied that the health risk condition is fulfilled with respect to that business,*
    the court shall by an order impose the appropriate prohibition.
(2) *The health risk condition is fulfilled with respect to any food business if any of the following involves risk of injury to health, namely –*
    (a) *the use for the purposes of the business of any process or treatment;*
    (b) *the construction of any premises used for the purposes of the business, or the use for those purposes of any equipment; and*
    (c) *the state or condition of any premises or equipment used for the purposes of the business.*
(3) *The appropriate prohibition is –*
    (a) *in a case falling within paragraph (a) of subsection (2) above, a prohibition on the use of the process or treatment for the purposes of the business;*
    (b) *in a case falling within paragraph (b) of that subsection, a prohibition on the use of the premises or equipment for the purposes of the business or any other food business of the same class or description;*
    (c) *in a case falling within paragraph (c) of that subsection, a prohibition on the use of the premises or equipment for the purposes of any food business.*
(4) *If –*
    (a) *the proprietor of a food business is convicted of an offence under any regulations to which this section applies by virtue of s. 10(3)(b) above;*
    and
    (b) *the court by or before which he is so convicted thinks it proper to do so in all the circumstances of the case,*
    the court may, by an order, impose a prohibition on the proprietor participating in the management of any food business, or any food business of a class or description specified in the order.
(5) *As soon as practicable after the making of an order under subsection (1) or (4)*

above *(in this Act referred to as a 'prohibition order'), the enforcement authority shall –*

(a) *serve a copy of the order on the proprietor of the business; and*

(b) *in the case of an order under subsection (1) above, affix a copy of the order in a conspicuous position on such premises used for the purposes of the business as they consider appropriate;*

and any person who knowingly contravenes such an order shall be guilty of an offence.

(6) *A prohibition order shall cease to have effect –*

(a) *in the case of an order under subsection (1) above, on the issue by the enforcement authority of a certificate to the effect that they are satisfied that the proprietor has taken sufficient measures to secure that the health risk condition is no longer fulfilled with respect to the business;*

(b) *in the case of an order under subsection (4) above, on the giving by the court of a direction to that effect.*

(7) *The enforcement authority shall issue a certificate under paragraph (a) of subsection (6) above within three days of their being satisfied as mentioned in that paragraph; and on an application by the proprietor for such a certificate, the authority shall –*

(a) *determine, as soon as is reasonably practicable and in any event within 14 days, whether or not they are so satisfied; and*

(b) *if they determine that they are not so satisfied, give notice to the proprietor of the reasons for that determination.*

(8) *The court shall give a direction under subsection (6)(b) above if, on an application by the proprietor, the court thinks it proper to do so having regard to all the circumstances of the case, including in particular the conduct of the proprietor since the making of the order; but no such application shall be entertained if it is made –*

(a) *within six months after the making of the prohibition order; or*

(b) *within three months after the making by the proprietor of a previous application for such a direction.*

(9) *Where a magistrates' court or, in Scotland, the sheriff makes an order under s. 12(2) below with respect to any food business, subsection (1) above shall apply as if the proprietor of the business had been convicted by the court or sheriff of an offence under regulations to which this section applies.*

(10) *Subsection (4) above, shall apply in relation to a manager of a food business as it applies in relation to the proprietor of such a business; and any reference in subsection (5) or (8) above to the proprietor of the business, or to the proprietor, shall be construed accordingly.*

(11) *In subsection (10) above 'manager', in relation to a food business, means any person who is entrusted by the proprietor with the day to day running of the business, or any part of the business.*

In situations where there is an immediate risk to public health, that action must be taken as a matter of urgency. Sections 12 and 13 provide powers for the taking of such emergency action. Section 12 enables an enforcement officer who has been duly authorized to do so, to take urgent action against an individual food business proprietor by serving emergency prohibition notices or applying to the court for emergency prohibition orders.

Section 12 provides:

(1) *If an authorised officer of an enforcement authority is satisfied that the health risk condition is fulfilled with respect to any food business, he may, by a notice served on the proprietor of the business (in this Act referred to as an 'emergency prohibition notice'), impose the appropriate prohibition.*

(2) *If a magistrates' court or, in Scotland, the sheriff is satisfied, on the application of such an officer, that the health risk condition is fulfilled with respect to any food business, the court or sheriff shall, by an order (in this Act referred to as an 'emergency prohibition order'), impose the appropriate prohibition.*

(3) *Such an officer shall not apply for an emergency prohibition order unless, at least one day before the date of the application, he has served notice on the proprietor of the business of his intention to apply for the order.*

(4) *Subsections (2) and (3) of section 11 above shall apply for the purposes of this section as they apply for the purposes of that section, but as if the reference in subsection (2) to risk of injury to health were a reference to imminent risk of such injury.*

(5) *As soon as practicable after the service of an emergency prohibition notice, the enforcement authority shall affix a copy of the notice in a conspicuous position on such premises used for the purposes of the business as they consider appropriate; and any person who knowingly contravenes such a notice shall be guilty of an offence.*

(6) *As soon as practicable after the making of an emergency prohibition order, the enforcement authority shall –*
   (a) *serve a copy of the order on the proprietor of the business; and*
   (b) *affix a copy of the order in a conspicuous position on such premises used for the purposes of that business as they consider appropriate; and any person who knowingly contravenes such an order shall be guilty of an offence.*

(7) *An emergency prohibition notice shall cease to have effect –*
   (a) *if no application for an emergency prohibition order is made within the period of three days beginning with the service of the notice, at the end of that period;*
   (b) *if such an application is so made, on the determination or abandonment of the application.*

(8) *An emergency prohibition notice or emergency prohibition order shall cease to have effect on the issue by the enforcement authority of a certificate to the effect that they are satisfied that the proprietor has taken sufficient measures to secure that the health risk condition is no longer fulfilled with respect to the business.*

(9) *The enforcement authority shall issue a certificate under subsection (8) above within three days of their being satisfied as mentioned in that subsection; and on an application by the proprietor for such a certificate, the authority shall –*
   (a) *determine, as soon as is reasonably practicable and in any event within 14 days, whether or not they are so satisfied; and*
   (b) *if they determine that they are not so satisfied, give notice to the proprietor of the reasons for that determination.*

(10) *Where an emergency prohibition notice is served on the proprietor of a business, the enforcement authority shall compensate him in respect of any loss suffered by reason of his complying with the notice unless –*

(a)   an application for an emergency prohibition order is made within the period
      of three days beginning with the service of the notice; and
(b)   the court declares itself satisfied, on the hearing of the application, that the
      health risk condition was fulfilled with respect to the business at the time
      when the notice was served;
and any disputed question as to the right to or the amount of any compensation
payable under this subsection shall be determined by arbitration or, in Scotland,
by a single arbiter appointed, failing agreement between the parties, by the
sheriff.

Section 13, in contrast to s. 12, allows the Minister to take emergency action affecting
a range of businesses, or a whole class of businesses where there is a widespread and
immediate risk to health. Section 13 provides:

(1)   If it appears to the Minister that the carrying out of commercial operations with
      respect to food, food sources or contact materials of any class or description
      involves or may involve imminent risk of injury to health, he may, by an order
      (in this Act referred to as an 'emergency control order'), prohibit the carrying
      out of such operations with respect to food, food sources or contact materials of
      that class or description.
(2)   Any person who knowingly contravenes an emergency control order shall be
      guilty of an offence.
(3)   The Minister may consent, either unconditionally or subject to any condition that
      he considers appropriate, to the doing in a particular case of anything prohibited
      by an emergency control order.
(4)   It shall be a defence for a person charged with an offence under subsection (2)
      above to show –
      (a)   that consent had been given under subsection (3) above to the contraven-
            tion of the emergency control order; and
      (b)   that any condition subject to which that consent was given was complied
            with.
(5)   The Minister –
      (a)   may give such directions as appear to him to be necessary or expedient for
            the purpose of preventing the carrying out of commercial operations with
            respect to any food, food sources or contact materials which he believes, on
            reasonable grounds, to be food, food sources or contact materials to which
            an emergency control order applies; and
      (b)   may do anything which appears to him to be necessary or expedient for that
            purpose.
(6)   Any person who fails to comply with a direction under this section shall be guilty
      of an offence.
(7)   If the Minister does anything by virtue of this section in consequence of any
      person failing to comply with an emergency control order or a direction under
      this section, the Minister may recover from that person any expenses reasonably
      incurred by him under this section.

Protecting the consumer

Sections 14 and 15 of the FSA 1990 seek to protect the consumer from unconscionable practices. Section 14 makes it an offence to sell food not of the nature, substance or quality demanded, whilst s. 15 makes it an offence falsely or misleadingly to describe, advertise or present food. The consumer is also protected outside the 1990 Act by the Labelling of Food Regulations 1984 (SI 1984/1305). These Regulations contain restrictions upon the presentation of food. They also prescribe the basic information that must be given with the food. The information required includes a list of ingredients, an indication of minimum durability, any specific storage conditions, the name and address of the manufacturer, packer or seller.

Section 14 provides:

> (1) *Any person who sells to the purchaser's prejudice any food which is not of the nature or substance or quality demanded by the purchaser shall be guilty of an offence.*
>
> (2) *In subsection (1) above the reference to sale shall be construed as a reference to sale for human consumption; and in proceedings under that subsection it shall not be a defence that the purchaser was not prejudiced because he bought for analysis or examination.*

This section mirrors the previous provision in s. 2 of the Food Act 1984. The section requires that the offence is committed by a 'person'. This can be an individual or a corporate entity. In normal circumstances, the sale of the food will be conducted by a junior employee. This person could of course be prosecuted, but the authorities will want to prosecute either the manager or proprietor, or the business entity itself. A case which illustrates the liability of a company for the actions of its counter staff is *Booth v. Helliwell* [1914] 3 KB 252. An employer will not always be liable for the actions of its employees, notably when the employee has acted outside the scope of his or her employment

The sale of the food must be for human consumption, and the prosecution must prove that the purchaser of the food was prejudiced. Purchasers are not prejudiced if the seller clearly brings to their notice that fact that the article is not of the nature, substance or quality which the purchaser demands.

PRESTON v. GRANT [1925] 1 KB 177 (KB) *per* Hewart LCJ	Where a sale has taken place of an article of food which is not of the nature, substance or quality demanded, the presumption that the purchaser has been prejudiced is not rebutted by proof of the existence of a notice which he did not see and to which his attention was not called.

This view admits the possibility that such a notice may, if sufficiently drawn to the purchaser's attention, constitute a defence. Salter J in the same case opined:

> *Where, as here, the seller relies on written notice, he must prove that notice of any circumstances which he was required to make known was in fact conveyed to the purchaser. He must prove that the purchaser understood the notice. If the notice was conspicuous, the justices would be more likely to hold that the purchaser saw it, but here they have found as a fact that he did not see it, and for that reason the defence fails.*

It can be said, therefore, that a clear notice (or label attached to the food product) which informs the purchaser of the true nature, quality and substance of the article may amount to a defence.

Of what standard must the food supplied be? Food is not of the *nature* demanded by the purchaser if it is something different from that which is demanded by him – *Knight* v. *Bowers* (1855) 14 BD 845. Food is not of the *substance* demanded by the purchaser if it has been adulterated in some way and is therefore of a different composition. If food has been adulterated and is thereby rendered injurious to health, the proper course of action is to prosecute under ss. 7 or 8 FSA 1990 (above). However, if the process used upon the food does not render it injurious to health, a prosecution can be brought under s. 14(1) for the sale of food not of the substance demanded. 'Substance' will also cover the situation where the food does not meet the required standard set out for food of that type. However, not all food products are defined as being of a certain standard or as containing certain ingredients. The minister responsible may by virtue of ss. 16 and 26 FSA 1990 introduce regulations which set out the standard with which the food must comply. The sale of food which does not comply with the standard set out in the regulations may render the seller liable to prosecution under s. 14(1) FSA 1990. The courts will have to determine the appropriate standard in the light of the accepted commercial standards for food of that sort – *Tonkin* v. *Victor Value Ltd* [1962] 1 All ER 821. Food is not of the *quality* demanded by the purchaser if the food is not of the normal commercial quality for such a product. 'Quality' does not relate simply to the description or kind of product.

McDONALD'S HAMBURGERS LTD v WINDLE [1987] Crim. LR 200 (QBD)

McDonald's were convicted before the justices upon charges under what was s. 2(1)c FA 1984 with a selling food, namely Diet McDonald's Cola, which was not of the quality demanded by the purchaser.

McDonald's displayed at their restaurants a 'nutrition guide' which stated that a McDonald's Cola contained between 96 and 187 kilocalories per serving (depending on size). It also stated every size of 'Diet McDonald's Cola' contained less than 1 kilocalorie per serving. A sampling officer of the county council on two occasions sought to purchase Diet Cola but was supplied with ordinary McDonald's Cola.

The appellants appealed against their convictions. The Divisional Court dismissed the appeals, taking the view that offences under s. 2(1)c had been committed. The justices had been entitled to find as a matter of fact that the supply of ordinary Cola was a supply not of the quality demanded by the purchaser.

One further observation should be made with regard to the scope of s. 14(1). The words 'sells to the purchaser's prejudice any food' in s. 14(1) cover the situation where the defendant sells as food something which is not in fact food and this prejudices the purchaser. This point arose in the case of *Meah* v. *Roberts* [1978] 1 All ER 97 (QBD) (see p. 197).

Many of the cases brought under s. 14(1) FSA 1990 relate to food which contains some form of extraneous matter. In *Newton* v. *West Vale Creamery Co. Ltd* [1956] 120 JP 318, a fly was found in a bottle of milk. In *J. Miller Ltd* v. *Battersea Borough Council* [1956] 1 QB 43, a piece of metal was found in a cake. In *Smedleys Ltd* v. *Breed* [1974] AC 839 (HL), a caterpillar was present in a can of peas.

BARBER v.
CO-OPERATIVE
WHOLESALE SOCIETY
LTD [1983] Crim. LR 476
(QBD)

The prosecutor laid an information against the defendant company alleging an offence contrary to what was s. 2(1) FDA 1955, in that the defendants sold, to the prejudice of the purchaser, a bottle of milk which was not of the quality demanded by him, in that it contained a plastic straw. No evidence was adduced to show that the straw had infected the milk, or had otherwise affected it. The magistrates dismissed the charge, on the basis that evidence of the presence of the straw in the sealed bottle of milk was not itself sufficient to establish the offence charged. The prosecutor appealed to the Divisional Court by way of case stated.

Held: Allowing the prosecutor's appeal, an offence was committed contrary to s. 2(1) of what was the FDA 1955 if the quality of the food supplied was not that which the purchaser was, in all the circumstances of the case, entitled to expect. It is not necessary for the prosecution to prove that the presence of the extraneous matter was deleterious to the purchaser. All that need be proven is that the presence of the object would give rise to the consequence that a purchaser could reasonably object to its presence in the food.

Barber's case considers the principle to be found in *Newton* v. *West Vale Creamery Co. Ltd*, and *J. Miller Ltd* v. *Battersea Borough Council*. The presence of extraneous matter may render food 'not of the quality demanded by the purchaser', but will not inevitably do so. A common-sense approach seems to prevail. The presence of extraneous matter will render the food not of the quality or substance demanded by the purchaser only if a reasonable purchaser would object to its presence. Mere presence is not enough to prove a s. 14(1) offence; nor is it necessary, on the other hand, to show that its presence was deleterious to the purchaser.

The importance of extraneous matter in s. 14(1) FSA 1990 lies in the fact that the presence of the offending object renders the food 'not of the ... quality demanded'. The quality of the food is that which the purchaser demands, not necessarily a particular set standard. This point is one which was reinforced in *Barber* v. *Co-operative Wholesale Society Ltd*.

A food business may seek to rely on a defence to avoid liability for a s. 14(1) offence. Available defences are discussed on pp. 212–14.

Section 15 of the FSA 1990 creates an offence of falsely describing, advertising or presenting food. Section 15 provides:

> (1) Any person who gives with any food sold by him, or displays with any food offered or exposed by him for sale or in his possession for the purpose of sale, a label, whether or not attached to or printed on the wrapper or container, which –
> (a) falsely describes the food; or
> (b) is likely to mislead as to the nature or substance or quality of the food, shall be guilty of an offence.
> (2) Any person who publishes, or is a party to the publication of, an advertisement (not being such a label given or displayed by him as mentioned in subsection (1) above) which –
> (a) falsely describes any food; or
> (b) is likely to mislead as to the nature or substance or quality of any food, shall be guilty of an offence.

(3) *Any person who sells, or offers or exposes for sale, or has in his possession for the purpose of sale, any food the presentation of which is likely to mislead as to the nature or substance or quality of the food shall be guilty of an offence.*

(4) *In proceedings for an offence under subsection (1) or (2) above, the fact that a label or advertisement in respect of which the offence is alleged to have been committed contained an accurate statement of the composition of the food shall not preclude the court from finding that the offence was committed.*

(5) *In this section references to sale shall be construed as references to sale or human consumption.*

This section is a partial re-enactment of s. 7 of the Food Act 1984; however, it creates a wholly new offence of falsely presenting food. Section 15(3) creates an offence aimed at those persons who through means other than advertisements and labelling mislead purchasers. Section 53(1) excludes from the definition of presentation, the use of labelling and advertising; therefore presentation covers shape, appearance, packaging, etc.

The penalties upon conviction for an offence under s. 14 are the same for those under ss. 7 and 8 above. For an offence under s. 15 the maximum fine upon summary trial is £2000.

Food regulations

Sections 16, 17, 18 and 19 FSA 1990 provide wide-ranging powers for ministers to make regulations. The extensive regulations made under the 1955 and 1984 Acts remain in force – see s. 59 and Schedule 4 to the 1990 Act. Section 16(1) provides authority for ministers to issue regulations under this section in respect of all matters set out in Schedule 1 to the Act, namely:

* composition of food;
* fitness, etc. of food;
* processing and treatment of food;
* food hygiene;
* inspection of food sources.

Section 16(2) FSA also gives Ministers powers to regulate 'contact materials', i.e. articles and substances which are intended to come into contact with food. Section 17 deals with compliance with the European Community food controls. Section 18 controls 'novel foods'; these include food products created by the use of advanced food technology, e.g. slimming foods, high-energy foods, etc. Milk is also regulated by means of powers set out in s. 18(2).

New powers are provided to require premises which are being used for the purpose of a food business (or which are intended to be used as a food business) to be registered with the enforcement authorities. Any premises which are not property registered can, by reason of s. 19, be prohibited from being used for a food business. The registration particulars are to be set out in regulations.

Typical of the type of regulations made by such delegated responsibility are the Food Safety (General Food Hygiene) Regulations 1995 and the Food Safety (Temperature Control) Regulations 1995. These are described here.

Food Safety Regulations 1995

The main food hygiene regulations of importance to the caterer are the Food Safety (General Food Hygiene) Regulations 1995 and the Food Safety (Temperature Control) Regulations 1995. These implemented the EC Food Hygiene Directive (93/43/EEC). They replaced a number of different sets of regulations including the Food Safety (General) Regulations 1970.

Food Safety (General Food Hygiene) Regulations 1995

These regulations apply to all food retailers, caterers, processors, manufacturers and distributors. Under these regulations the owners of food businesses which are not subject to food specific regulations (e.g. The Dairy Products (Hygiene) Regulations 1995) have to assess the hazards within their business, decide on critical controls, implement these and review them on a regular basis. The main requirements of the regulations cover:

Schedule I, Chapter I – Food Premises
Food Premises (I.1): must be cleaned and maintained in proper repair
Layout, design, construction and size (I.2): premises must be designed and built so that they permit good hygiene practices
Sanitary and handwashing facilities (I.3): have adequate handwashing facilities and toilets, not to connect directly with food rooms
Washbasins (I.4): there must be hot and cold running water and materials for drying hands. Where necessary separate facilities for washing food and hands must be provided
Ventilation (I.5 and I.6): there must be adequate and suitable ventilation which must be accessible for cleaning
Lighting (I.7): there must be adequate lighting
Drainage (I.8): there must be adequate drainage
Changing facilities (I.9): there must be adequate changing facilities if necessary.

Chapter II – Food Rooms
Food rooms (II.1): floors, walls, ceilings and other surfaces must be adequately maintained, easy to clean and disinfect, where necessary
Tools, utensils and equipment – cleaning (II.2): there must be adequate facilities, tools and equipment for cleaning purposes
Washing of food (II.3): there must be adequate facilities for washing food where necessary

Chapter III – Movable or Temporary Premises
Premises and vending machines (III.1): must be designed and sited to avoid contamination
Working practices for movable or temporary premises (III.2[a]): must have appropriate facilities for personal hygiene
Surfaces (III.2[b]): must be easy to clean and disinfect, where necessary
Cleaning of utensils and foodstuff (III.2[c] and [d]): there must be adequate facilities for cleaning food and the cleaning and disinfecting of utensils and equipment
Hot and cold water supply (III.2[e]): an adequate supply of hot and cold water
Waste storage and disposal (III.2[f]): adequate arrangements for storage and disposal.

Chapter IV – Transport
Containers and vehicles (IV.1): designed to allow them to be adequately cleaned and disinfected

Chapter V – Equipment
Equipment requirements (V.1): utensils, fittings, equipment etc. that can come into contact with food must be made of materials that can be kept clean, and equipment should be movable so that surrounding areas can be kept clean

Chapter VI – Food Waste
Food and other waste (VI.1): accumulation to be avoided
Containers for food and other waste (VI.2): containers should normally be able to be closed and they should be able to be cleaned and disinfected
Arrangements for the storage and removal of refuse (VI.3): designed and built so that they can easily be cleaned and they must be pest-proof

Chapter VII – Water Supply
Water supply (VII.1): there must be an adequate supply of potable (drinking) water to avoid food contamination
Ice (VII.2): where ice is to be consumed (e.g. with drinks) it must be made from drinking water

Chapter VIII – Personal Hygiene
Personal hygiene (VIII.1): food handlers must wear suitable clean and where appropriate protective clothing
Infected food handlers (VIII.2): anyone suffering from, or who is a carrier, of a disease which can be transmitted through food should not handle food

Chapter IX – Foodstuffs
Raw materials (IX.1): raw materials which are contaminated, or are suspected of being contaminated, and which would be unfit after processing should not be used
Protection of raw materials from contamination (IX.2): food must be protected at all stages from contamination likely to make it unfit for human consumption

Chapter X – Training
Training (X.1): all food handlers must be supervised and trained in food hygiene to an appropriate level

In essence the 1995 regulations are similar in many respects to earlier regulations. However, as with Health and Safety legislation, the regulations place a strong onus on owners and managers to identify food safety risks and to design and implement appropriate preventive measures which may include management techniques such as Hazard Analysis and Critical Control Points (HACCP).

Food Safety (Temperature Control) Regulations 1995

These regulations replaced earlier and quite complex regulations. There are now only three important temperatures 8°C, 63°C (and 82°C in Scotland). Foods which may be 'subject to microbiological multiplication' must be held at no more than 8°C or above

63°C. There are a few exceptions which include food on display, which can be displayed for up to 4 hours, and also low risk and preserved foods which can be stored at ambient temperature. Manufacturers can vary upward the 8°C ceiling if there is a scientific basis to do so. Food which is to be served hot should be held at over 63°C. In Scotland food that is to be reheated must attain a temperature of 82°C unless this will adversely affect the food.

Defences

The key defence to proceedings brought under the FSA 1990 is contained in s. 21 of the Act. This is the defence of due diligence. Section 21 provides:

(1) *In any proceedings for an offence under any of the preceding provisions of this Part (in this section referred to as 'the relevant provision'), it shall, subject to subsection (5) below, be a defence for the person charged to prove that he took all reasonable precautions and exercised all due diligence to avoid the commission of the offence by himself or by a person under his control.*

(2) *Without prejudice to the generality of subsection (1) above, a person charged with an offence under section 8, 14 or 15 above who neither –*

    (a) *prepared the food in respect of which the offence is alleged to have been committed; nor*

    (b) *imported it into Great Britain,*

    shall be taken to have established the defence provided by that subsection if he satisfies the requirements of subsection (3) or (4) below.

(3) *A person satisfies the requirements of this subsection if he proves –*

    (a) *that the commission of the offence was due to an act or default of another person who was not under his control, or to reliance on information supplied by such a person;*

    (b) *that he carried out all such checks of the food in question as were reasonable in all the circumstances, or that it was reasonable in all the circumstances for him to rely on checks carried out by the person who supplied the food to him; and*

    (c) *that he did not know and had no reason to suspect at the time of the commission of the alleged offence that his act or omission would amount to an offence under the relevant provision.*

(4) *A person satisfies the requirements of this subsection if he proves –*

    (a) *that the commission of the offence was due to an act or default of another person who was not under his control, or to reliance on information supplied by such a person;*

    (b) *that the sale or intended sale of which the alleged offence consisted was not a sale or intended sale under his name or mark; and*

    (c) *that he did not know, and could not reasonably have been expected to know, at the time of the commission of the alleged offence that his act or omission would amount to an offence under the relevant provision.*

(5) *If in any case the defence provided by subsection (1) above involves the allegation that the commission of the offence was due to an act or default of another person, or to reliance on information supplied by another person, the person charged shall not, without leave of the court, be entitled to rely on that defence unless –*

(a) *at least seven clear days before the hearing; and*

(b) *where he has previously appeared before a court in connection with the alleged offence, within one month of his first such appearance,*

he has served on the prosecutor a notice in writing giving such information identifying or assisting in the identification of that other person as was then in his possession.

(6) *In subsection (5) above any reference to appearing before a court shall be construed as including a reference to being brought before a court.*

Section 21 sets out a general defence for a defendant who has taken all reasonable precautions and exercised all due diligence. There is a marked difference between this provision and the defence provisions set out in the Food Act 1984. The previous defence (see s. 100 Food Act 1984) applied only where a third party could be blamed for the offence, but the provisions in s. 21 of the 1990 Act are much broader than this. The 1990 Act does not, however, reproduce the 'written warranty defence' previously found in s. 102 of the 1984 Act. The provisions in s. 21 of the 1990 Act subsume the warranty defence as one aspect of due diligence. To avail himself of the due diligence defence a defendant must establish that he 'took all reasonable precautions and exercised all due diligence to avoid the commission of the offence by himself or someone under his control' – see s. 21(1).

Where the defendant can show that the offence was committed owing to the act or default of another person who was not under his control or to reliance upon information supplied by such a person, then provided certain conditions are met, the defence of due diligence is deemed to have been satisfied in relation to offences under s. 8, 14 or 15 of the Act. Doubtless what amounts to 'reasonable precautions and all due diligence' will vary, not least according to the resources available to the defendant. Reasonable precautions and due diligence in the context of a multi-million pound food business may differ from those applicable to a corner café; higher standards may be expected from a larger organization than from a small business.

The act or default of another person was considered in *Tesco Supermarkets Ltd* v. *Nattrass* [1972] AC 153. In that case the House of Lords held that a store manager was 'another person' aside from the company. This case takes a very narrow view of the actions which could properly be attributed to the company. This means that the availability of a due diligence defence can have considerable utility for a defendant company. In Tesco's case the company satisfied the defence of due diligence by proving that the company had established a satisfactory system, and the company could not be held responsible for the failure of the shop manager to implement the system effectively. One view is that taking all reasonable precautions involves establishing a system whilst due diligence focuses on the mechanisms by which the company ensures that the system operates effectively.

The due diligence defence in the 1990 Act is broader than that contained in the 1984 Act, where proof of an act or default by another which caused the commission of the offence was a prerequisite to the operation of the defence. In one respect (the absence of the warranty defence) the due diligence defence seemed more harsh. The 1990 Act therefore specifies circumstances where the due diligence defence is deemed to have been satisfied in relation to prosecutions brought under ss. 8, 14 and 15 of the Act. This concession applies only where the defendant has neither prepared nor imported the food himself. The standard required of a defendant depends upon whether he is an 'own brander' or not. Section 21(4) sets out the conditions for a person who is not selling as an 'own brander' whilst s. 21(3) sets out those conditions which apply to an own brander.

A defendant wishing to rely on the due diligence defence, where the offence was due to the act or default of another person who was not under the defendant's control or to reliance upon information supplied by another, must comply with the notice procedures set out in s. 21(5). Failure to comply with this procedural requirement means that the defendant will not be able to rely on that defence at trial without the leave of the court. Section 20 provides for the prosecution of the person whose act or default caused the defendant to commit an offence under Part II of the 1990 Act. This is so whether or not proceedings are taken or continued against the defendant. This is sometimes known as a 'by-pass' prosecution.

A specific defence is provided by s. 22 for publishers and advertising agents where the offence committed consists of advertising food – s. 15(2). Section 22 provides:

> *In proceedings for an offence under any of the preceding provisions of this Part consisting of the advertisement for sale of any food, it shall be a defence for the person charged to prove –*
> *(a) that he is a person whose business it is to publish or arrange for the publication of advertisements; and*
> *(b) that he received the advertisement in the ordinary course of business and did not know and had no reason to suspect that its publication would amount to an offence under that provision.*

Enforcement process

Enforcement of the 1990 Act is vested in food authorities specified in s. 5. Basically these comprise Metropolitan Councils, the City of London, County Councils and District Councils. Section 6(2) provides that every food authority shall enforce and execute the provisions of the Act within its geographic area. This means that there are likely to be regional and local differences of approach to enforcement of the legislation. Enforcement authorities act through 'authorized officers', primarily environmental health officers and trading standards officers. These officers are given specific powers under the Act for entry to food premises (see s. 32). Many of the powers given to authorized officers (e.g. sampling) require the officer to exercise discretion in deciding what action is appropriate.

The food authority is liable for such actions taken within the scope of the officer's employment. Those steps which the officer may have taken which are considered outside the scope of his employment, he is personally liable for – see s. 44.

The processing of offences is a matter for the authorized officers and the courts and the legal advisers of the prosecuting authority and the defendant. Issues such as who is to be prosecuted – see s. 36 – for the liability of corporations, time limits for prosecutions and, following conviction, the appeal process are outside the province of this text.

Misleading pricing: Part III Consumer Protection Act 1987

Before the Consumer Protection Act 1987 (CPA) there was no unified offence of giving a misleading price indication. Section 11 of the Trade Descriptions Act 1968 dealt with certain aspects and the Price Marking (Bargain Offers) Order 1979 covered others. It had long been thought that these provisions were unwieldy and over-complicated. Part III of the CPA 1987 creates a new general offence of giving a misleading price indication (repealing s. 11 TDA and the Price Marking (Bargain Offers) Order 1979).

Section 20 CPA 1987 provides:

> *a person shall be guilty of an offence if, in the course of any business, he gives (by any means whatever) any consumers an indication which is misleading as to the price at which any goods, services, accommodation or facilities are available (whether generally or from particular persons).*

Liability under s. 20 attaches to any person who gives a misleading price indication 'in the course of any business of his'. This is broader than the supplier of the goods or service; it could include the person who markets the goods by publishing an advertisement in which the indication is made.

The 'consumer' to whom the misleading price indication is made is defined in s. 20(1):

> *'consumer'* –
> (a) *in relation to any goods, means any person who might wish to be supplied with the goods for his own private use or consumption;*
> (b) *in relation to any services or facilities, means any person who might wish to be provided with the services or facilities otherwise than for the purposes of any business of his; and*
> (c) *in relation to any accommodation means any person who might wish to occupy the accommodation otherwise than for the purposes of any business of his . . .*

The customer who purchases or seeks to purchase a meal or drink at a restaurant is clearly a consumer under s. 20(1)(a) and (b). Where that customer seeks to use the banqueting facilities the position is less clear, but appears to be covered by s. 20(1)(b) and (c). It should be emphasized that the consumer is acting other than in a business capacity.

What amounts to the 'price' of any goods, services, accommodation or facilities refers to the aggregate of the sums to be paid by the consumer – s. 20(6).

What is meant by a 'misleading' price indication?

A price indication may be misleading in any of the following ways:
1   Section 21(1): it may be misleading at the time when it is given.
2   Section 20(2): it may have become misleading as the result of subsequent events.
3   Section 21(2): where no fixed price is involved, the method of determining the price may be stated in a misleading fashion.

Presently misleading price indications – s. 21(1). A price indication is misleading if a consumer might reasonably infer any of the following:

(a) The price is less than in fact it is.
(b) The price is unconditional, when in fact the price depends on one or more conditions, e.g. purchase by given date.
(c) The price is fully inclusive, in that there are no additional charges, when further charges are required, e.g. essential items are charged as additional to the price indicated.
(d) The price is to be increased or reduced or maintained at its present or future level, when the person giving the price indication has no expectation that the price is to be altered or maintained.
(e) Where the price advertised is compared to some other price, to the value of the subject matter or to the price or value of any other subject matter, and the facts on which the comparison is based are not stated.

Price indications which become misleading. If a price indication was accurate at the time it was given, but has become misleading due to subsequent events, the person giving the indication commits an offence under s. 21(2)(a), where two conditions are satisfied:
1   It could reasonably be expected that consumers to whom the indication was originally given might rely upon it after it has become misleading – s. 20(2)(b). *and*
2   The person giving the indication has failed to take other reasonable steps to prevent reliance by these consumers – s. 20(2)(c).

Misleading indications as to the method of determining a price. An indication is misleading as to the method of determining the price if a consumer might infer from the indication any of the following (s. 21(2)):
(a) The method is not what it in fact is.
(b) The method is unconditional when in fact it rests upon other facts or circumstances.
(c) The method will produce a fully inclusive price when in fact further charges are to be imposed.
(d) The method is to be changed or maintained when in fact the person giving the indication has no such expectation.
(e) Where the method advertised is compared to some other method, the comparison is based upon facts or circumstances other than those on which it is in fact based.

Defences to the charge of giving a misleading price indication

A number of defences are available to a charge of giving a misleading price indication, and to a charge of giving a price indication which has become misleading.

Where a person is charged with giving a misleading price indication it is a defence for him or her to show that he or she took all reasonable steps and exercised all due diligence to avoid committing the offence (see s. 39 CPA 1987).

A person who is not seeking to promote a product through advertising but who is merely providing information about the product has a defence under s. 24(2). Similarly, publishers of advertising material and advertising agencies, etc. may avail themselves of a 'third party defence' under s. 24(3), where at the time of publication they neither knew nor had grounds for suspecting that publication would involve the commission of an offence.

Misdescribed food and drink

The principal provision here is s. 1 TDA 1968:

> *Any person who in the course of a trade or business,*
> *(a) applies a false description to any goods; or*
> *(b) supplies or offers to supply any goods to which a false trade description is*
> *applied, shall . . . be guilty of an offence.*

This offence raises three questions: (1) What is a trade description? (2) What does 'false' mean? (3) What does 'applies' mean? 'Trade description' is defined by s.2 TDA 1968:

> *A trade description is an indication, direct or indirect, by whatever means given, of*
> *any of the following matters with respect to the goods:*

The Act then goes on to state the full range of trade descriptions, of which the following are examples relevant to the hotel and catering industry and the sale of food and drink:
(a) quantity, size, etc. (e.g. 100 grams);
(b) method of manufacture, processing, etc. (e.g. home-made);
(c) composition (e.g. 100 per cent beef);
(d) fitness for purpose (e.g. suitable for diabetics);
(e) testing by any person and results thereof (e.g. eight out of ten mothers said their children preferred 'Stodge' to ordinary porridge);
(f) approval by any person, etc. (e.g. Egon Ronay recommended or RAC approved);
(g) place or date of manufacture, production, processing, etc. (e.g. 1982 Chateau Jones, bottled in France);
(h) person by whom manufactured, produced or processed (e.g. bottled by San Carlos of Spain);
(i) other history, etc. (e.g. matured in oak casks for six years).
The Trade Descriptions Act in s. 12 also covers the situations where sellers falsely indicate royal patronage or approval of their goods, and where there is a false indication that goods are of a kind supplied to any person, e.g. 'supplier of fruit and vegetables to Oxford University colleges'.

The trade description may be applied to the goods by any person. This covers both individuals and companies – s. 20 TDA 1968. Where the application of a false trade description is due to the actions or default of an employee of the company, the company, if charged under the Act, may rely upon the third party defence in s. 24(1)a – *Beckett* v. *Kingston Bros Ltd* [1970] 1 QB 606. The trade description must be false ('false' is defined by s. 3 TDA 1968) to a material degree before an offence has been committed; an insignificant inaccuracy will not suffice. The description must be sufficiently false to matter, although misleading descriptions will be treated as false descriptions.

The false trade description must be applied to the goods before the offence has been committed. The term 'applies' is covered by ss. 4 and 5 TDA. Section 4(1) states:

A person applies a trade description to goods if he:

(a) *affixes or annexes it to or in any manner marks it or incorporates it with the goods themselves or on anything in, or with which the goods are supplied; or*

(b) *places the goods in, on or with anything which the trade description has been affixed or annexed to or marked on or incorporated with, or places any such thing with the goods; or*

(c) *uses the trade description in any manner likely to be taken as referring to the goods.*

Section 4(2) allows for oral application of a trade description to goods. Hence, a waiter in a restaurant who remarks to a customer that the sherry trifle is home-made and is served with real cream, if in fact it is bought in and served with a synthetic cream substitute, has applied a false trade description to goods. We can also say that an offence under ss. 15 and 14 of the Food Safety Act 1990 has been committed when the food is purchased.

A trade description may also be applied to goods by means of an advertisement (s. 5 TDA 1968).

Weights and measures legislation, namely, the Weights and Measures Act 1963, provides for the enforcement of trading standards as to the quantity of food and drink provided. An example of how the legislation operates may be seen in relation to the sale of draught beer and cider – *Bennett* v. *Markham* [1982] 1 WLR 1231 (QBD).

When is it home-made?

Many catering businesses use descriptions such as 'home-made'. Such descriptions, as discussed above, are covered by the Trade Descriptions Act and the Food Safety Act. The description 'home-made' should be applied to prepared foods which have been prepared from basic ingredients in a domestic-style kitchen and not foods bought in, which were produced in factory-like conditions. Using modern large-scale ovens and other catering scale equipment which are not of a domestic type would not preclude the use of the description 'home-made'. Foods prepared in a factory or a manufacturing type of kitchen do not meet the description 'home-made'.

Foods may be prepared in domestic-type kitchens away from a restaurant, pub or hotel and still be described as 'home-made'. This is often the case with foods such as cakes and pies which may be made off the premises. Beware, however, of responsibilities under the Food Safety Act, i.e. the responsibility to ensure that the foods are of the nature, substance and quality which are not likely to be injurious to health. The caterer has a responsibility to exercise 'due diligence' in his or her methods of purchasing supplies.

There may be problems of description where 'home-made' dishes are made using bought-in ingredients such as prepared pastries and pie fillings (i.e. neither was actually home-made!). The description 'home-cooked' might be acceptable in such circumstances although it would be advisable to take advice from the local trading standards officer.

Other descriptions used include 'home-made style' and this can apply to factory-made foods, although it would not be advisable to apply that descriptions if the manufacturer has not done so.

6.4 REFUSING SERVICE TO THE CUSTOMER

It is not every person that enters the restaurateur's restaurant that the restaurateur is prepared to serve. The person may be drunk, unsuitably dressed or for some other reason unacceptable, e.g. the prospective customer appears unable to pay for the service. The restaurateur has a broad power to refuse service to a prospective customer, based on the principle of freedom of contract. However, if the restaurant is part of an inn the right of the restaurateur is restricted by the fact that innkeepers are under a duty to provide refreshment to travellers who are in a fit state to be received and who appear able to pay a reasonable sum for the service provided (see p. 151. The duty to provide refreshment). A failure to provide refreshment to such travellers is a criminal offence – *R.* v. *Higgins* [1948] 1 KB 165 (CA). There are also certain statutory restrictions placed on the right to refuse service to prospective customers by s. 29(1) of the Sex Discrimination Act 1975 and s. 20(1) of the Race Relations Act 1976. It amounts to unlawful discrimination to refuse service to a person either on grounds of their sex or on racial grounds. This has been fully discussed. The most pertinent case for present purposes is *Gill and Another* v. *El Vino Co. Ltd* [1983] 2 WLR 155 (CA).

Apart from the restrictions imposed by the Race Relations Act 1976 and the Sex Discrimination Act 1975, there is little further restraint placed upon the restaurateur's right to refuse service to a customer. The restaurateur's right to refuse service stems from the fact that it is the restaurateur who has control of the establishment and he or she may seek to impose whatever standards, e.g. of dress, he or she wishes within the parameters of the law. Only where the restaurant forms part of an inn can a customer claim a right to be served refreshment; however, this right is not absolute, and is subject to qualification. A restaurateur may lawfully refuse service to a customer for a number of reasons, some legitimate, others clearly unprincipled. Examples are:

1 The customer is gay. The refusal of service owing to the customer's sexual orientation does not amount to sex discrimination.
2 The customer's political views. The refusal of service to a customer because of his or her political views, be they extreme or otherwise, does not give rise to a right of action on the part of the customer.
3 The customer's appearance. Even at inns, where innkeepers are under a duty to receive travellers, they may refuse service on the ground that the traveller is not in a fit state to be received. Hence tramps *et al.* may be refused service in a restaurant.
4 The customer's behaviour. The customer's behaviour, e.g. drunkenness or abusive conduct towards staff or other customers, may be a reason for the refusal of service. This also covers the customer's behaviour on a previous occasion causing the customer to be banned and therefore the refusal of service on a subsequent visit to the restaurant.
5 The customer's religion. It is not unlawful discrimination to discriminate against a person on the grounds of his or her religion, e.g. Catholic or Protestant. However, some religions, e.g. Sikh, are covered by the Race Relations Act 1976, as constituting ethnic groups – *Mandla* v. *Dowell Lee* [1983] 2 WLR 620 (HL). Therefore, to refuse service on the grounds of the customer's religion is not unlawful discrimination under the Race Relations Act 1976. (See p. 158.)
6 In *Commission for Racial Equality* v. *Dutton* [1989] 2 WLR 17 (CA) it was held that a sign in a public house which read 'No travellers' applied to Romanies, who were an ethnic group within the Race Relations Act 1976. (See p. 159.)

6.5 THEFT BY CUSTOMERS

It is not unknown for customers to walk out without paying for the food and drink or service provided by the restaurateur or caterer. This phenomenon brought about a change in the law of theft and the creation of a specific offence, under s. 3 of the Theft Act 1978, to deal with the situation. Section (3)1 states:

> *A person who, knowing that payment on the spot for any goods supplied or service done is required or expected from him, dishonestly makes off without having paid as required or expected, and with intent to avoid payment of the amount due shall be guilty of an offence.*

Furthermore, s. 3(4) provides a power of arrest for any person; i.e. restaurateurs may arrest anyone who is, or whom they, with reasonable cause, suspect to be, committing or attempting to commit a s. 3(1) offence. The elements of the s. 3(1) offence are:

(a) The defendant must know that payment on the spot is required for the goods supplied or service provided.
(b) The defendant must be dishonest.
(c) The defendant must 'make off'. In *R*. v. *McDavitt* [1981] Crim. LR 843, the defendant's friends had left him to pay the bill and he sought to leave by the front door. He was told by the restaurateur that the police were on their way and he thereafter hid in the toilet. The Crown Court held that the defendant had not 'made off'. 'Makes off' refers to the spot where payment is required or expected, namely the restaurant itself. Since the defendant had not departed from the restaurant, he was not guilty as charged and an acquittal was directed by the trial judge.
(d) The defendant must make off without having paid.
(e) The defendant must intend to avoid payment.

R. v. ALLEN [1985] 2 All ER 641 (HL)   In this case the defendant had booked a room at a hotel for ten nights and had stayed on for some while after, incurring a total bill of £1286. He left without paying. Two days after departing he telephoned the hotel to explain that he was in financial difficulties and arranged to return to the hotel to collect his belongings and to leave his passport as security for the debt. Upon his return to the hotel he was arrested and charged with the offence of making off without payment contrary to s. 3(1) of the Theft Act 1978.

At his trial the defendant was convicted and appealed to the Court of Appeal, which allowed his appeal. Thereafter the Crown appealed to the House of Lords, who dismissed their appeal on the basis that the defendant did not have, at the time of making off from the hotel, a dishonest intention never to pay the sum due.

The significance of this decision of the House of Lords in *R*. v. *Allen* is that s. 3 of the Theft Act 1978 has been interpreted so that it must now be proven that the person who 'makes off' must do so intending never to pay. Previously it had been thought that the necessary guilty mind could be established by proof that the defendant intended to avoid payment there and then; thus it was assumed that a person would be guilty of the offence if he or she intended to avoid paying 'on the spot', although intending to pay at some time in the future.

CASE STUDY

Adam and Eve were dining at the Dead Rat Restaurant. Adam purchased game pie for Eve. Eve cut into the pie and ate a small amount, only to notice that inside it was a glass eye. Eve was thereupon sick.

Mary, another diner at the restaurant, purchased a cake described as 'made with fresh cream'. The cream was in fact artificial and the cake stale. Mary was taken ill after eating the cake.

The restaurant's menu contained the following clause: 'The restaurant will in no way be liable for any breach of a contractual term, be it express or implied by statute or common law. Furthermore, the restaurant accepts no liability for any personal injury sustained by diners, whatever the cause.'
(a) Advise Adam, Eve and Mary as to their respective rights of action against the Dead Rat Restaurant's proprietor, Roland.
(b) What, if any, criminal offences, as disclosed by the above facts, may have been committed by the proprietor of the Dead Rat Restaurant?

(a) Adam's rights of action against Roland. Adam is in a contractual position with Roland. He can commence an action for breach of contract, based on breach of one of the implied conditions of law:
1   s. 14 SGA 1979 (p. 177);
2   s. 13 SGA 1979 (p. 176).
Liability for breach of either term cannot be excluded (see s. 12 UCTA 1977).

Adam may also commence proceedings for the statutory strict liability tort under s. 2(1) Consumer Protection Act 1987 (see p. 186). He may also commence proceedings in the tort of negligence following from *Donoghue* v. *Stevenson* (see p. 183).

However, it should be noted that in order to succeed under either the Consumer Protection Act 1987 or the tort of negligence, the plaintiff must prove loss. Additionally, with the tort of negligence the plaintiff must prove fault on the part of the defendant.

(a) Eve's rights of action against Roland. Eve has a tortious claim under the Consumer Protection Act 1987 (see p. 185) and under the tort of negligence. She does not have a contractual claim against Roland, since she is not privy to any contract with him. Eve does suffer physical injury, and therefore the hurdle of proving loss is overcome.

(a) Mary's rights of action against Roland. Mary has the same rights of action as Adam. Mary, however, does suffer physical injury, unlike Adam, and may succeed in a claim under the CPA 1987 and the tort of negligence.

It should be noted that Roland's exclusion of liability for personal injury to customers is inoperative due to s. 2(1) UCTA 1977.

(b) The criminal offences which Roland may have committed.
1   Section 14 FSA – food not of the quality demanded by the purchaser. A glass eye is extraneous matter – *Barber* v. *Co-operative Wholesale Society Ltd* (see p. 208).
2   Section 7 FSA – sale of food injurious to health, if the glass eye had infected the food (see pp. 194–5).

3   Section 8 – sale of food which fails to comply with a food safety requirement –
     see s. 8(2)c (see p. 195).
4   Section 15 – falsely describing, advertising or presenting food, misuse of 'cream'
     with regard to the cake (see pp. 208–9) – see also s. 1 TDA 1968 (p. 217).

SEVEN

Commercial contracts and the caterer

We are not concerned here with contractual relationships between hoteliers or caterers and their clientele, but with the contractual arrangements entered into by caterers and hoteliers with other commercial organizations. The hotelier, caterer and restaurateur in offering their professional services to the public rely on other business organizations in order to provide their services. Caterers will have to enter into various contracts of supply with butchers, fruiterers and other suppliers for the food which they prepare for their clients. Similarly, restaurateurs will enter into contracts for either the purchase or the hire of equipment for their kitchens. Hoteliers may enter into a service contract with a laundry to provide clean linen for their guests' rooms, or with a florist to provide and care for plants and flower arrangements in the public rooms of the hotel. The various organizations on which professional caterers rely in order to perform their services for their customers are numerous and vary from kitchen suppliers to florists and entertainers. Equally, most hotel and catering businesses retain the services of professional advisers, such as solicitors and accountants. Some may utilize the services of interior designers, architects, security contractors and advertising agencies. All these facets of the catering enterprise involve commercial contracts between the caterer and other businesses.

7.1 STANDARD FORM CONTRACTS

Perhaps one of the longest-standing legal fictions is the doctrine of freedom of contract. Freedom of contract encompasses the notion that contracts are entered into voluntarily and therefore the parties are able to negotiate freely the terms on which they wish to contract. This may be described as a fiction because in the vast majority of contracts the terms are set by the offeror, and the offeree either accepts, in which case a contract is entered into and the offeree is bound by its terms, or rejects the offeror's terms and possibly contracts with another offeror offering more favourable terms. We can see this in relation to the booking of a holiday with a tour operator. A standard booking contract is appended to the brochure and clients either accept the terms contained therein and contract with the tour operator, or they book with another travel company offering better terms. With commercial contracts, in the vast majority of cases the parties contract on the standard terms of one party. A supplier of foodstuffs will normally, when an order is placed by the caterer, draw up an order form for the foodstuffs to be supplied. The order form will normally have terms and conditions on the back; these are the terms on which the supplier is prepared to supply the foodstuffs and constitute an offer to contract. When the foodstuffs are delivered to the caterer's premises the proprietor, or whoever is responsible for the food store, will sign the order form and this will amount to acceptance of the terms and conditions of the order form. The sort of terms which will be incorporated into a contract of supply will vary according to the nature of the goods or services supplied under the contract.

The difficulty with standard form contracts arises where both parties use standard forms and there is a conflict between the terms used in them. If there is a conflict, in that the standard form by which the offeree purports to accept the offeror's offer to contract introduces new terms and conditions, a contract does not arise on the original terms. There is no agreement between the parties: each believes the terms of the contract to be different. An example of this problem can be seen in the following case.

BUTLER MACHINE TOOL CO. LTD v. EX-CELL-O CORPORATION (ENGLAND) LTD [1979] 1 WLR 401 (CA)   The seller of a machine tool offered to deliver a machine tool. The terms of the offer stated that orders were accepted only on the seller's standard terms, which included a price variation clause which stated that the final contract price would be determined on the date of delivery. The buyer replied to the seller's offer with an order form containing different terms and conditions from those of the seller. This order form had a tear-off acknowledgment slip for signature and return. The order form fixed the total contract price as that which existed on the date of acknowledgment. The seller returned the acknowledgment slip duly signed. The seller later tried to invoke the price variation clause in his initial offer. The Court of Appeal held that the buyer's order was not an acceptance of the seller's offer to contract. The buyer's order amounted to a counter offer, which the seller had accepted by means of the acknowledgment slip. A contract had arisen on the terms of the buyer's order form, hence the seller could not rely on the price variation clause.

This case illustrates the likely effect of a conflict of standard terms: either no contract arises, or a contract arises on the terms stated in the 'counter offer' if this is accepted by the other party.

Increasingly, competitive tendering is used by public authorities and commercial organizations when they are seeking to establish a contract for the supply of goods, or more likely a service. The tendering process may give rise to issues of when, if at all, a binding contract has been formed. In *Blackpool and Fylde Aero Club Ltd* v. *Blackpool Borough Council* [1990] 3 All ER 26 the Court of Appeal considered the issue of tendering and the creation of contractual obligation. The defendants, a local authority, which owned and managed the local airport, had since 1975 granted to the plaintiffs, a flying club, a concession to operate pleasure flights from there. In 1983 the grant of the concession came up for renewal and the defendants prepared invitations to tender that they sent to the plaintiffs and to six other parties. It was stated on the form of tender that the defendants 'do not bind themselves to accept all or any part of any tender. No tender which is received after the last date and time specified shall be admitted for consideration.' The plaintiffs' tender for the concession was posted by hand in the defendants' letter-box before the expiry of the deadline. Because the town clerk's staff failed to empty the letter-box when they should have the defendants received the plaintiffs' tender too late for their consideration. The defendants accepted a tender lower than that submitted by the plaintiffs. The plaintiffs claimed damages against the defendants for breach of contract and negligence. The judge, at a hearing to determine the issues of liability only, held that the express request for tenders by the defendants gave rise to an implied obligation on them to perform the service of considering tenders duly received. He concluded that the defendants were liable under both heads of claim.

On appeal by the defendant borough council it was held, dismissing the appeal, that an invitation to tender was normally no more than an offer to receive bids, but circumstances could exist whereby it gave rise to binding contractual obligations; that although the defendants' form of tender did not explicitly state that they would consider timely and conforming tenders, and although contracts were not to be lightly implied, an examination of what the parties said and did established a clear intention to create a contractual obligation on the part of the defendants to consider the plaintiffs' tender in conjunction with all other conforming tenders or at least that the plaintiffs' tender would be considered if others were; and that, accordingly, the defendants' failure rendered them contractually liable to the plaintiffs.

7.2 THE TERMS OF A COMMERCIAL CONTRACT

It is important to understand that a contract does not only contain express terms agreed upon by the parties but will usually also include implied terms. We must now consider both the express terms and the implied terms which may be included in a commercial contract.

Consideration

Consideration is not normally an issue over which there is much litigation in commercial contracts. Normally it is the purchase price paid by the promisee for the goods or services supplied by the promisor. However, on occasions where a party has entered into the contract on terms which have ceased to be economic for him he may seek to renegotiate the purchase price. Such a case was *Williams* v. *Roffey Bros Ltd* [1990] 2 WLR 1153 (CA). In that case it was held that where a party to an agreement promises to make an additional payment in return for the other party's promise to perform his existing contractual obligations (in this case, the refurbishment of properties) and as a result has secured a benefit and avoided a detriment, the commercial advantage secured by the promise to make the additional payment was capable of amounting to good consideration (in this case it did so).

Express terms

The nature of the express terms to be included in a commercial contract will vary according to the subject matter of the contract. One need hardly say that the terms contained in a commercial contract for the supply of foodstuffs to a restaurant will differ from those contained in a contract for the supply of capital equipment, e.g. a chip fryer, to the same establishment. Equally, some commercial contracts relate to the hire rather than to the purchase of goods, and may also relate to the provision of a service. The terms to be found in a commercial contract for the supply of goods (e.g. processed food products) will normally include the following:

(a) A clause stating that the terms of the order form are not to have effect, overriding any other stated terms, i.e. those terms which may be introduced by the buyer. The purpose of such a clause is to make clear to the buyer that the terms on which the supplier is willing to contract are those of the supplier. This clause is put into the contract to prevent the problem of a counter offer arising, as in the *Butler Machine Tool* case.
(b) Date of delivery.
(c) Cost of delivery.
(d) Terms of payment.
(e) Lost goods.
(f) Limitation or exclusion of liability.
(g) Price.
(h) Cancellation and variation of contract.
(i) Applicable law.

Whilst it is perfectly possible for the parties to draw up the express terms of a contract to cover or exclude liability as they wish, the law may limit the extent to which the express terms of the contract are to have effect, e.g. Unfair Contract Terms Act 1977.

Implied terms

Terms may be implied in a contract in either of two ways: implied terms of fact and statutorily implied terms. Implied terms of fact arise where the fact that the parties have expressly agreed certain terms implies that certain other terms have been agreed upon, e.g. that fresh fruit is, in fact, fresh. These other terms are known as implied terms of fact. The question of whether the contract contains such implied terms is one for the court to determine. The test which is used to determine this question is the 'officious bystander test', as explained by MacKinnan LJ in *Shirlaw* v. *Southern Foundries Ltd* [1939] 2 KB 206:

> Prima facie *that which in any contract is left to be implied and need not be expressed is something so obvious that it goes without saying; so that, if while the parties were making their bargain an officious bystander were to suggest some express provision for it in their agreement, they would testily suppress him with a common 'Oh, of course'.*

Statutorily implied terms are of far greater significance than implied terms of fact. The statutes with which we are concerned are the Sale of Goods Act 1979 and the Supply of Goods and Services Act 1982. The terms implied by these statutes are also affected by the provisions of the Unfair Contract Terms Act 1977.

The EC Directive (Unfair Terms Directive 93/13) covers similar but not identical subjects as the UK Unfair Contract Terms Act 1977. Under both sets of legislation certain unfair or unreasonable clauses in contracts and conditions of sale are void in law, i.e. they cannot be enforced through the courts.

The Directive applies to consumer contracts for goods and services. Contracts between businesses are not affected by the directive.

Sale of Goods Act 1979, as amended by the Sale and Supply of Goods Act 1994

The Sale of Goods Act 1979 (SGA) applies only to contracts for the sale of goods. A contract for the sale of goods is defined by s. 2(1) SGA thus:

> *A contract whereby the seller transfers or agrees to transfer the property in the goods to the buyer for a money consideration called the price.*

Hence, not all commercial contracts into which the caterer is likely to enter are covered by the SGA 1979, only those by which goods are transferred to the caterer for monetary consideration. An example for a contract which is not covered by the SGA is a contract for a service such as may be provided by a florist or a laundry. Where the contract is for the sale of goods and is covered by the SGA 1979, certain terms are implied by that statute into the contract. These terms take effect as if they were conditions expressly agreed upon by the parties.

Right to sell. Section 12(1) SGA 1979 implies into a contract for the sale of goods a condition that the seller has the right to sell the goods to the buyer.

Sales by description. Section 13(1) SGA 1979 provides:

> *Where there is a contract for the sale of goods by description, there is an implied condition that the goods will correspond to that description.*

By s.13(2):

> *If the sale is by sample as well as by description it is not sufficient that the bulk of the goods corresponds with the sample if the goods do not also correspond with the description.*

By s.13(3):

> *A sale of goods is not prevented from being a sale by description by reason only that being exposed for sale or hire, they are selected by the buyer.*

A sale by description is clearly explained by Lord Wright in *Grant* v. *Australian Knitting Mills* [1936] AC 85 (PC), where he says:

> there is a sale by description even though the buyer is buying something displayed
> before him on the counter; a thing is sold by description, though it is specific, so
> long as it is sold not merely as the specific thing but as a thing corresponding to a
> description.

The essence of a sale by description is that, in deciding to buy, the buyer placed some, but not necessarily total, reliance upon the description. The relevance of the provision for our present purposes is as follows. Mr Cumberland, a representative of a sausage and meat pie supplier, calls at the catering premises. He leaves twelve pounds of sausages with the proprietor for use as a sample, and sales literature which describes the sample sausages as '100 per cent pork meat'. The proportion of pork meat to other ingredients in the sausages was in fact 70 per cent. The proprietor purchases forty packs of pork sausages on a monthly order. The proprietor reads the food label on the sausages, which declares the true percentage of pork meat to other ingredients, and wishes to cancel his order for further sausages and claim damages from the supplier. Can he?

The supplier is in breach of s. 13 SGA 1979. This is clearly a situation where the proprietor of the catering premises has relied partly on the sample and the description of the goods in the sales literature. Section 13(2) applies here, and provided the caterer can show that he did rely in part upon the description (*Grant* v. *Australian Knitting Mills*) he may treat the contract of supply as at an end and claim damages.

One important qualification to the use of the remedy under s. 13 SGA may be seen in the following case.

ASHINGTON PIGGERIES v. CHRISTOPHER HILL [1971] 2 WLR 1051 (HL)   The sellers supplied to the buyer 'herring meal'. The goods were to be used to feed minks. 'Herring meal' comprises herrings processed with a preservative. The preservative in the meal supplied had reacted with the herrings to produce a chemical poisonous to minks. The minks fed on the meal died. The question arose of whether the sellers were in breach of the implied conditions as to description. The House of Lords held that they were not. The goods were described as 'herring meal' and were in fact 'herring meal', although they possessed a quality which caused damage to the buyer's animals.

The essential point, therefore, is that s. 13 SGA relates to identification of the goods by a description; it does not relate to the quality of the goods. If the goods are as described but not of sound quality the remedy of the buyer lies not in s. 13 but in s. 14 of the SGA 1979.

Quality of the goods. Section 14 SGA 1979 implies terms as to the quality of the goods purchased. Section 14(2) states:

> Where the seller sells goods in the course of a business, there is an implied condition
> that the goods supplied under the contract are of satisfactory quality, except there is
> no such condition –

(a) as regards defects specifically drawn to the buyer's attention before the contract
     is made;

or

(b) if the buyer examines the goods before the contract is made, as regards defects
     which the examination ought to reveal.

Satisfactory quality is defined for the purposes of s. 14(2) by s. 14(6):

> Goods of any kind are of satisfactory quality . . . if they are as fit for the purpose or
> purposes for which goods of that kind are commonly bought as it is reasonable to
> expect having regard to any description applied to them, the price (if relevant) and
> all the other relevant circumstances.

It is important to assess the quality of the goods against the description given. Hence, like goods must be compared with the goods in question (e.g. 100 per cent pork sausages must be compared with other similarly described sausages) to see if the goods in question are of satisfactory quality.

The scope of s. 14(2) is limited by sub-paragraphs (a) and (b). Defects which have been specifically drawn to the buyer's attention (e.g. a scratch on a cooker, or a broken switch), or such defects as ought to be revealed by the buyer's examination of the goods prior to purchase, cannot be relied upon as rendering the goods not of satisfactory quality.

Satisfactory quality may be contested more clearly where the goods purchased are of a simple construction or composition, e.g. a table-cloth, bed linen or fruit and vegetables. It is much more difficult to establish that the goods were not of merchantable quality where the goods are, for instance, complicated machinery. How many times must a freezer malfunction before it is not of satisfactory quality? The buyer's expectation of a sophisticated and complex mechanical or electronic product may well be different from his or her expectation of a simpler and cheaper item, but would a buyer be entitled to reject such a product on the basis of a simple malfunction? In *Bernstein* v. *Pamson Motors (Golders Green) Ltd* [1987] 2 All ER 220 (HC), it was concluded that a drop of sealant which caused the engine of a three-week-old car to seize up rendered it unmerchantable. Prior to the SSGA 1994 the test was of 'merchantable' quality rather than 'satisfactory' quality. The breach, however, did not entitle the buyer to reject the vehicle and return it to the garage, because under s. 35 of the SGA he had accepted the goods and had lost his right to recission. In *Rogers* v. *Parish (Scarborough) Ltd* [1987] QB 933, a new Range Rover was found to have a defective engine, gearbox, bodywork and oil seals. The car could still be driven but these faults needed repair. The court took a broad view of the 'purpose or purposes' for which a car is bought:

> the purpose . . . would include . . . not merely the buyer's purpose of driving the car
> from one place to another but of doing so with the appropriate degree of comfort,
> ease of handling and reliability . . . and pride in the vehicle's outward and interior
> appearance.

The court concluded that there was a breach of the implied condition of merchantable quality.

Section 14(3) provides a further implied condition as to the quality of goods purchased:

> *Where the seller sells goods in the course of a business and the buyer, expressly or by implication, makes known (a) to the seller any particular purpose for which the goods are being bought, there is an implied condition that the goods supplied under the contract are reasonably fit for that purpose, whether or not that is a purpose for which such goods are commonly supplied, except where the circumstances show that the buyer does not rely, or that it is unreasonable for him to rely, on the skill or judgement of the seller . . .*

This section is of particular importance where a caterer wishes to purchase from a supplier a piece of complex machinery, e.g. an oven, hob or freezer. Caterers may seek the advice of the supplier by stating that the freezer must have a certain star rating or a given capacity, or perhaps that an oven is of a certain size or is capable of dealing with a given amount of use. The caterers have therefore expressly made known to the supplier their requirements and the purpose for which they are purchasing the goods. If the goods are not 'reasonably fit for that purpose' or not for a purpose for which such goods are commonly supplied, then the caterers may sue for breach of the implied condition under s. 14(3) SGA 1979. It is important to stress that the caterers, when buying the goods, must have relied on the seller's expertise, and that it is reasonable for them to rely on the seller's skill and judgement. If such reliance cannot be proven, or it would be unreasonable for them so to rely, they cannot bring an action under s. 14(3).

Breach of an implied condition under ss. 12–14 SGA 1979 will entitle the buyer to rescind the contract and treat it as at an end and sue the seller for damages.

Can liability under the implied terms be excluded by a properly worded exclusion clause? Section 55 SGA 1979 provides:

> *Where a right, duty or liability would arise under a contract of sale of goods by implication of law it may (subject to the Unfair Contract Terms Act 1977) be negatived or varied by express agreement, or by the course of dealing between the parties, or by such usage as binds both parties to the contract.*

A properly worded exclusion clause may therefore limit or exclude the seller's liability for breach of the implied terms under ss. 12–14 SGA 1979, in so far as it is allowed to operate by the Unfair Contract Terms Act 1977.

The effect of the Unfair Contract Terms Act 1977 (UCTA) will depend upon whether the buyer in question 'deals as a consumer or on the other's written standard terms' (see s. 3(1) UCTA). In the situation where a caterer purchases goods from a supplier, the caterer does not 'deal as a consumer' (see s. 12(1) UCTA). However, he or she will normally be contracting on the seller's 'written standard terms', and where this is so s. 3(2) UCTA 1977 applies:

> *As against that party the other cannot by reference to any contract term –*
> *(a) when himself in breach of contract, exclude or restrict a liability of his in respect of the breach; or*

(b) claim to be entitled -
    (i) *to render a contractual performance substantially different from what was reasonably expected of him; or*
    (ii) *in respect of the whole or any part of his contractual obligation, to render no performance at all*
except insofar as (in any of the cases mentioned above in this sub-section) the contract term satisfies the requirement of reasonableness.

The requirement of reasonableness is explained by s. 11(1) UCTA, namely

that the term shall have been a fair and reasonable one to be included having regard to the circumstances which were, or ought reasonably to have been known to or in the contemplation of the parties when the contract was made.

The effect of s. 3(2) is therefore that such exclusion clauses may operate provided that they are reasonable.

Section 6(3) UCTA deals specifically with ss. 13 and 14 SGA and the statutorily implied terms contained therein.

As against a person dealing otherwise than as a consumer the liability specified . . . (under ss. 13, 14 and 15 SGA) can be excluded or restricted by reference to a contract term, but only insofar as the term satisfies the requirement of reasonableness.

The modern approach to the test of reasonableness is laid out by Lord Bridge in the leading case of *George Mitchell (Chesterhall) Ltd* v. *Finney Lock Seeds Ltd* [1983] 2 AC 803 (HL). He emphasizes that determining the questions of whether a clause is fair and reasonable is an exercise of disaction. The court must look at the whole range of considerations and put them in the balance, then decide on which side the balance comes down. This means, in effect, that the question becomes almost exclusively one for the trial judge.

Supply of Goods and Services Act 1982

The Supply of Goods and Services Act 1982 is intended to afford similar protection to the SGA 1979 for those contracts which are not for the sale of goods. We have seen that the operation of the SGA is confined to 'contracts for the sale of goods' as defined by s. 2(1) of that Act. The Supply of Goods and Services Act 1982 (SGSA) applies to 'contracts for the transfer of property in goods' (s. 1 SGSA 1982) and 'contracts for the hire of goods' (s. 6 SGSA).

We must draw a line, therefore, between contracts for the sale of goods and contracts of hire purchase, with which the SGA 1979 deals, and contracts for the 'transfer of property in goods', or 'for the hire of goods', with which the SGSA 1982 deals. Hence, the SGA 1979 would deal with the situation where a caterer purchases a piece of kitchen equipment, or buys it on hire purchase. The SGSA 1982 would deal with the situation where the kitchen equipment was acquired under a contract other than one covered by the SGA 1979, or where the equipment was hired – s. 1(2) SGSA 1982. Section 2 SGSA 1982 implies terms as to the transferrer's right to title in the goods and s. 4 SGSA 1982 implies terms as to the quality and fitness of the goods transferred. Section 6 SGSA defines contracts of hire and s. 7 deals with the hirer's right to transfer possession of the goods. Section 9 deals with the quality and fitness for the purpose of the goods hired under the contract. Section 8 SGSA provides for hire by description, namely, that the goods hired to the party must correspond to the description of the goods for hire. The provisions of the SGSA 1982 are parallel to those contained in the SGA and are to the same effect.

Section 11 SGSA deals with the attempted exclusion by the transferrer, or hirer, of the implied terms contained in the 1982 Act. Section 11(1) states:

> *Where a right, duty or liability would arise under a contract for the transfer of goods or a contract for the hire of goods by implication of law, it may (subject to s. 11(2) of the 1977 Act) be negatived or varied by express agreement, or by the course of dealing between the parties, or by such usage as binds both parties to the contract.*

By s. 11(2):

> *An express condition or warranty does not negative a condition or warranty implied by the preceding provisions of the Act unless inconsistent with it.*

By s. 11(3):

> *Nothing in the preceding provisions of this Act prejudices the operation of any other enactment or any rule of law whereby any condition or warranty (other than one relating to quality or fitness) is to be implied in a contract for the transfer or a contract for the hire of goods.*

Sections 11(1) and 11(2) have the same effect for contracts covered by the SGSA 1982 as s. 55 SGA 1979 does for contracts covered by that Act (see above). By virtue of ss. 11(1) and 11(2), UCTA 1977 has equal effect *vis-à-vis* contracts covered by the 1982 Act as it has with regard to contracts covered by the 1979 Act.

Whilst this may all seem rather complex and confusing, we may summarize and simplify the law by saying that the SGSA 1982 provides parallel legislation for two classes of contract outside the operation of the SGA 1979 which previously were not afforded such protection.

Contracts for the supply of a service are also covered by the 1982 Act. A 'contract for the supply of a service' is defined by s. 12(1) SGSA 1982:

> *In this Act a 'contract for the supply of a service' means subject to s. 12(2) below, a contract under which a person ('the supplier') agrees to carry out a service.*

The definition is qualified by s. 12(2) so as to exclude 'a contract of service' (i.e. a contract of employment) from the definition. Section 12(3) provides that a contract may still be within the s. 12(1) definition although, incidental to the contract, goods are transferred or hired. The terms implied by the Act into contracts 'for the supply of a service' are contained in ss. 13, 14 and 15.

Section 14 implies a term to the effect that if there is not a fixed date for the performance of the service, the service shall be performed 'within a reasonable time'. What may be a reasonable time will depend on each case, since it is a question of fact and not a question of law. If the service has not been performed within a reasonable time, the customer may treat the contract as at an end and sue the supplier for damages. The proper approach would be for the customer to write to the supplier after the passing of 'a reasonable time' thereby giving notice and fixing a time by which the customer requires the supplier to perform the service, e.g. fourteen days. If the service is not performed within that period thereafter, the customer may then treat the contract as at an end and claim damages.

Section 15 covers contracts where the 'contract price' is not a fixed sum; it provides that the customer will 'pay a reasonable charge' for the service. What is 'a reasonable charge' is a question of fact in each case to be determined by the court.

Section 13 affords protection to the customer in a manner previously not recognized by statute:

In a contract for the supply of a service where the supplier is acting in the course of a business, there is an implied term that the supplier will carry out the service with reasonable care and skill.

This is an area of the law which has developed from the nineteenth-century case of *The Moorcock* (1889) 14 PD 64, which established the principle that in business contracts the law attempts to give effect to such business efficacy as must have been intended by the parties. Therefore, people who hold themselves out as being prepared to carry out a service must exercise the skill of reasonably competent members of that trade or profession in providing the service. The obligation implied by s. 13 merely restates the common law. Hence, if a business with which a caterer contracts undertakes to perform a service for the caterer, the caterer is entitled to claim damages for a breach of s. 13 SGSA 1982 if the supplier of the service fails to provide a service in the same manner as the caterer would reasonably expect a competent member of the same trade or profession as the supplier to supply the service. Where the supplier uses shoddy materials, or the workmanship is poor, the caterer would be able to claim under s. 13 SGSA 1982. There is a clear parallel here with liability under the tort of negligence, i.e. that the supplier has failed to exercise reasonable care and skill and has thereby caused 'injury' to the plaintiff. The points of distinction are clear:
1 With s. 13 liability the party bringing the action and the supplier must both be parties to a 'contract for the supply of a service'. Under negligence liability, provided the neighbour test is satisfied, the plaintiff may be a third party, i.e. X contracts to supply a service to Y and in so doing he causes damage to Z's property. Z claims in negligence, not under s. 13, since he is not privy to the contract for the supply of a service by X.
2 Section 13 is not 'fault' based whereas negligence liability is.
Section 16 SGSA 1982 provides for limitations on the supplier's right to limit or

exclude liability for a breach of an implied term under ss. 13, 14 or 15. The effect of s. 16 is to permit suppliers of service to exclude or limit their liability subject to the provisions of UCTA 1977, i.e. it applies in the same way as s. 11 SGSA applies to contracts for the transfer or hire of goods.

The importance of SGSA 1982 to the caterer. It was not clear whether some of the contracts into which the caterer was likely to enter (e.g. contracts for the hire of linen) were covered by the SGA 1979. The 1982 Act clarifies the point by creating two new classes of contract to which implied terms kindred to those provided by the 1979 Act apply: contracts for hire and contracts for transfer of property in goods.

SGSA 1982 provides protection by means of the implied terms in ss. 13, 14 and 15 for contracts for the supply of a service. Section 13 gives rise to a new statutory action for breach of an implied term of 'care and skill' in the supply of the service. Hence, a caterer has a contractual remedy, without proof of fault, where a business which he or she has contracted has provided an inadequate service. An example might be where a florist undertakes to provide flower arrangements and table settings, and the service provided is irregular, the flowers used are of poor quality, or the flower arrangements are inadequate and unattractive. The caterer may now have a remedy under s. 13 SGSA 1982 for breach of the implied term in the contract with the florist as to care and skill.

A point which I find perplexing arises where the service is one such as that provided by a comic entertainer or singer, and the entertainment they provide fails to please the caterer's customers or leads to numerous complaints from his or her clients. Does s. 13 apply to such a contract?

The safety of goods

The Consumer Protection Act 1987 (CPA) created a new criminal offence where any person supplies, offers or agrees to supply or possesses for supply consumer goods which do not conform to the general safety requirement – s. 10(1) CPA 1987. This is a criminal matter, not a civil one; breach of the general safety requirement does not itself give rise to an action in tort for breach of a statutory duty – s. 41(2) CPA 1987. The CPA is aimed at enforcing standards of safety in consumer products.

The offence is committed by a 'supplier' who, acting in the course of business, 'supplies' goods in breach of the 'general safety requirement'. In order to comply with the general safety requirement, goods must be 'reasonably safe'. By s. 19(1) CPA, goods are safe only if they pose no risk, or a risk reduced to the minimum, of death or personal injury. Potential danger to other products, and defects which render the goods useless but not dangerous, are irrelevant for the purposes of the general safety requirement.

This requirement does not apply to all goods. It applies only to consumer goods – s. 10(7) CPA. Consumer goods are goods ordinarily intended for private use or consumption. Obviously some items which a caterer or hotelier may purchase are outside the scope of this definition; they are in essence industrial goods. Others, however, may clearly be within the definition. It is important to note that not all those things which we might call consumer goods are within the scope of s. 10(7); some are specifically excluded, notably food – s. 10(7)(b).

The CPA provides a range of defences to those charged under s. 10. There is a general defence (s. 39 CPA) of due diligence. This requires the defendant to prove that he or she took all reasonable steps and exercised all due diligence to avoid committing the offence.

Section 10(4)(b) provides a defence where a person can show *both*
(a) that the goods were supplied, offered or displayed by him or her in the course of
    a retail business;
and
(b) that at the date of the alleged offence he or she neither knew nor had
    reasonable grounds for believing that the goods failed to comply with the
    general safety requirement.
Further defences apply to goods intended for export – s. 10(4)(a) – and second-hand
goods – s. 10(4)(c).

Safety regulations. Section 11 of the Consumer Protection Act empowers the Secretary
of State to make safety regulations in respect of goods covered by the Act. The purposes for which such regulations are to be established are:
(a) to ensure that safety standards are established and approved for the safety of
    goods;
(b) to ensure that goods are safe, and that unsafe goods do not reach the market;
(c) to ensure that goods which might be unsafe in the hands of particular persons
    or classes of persons (e.g. minors) are not supplied to them;
(d) to ensure that appropriate information is supplied with goods.
The CPA expressly refers to the following matters concerning which regulations
should be made:
(a) composition, contents, design, construction and packing of goods;
(b) requiring goods to be approved under regulation;
(c) testing or inspection of goods;
(d) requiring a warning or other information to accompany goods;
(e) prohibiting the supply, etc. of certain goods, component parts or raw materials.
What is the effect of any breach of a regulation? A breach of a safety regulation can
give rise to action in tort for breach of a statutory duty – s. 41(1) CPA. The plaintiff
must prove loss in consequence of the breach of the regulation. A breach of a safety
regulation may give rise to criminal liability only where the breach falls within the
scope of s. 12(1)–(4) CPA 1987.

CASE STUDY

Rex, the proprietor of the Dog and Flea public house, purchases a dishwasher from
Vomet Super Store. The dishwasher is to be used in the kitchen of the pub to clean
plates and cutlery. There is a heavy demand for snacks at the pub, and the dishwasher
is very slow and keeps clogging, flooding the kitchen. It breaks down twice in the first
week of use and Rex is told by the man who calls to fix it that it needs a new pump
and that this type of machine is wholly inappropriate for use in a busy pub kitchen.

Rex wishes to return the dishwasher to Vomet Super Store and get his money back.
Advise him.

Rex may seek to argue that the dishwasher was not of satisfactory quality and thus
Vomet are in breach of the statutorily implied term under s. 14(2) SGA 1979. Much can
be said about the meaning of 'satisfactory quality', particularly in relation to merchandise which is complex and sophisticated (see p. 229). In particular, reference should be

made to *Bernstein* v. *Pamson Motors Ltd*, *Rogers* v. *Parish (Scarborough) Ltd*, and *Shine* v. *General Guarantee Corporation*.

Section 14(3) is also of importance (see p. 230). Did Rex draw to the attention of Vomet's salesperson, when he purchased the goods, the particular purpose for which the dishwasher was to be used?

Can Rex rescind the contract? Not according to *Bernstein* v. *Pamson Motors*. This is by reason of s. 35 SGA, in that by using the goods he accepted them, and has thereby lost the right to rescind.

EIGHT

Licensing law

Liquor licensing was at the forefront of legislative reform in the late 1980s after much lobbying from the hotel, catering and licensed trades. The reforms which were made to the principal legislation, the Licensing Act 1964, are to be found in the Licensing Act 1988.

The purposes of this chapter are:

- to examine the legislative provisions made regarding the sale and supply of alcoholic beverages;
- to review how liquor licensing operates in relation to restaurants, hotels and clubs;
- to consider the relevant law on the conduct of licensed premises and a licensee's responsibility for the behaviour of those to whom he or she serves liquor;
- to provide an overview of other forms of licence.

8.1 LIQUOR LICENSING

The Licensing Act 1964 (LA 1964) consolidated the earlier licensing legislation and, although it has been amended by the Licensing Act 1988 (LA 1988), the Deregulation and Contracting Out Act 1994, and the Licensing (Sunday Hours) Act 1995, it remains the principal statute relating to liquor licensing. The legislation is coherent, though complex. Part I of the LA 1964 establishes the general licensing system.

The licensing system

It is a criminal offence contrary to s. 160 LA 1964 to sell or expose for sale any intoxicating liquor without a justices' licence. Not every sale of intoxicating liquor requires the vendor to possess a justices' licence; the following retail sales do not require one:
(a) the sale of liquor in a theatre;
(b) the supply of liquor to a member of a registered club;
(c) the sale of liquor on board a ship or aircraft which is *en route*, or its sale on a train to passengers who may, if they wish, be supplied with food;
(d) sale of liquor to service personnel in naval or military canteens.
'Intoxicating liquor' includes wine, spirits, cider, and 'any other fermented, distilled or spirituous liquor'. 'Retail sale' means no more than 9 litres or one case of spirits or wine, and 20 litres or two cases of beer or cider.

The law and practice of liquor licensing under the LA 1964 have been that the licensing system in England and Wales is controlled by local licensing justices. These are formed into committees of between five and fifteen members of the local bench of magistrates. It is the function of this body to grant, renew, transfer or remove justices' licences within their district. A licensing meeting is held annually. This used to be known as 'the general annual licensing meeting', and is held in the first fortnight of February. Liquor licences are reviewed each year at this meeting and any objections to renewal will be heard. The meeting must be advertised so that interested parties can attend, and 21 days' notice of the date of the meeting must be given by the justices.

The licensing justices may also hold between four and eight transfer sessions annually. It is at these meetings that applications other than ordinary renewals are heard. The transfer sessions are held before at least three members of the licensing committee for the district. It is a requirement of office that any magistrate sitting on the licensing committee must not have any financial interest in the brewing or retailing of liquor, or hold shares in a company which is so interested. Licensing sessions are akin to administrative tribunals in the way they operate. They do not try cases; nor are they subject to strict rules of evidence; and they have no power to make an order for costs. Hearings, however, are heard in public and the justices must act judicially.

The material ways in which the law and practice of liquor licensing were affected by the LA 1988 are:
1   The duration of a justices' licence to sell intoxicating liquor is three years (s. 11 LA 1988). Thus the utility and function of the general annual licensing meeting decreased.
2   Section 14 LA 1988 modified the constitution and procedure of licensing justices. In s. 14(1) LA 1988, the previous maximum of eight transfer sessions was abolished. Section 14(2) LA 1988 inserted a new section, s. 192A, into the LA 1964. This provides that where a majority of licensing justices present at a licensing session resolve to do so, they may constitute themselves into two or more divisions. A division, where constituted, may exercise all the powers of licensing justices under the LA 1964. The quorum of a division of justices constituted under this provision is three. Section 14(3) LA 1988 amended Schedule 1 to the LA 1964 so as to extend the number of justices constituting the licensing committee to twenty or such other number as authorized by the Secretary of State.

Applying for a licence

In England and Wales there is a set procedure to be followed when making a licence application:

1   At least 21 days prior to the date fixed for the hearing the applicant shall give notice in writing of his or her intention to make an application. Notice is given to: (a) the clerk to the justices; (b) the chief officer of police for the district; and (c) the local authority. The clerk to the justices' copy shall have attached to it a plan of the premises in respect of which the licence is applied for. A copy of the notice plus a plan will also be sent to the local fire authority.

2   During the 28-day period prior to the date set for the hearing, applicants must display a copy of their notice of intended application at or near the premises to be licensed. The notice must be displayed in such a way that it may be conveniently read by members of the public, and must be displayed for a minimum of seven days.

3   Between 28 and 14 days prior to the date of the hearing, the applicant shall publish a copy of the notice of intended application in a local newspaper. It is usual practice for the justice to state when this should be done.

The aforementioned notices are normally standard forms available from the clerk to the justices. The notices will in any event include the following information: (a) the name and address of the applicant; (b) the location of the premises for which the licence is sought; (c) the type of licence sought; and (d) the applicant's occupation for the past six months. They must be signed by the applicant. Where the premises for which a licence is sought are owned by a company, the licence is applied for in the name of the person who will manage the premises.

The applicant is invariably required to attend the licensing session in person. He or she is entitled to legal representation. Witnesses may be required by the justices to attend and give evidence. A licence may be granted to anyone who is not disqualified from holding a licence, and whom the licensing justices consider to be a fit and proper person to hold a licence. The main point to be established by an applicant is, therefore, that he or she is such a fit and proper person. The justices are also concerned about the suitability of the premises. Certain people are disqualified from holding a justices' licence:

(a) any public official executing the legal process;
(b) any person convicted of permitting licensed premises to be used as a brothel;
(c) any person disqualified for selling liquor without a licence;
(d) any person who has been convicted of forgery of a justices' licence or of its fraudulent use.

If a licence is issued to a person who is disqualified it is of no legal effect whatsoever.

New on-licences (other than for wine alone) may have conditions imposed upon them at the justices' discretion. Such conditions may restrict the licence to the sale of certain types of liquor, or may restrict sale to certain parts of the premises. The justices must decide whether the premises in question are structurally suitable before granting an on-licence. The licensee may be required to make alterations, e.g. provide more exits or further fire precautions. Breach of a condition imposed by the licensing justices is not itself an offence, though it may lead to the commission of an offence if, thereafter, liquor is sold at the premises.

Certain premises are in fact disqualified from use as licensed premises: (a) premises which form part of a motorway service area; (b) premises where, within a period of two years, two separate licensees have forfeited their licences for the same premises;

such premises are disqualified from receiving a justices' licence for twelve months following the second forfeiture; (c) by s. 10 LA 1988, which inserted new provisions, s. 9(4A) and 9(4B), into the LA 1964.

> *(4A) Premises shall be disqualified for receiving a justices' licence if they are primarily used as a garage or form part of premises which are primarily so used.*
>
> *(4B) In subsection (4A) of this section, the reference to use as a garage is a reference to use for any one or more of the following purposes, namely, the retailing of petrol or derv or the sale or maintenance of motor vehicles.*

Anyone may object to the grant of a justices' licence without giving notice. The grounds on which such objections are based may vary: a local resident may be worried about the effect the licensed premises might have on a residential area, local licensees may be fearful of lost trade, etc. The justices will thereafter make a decision: either they will grant a licence or refuse the application. In the event of a refusal the applicant has a right of appeal to the Crown Court. Where a licence is granted, the objectors have a similar right of appeal against the grant. Notice of an appeal must be served on the clerk to the justices within 21 days of the hearing. The licensing appeal bench consists of a Crown Court judge sitting with four licensing justices, two of whom are from the division concerned. No justice may hear an appeal against a decision in which he or she took part.

By virtue of s. 15 LA 1988 (which inserted a new provision, s. 193B, into the LA 1964), the licensing justices may, on hearing an application under the Licensing Act relating to licensed premises, make such order as they think just and reasonable for the payment of costs, to the applicant by any person opposing the application or by the applicant to any such person. The purpose of this provision is to ward off vexatious and to promote bona fide objections to licence applications.

A provisional grant of a licence may be made where premises are being constructed or altered, provided plans of the premises are deposited with the justices and found by them to be satisfactory. The licensing justices must declare the provisional grant of a licence final if the premises are thereafter completed in accordance with the plans, provided the licensee is a fit and proper person to hold a licence. Section 9 LA 1988 inserted a new section, s. 6(4A), into the LA 1964; this enables the holder of a provisional licence to apply, before the premises have been completed, to have the provisional grant made final before the date appointed for the next licensing sessions; and the licensing justices may (if they are satisfied that the premises are likely to be completed) direct that the declaration be made before the next licensing sessions by a single licensing justice.

Where s. 6(4A) applies, a single licensing justice, after such notice has been given as he or she may require, will declare the provisional grant final, provided he or she is satisfied that the premises have been completed in accordance with the plans deposited or as modified under s. 6(3) LA 1964.

For how long does a justices' licence last? Prior to the LA 1988, by s. 26 LA 1964, a licence lasted from the time of its grant until and including the following 4 April or, if granted in the last three months of the licensing year, until 4 April the following year. The LA 1988 radically altered the duration of a justices' licence. Section 11 LA 1988 amends s. 26 LA 1964 thus:

... *a justices' licence* –
(a) *if granted before 5th January 1989, shall be granted to have effect from the time of the grant until 4th April 1989;*
(b) *if granted after 4th January and before 5th April 1989, shall be granted to have effect from the time of the grant until 4th April 1992; and*
(c) *if granted after 4th April 1989, shall be granted to have effect from the time of the grant until the expiry of the current licensing period or, if granted in the last three months of that period, until the end of the next licensing period;*
but shall be superseded on the coming into force of a licence granted by way of renewal, transfer or removal of it.

In s. 26(5) LA 1964, which used to define 'licensing year', it is now provided that:

In this Act 'licensing period' means a period of three years beginning with 5th April 1989 or any triennial of that date.

The net effect of these amendments is that a justices' licence will now last for three years, rather than one. When a new licence is granted after an objection, s. 27 LA 1964 provides that the licence will not come into force until the expiration of 21 days after the hearing. This is the period within which an appeal against the grant of the licence must be lodged.

The LA 1988 made a new provision for the revocation of a justices' licence; s. 12 LA 1988 inserted s. 20A into the LA 1964, which provides (s. 20A(1):19):

Licensing justices may revoke a justices' licence at any licensing sessions, other than licensing sessions at which an application for renewal of the licence fails to be considered, either of their own motion or on the application of any person.

Section 20A(2) outlines when a justices' licence may be revoked under this section, namely on any ground on which licensing justices might refuse to renew a justices' licence (see below).

The procedure to be followed where the power of revocation is contemplated is set out in s. 20A(3):

Licensing justices may only exercise the power conferred by this section if, at least twenty-one days before the commencement of the licensing sessions in question, notice in writing of the proposal to exercise the power or, as the case may be, to make the application has been given to the holder of the licence and, in the case of a proposed application, to the clerk to the licensing justices, specifying in general terms the grounds on which it is proposed the licence should be revoked.

When revocation comes into effect is laid down in s. 20A(5):

A decision under this section to revoke a justices' licence shall not have effect –
(a) *until the expiry of the time for appealing against the decision; or*
(b) *if the decision is appealed against, until the appeal is disposed of.*

For an interesting article entitled 'Revoking a liquor licence', see Tony Wilkinson's article in the Law Society's *Gazette*, 31 October 1990.

Renewal of a licence

All justices' licences must be renewed before 4 April, which is the date of their expiry. Renewals of justices' licences under the LA 1964 could be granted by the justices only at their annual licensing meeting. Provision has been made in s. 13 LA 1988 for the clerk to the licensing justices to grant unopposed renewals of justices' licences. Prior to this power, most renewals had been granted *en bloc* after the annual reports at the annual licensing meeting. It was not necessary for a licensee to send a formal notice of his or her intention to apply for a renewal. (This was taken for granted.) Renewals are for three years.

The provision governing renewal of a justices' licence is s. 7 LA 1964. Section 7, as amended by the LA 1988, provides:

> (1) *Licensing justices may not renew a justice's licence at transfer sessions, except where the licence was due for renewal at the preceding general annual licensing meeting and the justices are satisfied that the applicant had reasonable cause for not applying for renewal at that meeting.*
>
> (2) *A person intending to oppose an application for the renewal of a justice's licence shall give notice in writing of his intention to the applicant, specifying in general terms the grounds of the opposition, not later than seven days before the commencement of the licensing sessions at which the application is to be made, and unless notice has been so given the licensing justices shall not entertain the objection.*

Section 13 LA 1988 made provision for the grant of an unopposed renewal by the justices' clerk; it did so by inserting a new section, s. 193A, into the LA 1964. This section provides:

> (1) *This section has effect in relation to applications for the renewal of justices' licences and canteen licences made to the general annual licensing sessions immediately preceding the expiry of a licensing period.*
>
> (2) *The clerk to the licensing justices may exercise on behalf of the justices their powers with respect to an application for the renewal of a justice's licence or canteen licence if:*
>   (a) *the application is not opposed; or*
>   (b) *where under this Act the application may only be refused on specified grounds, it is not opposed on a ground on which renewal may be refused.*
>
> (3) *An application may not be dealt with under this section if:*
>   (a) *the justices so direct;*
>   (b) *it is made in conjunction with any other application or request with respect to the licence sought to be renewed; or*
>   (c) *in the case of an application for the renewal of a justices' licence, there is a relevant entry in the register of justices' licences maintained under this Act which relates to the applicant or the premises for which the licence is sought.*

On the renewal of an on-licence, the licensing justice may require a plan of the premises to be deposited and, if they think it necessary, order structural alterations to be carried out in any part of the premises where liquor is sold or consumed (s. 19 LA 1964).

Transfer of a licence (s. 8 LA 1964)

A justices' licence is granted to a named person in respect of specified premises. Therefore, where the person to whom the licence is granted with respect to given premises changes, a transfer of the licence concerning those premises is required. The vast majority of transfers are made when the holder of the licence gives up occupation of the premises, e.g. where there has been a sale of the premises, or where there is a new tenant or manager.

The applicant for a transfer will be the person intending to take over the licence. Notice must be given in the same way as if the person seeking the transfer were applying for a new licence (see above). A copy of the notice must be sent to the current licensee. There is no need for display of the notice at the premises, or for publication in the local newspaper. The applicant, the current licensee and any witnesses may be required to appear before a transfer session of the licensing justices in person to give evidence. The transfer of a justices' licence may be granted only in certain circumstances:

1 On the death of the licensee, transfer may be made to his or her personal representatives, or the new occupier or tenant of the premises.
2 Where the licensee has become either physically or mentally incapable of carrying on the business, the licence may be transferred to his or her assigns, or to the new occupier or tenant.
3 Where the licensee has been declared bankrupt, the licence may be transferred to the licensee's trustees in bankruptcy, or to a new tenant or occupier.
4 Where the licensee has given up, is giving up, or is about to give up the occupation of the premises, or the carrying on of the business, the licence may be transferred to the new occupier or tenant.
5 Where the licence holder has, on the point of quitting the premises, wilfully omitted to apply for the renewal of the licence, a transfer may be granted to the new tenant or occupier.
6 Where the owner (or his or her agent) has obtained a 'protection order' in respect of the premises, the licence may be transferred to the owner (or the owner's agent).

The transfer should in each case be granted prior to the date of the proposed changeover.

Where there is an urgent need to transfer a licence prior to the next transfer sessions of the licensing justices, the applicant may apply for a 'protection order'. The protection order is in effect a temporary transfer, an interim measure until something more permanent may be arranged. In all cases other than the death or bankruptcy of the licensee, the application for a protection order is made to the local magistrates, with seven days' notice to the police (giving the same details as are required upon an application for a new licence). A protection order, when granted, lasts until the close of the next but one transfer session of the licensing justices. The authority conferred by a protection order is the same as that given by a justices' licence. Protection orders are provided for by s. 10 LA 1964.

Removal of a licence

When the holder of a licence wishes to move the licence from premises X to premises Y, he or she makes use of a system known as removal. An application is made to the justices in whose district the proposed premises (Y) are situated. The applicant is required to give the same notices as if he or she were applying for a new licence. An additional copy must be sent to the owner of the present premises (X). The justices have a discretion to refuse the removal, in the same way as they have a discretion to refuse the grant of a new licence. It should be noted that neither a residential nor a restaurant licence may be 'removed' by this procedure; the proper course of action is to apply for a new licence in respect of the new premises.

The various types of justices' licence

Full on-licence

A full on-licence enables the licensee to sell liquor for consumption either on or off the premises to any member of the public who is permitted by the law to consume it. This is the broadest form of justices' licence, and is the form of licence which applies to public houses. The justices have a complete discretion whether or not to grant a full on-licence. The most important factor to be borne in mind is whether or not there is a need within the district in question for further premises licensed in this way.

Off-licence

An off-licence permits the sale of liquor for consumption off the premises. The only question of importance raised by this area of the law has been whether licensing justices, when granting an off-licence, can impose terms as to its grant. In *R. v. Edmonton Licensing Justices Ex Parte Baker and Another* [1983] 2 All ER 545, it was held that licensing justices had no power to impose a legally enforceable undertaking as a condition of the grant of an off-licence. The licensing justices may of course seek assurances from applicants as to how they propose to conduct the premises and, bearing these in mind, consider whether or not to grant the licence. However, such assurances, once given, are unenforceable and can be disregarded with impunity by the licensee after the licence has been granted.

Occasional licences

An occasional licence is granted to a person who already holds an on-licence for one set of premises and who wishes to sell liquor at some special event which is to be held at premises which are normally unlicensed. This will cover parties and balls, fetes, wedding breakfasts and twenty-first birthday parties. However, in *R. v. Bow Street Justices Ex Parte Commissioner of Metropolitan Police* [1983] 2 All ER 915, it was held that the grant of an occasional licence may cover the situation where the applicant has held two licences, one of which is continuing and the other which has by mistake been allowed to run out; the occasional licence may be granted to enable the sale of liquor at the premises where the previous licence has run out.

Application for an occasional licence may be made to the local magistrates. The applicant must state: (a) his or her name and address; (b) the location of the premises for which the licence is sought; (c) the nature of the event; and (d) the duration for which the licence is sought. The applicant must give 24 hours' notice to the police of his or her intention to apply. The police have the right to attend the hearing and object to the grant of the licence.

An alternative procedure is laid down whereby if the applicant gives 28 days' notice to the clerk of the court prior to the date set for the hearing, the magistrates may grant the licence without calling the applicant to a hearing. Upon receipt of the notice the clerk will notify the police, who have seven days to lodge an objection. If no objection is lodged the licence may be granted in this way. An occasional licence may not be granted for certain days, e.g. Christmas Day.

Occasional permissions

The Licensing (Occasional Permissions) Act 1983 empowers licensing justices in England and Wales to grant to representatives of organizations not carried on for private gain occasional permissions authorizing the sale of intoxicating liquor at functions connected with the activities of such organizations.

Licensing justices may grant to an officer of an eligible organization, or a branch of such an organization, a permission authorizing the sale of intoxicating liquor during a period not exceeding 24 hours at a function held by the organization or branch in connection with the organization's activities (s. 1(1), L(OP)A 1983) (see also *R*. v. *Bromley Justices Ex Parte Bromley LVA* [1984] 1 All ER 794). Before granting an 'occasional permission' the justices must be satisfied as to the following matters set out in s. 1(2) of the Act:
(a) that the officer is a fit and proper person to sell intoxicating liquor and is resident in their licensing district;
(b) that the place where the function is to be held will be a suitable place for intoxicating liquor to be sold and is situated in that district; and
(c) that the sale of intoxicating liquor at the function is not likely to result in disturbance or annoyance being caused to residents in the neighbourhood of that place, or in any disorderly conduct.
An occasional permission will be in writing and will specify (see s. 1(3) of the Act):
(a) the place where intoxicating liquor may be sold by virtue of the permission;
(b) the kind or kinds of intoxicating liquor that may be sold there by virtue of the permission; and
(c) the hours between which such liquor may be so sold and the date (or dates) on which those hours fall.
In granting the permission the justices may attach any condition that they think proper to the grant of the permission.

There is a limit to the number of times any single organization may seek to utilize 'occasional permission'; this limitation is set out in s. 1(4) of the Act. It limits the number of occasional permissions to a maximum of four per organization in any period of twelve months.

Who may apply for the grant of an occasional permission? Only an 'eligible organization' may apply. Section 1(6) defines this term:

> *'eligible organisation' means any organisation not carried on for purposes of private gain; and, except in the case of an organisation carrying on a commercial under-taking, a purpose which is calculated to benefit an organisation as a whole shall not*

be taken to be a purpose of private gain by reason only that action in fulfilment of the purpose would result in benefit to any person as an individual.

Section 2 of the L(OP)A 1983 sets out the procedure for applying for an occasional permission:

(1) *An application for an occasional permission shall be in writing and shall contain the following particulars: -*
   (a) *the name and address of the applicant and the date and place of his birth;*
   (b) *the name of the organisation in connection with whose activities the function in question is to be held, the purposes for which the organisation is carried on, and (where appropriate) the name of the branch holding the function;*
   (c) *the nature of the applicant's office in the organisation or branch holding the function;*
   (d) *the date and nature of the function and the place where it is to be held;*
   (e) *the kind or kinds of intoxicating liquor proposed to be sold at the function and the hours between which it is proposed that such liquor should be sold;*
   (f) *details of any occasional permissions granted by the licensing justices in the twelve months preceding the date of the application in respect of functions held by the organisation or branch holding the function.*
(2) *An application for an occasional permission shall be made by serving two copies of the application on the clerk to the licensing justices not less than one month before the date of the function in respect of which the application is made.*
(3) *On receiving an application under subsection (2) above the clerk shall serve notice of the application on the chief officer of police by sending him a copy of it.*
(4) *An application for an occasional permission shall be heard by the licensing justices at the next licensing sessions following its receipt by the clerk or, where those sessions are to be held fifteen days or less after its receipt, at the licensing sessions next following those sessions.*
(5) *The clerk shall send to an applicant notice of the date, time and place of the licensing sessions at which his application is to be heard in accordance with subsection (4) above: and the list kept for those sessions under paragraph 6 of Schedule 2 to the principal Act shall show the name and address of the applicant, the nature of the application and the place where the function in question is to be held.*
(6) *On the consideration of an application for an occasional permission the applicant shall, if so required by the licensing justices, attend in person, and licensing justices may postpone consideration of such an application until the applicant does attend.*

Section 3 and Schedule I to the Act set out offences with respect to the sale of liquor under the Act; these mirror those contained in the LA 1964.

For residential licences, restaurant licences and combined licences, see below.

8.2 RESTAURANTS, HOTELS AND CLUBS

These three forms of catering establishment get separate attention with respect to the licensing of premises. Restaurants in particular were singled out for limited reform of permitted hours by the Licensing (Restaurant Meals) Act 1987.

Restaurants (s. 93 LA 1964)

There are two kinds of licence that a restaurant may apply for in order to serve drinks with meals:

(a) an ordinary justices' licence with a condition that a drink may be served only with a meal; and

(b) a restaurant licence.

The more common application is for a restaurant licence, since the licensing justices may refuse an application for a restaurant licence only on certain limited grounds. Furthermore, there are likely to be fewer objections from local licensees to the grant of a restaurant licence.

A restaurant, for the purposes of the grant of a restaurant licence, is 'premises structurally adapted and *bona fide* used, or intended to be used, for the purpose of providing the customary main meal at midday or in the evening, or both, for the accommodation of persons frequenting the premises'. An application for a restaurant licence is made to the licensing justices in the same manner as that described in the section on the licensing system.

The justices may refuse a restaurant licence only on the following grounds (s. 98 LA 1964):

1 The applicant is under 21 years old.
2 The proposed premises are not suitable.
3 The applicant is not a fit and proper person.
4 The premises will not be used to provide proper meals.
5 During the previous twelve months, the premises have been conducted improperly.
6 During the previous twelve months, soft drinks (including water) were not made as available as alcoholic drinks.
7 The main business of the restaurant is not that of providing table meals.
8 There would be a self-service method of selling drink.
9 The majority of customers were under eighteen years of age and were not accompanied by adults who purchased the drink.
10 The fire authority, local authority or police have been unable to inspect the premises after taking all reasonable steps to do so.

Where the justices refuse to grant a restaurant licence reasons must be given for their refusal; furthermore, the applicant has a right of appeal to the Crown Court.

The justices, when granting a restaurant licence, may attach certain conditions. However, they *must* attach the following two conditions:

1 The restaurant must be able to serve both water and soft drinks as well as alcohol.
2 Alcohol can be served only to those taking table meals.

Renewal and transfer of restaurant licences operate in the same way as outlined above.

Hotels

A residential licence authorizes the sale of liquor to residents of a hotel. It may be granted in respect of premises which are '*bona fide* used, or intended to be used, for the purpose of habitually providing for reward board and lodging, including breakfast and one other meal at least of the customary main meals'. The justices must be satisfied that the premises are suitable for use as a licensed hotel. Two conditions are attached to the grant of a residential licence: other beverages (including water) must be available with meals; and adequate seating must be provided in a room at the hotel which is not used as sleeping accommodation or for the service of food, and in which there is neither supply nor consumption of intoxicating liquor.

The only grounds on which a residential licence may be refused are those which are grounds for the refusal of a restaurant licence (1–10 above, excluding 7).

It may of course be the case that the hotel is an 'inn' as defined by s. 1(3) Hotel Proprietors Act 1956, in which case the usual form of licence is a full on-licence.

Combined licences

It is possible to combine a residential licence with a restaurant licence. This enables liquor to be sold to residents and to members of the general public who are dining in the restaurant. This form of licence is most useful to small and medium-sized hotels which have a restaurant which is open to the public. The grant and refusal of such a combined licence are subject to the same conditions and restrictions as those which apply to each form of licence separately.

A residential, restaurant or combined licence may be forfeited if the licensee is convicted of:
(a) selling drink without a licence;
(b) breaching the conditions of a licence;
(c) permitting drunkenness or disorderly conduct at the premises;
(d) permitting unlawful gaming (darts, dominoes, draughts, cribbage and chess are not gaming);
(e) passing betting slips, etc.;
(f) allowing prostitutes to meet habitually at the premises;
(g) permitting the premises to be used as a brothel (this carries automatic forfeiture of the licence).
Alternatively, the licensee may be disqualified from holding such a licence for up to five years, and the court may in addition prohibit the use of the premises as a restaurant for a period of up to five years. A licensee may appeal to the Crown Court against such a disqualification.

Clubs

For the purposes of the licensing laws there are two kinds of clubs: licensed clubs and registered clubs.

A licensed club, unlike a registered club, is a business set up to make a profit. In order to sell drink legally, such clubs must have a justices' licence.

A registered club is one where the profits go to the members and club property is owned in equal shares by the members. In order to sell liquor the club must have a registration certificate, which is obtainable from an ordinary session of the Magistrates' Court. An application to a licensing session of the justices is not required.

Registered clubs are not classed as 'bars in licensed premises', so the prohibition of children being in a registered club does not apply. Also, because the alcoholic stocks belong to the members, 'sales' do not take place when alcoholic beverages are supplied to members. Instead, the supply of alcoholic beverages to members can be perceived as a transfer of assets. As no 'sale' takes place the Weights and Measures Act 1985 does not apply either. Most registered clubs, however, deem it good sense to use the commonly used legal measures for the supply of alcoholic beverages. In those cases where a registered club makes a sale of alcoholic beverages to non-members, the Weights and Measures Act does apply.

Licensed clubs

An application for a justices' licence by a club is made to the licensing justices; the procedure for this is outlined above. In addition to the normal documentation, the club's rules must be sent to the clerk to the justices. The provisions for transfer and renewal are also the same as with other forms of justices' licence.

Registered clubs

In order to be a registered club, a club must have a registration certificate, which will be granted only if the club complies with certain requirements:
1   The club must be established and conducted in good faith as a club.
2   There must be at least 25 members.
3   At least two days must elapse between a new member applying for membership and his or her using the club as a member.
4   No one must gain any financial benefit from the supply of alcohol by the club.
5   The purchase and supply of drink must be supervised by the club's committee, or by a sub-committee whose members serve between one and five years.
6   Alcohol can be supplied only on behalf of the club.
To obtain registration, an application is sent to the clerk to the justices, who will forward copies to the police, the fire authority and the local authority. The application must be signed by the club's chairperson or secretary and a copy of the club's rules should be attached to it. The clerk, on receipt of the application for registration, must allow 28 days in which the police, fire authority or local authority may lodge an objection. Applicants must also give public notice of their application, which must be done within seven days of lodging the application with the clerk to the justices. In granting a registration certificate, the magistrates may impose conditions. Appeal is to the Crown Court, either against the magistrates' refusal of registration or against any conditions imposed for registration.

Objections to the proposed registration of a club may be made only by the police, the fire authority, the local authority, or anyone occupying neighbouring premises who could be affected. Furthermore, the grounds for objection are limited to the following:
(a) that the application has not been made as stipulated by law;
(b) that the premises are unsuitable;
(c) that the club cannot legally be a registered club since it fails to fulfil the conditions;
(d) that the premises have already been forbidden by a court to be a club;

(e) that the proposed manager of the club has been shown in court to be unfit to manage a club;
(f) that during the preceding year a licence in respect of the club premises has been forfeited;
(g) that the club already has other premises with different permitted hours (to prevent the club having three separate premises with different permitted hours so that the members, by moving from one site to another, may escape the rigours of the licensing laws);
(h) that the club is disorderly;
(i) that the club premises are habitually used by criminals or sots;
(j) that there have been illegal sales of drink or that unaccompanied non-members have habitually been admitted to the club.

If an authority or person wishes to object he or she must send two copies of the objection to the clerk of the court within 28 days of the application being made. At the hearing an adjournment may be granted if the police or the two authorities wish further time to inspect the premises. If this adjournment is granted, the time for making objections is extended. The applicant should be present at the hearing. The justices have power to award costs against the objector or the club.

Where a registration certificate is granted, the police, fire authority or local authority may take out a summons seeking the cancellation of the certificate. In order to establish sufficient grounds for the cancellation of the certificate, one of the following must be established:

(a) that the registered club does not fulfil the qualifications of a registered club;
(b) that the person managing the club has been shown in court to be unfit to do so;
(c) that in the previous twelve months a licence in respect of the same premises has been forfeited;
(d) that the club has other premises with different permitted hours;
(e) that the club premises have been disqualified by a court from being used as a club;
(f) that the club premises are habitually used by criminals or sots;
(g) that there have been illegal sales of drink at the club;
(h) that the club is disorderly.

A registration certificate must be renewed annually for the first two years of its issue. However, a club may request, when applying for the third time, that the certificate be issued for ten years, or for a shorter period. Where a club seeks renewal of registration the procedure to be followed is the same as that for a first application, though there is no requirement as to public notice and advertising.

If there is any alteration of the club's rules which invalidates the information held by the clerk of the court, the club must notify the clerk within 42 days and the secretary must notify the police and the local authority within 21 days. Failure to do so constitutes an offence.

Any club, whether licensed or registered, may lose its licence or registration certificate through misconduct. Misconduct covers:

(a) selling drink to people under eighteen years of age;
(b) employing people aged under eighteen in the bar;
(c) permitting children under fourteen in the bar; (excepting in registered clubs)
(d) after-hours drinking;
(e) disorderly conduct;
(f) breach of the conditions on which the licence was granted.

A very useful article on licensing problems with registered clubs is to be found in *The Legal Executive Journal*, March 1991, p. 14.

8.3 PERMITTED HOURS

It is a criminal offence under s. 59 LA 1964 for any person to sell or supply intoxicating liquor, either personally or through an employee or agent, on licensed premises or the premises of a registered club, except during permitted hours. A customer who consumes liquor outside permitted hours is also committing a separate, though related, offence. Section 59 does not apply to an occasional licence; nor does it apply to a situation where an extension of permitted hours has been obtained. Where the licensee or the person in charge of the licensed premises entertains his friends after hours at his expense, this is not an offence. A licensee is not required to close the premises outside the permitted hours, provided no liquor is sold or supplied; equally, there is nothing which requires the licensee to remain open during permitted hours.

On-licences

The permitted hours for licensed premises on weekdays other than Christmas Day or Good Friday are from 1100 hours to 2300 hours. On Sundays, (other than when Christmas Day falls on a Sunday) and Good Friday, the permitted hours are 1200 hours to 2230 hours. On Christmas Day, the permitted hours are 1200 hours to 1500, and 1900 to 2230 hours.

Licensing Justices, if satisfied that the requirements of their district make it desirable, have power to vary the weekday hours for their area by fixing an earlier opening hour but not earlier than 1000 hours. Where the Justices vary the permitted hours in this way they may do so for different weekdays and for different periods of not less than eight consecutive weeks.

The powers of the Licensing Justices to fix the hours for the licensing district can only be exercised at the Annual Licensing Meeting and the hours must be the same for the whole of the licensing division.

Where Justices intend to consider any proposal for the variation of the permitted hours in their district, a notice in the prescribed form must be published in two newspapers circulating in the district and, if they think fit, in such further manner as they may direct. When the proposal is considered the Justices must take into account local opinion and hear the views of those who they consider may be able to give expression to that opinion.

Off-licences

The permitted hours on weekdays, other than Christmas Day, are from 0800 hours until the evening terminal hour which will be either 2230 hours or 2300 hours as the case may be. The permitted hours on Sundays, other than Christmas Day, shall begin at 1000 hours. On Christmas Day the hours are the same as for on-licensed premises.

On-licensed premises which have a separate off-licence department, in respect of which there is no internal communication for customers between that part and any part of the premises where sales or consumption on the premises take place, can obtain permission from the Licensing Justices to have the full off-licence hours for that part.

Registered clubs

The permitted hours for registered clubs are set out in s. 62(1) LA 1964 as amended by s.1(5)LA 1988:

> *The permitted hours in premises in respect of which o club is registered shall be: –*
> (a) *on weekdays, other than Christmas Day or Good Friday, the general licensing hours; and*
> (b) *on Sundays, Christmas Day and Good Friday, the hours fixed by or under the rules of the club in accordance with the following conditions: –*
>   (i)   *the hours fixed shall not be longer than five and a half hours and shall not begin earlier than twelve noon nor end later than half past ten in the evening;*
>   (ii) *there shall be a break in the afternoon of not less than two hours which shall include the hours from three to five; and*
>   (iii) *there shall not be more than three and a half hours after five.*

Drinking-up time (s. 63 LA 1964)

After the end of the hours during which sales are permitted, 'drinking-up time' is allowed. The LA 1988, by s. 2, extended the premises' drinking-up time of ten minutes to twenty minutes.

Restriction orders

The LA 1988, whilst liberalizing to a very large degree the permitted hours when intoxicating liquor may be served at licensed premises, also provides for a limited degree of restriction upon permitted hours. The Act does this in s. 3, which introduced a new provision, s. 67A, into the LA 1964. Section 67A provides:

> (1) *An order under this section may be made with respect to: –*
>   (a) *any licensed premises or part of licensed premises, other than premises licensed for the sale of intoxicating liquor for consumption off the premises only and any premises for which an occasional licence is in force; and*
>   (b) *any premises in respect of which a club is registered.*
> (2) *An order under this section is referred to in this section as a 'restriction order'.*
> (3) *Where a restriction order is in force with respect to any premises or part of any premises, the permitted hours in those premises or that part shall not include any time specified in the order.*
> (4) *A restriction order may specify any time between half past two and half past five in the afternoon and may apply in relation to particular days of the week specified in the order and in relation to particular periods of the year so specified.*
> (5) *The power to make a restriction order shall be exercisable: –*
>   (a) *with respect to licensed premises, by licensing justices, and*

    (b) *with respect to premises in respect of which a club is registered, by a magistrates' court,*

on application being made to them under this section.

  (6) *An application for a restriction order may be made by: –*

    (a) *the chief officer of police;*

    (b) *any person living in the neighbourhood, or anybody representing persons who do;*

    (c) *any person carrying on a business in the neighbourhood or managing or otherwise in charge of it in the neighbourhood; or*

    (d) *the head teacher or other person in charge of any educational establishment in the neighbourhood.*

  (7) *A restriction order may be made: –*

    (a) *on the ground that it is desirable to avoid or reduce any disturbance of or annoyance to: -*

      (i) *persons living or working in the neighbourhood,*

      (ii) *customers or clients of any business in the neighbourhood, or*

      (iii) *persons attending, or in charge of persons attending, any educational establishment in the neighbourhood,*

due to the use of the premises or part of the premises; or

    (b) *on the ground that it is desirable to avoid or reduce the occurrence of disorderly conduct in the premises or part of the premises or the occurrence in the vicinity of the premises of disorderly conduct on the part of persons resorting to the premises or part of the premises.*

  (8) *The terms of a restriction order shall be such as the licensing justices or, as the case may be, the magistrates' court think fit.*

  (9) *A restriction order shall have effect as from the date specified in it and (unless revoked or varied or the licence or registration ceases to be in force) for the period specified in it, which shall not exceed twelve months.*

The restriction order provisions are designed to limit licensing hours in accordance with local conditions. The restriction order is in many ways a recognition of legitimate opposition to an extension of licensing hours in a given locality. Under s. 67A(6), not only may the police apply for a restriction order, but so may any person living in the neighbourhood, or any person carrying on a business in the neighbourhood. The concerns of head teachers with high truancy levels that licensed premises might attract students away from their studies, etc. are also recognized, since head teachers may also apply for a restriction order. The grounds on which a restriction order may be granted are: first, that it is desirable to avoid or reduce any disturbance or annoyance to people living or working in the neighbourhood, or to customers or clients of any business in the neighbourhood, or to people attending, or in charge of people attending, any educational establishment in the neighbourhood, due to the use of the premises; and secondly, it is desirable to avoid or reduce the occurrence of disorderly conduct in the premises, or in the vicinity of the premises, on the part of people using the premises.

The justices can impose such restrictions as they think fit, but such an order cannot last longer than twelve months.

Section 67B provides a right of appeal on the part of the licensee:

  (1) *Any holder of a justices' licence, any club or any proprietor of a theatre aggrieved by a decision of licensing justices or a magistrates' court:*

(a) granting a restriction order, or

(b) as to the terms of a restriction order,

may appeal to the Crown Court against the decision.

(2) On an appeal under this section against a restriction order the applicant for the order shall be respondent in addition to the licensing justices or magistrates' court, as the case may be.

(3) Where an appeal is brought under this section against a restriction order, the operation of the order shall be suspended until the disposal of the appeal, unless the licensing justices or magistrates' court, as the case may be, or the Crown Court otherwise order.

(4) The judgment of the Crown Court on any appeal under this section shall be final.

Where a restriction order is in force, the licensee may apply to the licensing justices (or Magistrates' Court in respect of a registered club) who made the order to have it revoked or its terms varied – s. 67C(1). However, no application for the revocation or variation of a restriction order can be made within a period of six months of the date on which the order came into force. Where such an application is made, s. 67C(3) provides:

the licensing justices or the magistrates' court may, if they think fit: –

(a) where revocation of the order is sought, either revoke it or make such an order varying its terms as they think fit; and

(b) where variation of the terms of the order is sought, make such an order varying its terms as they think fit.

At licensed premises where a restriction order is in force, the licensee shall keep posted in some conspicuous place there a notice stating the effect of the order on the permitted hours – s. 67D.

A restriction order may be imposed on part of the licensed premises, rather than on the whole premises. In this case the notice by s. 67D must be displayed in the part to which the restriction order applies.

The procedural requirements to be followed where an application is made for a restriction order are set out in Schedule 2 to the LA 1988, which takes effect as Schedule 8A to the LA 1964.

Extended hours orders (s. 70 LA 1964)

Justices may make an extended hours order extending the permitted hours for a further hour on weekdays (except Good Friday, Maundy Thursday and Easter eve) in any part of licensed premises where there is a supper hour certificate in force and where substantial refreshment and live entertainment are provided to which the sale of intoxicating liquor is ancillary. The making of an extended hours order is discretionary, and anyone may object to an application for such an order. The police may apply for revocation of an extended hours order once made by the justices.

Until the LA 1988, an extended hours order lapsed when the licence was renewed, transferred, etc. Section 4 LA 1988 amended s. 71(2) LA 1964 so as to provide:

Any such order:
(a)   shall lapse when the licence ceases to be in force otherwise than on its being superseded on renewal or transfer; and
(b)   may be varied by a further such order.

Special hours certificates (s. 77 LA 1964)

This form of extension exists for the benefit of restaurants, etc., where the sale of liquor accompanies, and is ancillary to, the service of substantial refreshment, and where music and dancing are provided.

Section 77 LA 1964 (as amended) provides:

If, on an application made to the licensing justices with respect to licensed premises . . . the justices are satisfied;
(a)   that a music and dancing licence is in force for the premises, and
(b)   that the whole or any part of the premises is structurally adapted, and bona fide used, or intended to be used, for the purpose of providing for persons resorting to the premises music and dancing and substantial refreshment to which the sale of intoxicating liquor is ancillary,
the licensing justices may grant with or without limitations a special hours certificate for the premises or, if they are satisfied that part only of the premises is adapted or used or intended to be used as mentioned in paragraph (b) of this section, for that part.

Section 78 LA 1964 (as amended) applies identical requirements for registered clubs. By s. 5(2) LA 1988, a limitation is imposed on the grant of special hours certificates, by inserting s. 78A into the LA 1964, which provides:

(1)   On an application for a special hours certificate the licensing justices or, as the case may be, the magistrates' court may grant a certificate under section 77 or 78 of this Act limited in any of the following respects.
(2)   The limitations referred to are limitations:
(a)   to particular times of the day;
(b)   to particular days of the week;
(c)   to particular periods of the year.
(3)   Different limitations may be imposed by virtue of subsection (2)(a) above for different days.
(4)   Where a special hours certificate is subject to limitations under this section the licensing justices or, as the case may be, the magistrates' court may, on the application of the licensee or the club, vary any limitation to which it is so subject.

Limitations can be imposed on the grant of a special hours certificate, by s. 81A LA 1964, as set out in s. 5(4) LA 1988.

(1) *Limitations to particular times of the day may also be attached to special hours certificates by licensing justices or, as the case may be, a magistrates' court as provided by subsections (2) and (3) below; and different limitations may be imposed under this section for different days.*

(2) *On an application for revocation of such a certificate under section 81(2) of this Act, the justices or court may, instead of revoking the certificate, attach any limitation authorised by subsection (1) above or vary any such limitation to which the certificate is subject under section 78A of this Act.*

(3) *Any time while such a certificate is in force (other than for any premises situated as mentioned in section 76(3) of this Act) the justices or court may, on the application of the chief officer of police, attach any limitation authorised by subsections (1) above or vary any such limitation to which the certificate is subject under section 78A of this Act.*

(4) *Where a special hours certificate is subject to limitations under subsection (2) or (3) above, the licensing justices or, as the case may be, the magistrates' court may, on the application of the licensee or the club, vary any limitations to which it is so subject.*

A special hours certificate, where in force, may extend licensing hours to 2.00 a.m. (3.00 a.m. in the Metropolitan special hours area) on weekdays other than Good Friday. On Maundy Thursday and Easter eve, and on any day when there is no music and dancing after midnight, the permitted hours end at midnight.

Exemption orders (s. 74 LA 1964)

Applications may be made either for a general order of exemption for market areas or for a special order of exemption for special occasions. (N.B. The hours a business may open are also subject to planning law.)

Liquor licensing and sports grounds

The Sporting Events (Control of Alcohol, etc.) Act 1985 regulates liquor licensing at sports grounds. Section 1 of the Act creates a criminal offence with regard to liquor on coaches and trains used for carrying passengers to and from a 'designated sporting event'. Section 2 creates a criminal offence in connection with alcohol containers, etc., at sports grounds. The section provides:

(1) *A person who has intoxicating liquor or an article to which this section applies in his possession:*
     (a) *at any time during the period of a designated sporting event when he is in any area of a designated sports ground from which the event may be directly viewed, or*

    (b) while entering or trying to enter a designated sports ground at any time during the period of a designated sporting event at that ground, is guilty of an offence.

(2) *A person who is drunk in a designated sports ground at any time during the period of a designated sporting event at that ground or is drunk while entering or trying to enter such a ground at any time during the period of a designated sporting event at that ground is guilty of an offence.*

(3) *This section applies to any article capable of causing injury to a person struck by it, being:*

    (a) a bottle, can or other portable container (including such an article when crushed or broken) which:

        (i) is for holding any drink, and

        (ii) is of a kind which, when empty, is normally discarded or returned to, or left to be recovered by, the supplier, or

    (b) part of an article falling within paragraph (a) above; but does not apply to anything that is for holding any medicinal product (within the meaning of the Medicines Act 1968).

Section 3 of the Act deals with liquor licensing hours within sports grounds. The permitted hours for the sale of intoxicating liquor must *not* include any part of the period of any designated sporting event at the sports ground. Section 3(2) enables a Magistrates' Court, where licensed premises or registered club premises are so situated, to make an order:

    (a) that the permitted hours in the premises or any part of them shall during so much of the period of any designated sporting event at the designated sports ground as would (apart from this section) be included in the permitted hours, include such period as may be determined under the order, and

    (b) that during the period so determined such conditions as may be specified in the order (including conditions modifying or excluding any existing conditions of the justices' licence or, as the case may be, the registration certificate) shall apply in respect of the sale or supply of intoxicating liquor in the premises.

Section 3(4) provides:

    It shall be a condition of any order under this section that there shall be in attendance at the designated sports ground throughout the period of any designated sporting event a person:

    (a) who is responsible for securing compliance with this section, being the holder of the justices' licence or a person designated by him or, in the case of registered club premises, a person designated by the club, and

    (b) written notice of whose name and current address has been given to the chief officer of police.

Further provision is made in the Act for the variation of orders made under the Act. The Act makes clear provision where alcohol is sold in breach of the provisions of the Act. Section 3(10) provides:

A person who sells or supplies or authorises the sale or supply of intoxicating liquor at any time that is excluded from the permitted hours by virtue of this section or in contravention of conditions imposed under this section shall be guilty of an offence under this subsection if:

(a) he is the holder of the justices' licence or, as the case may be, an officer of the club, or

(b) he knows or has reasonable cause to believe the sale or supply to be such a contravention.

Furthermore, s. 6(1) of the Act deals with the situation where things get 'out of hand' in any particular bar at which alcohol is served at a sports ground. It provides:

(1) If at any time during the period of a designated sporting event at any designated sports ground it appears to a constable in uniform that the sale or supply of intoxicating liquor at any bar within the ground is detrimental to the orderly conduct or safety of spectators at that event, he may require any person having control of the bar to close it and keep it closed until the end of that period.

(2) A person who fails to comply with a requirement imposed under subsection (1) above is guilty of an offence, unless he shows that he took all reasonable steps to comply with it.

8.4 THE CONDUCT OF LICENSED PREMISES

There are many requirements to be met in order to conduct licensed premises within the parameters of the law. We are principally concerned with licensing offences, which are discussed below.

Selling liquor without a licence (s. 160 LA 1964)

No licensee may sell, or expose for sale, any liquor for the sale of which he or she is not licensed. The maximum penalty for selling liquor by retail without a justices' licence authorizing the sale is six months' imprisonment and/or a fine. On a second or subsequent conviction, defendants who are licensees automatically forfeit their licences. On a second conviction, a defendant may be disqualified from holding a licence for up to five years, and on a third or subsequent conviction for life or for any other period. If licensees are convicted the court may declare liquor found in their possession, and the vessels containing it, to be forfeited.

Sale or supply of liquor in breach of licence conditions

Where the licensee sells or supplies any liquor in breach of the conditions of his or her licence this is an offence contrary to s. 161 LA 1964.

The sale of liquor on credit (s. 166 LA 1964)

Except for the duration of a meal being eaten, or where the person concerned is residing in a hotel, it is an offence to sell liquor on credit.

The protection of people under eighteen

The provisions contained in s. 169 LA 1964 make it clear that a licensee of licensed premises is not permitted knowingly to sell liquor to a person under eighteen, to allow a person under eighteen to consume liquor in a bar, or to allow anyone else to make such a sale. A person under eighteen is not permitted to buy liquor in licensed premises, or to consume liquor in a bar. No person is allowed to buy liquor for consumption in a bar in licensed premises for a person under eighteen. It is required, however, that a sale to a person under eighteen must be made 'knowingly' in order to convict a licensee or an employee of the offence (*Wallworth* v. *Balmer* [1965] 1 WLR 16). The Divisional Court considered the requirement of knowledge in s. 169 offences in the following case.

BUXTON v. CHIEF CONSTABLE OF NORTHUMBRIA *The Times* 19 July 1983 (QBD) A licensee who had taken steps to prevent the serving of drinks to those under eighteen, but who recognized that under the system operated it was inevitable that people under eighteen would be admitted and buy or consume intoxicating liquor, was not guilty of offences under s. 169(1) LA 1964 of knowingly allowing the consumption of intoxicating liquor by persons under eighteen and of knowingly allowing a person to sell intoxicating liquor to persons under eighteen. The defendant's appeal against conviction was allowed. The defendant licensee managed an entertainments complex where musical events took place; on the day in question a heavy metal rock session was held. The policy of the management was to allow only people over the age of eighteen into the premises. However, sixteen-year-olds and seventeen-year-olds were attracted to the event. Entry was regulated by a visual assessment of age. It was inevitable that some people aged under eighteen would gain entry and buy drinks. The licensee was charged under s. 169(1).

Goff LJ observed: 'if the facts had proved that although the licensee did not actually know because he turned his head away deliberately, in order not to know, then it was open to the court to convict. A defendant could not deliberately avoid the means of having knowledge. But, on the facts, the defendant did not deliberately turn away or avoid knowing what was happening. He was doing his best to enforce a system, knowing that it was inevitable some would escape the net ... The defendant was not turning a blind eye. He was doing his best but recognising the inevitable. It could be said that he knowingly allowed the sale of intoxicating liquor ... [to persons under the age of eighteen].'

The LA 1988 has, by s. 16, amended s. 169 of the LA 1964 so that it now provides:

> (1) *Subject to subsections (4) and (10) of this section, in licensed premises the holder of the licence or his servant shall not sell intoxicating liquor to a person under eighteen or knowingly allow a person under eighteen to consume intoxicating liquor in a bar nor shall the holder of the licence knowingly allow any person to sell intoxicating liquor to a person under eighteen.*

(2)   *Subject to subsection (4) of this section, a person under eighteen shall not in licensed premises buy or attempt to buy intoxicating liquor, nor consume intoxicating liquor in a bar.*

(3)   *No person shall buy or attempt to buy intoxicating liquor for consumption in a bar in licensed premises by a person under eighteen.*

(4)   *Subsections (1) and (2) of this section do not prohibit the sale to or purchase by a person who has attained the age of sixteen of beer, porter, cider or perry for consumption at a meal in a part of the premises usually set apart for the service of meals which is not a bar.*

(4A)   *Where a person is charged under subsection (1) of this section with the offence of selling intoxicating liquor to a person under eighteen and he is charged by reason of his own act, it shall be a defence for him to prove:*

(a)   *that he exercised all due diligence to avoid the commission of such an offence; or*

(b)   *that he had no reason to suspect that the person was under eighteen.*

(4B)   *Where the person charged with an offence under subsection (1) of this section is the licence holder and he is charged by reason of the act or default of some other person, it shall be a defence for him to prove that he exercised all due diligence to avoid the commission of an offence under that subsection.*

(5)   *Subject to subsection (7) of this section, the holder of the licence or his servant shall not knowingly deliver, nor shall the holder of the licence knowingly allow any person to deliver, to a person under eighteen intoxicating liquor sold in licensed premises for consumption off the premises, except where the delivery is made at the residence or working place of the purchaser.*

(6)   *Subject to subsection (7) of this section, a person shall not knowingly send a person under eighteen for the purpose of obtaining intoxicating liquor sold or to be sold in licensed premises for consumption off the premises, whether the liquor is to be obtained from the licensed premises or other premises from which it is delivered in pursuance of the sale.*

(7)   *Subsections (5) and (6) of this section do not apply where the person under eighteen is a member of the licence holder's family or his servant or apprentice and is employed as a messenger to deliver intoxicating liquor.*

(8)   *A person guilty of an offence under this section shall be liable to a fine not exceeding level 3 on the standard scale; and on a person's second or subsequent conviction of such an offence the court may, if the offence was committed by him as the holder of a justices' licence, order that he shall forfeit the licence.*

By removing the requirement of 'knowledge' in the sale of intoxicating liquor to people under the age of eighteen, Parliament has sought to address the problem of under-age drinking. Licensees, it is hoped, will take a more stringent view of the sale of alcohol to minors.

Licensees may not be convicted of an offence under s. 169 LA 1964 on the basis of the fault of one of their employees where it can be established that the licensee had no knowledge of this and had used all due diligence to prevent the offence from occurring (Schedule 12 Criminal Law Act 1977).

Although the general rule is that a person under eighteen must not be served liquor, a person aged over sixteen but under eighteen may purchase beer, porter, cider or perry for consumption with a meal in a restaurant (s. 169(4) LA 1964).

Nobody must allow children aged under 14 to be present in a bar during permitted hours (s. 168 LA 1964). This does not apply to the licensee's child, a child resident though not employed at the premises, or a child passing through a bar, e.g. *en route* to the toilet.

Children's Certificates

The Deregulation and Contracting Out Act 1994, by amending the Licensing Act 1964, created Children's Certificates which permit licensees to allow children into an ordinary bar from which children would normally be prohibited during permitted hours. The Certificate allows children, under 14 years of age, when accompanied by an adult, to be in a bar until 2100 hours (or later if specified). The licence is granted by the licensing magistrates, who have to be satisfied that the environment is suitable for persons under 14 years of age to be present. Meals and non-intoxicating drinks have to be available, although the children in the bar do not have to consume them (Section 168, Licensing Act 1964).

Should an application for a Children's Certificate be refused an appeal can be made to the Crown Court.

Employing young persons

Section 170 LA 1964 prohibits people under the age of eighteen from being employed, whether for wages or otherwise, in hours while the bar is being used for the sale of liquor. An employee under eighteen may, however, work in the dispense bar and/or dining room of a hotel restaurant, etc. where alcoholic beverages are consumed. This situation was under review in 1996, with the intention of allowing certain categories of trainee to work in a bar.

TABLE 8.1 Children, young persons and alcohol.

Age	
Under 5	It is an offence to give alcohol of any sort to a child aged under 5 except on a doctor's orders or in a medical emergency when a responsible person considers the alcohol necessary
5–13	Children aged 5–13 may drink alcoholic drinks in a restaurant with a meal but cannot buy it or be served with it by the staff (i.e. parents or guardians must serve it)
Under 14	Children, when accompanied by an adult, may be permitted into a bar, which is subject to a Children's Certificate (see above for more details)
14–17	May be allowed into a bar at the licensee's discretion but must not consume alcoholic drinks there, although they may consume low alcohol beers i.e. under 0.5% of alcohol by volume
16–17	Young persons aged 16 and 17 may buy beer, cider or perry but not wine (wine is permitted in Scotland), to be consumed as an ancillary to a meal, in a restaurant or area used exclusively for the service of meals

Sale of intoxicating liquor at wholesale premises

One of the retailing developments of recent years has been the 'wholesaling' of liquor to the public. Section 181 LA 1964 provides for the resale of alcohol through wholesale outlets. A wholesaler of intoxicating liquor may, at the premises from which he or she deals wholesale, sell by retail without a justices' licence any intoxicating liquor, other than cider, in which he or she deals wholesale if:

(a) those premises are used exclusively for the sale of intoxicating liquor and mineral waters, or other non-intoxicating drinks, and have no internal communication with the premises of any person who is carrying on any other trade or business; and

(b) the sale by retail is:
    (i) to a person lawfully carrying out a business of selling intoxicating liquor by retail; or
    (ii) to an officers' mess or registered club; or
    (iii) to a person engaged at those premises or elsewhere in any business carried on by the wholesaler; or
    (iv) for delivery outside Great Britain.

This last exception appears in s. 181 of the 1964 Act, and since the wholesalers taking advantage of this provision do not require a justices' licence, it would seem that their premises are not 'licensed premises' for the purposes of s. 200(1) of the Act, and therefore are not covered by the normal 'permitted hours' laid down under the Act, nor are they covered by the other rules relevant to the sale of intoxicating liquor on 'licensed premises'.

Section 17 of the LA 1988 inserted s. 181A into the LA 1964. This section provides:

(1) *In any premises from which he deals wholesale the wholesaler or his servant shall not sell intoxicating liquor to a person under eighteen.*

(2) *In any premises from which he deals wholesale the wholesaler shall not allow a person under eighteen to make any sale of intoxicating liquor unless the sale has been specifically approved by the wholesaler or by a person of or over the age of eighteen acting on his behalf.*

(3) *A person under eighteen shall not in premises from which intoxicating liquor is dealt in wholesale buy or attempt to buy such liquor.*

(4) *In proceedings for an offence under subsection (1) of this section:*
    (a) *where the person is charged by reason of his own act, it shall be a defence for him to prove:*
      (i) *that he exercised all due diligence to avoid the commission of an offence under that subsection; or*
      (ii) *that he had no reason to suspect that the other person was under eighteen; and*
    (b) *where the person charged is charged by reason of the act of some other person, it shall be a defence for him to prove that he exercised all due diligence to avoid the commission of an offence under that subsection.*

(5) *A person guilty of an offence under subsection (1) or (3) of this section shall be liable to a fine not exceeding level 3 on the standard scale.*

(6) *A person guilty of an offence under subsection (2) of this section shall be liable to a fine not exceeding level 1 on the standard scale.*

(7) *In this section 'wholesaler' and 'wholesale' have the same meaning as in section 4 of the Alcoholic Liquor Duties Act 1979.*

The LA 1988 not only seeks to protect minors with regard to the sale of liquor to them, it also seeks to ensure that they do not themselves sell liquor at wholesale premises. It does this by virtue of s. 18, which inserted s. 171A into the LA 1964. This provides:

(1) *In any premises which are licensed for the sale of intoxicating liquor for consumption off the premises only or any off-sales department of on-licensed premises, the holder of the licence shall not allow a person under eighteen to make any sale of such liquor unless the sale has been specifically approved by the holder of the licence or by a person of or over the age of eighteen acting on his behalf.*

(2) *The reference in subsection (1) of this section to an off-sales department of on-licensed premises is a reference to any part of the premises for which a justices' on-licence has been granted which is set aside for use only for the sale of intoxicating liquor for consumption off the premises.*

(3) *A person guilty of an offence under this section shall be liable to a fine not exceeding level 1 on the standard scale.*

Licensing (Retail Sales) Act 1988

This legislation redefines 'sales by retail' as set out in s. 210 of the Licensing Act 1964. It incorporates some of the provisions of s. 181 of the LA 1964 and replaces that section.

Under this Act, sales in quantities of more than nine litres (or one case) of wine or spirits, or 21 litres (two cases) of beer or cider, are treated as sales by wholesale and not by retail, and do not require a justices' licence. Sales to a trader for the purpose of this trade, to a registered club for club purposes, and to any canteen or mess are also excluded from the definition, as is a sale to the holder of an occasional permission for the purpose of sales authorized by that permission. Otherwise, all sales of intoxicating liquor made at any one time to any one person are treated as sales by retail, and thus do not require a justices' licence.

This position is further qualified by s. 181, which provides that retail sales, i.e. sales in less than the quantities referred to above, do not require a justices' licence when made from premises used exclusively for the sale of beverages, intoxicating or otherwise, and the sale is to a person carrying on a retail liquor business, a mess or registered club, an employee or for delivery outside Great Britain.

Drunkenness and disorderly behaviour

It is an offence contrary to s. 172(1) LA 1964 to permit drunkenness on the premises. In cases where the licensee holds a residential, restaurant or combined licence, it can lead to disqualification of the licensee. Licensees must show that they took reasonable steps to prevent the alleged occurrence. It is also an offence contrary to s. 172(1) to permit violent or disorderly conduct. A further offence, of selling liquor to a person who is drunk, is provided for by s. 172(3). It shall be no defence for licensees to establish that they did not know that the person was drunk. A licensee may eject drunks from the premises (s. 174 LA 1964).

The Licensed Premises (Exclusion of Certain Persons) Act 1980 empowers a court, when convicting a person of an offence of violence or threatened violence on licensed premises, to make an exclusion order. Such an order bans the person from the licensed premises specified in the order. The ban may be imposed for any period of between two and three years. The order may cover a number of licensed premises. Breach of the order by the person excluded is itself an offence punishable by a fine or imprisonment.

Prostitutes (s. 175 LA 1964)

A licensee is not permitted to allow prostitutes to assemble on the premises. A licensee may allow a prostitute to remain on the premises for as long as it is necessary for her or him to obtain reasonable refreshment. Licensees who permit their premises to be used as brothels are liable under s. 177 LA 1964 to a fine and automatic forfeiture of their licences.

Gaming

It is an offence for licensees to allow gaming on their premises except dominoes, cribbage and any other game which may be permitted under the Gaming Act 1968.

The police

Licensees are liable for an offence if they knowingly allow a police officer who is on duty to remain on licensed premises, unless the officer is there in the execution of his or her duty (s. 178 LA 1964). Licensees will similarly be liable if they supply liquor or refreshment to an officer on duty except by authority of the officer's superior.

Notices

The full holder of a justices' licence (other than a residential licence) must display a notice in a conspicuous place on the premises. The notice must state *inter alia* the licensee's name and other details as required by s. 183 LA 1964.

8.5 WEIGHTS AND MEASURES

The Weights and Measures Act 1963, Schedule 4, requires the following:
1   Draught beer or cider may be sold only by retail in quantities of one-third pint, one-half pint, or multiples of one-half pint. When assessing the quantity of any beer or cider for the purposes of Schedule 4, the gas in any foam on the beer or cider will be disregarded by virtue of the Weights and Measures Act 1979.

What constitutes a pint of beer?

BENNETT v. MARKHAM AND ANOTHER [1982] 1 WLR 1231 (QBD)
Where a pint of beer was sold and delivered in public houses in brim-measure glasses and measured less than 20 fl. oz, the head of froth would be an integral part of the pint in areas where customers demanded beer with a head. It would be a matter for the court to determine whether the head of froth was unreasonable or excessive and would depend upon what the customer was taken as ordering at the time when ordering the pint.

2   Gin, rum, vodka and whisky may be sold for consumption on the premises only in quantities of 25 or 35 ml multiples thereof.
3   All liquor sold in sealed containers must be clearly marked with the quantity.
4   Wine sold for consumption on the premises, whether pre-packed or not, must be sold in quantities of 25 cl, 50 cl, 75 cl, or 1 litre, unless pre-packed in a securely closed bottle or sold by the glass. The sale of wine by the glass is to be regulated by a further Weights and Measures (Sale of Wine) Order.

Section 16(1) of the Weights and Measures Act 1963 creates an offence of having in one's possession for use for trade an unjust measuring system. The House of Lords' decision in *Bellerby* v. *Carle* (1983) 1 All ER 1031 considers how this position may affect the licensed premises.

BELLERBY v. CARLE [1983] 1 All ER 1031 (HL)
Carle and another were joint licensees of premises licensed to sell intoxicating liquor. The brewery owned pumps installed at the premises for the retail of beer. The brewery inspected the equipment and stamped and sealed the pumps as measuring one pint. Carle, who relied entirely upon the brewery for the accuracy of the measuring pumps, neither knew nor suspected that certain of them were defective. Carle and his joint licensee were charged under s.16(1). The magistrates dismissed the charges.

Held: The appeal was dismissed; a s. 16(1) offence is not committed unless the person charged has some degree of control over the measuring instrument. The mere fact that the joint licensees were the only people lawfully entitled to sell intoxicating liquor did not give them the degree of control required for there to be an offence; they were not 'in possession of' the equipment within the meaning given to those words by s. 16(1).

Metrication

From 1 October 1995 regulations were introduced which brought to an end the legal use, for pre-packed foods (including beverages), of most imperial measures such as the pound, the ounce, the gallon.

Draught beer and cider must be still be sold by the imperial measure i.e. the pint or half pint (milk also may continue to be sold by the pint).

Soft drinks, shandies etc.

Whilst beer and cider must still be sold in multiples of a half pint, soft drinks, shandies etc. **if sold by the measure**, have to be sold by metric measure. They may, however, be sold by description such as 'small' or 'large'.

8.6 MISCELLANEOUS LICENCES

There are a number of different forms of entertainments, etc. where a licence of some sort or another is required by law. Examples include music, dancing, billiards and gaming.

Gaming

The definition of 'gaming' is to be found in the Gaming Act 1968. Gaming is 'the playing of a game of chance for winnings in money or money's worth, whether any person playing the game is at risk of losing any money or money's worth or not'. Games such as darts and snooker are games of skill and not chance and are therefore excluded from the 1968 Act. Dominoes, however, are within the scope of the Act, since there is an element of chance involved.

The Gaming Act, with very limited exceptions, bans gaming without a licence or certificate. However, by virtue of s. 6, the playing of dominoes and cribbage for money is allowed in public houses, but the licensing justices may restrict this by imposing limits on the stakes played for. Furthermore, gaming must not be the main attraction of the premises.

Also exempted, by s. 41, is gaming organized in the form of entertainment other than for private gain, e.g. charity pontoon or whist drive, though this is subject to certain limitations.

Gaming machines are today a common sight in public houses, cafés and even hotel foyers. What is a gaming machine? Section 26 of the Gaming Act 1968 defines them thus: 'any machine which is constructed or adapted for playing a game of chance, and which has a slot or aperture for the insertion of money or money's worth in the form of cash or tokens'. Only those machines which are covered by a local justices' permit under s. 34 of the Gaming Act 1968 are allowed on licensed premises other than registered clubs. A machine, to be covered by such a permit, must comply with certain requirements as to prize money, etc. laid down by the 1968 Act. Licensing justices hear applications made by the licensee for a s. 34 permit. The justices have full discretion whether or not to grant a permit.

Video games are a feature of many public houses. The House of Lords has considered whether such games require licensing by local authorities under the Cinematograph Act 1909.

BRITISH AMUSEMENT CATERING TRADES ASSOCIATION v. WESTMINSTER CITY COUNCIL [1988] 1 All ER 740 (HL)

The first appellant was a trade association for operators of amusement arcades and similar places. The second appellant operated an amusement arcade where coin-operated video games were played and was a member of the association. The licensing authority for the area in which the second appellant's arcade was situated took the view that the premises were required to be licensed under s. 1(1)(a) of the Cinematograph Act 1909 on the grounds that video games constituted a cinematograph exhibition within s. 1(3), which defined a 'cinematograph exhibition' as 'any exhibition of moving pictures' which was produced other than by the simultaneous reception and exhibition by television programmes. On the appellant's application for the court's determination of the true construction of s. 1, the judge made a declaration that operation of video games constituted an exhibition of moving pictures within s. 1(3) and therefore the premises were required to be licensed under s. 1(1). The appellants appealed to the Court of Appeal, which dismissed the appeal on the ground that, since the screen of a video game displayed moving objects, there was an exhibition of moving pictures within the meaning of the 1909 Act. The appellants appealed to the House of Lords.

Held: On the true construction of s. 1(3) of the 1909 Act, an 'exhibition of moving pictures' denoted the showing of moving pictures to an audience rather than a display of moving objects on a video screen. Accordingly, a video game was not a cinematograph exhibition within s. 1(3) and the second appellant's premises were not required to be licensed under s. 1(1) of the 1909 Act. The appeal would therefore be allowed.

Music, dancing and theatre

A licence may be required for the public performance of music. The licensing of music and dancing operates capriciously; certain local authorities operate a licensing system, whereas others do not. Normally, where the local authority operates a licensing system for 'public' performances, a licence is not required where a performance is private. However, by virtue of the Private Place of Entertainment Act 1967, a local authority which operates a system of licensing for public performances may require that a licence be taken out for private events organized for private gain. Any event for charity or to raise clubs' funds is outside the scope of this provision, since such events are not organized for private profit.

Some large public houses provide serious theatrical entertainment; such theatres require a licence. A licence is required under the Theatres Act 1968 for any premises used for the public performance of dramatic work. Such a licence is obtained from the local authority. Restrictions as to the service of liquor, etc. may be imposed by the licensing authority.

Performing copyright music etc.

Under the Copyright, Designs and Patents Act 1988 music is the personal property of the composer. The copyright lasts for the lifetime of the composer and for a further 50 years. Copyright music can only be played in public places e.g. public houses, restaurants etc., if a licence has been granted by the owner of the copyright. Effectively, this means the Performing Rights Society which acts on behalf of the composers of music and is located in London. This licence is required for both live and recorded music. In the case of recorded music another licence, this time for the benefit of the recording company is required. This is obtained from Phonographic Performance Ltd., also located in London. The domestic TV licence does not permit the public performance of copyright material. A special licence has to be obtained.

8.7 LIABILITY FOR INTOXICATED CUSTOMERS

An interesting question arose in the case of *Munro* v. *Porthkerry Holiday Estates Ltd* (*The Times*, 9 March 1984 (QB)) where a young man fell to his death having consumed a considerable amount of alcohol at the licensee's premises. The parents of the deceased brought a civil action claiming that the licensee owed a duty of care to the deceased because the licensee had served him with alcohol, by reason of which he was no longer capable of looking after himself. Whilst the High Court recognized that such a duty may exist, on the facts the deceased was not so drunk as to give rise to such a duty on the part of the licensee.

CASE STUDY

Outline the ways in which the Licensing Act 1988 and the Deregulation and Contracting Out Act 1994 have brought about the changes in liquor licensing law.

The Licensing Act 1988 (LA 1988) is complementary to the Licensing Act 1964 (LA 1964) and amends this legislation.

The first area in which the LA 1988 brings about change is with regard to the contribution of licensing justices (see s. 14 LA 1988) and the duration of a liquor licence when granted, which is now three years rather than one (see s. 11 LA 1988). The LA 1988 provides the justices with new powers as to costs (s. 15 LA 1988), and to speed up procedures for renewal of licences the clerk to the justices may grant an unopposed renewal of a licence (see s. 13 LA 1988). The extension of the duration of a liquor licence has brought with it a power of revocation (see s. 12 LA 1988).

The most far-reaching provisions of the LA 1988 relate to permitted hours. Section 1 LA 1988 amends s. 60 LA 1964 to enable licensees to sell liquor between the hours of 11.00 a.m. and 11.00 p.m. on weekdays, and between 12.00 midday and 3.00 p.m., and 7.00 p.m. and 10.30 p.m., on Sundays, Christmas Day and Good Friday. The extension of permitted hours to all licensed premises has meant the repeal of the Licensing (Restaurant Meals) Act 1987, and in practical terms will require breweries, their licensees and management to reconsider the terms and conditions of staff operating new work patterns to accommodate the amended licensing hours. The increased hours of opening will also have a practical significance with regard to overheads, i.e. heating, lighting, wear and tear on furnishings and fittings, etc.

The flexible opening hours may be restricted as local circumstances dictate, where an application is made to the justices for a restriction order (see s. 3 LA 1988).

The LA 1988 also makes amendments to special hours certificates (see s. 5 LA 1988).

A substantial change brought about by the LA 1988 in relation to the conduct of licensed premises is in relation to the sale of liquor to people under the age of eighteen. Section 169 of the LA 1964 is amended by s. 16 LA 1988, to remove the requirement of knowledge that the person to whom the liquor was sold was under age.

The LA 1988 makes amendment to the sale of liquor at wholesale premises by people under eighteen and to people under eighteen (see s. 17 and s. 18 LA 1988).

The LA 1988 prohibits the sale of intoxicating liquor at garages (see s. 10 LA 1988).

The Deregulation and Contracting Out Act 1994 amends Section 168 of the Licensing Act 1964. This amendment permits licensees to apply for a certificate which permits children into an ordinary bar from which children would normally be prohibited during permitted hours. The Certificate allows children, under 14 years of age, when accompanied by an adult, to be in a bar until 2100 hours (or later if specified). Before a Children's Certificate is granted the licensing magistrates have to be satisfied that the environment is suitable for persons under 14 years of age to be present. Meals and non-intoxicating drinks have to be available, although the children in the bar do not have to consume them.

NINE

The caterer and the staff I: Individual rights and duties in relation to the contract of employment

Employment law is extremely complex and constantly changing; it is also highly technical and almost wholly a creature of statute. Furthermore it is subject, more than most law, to the vagaries of political change. However, it is perhaps one of the most important areas of law with which a caterer will deal. If we are employees we should understand the law and thus ensure that the rights which we have been statutorily given by Parliament are not infringed by either our employer or others, e.g. a trade union. If we are employers involved in a dispute with our staff, or with a trade union, we must understand the law so as to know what are the respective rights of the employer, the employee and the trade union in the dispute. Employment law affects us all and we should all seek to understand the principles contained therein as well as the practice of good employment relations in the workplace. It is important to understand the breadth of the topic: employment law is not simply concerned with wages, strikes and dismissals; it covers a great number of important rights and duties such as health and safety at work, discrimination on the grounds of race or sex, and trade union activities. However, the scope of this text does not allow for a full and in-depth analysis of the whole range of laws relating to work. In this chapter we consider the contract of employment and the rights and duties arising in consequence of the relationship of employer and employee. In Chapter 10 we consider aspects of health and safety at work, and in Chapter 11 we turn our attention towards the collective aspects of employment law and the relationship between the employer, members of staff who are trade unionists and the trade union itself.

9.1 THE CONTRACT OF EMPLOYMENT

It is important from the outset to appreciate the need to classify a person as either being an employee of the employer or as having some other status, e.g. subcontractor.

Why? Simply because the rights, obligations and duties which we are to discuss apply solely to employees. More or less all duties owed by an employer are owed exclusively to his or her employees, and the status of an employee confers rights upon a person (e.g. a right not to be unfairly dismissed or a right not to be made redundant without compensation) which are *not* conferred upon non-employees. It should be added that these rights may be subject to qualification and exclusion. Therefore, the fact that someone is an employee does not always confer an automatic right.

Who is an employee?

The starting point for formulating a definition is s. 153(1) of the Employment Protection Consolidation Act 1978 (EPCA):

> *'employee' means an individual who has entered into or works under (or, where the employment has ceased, worked under)* a contract of employment.

Such a definition is of little help, since it does not enable one immediately to identify a particular relationship as one of employer and employee. A contract of employment is also defined in s. 153(1) as 'a contract of service'. This takes us little further; hence we must look outside the Act to establish a test as to whether one person is an employee of another. Various tests have been put forward.

The control test

This is the traditional approach. Does the employer have sufficient control over the person to make that person an employee (*Performing Rights Society Ltd* v. *Mitchell & Booker* [1924] 1 KB 762). An employee works sufficiently under the control of another where the other may tell the employee not only what to do but also when and how to do it (*Yewens* v. *Noakes* [1880] 6 QBD 580). The greater the degree of control exercised the more likely it is that the person subject to control is an employee. A kitchen porter or waitress is clearly an employee under this test. Is the head chef? An employer may use the skills of highly trained personnel, e.g. head chef, whom he or she cannot tell how to perform their work. Are these people still employees? The greater the skill required for an employee's work, the less significant is the control test in determining whether the employee works under a contract of service (*Beloff* v. *Pressdram Ltd* [1973] 1 All ER 241).

The business integration test

This test considers to what extent the work of the so-called employee is integrated with the work of the employer's business organization. The test was explained by Denning LJ (as he then was) in *Stevenson Jordon & Harrison Ltd* v. *Macdonald & Evans* (1952) 1 TLR 101 (CA):

> *under a contract of service, a man is employed as part of the business. Whereas under a contract of services, his work although done for the business, is not integrated into it but is only accessary to it.*

It can be said, therefore, that a window cleaner or a cabaret artiste is clearly not an employee. That which these people contract to do is done for the hotelier, but not as part of his or her business organization. Such people are subcontractors. However, in *Whittaker* v. *Minister of Pensions and National Insurance* [1966] 3 All ER 531, a circus artiste broke her wrist whilst performing her act. The court held that she was an integral part of the business organization of the circus, and therefore an employee for the purpose of claiming industrial injuries benefit. It may be argued, therefore, that people such as holiday-camp hosts are clearly employees, whereas a comedian who performs twice weekly at a hotel is not an employee.

In *Withers* v. *Flackwell Heath FC Supporters' Club* [1981] IRLR 307 (EAT), the complainant (Mr Withers) worked as a bar steward at the football club. The question of whether he was or was not an employee arose. Bristow J took the view: 'If you had asked Mr Withers while he was running the club bar, "Are you your own boss?", could he have honestly given any other answer than "No"? In our judgment clearly not.'

This 'lay' approach fits in with that taken by the Court of Appeal in *O'Kelly and Others* v. *Trusthouse Forte plc* [1983] IRLR 369 (below).

The multiple test

The law evolved in the 1960s and early 1970s to recognize that a single test would not be applicable to all employees:

READY-MIXED CONCRETE (SOUTH EAST) LTD v. MINISTER OF PENSIONS AND NATIONAL INSURANCE [1968] 1 All ER 433 (QBD)	Mackenna J said 'A contract of service exists if the following three conditions are fulfilled: (i) The servant agrees that in consideration of a wage or other renumeration he will provide his own work and skill in the performance of some service for his master. (ii) He agrees, expressly or impliedly, that in the performance of that service he will be subject to the other's control in a sufficient degree to make that other master. (iii) The other provisions of the contract are consistent with its being a contract of service.'

This multiple test adopts a broader approach, not determining the definition of an employee on the basis of a single factor. It contains elements of the control test, but element (iii) enables all the surrounding circumstances to be taken into account. In *Ferguson* v. *John Dawson & Partners (Contractors) Ltd* [1976] 3 All ER 817, the Court of Appeal approved this threefold approach. The Court of Appeal say that one can determine the issue only by looking at the whole relationship.

Is a statement by the parties of their respective positions conclusive in determining whether the relationship is one of employer and employee? In *Ferguson* v. *John Dawson* it was said that a statement by the parties that the relationship was one of contractor and subcontractor was not conclusive, and on the facts of the case the plaintiff was found to be an employee of the defendants. A label placed upon the relationship by the parties themselves is insufficient to determine the true nature of the relationship. However, in *Massey* v. *Crown Life Insurance Co.* [1978] 2 All ER 576 (CA), Denning MR took the view that if the relationship between the parties is ambiguous and is capable of being either one of contractor and subcontractor or employer and employee, then the ambiguity may be resolved by assessing any label placed upon the relationship by the parties to the contract between them.

Other factors, such as the method of payment, may help to determine the question. In *102 Social Club and Insitute Ltd* v. *Bickerton* [1977] ICR 911, the fact that a club steward was paid an honorarium rather than a salary was inconsistent with there being a contract of employment.

The courts have, in recent years, increasingly emphasized the factor of dependence and the related notion of an on-going obligation as evidence for the existence of a contract of employment: see, e.g., *McLeod* v. *Hellyer Brothers Ltd* [1987] IRLR 232 (CA). Such an approach will, therefore, tend to exclude the casual worker (see *O'Kelly* v. *Trusthouse Forte*, below) and even the part-time worker. It is notable, however, that in practice such a multi-factor approach allows for wide judicial discretion. Assessment of the width of case law on this topic provides illustration of the variety of approaches adopted: see e.g. *Withers* v. *Flackwell Heath FC and Supporters' Club* [1981] IRLR 307; *Airfix Footwear Ltd* v. *Cope* [1978] IRLR 396; *Mailway Ltd* v. *Wilsher* [1978] IRLR 322.

Directors

In many small catering enterprises which are constituted as limited companies the main people working for the company are also directors. Where an individual is appointed as a director, that person, by reason of his or her appointment, is the holder of an office of the company and not an employee. However, a director may at the same time as being the holder of such office be an employee if he or she works under a service contract. There may be an express oral or written service contract. However, a service contract may be implied from the surrounding circumstances; this will be a question of fact in each case. In *Parsons* v. *Albert J. Parsons & Sons Ltd* [1979] IRLR 117 (CA), the applicant was a director of a family company. After arguments with other directors he was removed from the office of director. He claimed that this constituted unfair dismissal. It was held by the Court of Appeal that the applicant was not an employee and thus was unable to claim unfair dismissal. The court took the view that he was not an employee since: (a) there was no express contract of service; (b) no record was kept pursuant to s. 26(1) of the Companies Act 1967 of details of the applicant's contract of service; (c) all directors including the applicant paid self-employed national insurance contributions; (d) the monies paid to him by the company had been by way of fees and expenses and not by way of a salary.

Although the initial presumption is therefore that directors of a company are office holders, this presumption is rebuttable.

Directors are in a special position in the eyes of the law, thus s. 318 of the Companies Act 1985 requires that the service contracts of company directors are open to inspection.

Partners

A partner is a self-employed person who is remunerated by a share in the profits of the partnership. Partners are clearly, on this basis, not employees of the partnership. In a small catering business (e.g. a tearoom) where two people have formed a partnership and both draw an agreed monthly 'salary' from the partnership account, this may at first sight point towards a contract of service. Such a view would, however, be incorrect, since partners pay self-employed national insurance contributions and Schedule D income tax. Furthermore, they are entitled to tax relief not applicable to PAYE taxpayers under Schedule E.

Casual workers

Within the hotel and catering industry many casual workers are employed due to the fluctuating demand for services and the seasonal nature of the work. Are casual workers employees within s. 153(1) EPCA 1978.

O'KELLY AND OTHERS v. TRUSTHOUSE FORTE plc [1983] IRLR 369 (CA)

THF carried on two forms of business at the Grosvenor House Hotel: the business of a hotel and restaurant and the provision of banqueting and conference facilities. Thirty-four permanent staff were employed on the conference and banqueting work. In addition to these 34 employees, casual staff were employed as and when there was sufficient work to require further personnel. A list of some 300 casual workers was maintained. Of these a 'regulars' list of 100 was kept. A 'regular' could be relied on by THF to do regular work and in return THF showed 'regulars' preference in the allocation of any available work. The applicants, 'regulars' on the casual list of THF, brought an action for unfair dismissal (alleging that they were dismissed for taking part in trade union activities). The Industrial Tribunal ruled on a preliminary point that the applicants were not 'employees' within s. 153 EPCA 1978 and were thus not qualified to bring an action for unfair dismissal. The applicants appealed against the preliminary ruling to the EAT, which allowed the appeal (*The Times*, 12 May 1983). THF appealed to the CA against the findings of the EAT, arguing that the question of whether the applicants were or were not employees was one of fact and the EAT could not consider whether on the facts as found the IT had reached the correct conclusion. THF's appeal against the decision of the EAT was allowed.

Held: The EAT was not entitled to interfere with the decision of the IT unless the IT had misdirected itself in law or the decision was one which no IT properly instructed could have reached on the facts, neither of which applied to the present case. The Master of the Rolls, Lord Donaldson, observed: 'Unpalatable as it might be on occasions an appellate court must legally accept the conclusions, the fact with which it was presented and, accepting those conclusions, it must be satisfied that there must have been a misdirection on a question of law before it could intervene.' On the facts, therefore, the applicants were not employees within s. 153.

The IT, which had investigated the facts most carefully, found that there was no obligation for the 'regular' casual worker to offer services and no obligation for the employer to provide work. The IT considered all the aspects of the relationship; the essential feature of a contract of employment was missing, and there was no mutual obligation of the parties, one to provide work the other to undertake it; 'it was a purely commercial transaction for the supply and purchase of services for specific events'. Each hiring was treated as a separate contract for the services of the person concerned.

O'Kelly's case is of some considerable importance to the hotel and catering industry. This decision in effect prevents many regular workers who in reality do the same work as full-time employees from gaining the protection offered by the EPCA 1978.

The significance of defining an 'employee'

Many important legal issues may be determined in consequence of defining a person as an 'employee':

1 Statutory rights arising under the EPCA 1978, e.g. the right not to be unfairly dismissed, apply only to employees.

2 Statutory duties may be owed only to employees, e.g. s. 2(1) of the Health and Safety at Work etc. Act 1974.

3 Taxation and national insurance: the class of taxation of employees differs from that of self-employed people, and tax allowances vary accordingly. National insurance contributions also vary.

4 An employer is vicariously liable only for the actions of his or her employees acting in the course of their employment.

5 An employer owes a common-law duty of care under the principles in *Wilsons and Clyde Coal Co. Ltd* v. *English* [1937] 3 All ER 628 (HL) only to his or her employees.

6 Employers are under a duty to pay wages to their employees where there is no express term in the contract dealing with remuneration.

7 An employee is under a duty to obey the reasonable orders and instructions of her employer.

8 A duty is imposed upon employees to take reasonable care and skill in doing their work under the contract of employment. An employee may in fact be sued by the employer for negligence in carrying out his or her work (*Janata Bank* v. *Ahmed* [1981] IRLR 457).

9 An employee owes to his or her employer a duty of fidelity, that is, a duty of confidence regarding the employer's trade and business secrets, etc.

10 An employee is entitled to expect the reasonable support of his or her employer. In *Woods* v. *W.M. Car Services (Peterborough) Ltd* [1981] IRLR 347, it was said: 'There is implied in a contract of employment a term that the employers will not, without reasonable and proper cause, conduct themselves in a manner calculated or likely to destroy or seriously damage the relationship of confidence and trust between employer and employee.'

A recent case analysing the extent of the implied duties owed by an employer to an employee is *Scally* v. *Southern Health and Social Services Board* [1991] ICR 771 (HL).

9.2 THE TERMS OF THE CONTRACT OF EMPLOYMENT

A contract of employment comprises both express and implied terms. Express terms are negotiated and agreed upon by the parties and stated in the contract itself. Implied terms may arise from custom and practice or other surrounding circumstances in which the contract was made. The express terms of the contract may be freely negotiated between the employer and employee (as is often the case with senior management posts) or imposed on the employee (in the lower strata of the employment field). At the conclusion of the selection procedure and negotiations the parties will normally agree on the expressly stated terms which will then form the contract of employment. These terms will deal with remuneration, sickness benefits, holiday pay, bonus payments, etc. In any case where there is a dispute as to the terms of a particular contract of employment, the role of the court or industrial tribunal is to interpret the contract and give effect to the intentions of the parties at the time the contract was made. This will require taking into account both express and implied terms.

Example. Jack is appointed head waiter at the Riverside Hotel, Wapping. The hotel manager tells Jack that his role is to ensure the efficiency and smooth running of the service in the hotel dining room. Because of poor demand the hotel manager sacks waiting staff and thus requires Jack to wait on table as would an ordinary waiter. Jack refuses to do this on a regular basis, arguing that his job is to manage and organize the smooth running of the restaurant, not to do all the waiting himself.

The question whether Jack can be required to wait on table is a matter of construction of his contract of employment. In *Redbridge Borough Council* v. *Fishman* [1978] ICR 569, a teacher who was appointed in charge of a resource unit was gradually required to do more and more teaching. She refused and was dismissed. The question arose of whether she could be required to bear this increasing teaching load. A head teacher could require his or her staff to do work other than that for which they were engaged, provided that such requests were reasonable. On the facts of the case in question, the teacher was appointed in charge of a resource unit, and although some teaching would be ancillary to that job, the head teacher's instructions went beyond the contractual obligations placed on the teacher and were unreasonable. The teacher was held to be unfairly dismissed. Returning to our example, the question revolves around whether it is a reasonable request, and thus within Jack's contract of employment, to require him to serve meals on a regular basis. It probably is.

On rare occasions courts or industrial tribunals are prepared to imply a term into a contract of employment in circumstances where the parties themselves did not expressly provide for the situation. In *Mears* v. *Safecar Security Ltd* [1981] 1 WLR 1214 the Court of Appeal stated that the correct approach was to consider all the facts and surrounding circumstances, including the manner in which the parties had carried out the contract since it was formed. The purpose of implying terms into the contract is to make the contract work more effectively; therefore terms will be implied only where this objective will be achieved. It has been said that one term to be implied into a contract of employment is that the employer should treat employees with trust and respect and the employer should not act in a capricious way towards them (*Gardner Ltd* v. *Beresford* [1978] IRLR 63).

Can an employer vary an employee's contract of employment so as to require the employee to undertake different work? Any variation of the terms of a contract must be by the agreement of both parties. One party to a contract cannot unilaterally vary the terms of the contract. Therefore, if the employer does unilaterally vary the contract by insisting that the employee performs duties other than those contained in the contract, this will amount to a breach of contract on the part of the employer. If a hotelier were to require a receptionist to clean rooms, or if a restaurateur were to order the chef to wash up, these would be examples of a unilateral variation on the part of the employer. Careful employers should not allow such situations to arise, and they may avoid confrontations by including in the written contract of each employee a term to the effect that 'the employee may be required to perform such other duties as may be requested from time to time by the employer'. Of course such requests must be reasonable. A restaurant manager would rightly object if his employer required him to clean the toilets. If the contract is properly worded, some unilateral variations on the part of the employer may be provided for, e.g. change of shift system or the taking on of additional responsibilities.

Example. Mr Bunn, the restaurant manager of a small hotel, is required by his employer to take on the additional responsibility of managing the lounge bar after the resignation of the head bar steward. Mr Bunn refuses. Can he refuse within the terms of his employment if his contract states that his responsibilities are the supervision of restaurant staff and the general management of the dining room? The answer would appear to be that he can refuse; his contract does not include the management of the lounge bar. However, the question is to a large extent determined by fact. If the additional responsibilities reflect an unreasonable increase in workload he may refuse; otherwise he may not.

BOWATER CONTAINERS LTD v. McCORMACK [1980] IRLR 50 (EAT)

The applicant was a supervisor who, following a reorganization within the company, was required to supervise a further section. The applicant refused to accept these additional responsibilities, maintaining that they were outside the terms of his contract of employment, and therefore he was not obliged to undertake them. The employer dismissed the applicant.

Held: The Employment Appeal Tribunal, reversing the decision of the Industrial Tribunal, held that the dismissal was fair. The applicant's refusal to undertake the additional responsibility amounted to 'some other substantial reason' within s. 57(1)(b) EPCA 1978 and the employers had acted reasonably in dismissing the applicant.

The appropriate way for an employer to draft a contract of employment is to include clear though broadly stated terms which will permit a variation. An example of this is often seen in relation to the location of the workplace. A contract of employment may include a term requiring the employee to work at any location, as directed by the employer. Such a clause is of considerable importance to an employer who has a number of premises nationwide, e.g. a chain of hotels. An employment contract for supervisory and management staff should therefore include a term which would enable the hotelier to require them to work at any of the hotels. The wording of the contract is all-important. In *Bex* v. *Securicor Transport Ltd* [1972] IRLR 68, a term in a contract of employment was held to give the employer the right to alter the nature of the employee's work.

Employment: Accommodation as forming part of the contract of employment

It is important to make clear in any contract of employment the extent of the rights of occupation which any member of staff may have during his or her employment with the organization. This is particularly important where 'living in' forms a central element in the performance of the employee's contract of employment. The Court of Appeal has recently considered the issue of eviction of a former employee from residential accommodation which came with his former employment in *Norris* v. *Checksfield* [1991] NLJ 707. On the facts of that case (a coach mechanic occupying a house next door to his employer's garage) it was found that the employee's occupation of the house arose from a 'contractual licence' to reside in the house which terminated at the time when the employee's contract of employment with the employer was ended. The termination of an employee's permission to occupy does not have to comply with the notice provisions of s. 5(1A) of the Protection from Eviction Act 1977.

It is particularly important for employers in the hotel, licensed, catering and leisure industries to be clear and precise when drawing up employment contracts for staff who are to 'live in' at the employer's premises as to the terms on which the employee occupies the residential accommodation. Employers should draw up a licence by which they grant permission to the employee to reside in the accommodation for the purposes of fulfilling his or her obligations under his or her contract of employment, and stating clearly that the licence terminates when the contract of employment ends.

Written statement of terms and conditions

By s. 1 EPCA 1978 (as substituted by schedule 4, Trade Union Reform and Employment Rights Act 1993) an employee has a right, within two months of the commencement of employment, to a written statement of the terms and conditions of his or her contract of employment. It should be noted that this is a statement of terms and it is not the employee's contract of employment. Therefore, the particulars set out in the notice are not conclusive proof of all the terms of the contract (*Systems Floors (UK) Ltd* v. *Daniel* [1982] ICR 54; *Robertson* v. *British Gas* [1983] ICR 351(CA), in which the statement of particulars was held to be no more than strong evidence of the contractual terms). The purpose of the notice is to enable the employee to be made aware of the terms of the contract. Verbal notice of terms and conditions is insufficient.

Who is entitled to a written statement of terms and conditions?

Certain limited categories of employee are excluded from the requirements of s. 1. These are persons in Crown employment (s. 138), House of Commons staff (s. 139), and those employed outside Great Britain (s. 141). Part-time staff are entitled to a written statement upon completion of two months continuous service.

Contents of the statement

Because of changes introduced by the Trade Union Reform and Employment Rights Act 1993, a written statement may have to include most or all of the following items.
*   The names of the employer and the employee.
*   The date when the employment, which is covered by the statement began. This will be the date on which the employment began and not the date on which the employee first turned up for work.
*   The date on which the employee's period of continuous employment began, taking into account any employment with a previous employer which counts towards that period. This date will normally be the date when the employee began working for the employer but note Transfer of Undertakings Regulation (see below).
The written statement also needs to contain other particulars. They should be those which are applicable at a date which is no more than seven days before the statement containing the relevant particulars is given to the employee. They are as follows:
*   The scale or rate of remuneration or the method of calculating remuneration.
*   The intervals at which remuneration is paid – weekly, monthly or some other period.
*   Any terms and conditions relating to hours of work, including any terms and conditions relating to normal working hours.

- Any terms and conditions relating to holidays and holiday pay, including a calculation of any entitlement to holiday pay on termination of employment.
- Any terms and conditions relating to incapacity for work due to sickness or injury, including any provision for sick pay.
- Any terms and conditions relating to pensions and pension schemes. This should also specify if the relevant pension scheme is contracted out of the State Earnings Related Pension Scheme;
- The length of notice which an employee is obliged to give and entitled to receive.
- The title of the job which the employee is employed to do or a brief description of the work for which the employee is employed.
- Where the employment is not intended to be permanent, the period for which it is expected to continue or, if it is for a fixed term, the date when it is to end.
- Either an employee's place of work or, where an employee is required or permitted to work at various places, an indication of that fact and of the employer's address.
- Details of any collective agreements which directly affect the terms and conditions of the employment including, where the employer is not a party, the persons by whom they were made.
- Where an employee is required to work outside the United Kingdom for a period of more than one month:
  - the period of work outside the United Kingdom
  - the currency in which remuneration will be made whilst the employee is working outside the United Kingdom
  - any additional remuneration and benefits to be provided by reason of the work being outside the United Kingdom; and
  - any terms and conditions relating to the employee's return to the United Kingdom.

Written statements normally need to contain all of these, but some will not. In that event the statement should specify the items where there is no entitlement to the particulars.

- Grievance and discipline

Finally, the statement should include information:

- giving details of any disciplinary rules applicable to the employee
- specifying a person to whom the employee can apply if he or she is dissatisfied with any disciplinary decision and to raise any grievance, as well as the manner in which any such application should be made
- specifying a person to whom the employee can apply to raise any grievance and the manner in which any such application should be made; and
- explaining any further steps which can be taken after such an application has been made, if the employee wishes to appeal.

Exclusion of certain contracts

An employer is not obliged to issue a s. 1 statement or notify changes under s. 4 if and for so long as the following conditions are fulfilled:
(a) the employee's contract of employment is a contract which has been reduced to

*writing in one or more documents, and which contains express terms affording
the particulars to be given under s. 1(3);*

(b) *the employee has been given a copy of the contract (with any variations made
from time to time) or he has reasonable opportunities of reading a copy in the
course of his employment, or a copy is made reasonably accessible to him in
some other way; and*

(c) *a note of the kind mentioned in s. 1(4) has been given to the employee or he has
reasonable opportunities of reading such a note in the course of his employment,
or such a note is made reasonably accessible to him in some other way.*

*If the above conditions cease to be fulfilled at any time a s. 1 statement must be given
within one month of that time.*

Section 5, Employment Protection (Consolidation) Act 1978

If there is a change in the terms of employment the employer is obliged within one
month of the change to notify the employee (s. 4(1) EPCA).

Are there sanctions for non-compliance with s. 1?

If the employer fails to comply with the requirements of s. 1 EPCA 1978 the employee
may apply to an industrial tribunal, by virtue of s. 11 EPCA 1978. An employee who
is dissatisfied because no written particulars at all have been received may refer the
matter to an industrial tribunal, which has the power to determine what particulars the
written statement should have included. In any case the particulars decided on by the
tribunal have effect as if they had been included in a s. 1 statement issued by the
employer (*Mears* v. *Safecar Security Ltd* [1982] IRLR 190). Section 11 EPCA would
seem to impose on the tribunal the duty to find the specified terms, and in the last
resort to draw them up and write them into the contract.

Job description

It is the proper practice for employers to draw up and send to their employees upon
appointment a description of the duties they are to perform. This job description
should be worded in sufficiently clear terms as to identify the specific duties of the
employee. However, it must be broad enough to enable variations in the employee's
duties to be instituted within the parameters of his or her contract of employment.
Flexibility is of considerable importance where the number of employees is small, as
in a restaurant, inn or small hotel. Letters of appointment and s. 1 notices should
therefore contain a brief description of the work required of the employee.
Furthermore, it should be made clear that the description contained therein is not
exhaustive and that the employee may be required to undertake other duties.

9.3 REMUNERATION

The rate and intervals at which remuneration (i.e. wages or salary) is to be paid to the
employee are set out in the employee's contract of employment, as is the method of
calculation. We are concerned here with the process by which remuneration is agreed

upon within the hotel and catering industry, as well as with any statutory obligations that relate to remuneration.

Payment of wages and salaries

The law relating to the payment of wages has two major aspects: the method by which payment is made; and deductions from the wages of employees.

The payment of wages and deductions therefrom are now covered by the Wages Act 1986. Unlike the previous law in the Truck Acts 1831–40, which applied only to manual workers, the Wages Act 1986 applies to all workers. Section 8(1) of the Act defines a worker as being:

> *an individual who has entered into or works under (or, where the employment has ceased, worked under) one of the contracts referred to in subsection (2), and any reference to a worker's contract shall be construed accordingly.*

Section 8(2) states:

> *Those contracts are –*
> (a) *a contract of service;*
> (b) *a contract of apprenticeship; and*
> (c) *any other contract whereby the individual undertakes to do or perform personally any work or services for another party to the contract whose status is not by virtue of the contract that of a client or customer of any profession or business carried on by the individual,*
> *in each case whether such a contract is express or implied and, if express, whether it is oral or in writing.*

This is a very broad definition indeed.

The Truck Acts had placed restrictions on both the method of payment and the deductions which an employer could make from an employee's pay. Section 11 of the Wages Act 1986 removes all restrictions on the way in which payment of wages to manual and other workers is made. The method of payment is determined by the contract of employment.

Deductions from pay

No deductions from a worker's wages may be made unless either:
(a) it is required or permitted by a statutory or contractual provision; *or*
(b) the worker has given his or her prior written consent to the deduction.
If the deduction is made pursuant to a contractual provision, the terms of the contract must have been shown to the worker or, if the contract is not in writing, its effect notified in writing to the worker before the deduction is made.

The above provisions do not apply to:

(a) deductions made pursuant to any statutory disciplinary proceedings;
(b) statutory payments due to a public authority;
(c) deductions payable to third parties, for example trade union dues, made either pursuant to a contractual term the inclusion of which the worker has agreed to in writing, or otherwise with his or her prior written agreement or consent;
(d) deductions made from a worker's wages for taking part in a strike or other industrial action.

Such deductions are specifically covered by s. 1 of the Act.

Deductions from pay of workers in retail employment

Special provision is made by s. 2 of the Wages Act 1986 for deductions from pay of workers in retail employment. Retail employment is defined by s. 2(2) of the Act:

> *'Retail employment', in relation to a worker, means employment involving (whether on a regular basis or not) –*
> (a) *the carrying out by the worker of* retail transactions *directly with members of the public or with fellow workers or other individuals in their personal capacities, or*
> (b) *the collection by the worker of amounts payable in connection with* retail transactions *carried out by other persons directly with members of the public or with fellow workers or other individuals in their personal capacities.*

'Retail transactions' is defined as being 'the sale or supply of goods, or the supply of services (including financial services)'.

Clearly a considerable number of the staff employed in the hotel and catering industry fall within the scope of 'retail employment'.

By virtue of s. 2(1) of the Wages Act 1986 the employer of a worker in retail employment may not deduct for cash shortages or stock deficiencies more than one-tenth of the gross wages payable to the worker on a particular pay day.

In order for a deduction to be lawful (where made within the above limitations), ss. 3(1) and (2) require that the employer must:
(a) notify the worker in writing of his or her total liability to the employer in respect of that shortage or deficiency;
(b) make a demand for payment which is:
    (i)   in writing;
    (ii) on a pay day;
    (iii) after notification of total liability.

It should be noted that whilst s. 3(4) limits deductions to one-tenth of gross wages, this limitation does not apply to deductions made from the final payment of wages (see s. 4).

Where an employer makes any deduction from a worker's pay in breach of these statutory provisions the worker may present a complaint to an industrial tribunal. The nature of such a complaint may fall into any one of four categories:
1   An unauthorized deduction has been made contrary to s. 1(1).
2   An unauthorized payment has been received by the employer contrary to s. 1(2) or s. 3(1).
3   Deductions exceeding the limit set by s. 2(1) have been made.
4   The employer has received more than the limit set by s. 3(4).

The time limit for presenting a complaint to an individual tribunal under the Wages Act is three months commencing with the date of the deduction on the receipt of which complaint is made – s. 5(1). A tribunal may extend the time limit where it is satisfied that it was not reasonably practicable for the complaint to be presented within the period of three months.

Where an industrial tribunal finds that a complaint made to it under s. 5 is well founded, it will make a declaration to that effect.

Where an unlawful deduction is found to have been made by an employer, the tribunal will order the employer to pay the worker the amount of the deduction, pursuant to s. 5(4). Section 5(8) of the Act prohibits an employer who is ordered to pay or repay money wrongfully deducted from a worker's wages from recovering by any means that sum of money from the worker.

An employer may not seek, by means of the contract by which he or she employs a worker, to exclude or limit the operation of s. 5 procedures under the Wages Act 1986.

The House of Lords has recently considered the question of the Wages Act 1986 with regard to payments in lieu of notice in *Delaney* v. *Staples* [1992] IRLR 191.

Overpayment

Where an employer makes an overpayment of wages under a mistake of fact, and the employee is led to believe that he or she can treat the overpaid money as his or her own, and in reliance on such a representation spends some or all of it, the employer cannot recover the overpayment (*Avon County Council* v. *Howlett* [1983] 1 WLR 605).

Withholding payment

An interesting case of an employer withholding the pay of an employee where the employee was taking limited industrial action is *Wiluszynski* v. *Tower Hamlets London Borough Council* [1989] IRLR 259 (CA). On the facts of the case the employer withheld payment of all of the plaintiff's wages when the plaintiff refused to reply to councillors' enquiries, part of the plaintiff's contractual duties, albeit a small part in terms of the hours required, in pursuance of limited industrial action taken by NALGO (National and Local Government Officers' Association), of which he was a member. The plaintiff fully performed all his other duties.

Michael Davies J at first instance held that the defendant council must pay the plaintiff's wages plus interest. An employer was not entitled to withhold the whole of an employee's pay in circumstances where the employee has substantially fulfilled his contract but has failed fully to perform his duties due to industrial action taken by the trade union to which he belongs.

The Court of Appeal, in allowing the employer's appeal, held their actions to be lawful. The plaintiff had failed to show that he was ready and willing to discharge his full contractual obligations so that his actions had effectively amounted to a repudiatory breach of contract entitling the employer to decline to accept or pay for the proffered partial performance. The Court considered the duty to respond to councillors' enquiries as one holding constitutional importance and the corresponding breach consequently as not insubstantial. On the facts of the case the council had made it clear to the plaintiff that if he was not prepared to comply with his contract he was not required to work, and that if he did work (as he had continued to do) he did so voluntarily and would not be paid, a pronouncement which the Court considered as being meant to be taken seriously.

The central principle which emerges from this case and the earlier House of Lords decision in *Miles* v. *Wakefield Metropolitan District Council* [1987] ICR 368, a case involving part withholding an employee's pay in the context of minor industrial action, is that an employee is not entitled to remuneration under the contract of employment unless he or she is willing fully to perform the contract.

Wages councils

The Wages Act 1986 repealed the Wages Councils Act 1979, which had provided for the establishment of wages councils by the Secretary of State where there was no adequate machinery for effective regulation of the remuneration of specific groups of workers.

Currently there are no wages councils concerning the hospitality industry.

Employees' rights to an itemised pay statement

Every employee (including part-time employees) who has completed two years continuous employment has the right to be provided with an itemised pay statement by his or her employer. Section 8 EPCA 1978 states:

> *Every employee shall have the right to be given by his employer at or before the time*
> *at which any payment of wages or salary is made to him an itemized pay statement,*
> *in writing containing the following particulars, that is to say –*
> *(a) the gross amount of the wages or salary;*
> *(b) the amounts of any variable and, subject to s. 9, any fixed deductions from that*
> *   gross amount and the purposes for which they are made;*
> *(c) the net amount of wages or salary payable; and*
> *(d) where different parts of the net amount are paid in a different way, the amount*
> *   and method of each part-payment.*

A pay statement need not contain separate particulars of fixed deductions (s. 9 EPCA) provided the aggregate amount of all deductions is stated, and the employer has given the employee a standing statement of fixed deductions which outlines all the relevant details. The standing statement must be re-issued annually. Where an employer has failed to provide an itemized pay statement the employee may refer the matter to an industrial tribunal, which will determine the particulars which ought to be included in the statement.

Tips paid by customers to waiting staff are not part of the wages of the waiters and waitresses for the purposes of s. 8 EPCA (see *Cofone* v. *Spaghetti House Ltd* [1980] ILR 155).

Sick pay

When considering the issue of payment for periods of sickness, any of the following may apply:

1   They may be provisions in the individual employee's contract of employment which provide for sick pay.
2   Statutory sick pay (SSP) provides a statutory right to a specified level of sick pay.

Where statutory payments are made under SSP they are offset against payments made under the individual's contract of employment.

It should be noted that sickness and absence from work through ill health are of significance to the termination of employment. First, persistent and repeated illness (e.g. long-term sickness) may constitute 'incapacity' and therefore may amount to a bona fide reason for dismissal. Secondly, in rare cases, sickness may frustrate an employee's contract of employment.

Sick pay: the contract of employment

An employer may agree to pay his or her employees while they are absent due to ill health. Such payments commonly run for a specified period of time and are subject to conditions.

The written particulars given to an employee setting out the terms and conditions of his or her employment must state whether or not the employer makes payments for periods of absence due to sickness and, if so, on what terms. In *Mears* v. *Safecar Security Ltd* [1982] ICR 626, the Court of Appeal held that where such a term is not specified or agreed, the tribunal must consider all the facts and circumstances to ascertain the term implied. There is no presumption of a contractual right to sick pay. An industrial tribunal must look at all the facts and circumstances and at the conduct of the parties since the contract began.

Where there is a contractual right to sick pay, but no provision as to its duration, the court will infer a reasonable term (*Howman & Son* v. *Blyth* [1983] ICR 416).

Statutory sick pay (SSP)

This is a complex issue, and it is not our purpose here to deal with it in detail. Detailed and practical guidance can be found in *Employer's Guide to Statutory Sick Pay*.

How does SSP work? All employees, apart from those who fall into the category of 'excluded employees' (e.g. those over state pensionable age), are entitled to SSP from their employers. The entitlement to SSP is usually 28 weeks in any three-year period.

The entitlement provisions are to be found in the Social Security Contributions and Benefits Act 1992. The operative regulations are the Statutory Sick Pay Regulations 1982 and the Statutory Sick Pay (General) Amendment Regulations 1986.

The essential requirements for qualification for SSP are that an employee must:

(a)   have four or more consecutive days of sickness (including Sundays and holidays) during which he or she is too ill to be capable of doing his or her work; *and*
(b)   notify his or her absence to his or her employer, subject to certain statutory requirements and any agreement between them; *and*
(c)   supply evidence of incapacity. This is also a matter for the employer; a common example of an employer's requirement would be:
   (i)   a 'self-certificate' for periods of four to seven days;
   (ii)   a doctor's certificate or other evidence of sickness for periods after the first seven days.

It should be emphasized that employers cannot contract out of the SSP provisions, nor can they require employees to contribute towards payments.

Smaller employers qualify for some relief (SER), i.e. they may recover a proportion of the SSP paid to employees.

9.4 THE RIGHTS OF EMPLOYEES DURING EMPLOYMENT

Certain rights are accorded to employees, e.g. the right to a notice of terms and conditions of employment pursuant to s. 1 EPCA 1978 as amended by the Employment Acts 1980 and 1982. Here we shall examine some of those rights, particularly the right not to be discriminated against on grounds of race or sex, the right to equal pay, and the right to maternity benefits. Women comprise a major part of the workforce in the hotel and catering industry, so it is particularly important to study those rights which relate specifically to women. We shall consider in section 9.5 the right of all employees (subject to qualifications) not to be unfairly dismissed, and the right (subject to qualification) to claim a redundancy payment where the dismissal is by reason of redundancy. In Chapter 11 we shall also consider the rights of an employee as a trade union member, or as an official of a recognized trade union.

Sex discrimination

The legislation dealing with sex discrimination – the Sex Discrimination Acts 1975 and 1986 and Employment Act 1989 – covers more than discrimination against women. Section 2 SDA 1975 provides that the statutory restrictions on discrimination shall apply to discrimination against men, whilst s. 3 SDA 1975 provides for discrimination against married people on the grounds of their marital status. The Sex Discrimination Acts do not cover discrimination against a person on the ground that he or she is unmarried; nor does it cover discrimination against a person on the grounds of that person's sexual orientation, i.e. if he or she is gay.

The 1986 Act and relevant provisions of the 1989 Act were designed to bring UK law into line with European Community Law and to plug some of the more obvious gaps in the 1975 Act which had been exposed by cases being brought, particularly before the European Court.

The division of function between the sex discrimination legislation still remains, but flaws in the Equal Pay Act 1970 have been dealt with to some extent by the Equal Pay (Amendment) Regulations 1983 and the SDA 1986.

The law on sex discrimination and equal pay has seen substantial case law and legislative developments in recent years, mainly brought about by the European context in which the UK law operates.

What does discrimination cover?

Discrimination may take place in three ways: direct discrimination, indirect discrimination and victimization.

In deciding whether discrimination has taken place the position of the person allegedly discriminated against will be compared with that of a person of similar skill and qualification: like must be compared with like (s. 5(3) SDA).

Section 1 SDA 1975 lays down the forms of discrimination against women:

A person discriminates against a woman in any circumstances relevant for the purposes of a provision of this Act if –
(a) *on the ground of her sex he treats her less favourably than he treats or would treat a man, or*
(b) *he applies to her a requirement or condition which applies or would apply equally to a man but –*
   (i) *which is such that the proportion of women who can comply with it is considerably smaller than the proportion of men who can comply with it, and*
   (ii) *which he cannot show to be justifiable irrespective of the sex of the person to whom it is applied, and*
   (iii) *which is to her detriment because she cannot comply with it.*

Section 1 covers two forms of discrimination: direct discrimination (s. 1(1)a) and indirect discrimination (s. 1(1)b).

Direct discrimination. This relates to the less favourable treatment of a person on the grounds of their sex. The clearest example would be where an employer refuses to employ a woman because the work is man's work. A classic situation in the hotel or catering trade is where an employer refuses employment to a barman because the employer wishes to have 'attractive female bar staff'. This constitutes direct discrimination against men and is provided for by s. 2 of the Act.

The dismissal of a woman because she is pregnant may amount to sex discrimination. In *Hayes* v. *Malleable Working Men's Club and Institute* [1985] ICR 703, the Employment Appeal Tribunal held that there was no principle of law preventing the Sex Discrimination Act from applying to a woman who has suffered discrimination in her employment because of her pregnancy, although such an act was not automatically discriminatory. In order for a pregnant applicant to succeed in such a claim she must show that her employer would have treated a male employee who needed time off or was not fully capable of fulfilling his contract of employment in a better manner than she was treated. This principle was applied in *Webb* v. *Emo Cargo (UK) Ltd* [1990] (EAT), where the tribunal rejected a claim of direct discrimination on grounds of pregnancy. On appeal [1992] IRLR 116) the Court of Appeal insisted that the proper basis of comparison was not simply that between a man and a woman, but between a woman and a man in the most nearly comparable circumstances, i.e. a man who required an equivalent amount of time off for a medical condition. The subsequent decision of the Court of Appeal in *Shoner* v. *B&R Residential Lettings Ltd* [1992] IRLR 317 adds support to the approach adopted in *Webb*.

Dismissal on grounds of pregnancy may also amount to unfair dismissal under s. 60 EPCA, which makes it automatically unfair for an employer to dismiss a female employee if the reason or principal reason for her dismissal is pregnancy 'or any other reason connected with her pregnancy' (see the section on 'grounds for unfair dismissal'). It should, however, be noted here that protection under s. 60 is limited by qualification in terms of continuous employment and is also subject to statutory exceptions favouring the employer. The Sex Discrimination Act consequently provides a more widely based right.

In *Berrisford* v. *Woodland Schools (MD) Ltd* (1991) 6 March (EAT) (unreported), it was found that discrimination could not be established under s. 1(1) of the SDA 1975 when an unmarried school matron who became pregnant was dismissed in circumstances where she refused to marry the child's father.

It should also be noted that to make a woman redundant whilst she is on maternity leave will give rise to a claim of unfair dismissal – *Community Task Force* v. *Rimmer* [1986] ICR 491. Although analogous, this situation is not one giving rise to a claim of sex discrimination; it relates to the specific maternity rights provided by the EPCA.

Indirect discrimination. This occurs in circumstances where the employer applies a condition or requirement to an employee (or a prospective employee) which is such that the proportion of people of one sex who can comply with the condition or requirement is considerably smaller than that of the other sex and the condition or requirement cannot be justified irrespective of sex, and is a detriment to that person since he or she cannot comply with it. Indirect discrimination covers the situation where an innkeeper or hotelier advertises for an 'attractive bar person to work in discothèque – must be prepared to wear uniform' and the uniform which the bar person must wear is a 'bunny girl' outfit! Indirect discrimination may also occur in less dramatic ways.

HURLEY v. MUSTOE   A married woman who had four young children applied for a
[1981] IRLR 208 (EAT)   job as a waitress. The proprietor had a policy of not employ-
                          ing women with young children since he took the view that
                          they were unreliable. The manager gave the applicant a trial
but on her first night as a waitress she was asked to leave by the proprietor.

Held: The EAT held firstly that the applicant had been directly discriminated against contrary to s. 1(1)a. Secondly, indirect discrimination had occurred contrary to s. 3(1)b on the grounds of the applicant's married status. The employer's requirement (i.e. no married women with children) was not justifiable, since it applied to women yet not to men. Lastly, each applicant should have his or her application dealt with on its merits; there are ways of determining the reliability of potential employees without imposing an exclusionary rule applicable only to one class of applicant, e.g. women with children.

Where the employer seeks to impose a particular requirement or condition, the industrial tribunal, when determining the case, should consider whether in practical terms the requirement or condition is one with which both women and men could comply equally – *Price* v. *Civil Service Commission* [1978] 1 All ER 1228 (EAT). The requirement or condition must also act as an 'absolute bar' to selection: *Perera* v. *Civil Service Commission and Department of Customs and Excise (No. 2)* [1983] IRLR 166 (CA).

The question of justification and the width of the employer's defence to an alleged discriminatory practice have proven contentious in recent years. The original standard adopted by the courts was one of 'business necessity' (*Steel* v. *UPW* [1978] ICR 181 (EAT)), i.e. unless a practice was 'necessary', rather than merely convenient, it was not justifiable. Later cases, however, tended to weaken this standard by applying subjective criteria: see e.g. *Ojutiku* v. *MSC* [1987] ICR 661 (CA). Following the decision of the European Court in *Bilka-Kaufhaus GmbH* v. *Weber von Hartz* [1986] 2 CMLR 701, the possibility of an objective standard being adopted in determining the issue of justification in cases of alleged discrimination has arisen, so that only measures which 'correspond to a real need on the part of the undertaking, are appropriate with a view to achieving objectives pursued and are necessary to that end' are justifiable. Such a standard was held to be applicable to sex discrimination cases by Lord Keith in the case of *Rainey* v. *Greater Glasgow Health Board* [1987] IRLR 26 (HL).

Victimization. If an employer treats any person less favourably than others because that person threatens to bring proceedings, to give evidence or information, or to take any action or make any allegation concerning the employer with reference to the SDA 1975 and 1986 or the Equal Pay Act 1970, or has already done any of those things, then the employer is guilty of discrimination by victimization. This arises from s. 4(1) SDA 1975. Where the allegation made against the employer is false and not made in good faith, any unfavourable treatment of that person by reason of that allegation will not be considered discriminatory (s. 4(2) SDA 1975). There must be a causal link between the victimization and acts done under or by reference to the relevant statute: see *Aziz* v. *Trinity Street Taxis Ltd* [1988] IRLR 204 (CA), a case concerning victimization under the Race Relations Act 1976, s. 4.

In what situations may sex discrimination occur at work?

Recruitment. The arrangements which an employer makes for the selection of applicants for employment should be non-discriminatory. Section 6(1)a SDA 1975 states:

> *It is unlawful for a person, in relation to employment at an establishment in Great Britain to discriminate against a woman –*
> *(a) in the arrangements he makes for the purpose of determining who should be offered the employment . . .*

The selection process normally commences with the advertisement of the vacancy. It is unlawful to advertise a vacancy in terms which indicate an intention on the part of the employer to discriminate on grounds of the applicant's sex (s. 38 SDA 1975). Advertisements including terms such as barmaid, club hostess or head waiter are therefore contrary to s. 38. Job descriptions in advertisements should avoid sexual connotations: bar person, club host or hostess or restaurant manager/manageress are the acceptable ways of advertising such jobs. The advert should be looked at as a whole; one might find a phrase such as 'Bograte Hotels Ltd are equal opportunity employers and all applications will be determined on their merit, irrespective of the applicants' sex, race or disability'. Albeit that an advertisement is non-sexist, there will be discrimination contrary to s. 6(1)a (above) if the applicant's further enquiries show that there is an intention on the part of the employer to discriminate – *McDonald* v. *Applied Art Glass Co.* [1976] IRLR 130. Equally, if the interviewing process, i.e. selection for interview and the employer's conduct at the interview, indicates an intention to discriminate, this will similarly be a breach of s. 6(1)a.

The offer of employment. It is unlawful to discriminate in the terms on which employment is offered (s. 6(1)b SDA 1975). This does not apply to wages and salaries; that aspect is covered by the Equal Pay Act. Where an employer refuses or deliberately omits to offer employment on the ground of the applicant's sex, this is unlawful discrimination contrary to s. 6(1)c.

The training, promotion and other facilities available to employees. It is unlawful discrimination contrary to s. 6(2)a to deny a woman promotion, transfer, access to training, or access to any other benefit, facility or service which is open to men. Some employers, quite wrongly, have taken the view that since younger female employees are likely to marry, leave work and have children, they should not have the company's money spent on them by affording them training and promotion opportunities. This is quite wrong and such a policy is contrary to s. 6(2)a SDA 1975. Equally, if a benefit, facility or service is offered by the employer to employees, it must be provided equally for both women and men.

Dismissal and action short of dismissal. Any dismissal which is due to the sex of the employee in question is unlawful. Section 2(3) of the SDA 1986 provides an extended definition of 'dismissal'. 'Dismissal' additionally covers a situation where a partnership comes to an end on the expiration of a certain period or on the occurrence of a certain event, and it is not immediately renewed on the same terms. Similarly, 'dismissal' covers where employees or partners terminate their employment or partnership by acceptance of their employer's or fellow partner's repudiatory breach of contract.

In *Monro* v. *Allied Suppliers* (1977) IRLIB a man who was offered the job of a cook was dismissed before undertaking his work, since the female employees of the employer indicated that they would not work with him. The dismissal was due to the applicant's sex and amounted to unlawful discrimination contrary to s. 2(2)b SDA 1975. What if a female employee, e.g. a waitress, intends to marry and the employer dismisses her upon the marriage? Is this unlawful discrimination? In *Bick* v. *Royal West of England Residential School for the Deaf* [1976] IRLR 326 it was held not to be. However, this case had been argued as coming within s. 3(1)a, and the possibility of a dismissal contrary to s. 6(2)b was not argued. In *McLean* v. *Paris Travel Services Ltd* [1976] IRLR 202, where a woman was dismissed upon her engagement, such a dismissal was held to be contrary to s. 6(2)b, and she was, in addition to compensation for unfair dismissal, awarded damages for injured feelings.

Does an employer discriminate on grounds of sex if he or she dismisses an employee because she is pregnant? Initially it was held that since no man can become pregnant this was not a situation where a woman could argue that she has been treated in an unequal way in relation to male employees – *Turley* v. *Allders Departmental Stores Ltd* [1980] IRLR 4. The courts have, however, adopted a less rigid approach in more recent cases and acknowledged that there is no principle of law preventing the Sex Discrimination Act from applying to a woman who has suffered discrimination in employment by reason of her pregnancy. Such an act is not, however, automatically discriminatory, the central test being for the pregnant woman to show that her employer would have treated a male employee needing comparable time off or not fully capable of fulfilling his contract in a better manner than she was treated: *Hayes* v. *Malleable Working Men's Club* [1985] IRLR 367 (EAT); *Webb* v. *Emo Cargo (UK) Ltd* [1992] (see p. 287). The alternative course of action is to pursue a claim for unfair dismissal on the ground of pregnancy or reason connected with pregnancy under s. 60 EPCA (see the section on grounds for unfair dismissal).

Sexual harassment. There is no express provision in the 1975 Act dealing with sexual harassment, but courts have been willing to acknowledge that such an act may amount to direct discrimination within an employment context by virtue of s. 6(2)b of the 1975 Act, which states:

> it is unlawful for a person, in the case of a woman employed by him at an establishment in Great Britain, to discriminate against her –
>
> . . .
>
> (b) by dismissing her, or subjecting her to any other detriment. . . .

This was first accepted in the Scottish case *Porcelli* v. *Strathclyde Regional Council* [1986] ICR 564 and has been recently well illustrated in the case of *Bracebridge Engineering Ltd* v. *Darby* [1990] IRLR 3 (EAT), where it was held that sexual harassment is a discriminatory act on grounds of sex and that a single incident, if sufficiently serious, would be enough to found a claim.

Pensions. In *Bilka-Kaufhaus GmbH* v. *Karin Weber von Hartz* [1986] IRLR 317 (EC), it was held that the exclusion of part-time workers from an occupational pension scheme was contrary to Article 119 of the EEC Treaty requiring equal pay for equal work where such a provision affected disproportionately more women than men. This was so unless the provision was attributable to objectively justified factors which were not related to any discrimination based on sex.

The application of Article 119 is dependent on the benefit in question being capable of falling within the definition of 'pay' established by that Article:

> ordinary basic or minimum wage or salary and any other consideration, whether in cash or in kind, which the worker receives, directly or indirectly, in respect of his employment from his employer.

In the *Bilka* case the pension entitlement was held to be capable of falling within such a definition because the scheme was based on an agreement within the employment context and provided a supplement to relevant social security provisions. The problem that has arisen in relation to UK pension schemes is whether they are social security or employment based. In *Newstead* v. *Department of Transport* [1988] CMLR 219 the European Court held Article 119 to be inapplicable; the given scheme being funded out of social security meant that the article dealing with social security was instead applicable. The recent decision of the European Court in *Barber* v. *Guardian Royal Exchange Assurance Group* [1990] 2 All ER 660 has, however, held that a contracted out pension scheme, established and wholly financed by the employer, amounts to consideration paid by the employer to the employee in respect of his employment and therefore falls within the definition of pay under Article 119. Age differentials based on sex relating to entitlement to the given pension on redundancy were consequently held to offend against the principle of equal pay set out in Article 119.

Part-time workers

Recently the Court of Appeal has had to consider the position of part-time female workers in relation to discriminatory treatment in the qualification period for unfair dismissal and redundancy. In *R.* v. *Secretary of State for Employment, Ex Parte Equal Opportunities Commission and Another* [1991] NLJ 1409, the fact that the less favourable treatment of part-time workers compared to full-time workers in respect of qualifying periods for eligibility for statutory rights to unfair dismissal and redundancy payments under the Employment Protection (Consolidation) Act 1978 adversely affects women because many more women than men work part-time does not necessarily have the consequence that the unfair dismissal and redundancy payments provisions in the Act constitute an infringement of Article 119 of the Treaty of Rome.

The Employment Protection (Part-time Employees) Regulations 1995 came into effect on 6 February 1995. This new legislation followed a House of Lords' decision that previous UK legislation discriminated against part-timers and contravened European Directives.

The new regulations have the effect of removing the complex employment rights which have been based upon the benchmarks of an employee working 8 or 16 hours per week. Previously employees had to complete 5 years' service in order to qualify for employment rights and employees working fewer than 8 hours never qualified for those rights.

Two years' continuous service is now the only service qualification required, regardless of number of hours worked, to become entitled to those rights.

Is it ever permissible to discriminate on grounds of sex? It is permissible, where the sex of the employee is a genuine occupational qualification for the job, to discriminate on grounds of sex. This operates only in so far as employers do not unlawfully discriminate on grounds of sex where they do not employ someone or where they deny to an employee an opportunity for promotion, transfer or training on the basis that there is a genuine occupational qualification. 'Genuine occupational qualification' is defined by s. 7(2) SDA 1975:

> *Being a man is a genuine occupational qualification for a job only where –*
> *(a) the essential nature of the job calls for a man for reasons of physiology (excluding physical strength or stamina) or, in dramatic performances or other entertainment, for reasons of authenticity, so that the essential nature of the job would be materially different if carried out by a woman; or*
> *(b) the job needs to be held by a man to preserve decency or privacy because –*
> > *(i)   it is likely to involve physical contact with men in circumstances where they might reasonably object to its being carried out by a woman, or*
> > *(ii) the holder of the job is likely to do his work in circumstances where men might reasonably object to the presence of a woman because they are in a state of undress or are using sanitary facilities; or*
> *(c) the nature or location of the establishment makes it impracticable for the holder of the job to live elsewhere than in premises provided by the employer, and*
> > *(i)   the only such premises which are available for persons holding that kind of job are lived in, or normally lived in, by men and are not equipped with separate sleeping accommodation for women and sanitary facilities which could be used by women in privacy from men, and*
> > *(ii) it is not reasonable to expect the employer either to equip those premises with such accommodation and facilities or to provide other premises for women; or*
> *(d) the nature of the establishment, or of the part of it within which the work is done, requires the job to be held by a man because –*
> > *(i)   it is, or is part of, a hospital, prison or other establishment for persons requiring special care, supervision or attention, and*
> > *(ii) those persons are all men (disregarding any woman whose presence is exceptional), and*
> > *(iii) it is reasonable, having regard to the essential character of the establishment or that part, that the job should not be held by a woman; or*
> *(e) the holder of the job provides individuals with personal services promoting their welfare or education, or similar personal services, and those services can most effectively be provided by a man, or*
>
> *. . .*

(g) the job needs to be held by a man because it is likely to involve the performance of duties outside the United Kingdom in a country whose laws or customs are such that the duties could not, or could not effectively, be performed by a woman, or

(h) the job is one of two to be held by a married couple.

Subsection (2)f was repealed by the Employment Act 1989, s. 3.

The 1975 Act also contained an important exception to the general rule against discrimination on grounds of sex or marital status where an act was done under statutory authority: s. 51 SDA. This gave blanket exemption from liability for discriminating actions which were necessary to comply with a statute passed before the 1975 Act. Following an opinion issued by the European Commission, which alleged that s. 51 was inconsistent with the requirements of the Equal Treatment Employment Directive (76/207/EEC) (equal treatment as regards 'access to employment, vocational training and promotion, and working conditions'), the government gave an undertaking that s. 51 would be retrospectively amended.

This has been achieved by the Employment Act 1989, which brings domestic law into line with the Directive by providing that any statute passed before the 1975 Act requiring discrimination in the field of employment or vocational training is overridden by the 1975 Act. A new s. 51 gives effect to this, but it must be noted that the prior blanket exception still applies in areas other than employment and vocational training, i.e. the reforms go no further than was considered necessary to comply with our European obligations.

Discrimination in training

Positive discrimination in favour of women or men, in affording access to training and encouragement to apply for particular work, is permitted to employers if at any time within the twelve months immediately preceding the doing of the act there was nobody of the sex in question among those doing that work, or the number of people of that sex doing that work was comparatively small (see s. 48 SDA 1975 and s. 4 SDA 1986).

Note also the provisions of the Employment Act 1989 with regard to vocational training, which extend the existing provisions under the 1975 Act to cover discrimination during the course of training, no matter who provides that training, and enable special treatment to be afforded to lone parents in connection with their participation in training schemes and other designated programmes – ss. 7 and 8 EA 1989.

Benefits on death or retirement

An employer used to be able to discriminate in relation to benefits on death or retirement. By virtue of s. 6(4) SDA 1975 discrimination in relation to death or retirement was excluded from the operative provisions of the Act. In *Roberts* v. *Cleveland AHA* [1979] ICR 558 a complaint based on the fact that women were required to retire earlier than men was dismissed because the retirement age was within s. 6(4) SDA 1975.

In *Garland* v. *British Rail Engineering Ltd* [1982] ICR 420, on a reference to it by the House of Lords, the European Court of Justice held that the provision by an employer of special travel facilities for male employees after retirement, some of which female employees did not receive, was discrimination against the female employees contrary to Article 119 of the Treaty of Rome. Thereafter, the House of

Lords held that s. 6(4) SDA ought as far as possible to be construed so as to carry out the obligations of and not to be inconsistent with the Treaty of Rome, and that the employers were guilty of unlawful discrimination.

Until the coming into force of the Sex Discrimination Act 1986, s. 6(4) SDA 1975 permitted discrimination in relation to death or retirement. However, the European Court of Justice, in *Marshall* v. *Southampton and South West Hampshire Area Health Authority (Teaching)* [1986] 2 WLR 780 held that:

> *For an employer to dismiss a woman employee after she has passed her 60th birthday pursuant to a policy of retiring men at the age of 65 and women at the age 60 and on the grounds only that she is a woman who has passed the age of 60 is an act of discrimination prohibited by Article 5(1) of Council Directive (76/207/EEC).*

The Article was held to be directly applicable against state authorities, who must now have the same retiring age for men and women.

Section 2 of the Sex Discrimination Act 1986 seeks to bring the English legislation into conformity with the Directive by enacting that (irrespective of whether the employer is a state employer) it is unlawful to discriminate, by virtue of provision in relation to retirement:

(a) in the terms on which a woman is offered employment as regards
  (i)   access to opportunities for promotion, transfer or training, and
  (ii) dismissal or demotion; *or*
(b) in the way the employer affords a woman access to opportunities for promotion, transfer or training or in refusing or deliberately omitting to offer such access; *or*
(c) in dismissing a woman or subjecting her to a detriment which results in dismissal or involves demotion.

It is now unlawful for an employer to dismiss a woman on the grounds that she has attained a particular retiring age, where that age is lower than the retirement age applicable to men.

It is worthy of note here that s. 16 of the Employment Act 1989 has the same effect, i.e. assimilation of age limits for men and women, in relation to redundancy payments.

Who is responsible under the Sex Discrimination Acts?

Anything done by a person in the course of his or her employment is treated for the purposes of the Act as done by his or her employer as well as by him or her, whether or not it was done with the employer's knowledge or approval. However, it is a defence for an employer to prove that he or she took such steps as were reasonably practicable to prevent the employee from doing that act, or from doing in the course of his or her employment acts of that description (see s. 41 SDA 1975). The 1975 Act also creates liability if a person knowingly aids another person to do an act made unlawful by the Sex Discrimination Act (s. 42 SDA).

How are the Sex Discrimination Acts enforced?

A complaint may be made to the industrial tribunal pursuant to s. 63 SDA 1975. The normal practice is for ACAS to intervene and seek conciliation in the dispute. If the matter is not resolved it will thereafter be heard by an industrial tribunal. If discrimination is established:

1	An order may be made declaring the rights of the complainant.
2	An award of compensation may be made (including an award for injured feelings) to a maximum sum of £10 000 (since 1 April 1991).
3	Either in addition to compensation or in substitution for it, a recommendation may be made as to future action to be taken to remove the discriminatory effect of the employer's actions. If this is not complied with, further compensation may be ordered.

A complainant must make his or her application to the industrial tribunal within three months of the alleged discrimination, or as soon as is reasonably practicable thereafter.

Discrimination – Gay Employees

Although the legislation is silent as to discrimination against an individual on the grounds of his/her sexual orientation there have been cases where the issue has been before the courts. The action brought by four former armed services personnel against their former employers for dismissal from the army, navy and air force on the ground of their being gay is perhaps the most high profile litigation. This case is based on the statutes which specifically cover the employment of members of the armed forces. Meanwhile, British Rail has had its equal opportunities policy challenged in the High Court, regarding the provision of concessionary travel passes for the partners of time-served personnel. A female catering operative who was unable to obtain a concessionary travel pass for her long-term female partner is arguing that British Rail has discriminated against her by non-compliance with BR's own equal opportunities policy. BR contends that the equal opportunities policy does not form part of individual contracts of employment and there is no contractual entitlement on the part of any partner of a BR employee to free travel. BR's equal opportunities policy and the travel rights are negotiated collectively, the travel rights are fiercely guarded and are perceived as a substantial benefit by BR employees. Is BR in refusing to provide passes for the gay partners of employees out of line with the practice of other large employers? British Airways, for example, allows unmarried employees to nominate a 'travel companion' without regard for the nature of that relationship – e.g. the nominated person could simply be a friend, a relative or a partner of the employee.

A key area of concern with respect to discrimination against gay people is the failure on the part of employers to recognize the employee's partner with regard to occupational pension schemes. Whereas the wife or husband is very often recognized, and some pension schemes recognize the rights of unmarried heterosexual partners, few if any recognize the partner in a homosexual relationship. It is likely that proceedings will be brought to establish the legality of such exclusions, some may argue that to deprive a long-term gay partner of the equivalent of a 'widow's pension' is unfair, if not discriminatory.

Racial discrimination

The provisions relating to racial discrimination at work are contained in the Race Relations Act 1976 (RRA) and are directly analogous to those contained in the Sex Discrimination Act 1975, discussed above. Discrimination may take one of three forms: direct discrimination, indirect discrimination or victimization.

Direct discrimination

Under s. 1(1)a **RRA** 1976, a person directly discriminates against another where on racial grounds he or she treats that other less favourably than he or she treats or would treat others. A clear example of direct discrimination is as follows:

ZARCZYNSKA v. LEVY   A barmaid was dismissed by an employer for refusing to obey
[1979] 1 All ER 814 (EAT)   an order not to serve coloured people at the pub where she
                            was employed. It was held by the Employment Appeal
                            Tribunal that s. 1(1)a covered such a situation. The matter
was remitted to the industrial tribunal, which found that no such unlawful instruction had been
given by the employer. See *Showboat Entertainment Centre* v. *Owens* [1984] IRLR 7 (EAT).
'Racial grounds' are defined by s. 3(1) of the 1976 Act.

Indirect discrimination

This is covered by s. 1(1)b **RRA** 1976:

> *A person discriminates against another in any circumstances relevant for the*
> *purposes of provision of this Act if –*
> *(a) [see above]*
> *(b) he applies to that other a requirement or condition which he applies or would*
> *   apply equally to persons not of the same racial group as that other but –*
> *   (i)   which is such that the proportion of persons of the same racial group as*
> *   that other who can comply with it is considerably smaller than the*
> *   proportion of persons not of that racial group who can comply with it; and*
> *   (ii) which he cannot show to be justifiable irrespective of the colour, race,*
> *   nationality or ethnic or national origins of the person to whom it is applied;*
> *   and*
> *   (iii) which is to the detriment of that other because he cannot comply with it.*

'Racial group' is defined by s. 3(1) of the 1976 Act.

An example of indirect discrimination and one which is highly relevant to the catering profession is:

PANESAR v. NESTLÉ &   The complainant, a Sikh, alleged indirect discrimination by
CO. LTD [1980] IRLR 64   the defendant company. A company rule (at the defendant's
(CA)   factory which processed food products) prohibited beards
                            and long hair. The complainant, because of his religious
                            beliefs, wore a beard and uncut hair. The Court of Appeal
held that the factory rule could be justified on grounds of safety and hygiene and therefore this
was not a case of indirect discrimination.

If a caterer wishes to employ kitchen staff for the preparation of food, and makes it a condition of employment that male staff should be clean-shaven, and two of the applicants are male, one a Jew and the other a Sikh, both of whom wear beards and refuse to shave them off, the caterer will not be discriminating on racial grounds if he refuses employment to either of these men under the rule in *Panesar* v. *Nestlé*.

However, following from the House of Lords' decision in *Mandla* v. *Dowell Lee* [1983] 2 WLR 620 where it was held that a 'no turban' school uniform rule amounted to indirect discrimination contrary to s. 1(1)b, this point may be open to doubt. If the facts should arise, the caterer would be able to argue, doubtless, that the interests of hygiene are paramount (the rule would be applied equally to all racial groups), and thus distinguish *Mandla*'s case, since in that case the rule served no function other than to enforce standards of attire.

It will also be discrimination contrary to s. 2 RRA 1976 to victimize a person for *inter alia* commencing proceedings under the RRA 1976.

Racial discrimination in the sphere of employment is legislated against by s. 4 RRA 1976. Section 4(1) states:

> *It is unlawful for a person, in relation to employment by him at an establishment in Great Britain, to discriminate against another –*
> *(a) in the arrangements he makes for the purpose of determining who should be offered that employment; or*
> *(b) in the terms on which he offers him that employment; or*
> *(c) by refusing or deliberately omitting to offer him that employment.*

Section 4(2) RRA 1976 states:

> *It is unlawful for a person, in the case of a person employed by him at an establishment in Great Britain, to discriminate against that employee –*
> *(a) in terms of employment which he affords him; or*
> *(b) in the way he affords him access to opportunities for promotion, transfer or training, or to any other benefits, facilities or services, or by refusing or deliberately omitting to afford him access to them; or*
> *(c) by dismissing him, or subjecting him to any other detriment.*

Section 4(2)c has been successfully used as the basis of claims of racial harassment: *British Leyland Cars Ltd* v. *Brown* [1983] IRLR 193 (EAT); *De Souza* v. *AA* [1986] IRLR 103 (CA). Section 4 in effect mirrors s. 6 of the SDA 1975, in relation to race rather than sex discrimination.

In *Dhatt* v. *McDonald's Hamburgers Ltd* [1991] 1 WLR 527 (CA) it was held that two Indian brothers who were entitled to work in England without work permits had not been unlawfully discriminated against on the grounds of their race when they were dismissed for refusing to provide evidence of their right to work.

The complainants had argued that, because they were asked to produce evidence of their right to work in circumstances where non-EC nationals were not so required, this amounted to unlawful discrimination. It was held that it did not.

Is it ever permissible to discriminate on grounds of race? Where being a member of a particular racial group is a 'genuine occupational qualification' for the job, then it is permissible to discriminate – s. 5 RRA 1976. Of the four genuine occupational qualifications set out in s. 5(2), only (c) is directly relevant to the hotel and catering industry.

Being of a particular racial group is a genuine occupational qualification for a job only where – ...

(c) *the job involves working in a place where food or drink is (for payment or not) provided to and consumed by members of the public or a section of the public in a particular setting for which, in that job, a person of that racial group is required for reasons of authenticity;*

Hence it is permissible for the proprietor of an Indian restaurant to employ only Indian staff, and likewise a Chinese restaurant Chinese staff. It would not be so where the speciality was English dishes and the proprietor sought to employ only white English staff. This would amount to unlawful discrimination, since the employment of English staff is not required for reasons of authenticity.

Three further points should be made with regard to racial discrimination:

1   Discriminatory advertising (s. 29 RRA 1976) – it is unlawful for a person to publish an advertisement which indicates an intent on the part of the advertiser to discriminate. Therefore (as with sex discrimination above) the wording of advertisements for jobs should make it clear that the job is open to all applicants regardless of race, ethnic origin, etc.

2   Section 30 RRA 1976 renders it unlawful for a person who has authority over another to instruct that other to undertake a discriminatory act. If X, the proprietor of a chain of hotels, tells the managers at each hotel not to employ black staff, this in itself constitutes a breach of s. 30 RRA 1976, regardless of whether or not a black person thereafter applies for a job and is refused.

3   Section 32 RRA 1976 states that anything done by a person in the course of his employment shall be treated as done by his employer as well as by him for the purposes of the 1976 Act, irrespective of whether it was done with the employer's knowledge or approval. As with the analogous provision under the SDA 1975 (s. 41) it is a defence for an employer to prove that he or she took such steps as were reasonably practicable to prevent the employee from doing that act, or from doing in the course of his or her employment acts of that description.

The 1976 Act also creates liability if a person knowingly aids another person to do an act made unlawful by the RRA (s. 33).

How is the Race Relations Act 1976 enforced?

Section 54 RRA 1976 allows for a complaint to be made by an individual to an industrial tribunal. On the issue of when a complaint may be brought see *Barclays Bank PLC* v. *Kapur* [1991] 2 WLR 401 (HL). This affords the same remedies as are available where a complaint of sex discrimination is alleged (see above). Recently the Court of Appeal has addressed the issue of damages in race bias cases. In *Alexander* v. *Home Office* [1988] IRLR 190 (CA), it was held that the objective of awards of damages for unlawful racial discrimination was restitution. Damages for injury to feelings caused by such discrimination should be restrained, whilst being neither nominal nor minimal.

This case has little to do with employment; the facts relate to the initial assessment written about the plaintiff (a prisoner) when serving in Parkhurst Prison. It is true to say, however, that the case reflects the general attitude of the courts to compensation for injured feelings in race cases, whether they are concerned with employment or otherwise.

Section 58 RRA 1976 allows for enforcement by means of an investigation by the Commission for Racial Equality.

Equal pay

The Equal Pay Act 1970 (EqPA) provides the legal framework to remove discrimination between the sexes in the terms of their contracts of employment. Since the introduction of the EqPA women have been able to claim equal pay to men. Britain's joining the EEC also affected women's rights to equal pay, since Article 119 of the Treaty of Rome provides:

> *Each member state shall during the first stage ensure and subsequently maintain the application of the principle that men and women should receive equal pay for equal work.*

The impact of this Article of the Treaty is discussed in Chapter 1 and in the discussion of sex discrimination above.

The EqPA has been amended by the Sex Discrimination Act 1975 and more recently by the Equal Pay (Amendment) Regulations 1983 and the Sex Discrimination Act 1986. The Equal Pay (Amendment) Regulations 1983 were introduced so as to bring UK law into line with EEC legislation. The Regulations introduced a right to claim equal treatment for work of equal value in circumstances where the jobs of the complainant and the person with whom he or she is seeking comparison have not been rated equivalent under a job evaluation scheme and there is no 'like work', i.e. the claim for work of equal value is a residual claim under the EqPA 1970.

The EqPA applies both to women and to men and requires that the contracts of employment of all women shall be deemed to include an equality clause. Section 1(2) Equal Pay Act 1970:

> *An equality clause is a provision which relates to terms (whether concerned with pay or not) of a contract under which a woman is employed (the 'woman's contract'), and has the effect that –*
>
> *(a) where the woman is employed on like work with a man in the same employment*
>
> > *(i) if (apart from the equality clause) any term of the woman's contract is or becomes less favourable to the woman than a term of a similar kind in the contract under which that man is employed, that term of the woman's contract shall be treated as so modified as not to be less favourable, and*
> >
> > *(ii) if (apart from the equality clause) at any time the woman's contract does not include a term corresponding to a term benefiting that man included in the contract under which he is employed, the woman's contract shall be treated as including such a term;*
>
> *(b) where the woman is employed on work rated as equivalent with that of a man in the same employment –*
>
> > *(i) if (apart from the equality clause) any term of the woman's contract determined by the rating of the work is or becomes less favourable to the woman than a term of a similar kind in the contract under which that man is*

> *employed, that term of the woman's contract shall be treated as so modified as not to be less favourable, and*
>
> (ii) *if (apart from the equality clause) at any time the woman's contract does not include a term corresponding to a term benefiting that man included in the contract under which he is employed and determined by the rating of the work, the woman's contract shall be treated as including such a term;*
>
> (c) *where a woman is employed on work which, not being work in relation to which Paragraph (a) or (b) above applies, is, in terms of the demands made on her (for instance under such headings as effort, skill and decision), of equal value to that of a man in the same employment –*
>
> (i) *if (apart from the equality clause) any term of the woman's contract is or becomes less favourable to the woman than a term of a similar kind in the contract under which that man is employed, that term of the woman's contract shall be treated as so modified as not to be less favourable, and*
>
> (ii) *if (apart from the equality clause) at any time the woman's contract does not include a term corresponding to a term benefiting that man involved in the contract under which he is employed, the woman's contract shall be treated as including such a term.*

An equality clause will not operate, however, where an employer can establish that the difference between the woman's contract and the man's is due to a material difference other than that of sex – s. 1(3) of the Equal Pay Act 1970 (see below).

There are a number of claims which may be made under the Equal Pay Act 1970. These are discussed below.

Where a woman is employed on like work *with a man who is, or was, in the same employment, but is treated less favourably.* 'Like work' is defined by s. 1(4) of the Equal Pay Act 1970.

> *A woman is to be regarded as employed on* like work *with men if, but only if, her work and theirs is of the same or a broadly similar nature, and the differences (if any) between the things she does and the things they do are not of practical importance in relation to terms and conditions of employment; and accordingly in comparing her work with theirs regard shall be had to the frequency or otherwise with which any such differences occur in practice as well as to the nature and extent of the differences.*

It has been stated by the Employment Appeal Tribunal in *Capper Pass Ltd* v. *Lawton* [1977] ICR 83 that:

> *In deciding whether the work done by a woman and the work done by a man is 'like work' within the meaning of s. 1(4), . . . the industrial tribunal has to make a broad judgment . . . In order to be like work within the Act's definition the work need not be of the same nature; it need only be broadly similar.*

The duties which each performs are not the only considerations to be taken into account when deciding whether a woman is engaged in like work. In *Eaton* v. *Nuttall* [1977] ICR 272, the EAT took the view that:

In considering whether there is like work, though the most important point is what the man does and what the woman does, the circumstances in which they do it should not be disregarded. One of the circumstances properly to be taken into account is the degree of responsibility involved in carrying out the job.

The following is an example of 'like work'. Ms Jones is employed as a barmaid in the lounge bar of the Hotel Splendide, at a wage of £3.80 per hour. Mr Johnson, who had left the employment of the Hotel Splendide, had been employed as lounge barman (until Ms Jones replaced him) at a wage of £4 per hour. Has Ms Jones a claim under the Equal Pay Act 1970? Yes. However, the answer may not be so clear-cut if Mr Johnson performed tasks (e.g. cellar work) which Ms Jones is not required to undertake.

SORBIE & OTHERS v. TRUSTHOUSE FORTE HOTELS LTD [1976] 3 WLR 918   Mrs Sorbie *et al.* were employed as waitresses at the Post House Hotel, Heathrow, at a wage of 85 pence per hour. There was only the one male waiter working in the restaurant with Mrs Sorbie and her colleagues; he was paid 97½ pence per hour. All the staff involved did identical work. The male employee (in anticipation of a claim for wage parity by the women employees) was re-graded as 'banqueting supervisor'. Mrs Sorbie and her female colleagues sought parity with the pay of the male waiter at the rate he was paid prior to re-grading (97½ pence per hour). It was held that Mrs Sorbie *et al.* were entitled to parity at 97½ pence per hour on a permanent basis; the waitresses were engaged upon 'like work' to that of the waiter.

NOBLE v. DAVID GOLD & SON (HOLDINGS) LTD [1980] IRLR 252 (CA)   In this case the men worked in a warehouse loading and unloading, whereas the women did less strenuous duties, e.g. sorting, labelling, etc. The Court of Appeal upheld the decision of the tribunal that the men and women were not employed on like work within s. 1(4). Nor could the work be said to be broadly similar, since the differences were of practical importance *vis-à-vis* the terms and conditions of employment.

Where a woman is employed on work in a job rated as equivalent with the job of a man who is, or was, in the same employment and the claim is based on a job evaluation study made by the employer set out in s. 1(5) of the Equal Pay Act. To establish a successful claim before the industrial tribunal the woman making the application must:
(a) specify the difference between her contract and that of the male employee;
(b) identify the male employee with whom she is making her comparison and show that he is, or was, employed by the same employer or by an associated company of the employer; and
(c) show that she carries out like work to that of the man; *or*
(d) show that her work and that of the male employee received the same rating under a job evaluation scheme.

Where a woman is employed on work which is not 'like work' or work which has not been 'rated as equivalent' to that of a male comparator, she may now claim equal pay with a man if her work is of equal value *to his in terms of the demands made upon her, e.g. effort, skill and decision.* Employees of one sex may use this provision to claim equal pay to that of those of the other sex doing a quite different job.

This subsection (s. 1(2)(c) EqPA) has led to substantial litigation, both in the UK and in the European Court. As a preliminary point it should be noted that the Court of Appeal, in *Leverton* v. *Clwyd County Council* [1989] 2 WLR 47, held that a woman could not succeed on a claim that her work was of equal value to that of a man employed by the same employer at a different establishment unless the terms and conditions of the man's employment were broadly similar to those of her employment. The decision was upheld in the House of Lords.

The most important case in this area is *Hayward* v. *Cammell Laird Shipbuilders Ltd* [1988] IRLR 257. This decision of the House of Lords has been hailed as a great victory for women's rights and pay equality. Ms Hayward was a cook at Cammell Laird Shipbuilders Ltd. She sought to argue that she carried out work of equal value to male workers at the shipyard, and that she was treated less favourably than the male comparators as to basic pay, overtime payments, etc. The House of Lords held that where a woman is engaged on work of equal value to that of a male comparator in the same employment (and so is entitled under the EqPA to receive equal treatment under the equality clause in her contract of employment) she can claim the same basic wage and overtime rates as the male. Her employer cannot say, after *Hayward*'s case, that although she gets less money than her male comparator does, this difference is cancelled out by other conditions of employment which favour her, such as better holiday entitlement, etc.

It should be remembered that, although this case is a landmark in equal pay, the decision is based on the established fact that the complainant is doing work of equal value to that of a male comparator. In a large number of cases this point is very difficult to establish. Where it cannot be established, of course the claim fails to get off the ground. Before equal value is proved, a claim must have been made to an industrial tribunal, an expert appointed by the tribunal must have produced an analysis of the jobs compared (following a job evaluation exercise), and a tribunal must have decided on the basis of that report that equal value exists between the jobs compared.

One problem in assessing equal value may be where the employer employs a token male, on the same terms and conditions as the female complainant, to do the job which she is doing. This may have the effect of frustrating a claim based on 'equal value', as an 'equal value' claim may not be successful where men are actually employed doing the same job as the complainant.

However, in *Pickstone and Others* v. *Freeman's plc* [1988] IRLR 357 the House of Lords held that if a female employee is employed on work of equal value to the work of a man doing another job for the same employer, she is entitled, under s. 1 (2)(c) of the Equal Pay Act 1970, to equal pay with that man, notwithstanding the fact that there is another man doing the same work as her for the same money.

The employer's defence

This involves s. 1(3) Equal Pay Act 1970, which states:

> An equality clause shall not operate in relation to a variation between the woman's contract and the man's contract if the employer proves that the variation is genuinely due to a material factor which is not the difference of sex and that factor –
> (a) in the case of an equality clause falling within subsection 2(a) or (b) above, must be a material difference between the woman's case and the man's; and
> (b) in the case of an equality clause falling within subsection 2(c) above, may be such a material difference.

This covers:

1 Work done at different times (e.g. night-shift work compared with day-shift work) should be ignored. It is not a genuine material difference, since a premium may be paid for unsocial hours. Therefore the basic pay for night-shift male workers and that for day-shift female workers engaged on 'like work' should be the same – *Dugdale* v. *Kraft Foods Ltd* [1977] 1 All ER 454.

2 Work done at different places (e.g. waitress X wishes for parity with waiter Y, who is employed by the same employer but at a different establishment). In *NAAFI* v. *Varley* [1977] ICR 11, the difference in location (where both employees were employed for the same hours in like work) was a genuine material difference within s. 1(3) and parity could not be established.

3 Can an employer who pays lower rates of pay to a woman doing work of 'equal value' to that of a man seek to justify the differential by reference to other terms and conditions which benefit the female worker but not the male? The answer, following the House of Lords' decision in *Hayward* v. *Cammell Laird Shipbuilders Ltd*, is no. However, the point is not as watertight as it may at first appear. Can an employer argue that the woman's claim for 'equal value' fails because the better 'perks' (e.g. holiday entitlement) constitute a 'material factor' under s. 1(3), justifying the pay differential between them? In *Rainey* v. *Greater Glasgow Health Board* [1986] 3 WLR 1017, Lord Keith set out those matters which should be considered when determining a 'material difference' under s. 1(3):

> *The difference must be 'material', which I would construe as meaning 'significant and relevant', and it must be between 'her case and his'. Consideration of a person's case must necessarily involve consideration of all circumstances of that case. These may well go beyond what is not very happily described as 'the personal equation', i.e. the personal qualities by way of skill, experience or training which an individual brings to the job. Some circumstances may on examination prove to be not significant or not relevant, but others may do so, though not relating to the personal qualities of the employee. In particular, where there is no question of intentional sex discrimination whether direct or indirect, a difference which is connected with economic factors affecting the efficient carrying on of the employer's business or other activity may well be relevant.*

In *Rainey* the House of Lords accepted that s. 1(3) could provide a defence to an employer who paid more to a man than a woman for doing the same job, when the extra pay was necessary in order to recruit staff to do the work at a particular time. Thus market forces can, by reason of s. 1(3), justify pay differentials between men and women doing the same work or work of equal value. Where such forces lack the taint of sex discrimination they may provide a defence to an employer under s. 1(3) Equal Pay Act. One such instance may be where the terms and conditions were freely negotiated between the employer and a trade union as part of a collective agreement.

Mention should also be made here of *Reed Packaging Ltd* v. *Boozer* [1988] ICR 391 (EAT), which considers procedural issues relevant to s. 1(2) EqPA and also adopts the approach advocated in *Rainey* and, before it, the *Bilka-Kaufhaus* decision, i.e. that such differences must be objectively justifiable, such justification being capable of incorporating economic and administrative reasons.

Maternity rights

It is vital that the hotelier and caterer understand the statutory maternity rights of their employees, since the number of female staff employed in the industry is considerable. Furthermore, all female workers should be aware that there are statutory rights which relate to pregnancy.

The rights of the pregnant woman whilst at work

A pregnant employee who on medical advice has made an appointment to receive antenatal care has the right not to be unreasonably refused time off work to keep the appointment. This right arises from s. 31A Employment Protection (Consolidation) Act 1978 (EPCA). Furthermore, the right is to paid time off. If the employer acts in breach of the provisions in s. 31A the employee may present a complaint to an industrial tribunal and, if proven, compensation may be ordered to be paid by the employer to the employee.

Pregnant employees are also protected in three other respects:

1 A pregnant employee may claim that she was unfairly dismissed if the dismissal was by reason of her pregnancy – s. 60 EPCA (see the section on grounds for unfair dismissal).
2 Subject to certain restrictions, a pregnant employee will be entitled, on leaving employment due to pregnancy, to receive maternity pay – Social Security Act 1986, ss. 46–50.
3 In certain circumstances an employee who has left her job due to pregnancy will have a right to return to work after the birth – ss. 33 and 45–8 EPCA.

New or expectant mothers' rights

Additional statutory maternity leave and maternity pay rights were introduced in October 1994 as a result of The European Directive on Pregnant Workers which contains requirements for protecting the health and safety of new and expectant mothers. Now the Management of Health & Safety at Work (Amendment) Regulations 1994, which took effect on 1 December 1994, apply to an employee who is pregnant, has given birth within the previous six months or is breastfeeding.

Under the new regulations employers are required to assess the health and safety risks to new and expectant mothers at work and to take appropriate measures to protect them. These may include:

• adjusting working conditions or hours of work
• offering alternative type of work in order to eliminate or reduce risks to an acceptable minimum.

If neither of these is possible then the employer may offer paid leave for as long as is necessary to protect her health and safety or that of her child.

Risks identified may include:

• manual handling of loads
• biological agents, eg Rubella, HIV
• certain chemicals
• working with VDUs.

The right to maternity pay

Section 46 of the 1986 Social Security Act (SSA 1986) lays down five preconditions which must be fulfilled:

1 The woman must have 26 weeks of continuous employment (by the fourteenth week before the expected week of confinement).
2 She must have ceased to work wholly or partly because of pregnancy or confinement.
3 Her normal weekly earnings must be not less than the lower limit with regard to National Insurance contributions.
4 She has become pregnant and has reached, or been confined before reaching, the commencement of the 11th week before the expected week of confinement.
5 She has given notice of such absence at least twenty-one days prior to the absence or as soon as is reasonably practicable.

How is maternity pay calculated? Where the above conditions are satisfied, the employee will be entitled to maternity pay for a maximum period of eighteen weeks (SSA 1986, s. 47) beginning with the 11th week before the expected week of confinement. SSA 1986, s. 48 creates two 'rates' of pay: a 'higher rate' and a 'lower rate'. The 'higher rate' is a weekly rate equivalent to nine-tenths of the woman's weekly earnings for the period eight weeks immediately preceding the fourteenth week before the expected week of confinement. The higher rate is payable for the first six weeks of maternity pay period, with the lower rate being paid for the remainder of the maternity pay period. Liability to pay maternity pay is placed on the employer and cannot be excluded, limited or modified in any way. It is, however, worthy of note that any contractual obligation with regard to maternity pay will go towards discharging the employer's liability to pay statutory maternity pay.

The right to return to work after pregnancy

Section 33 EPCA 1978 lays down five preconditions which must be fulfilled:

1 The employee's absence from work must be wholly or partly due to pregnancy or confinement.
2 The woman must continue to be employed until immediately before the eleventh week prior to the expected week of confinement.
3 The woman must have not less than two years' continuous employment by the employer at the eleventh week prior to the expected week of confinement. It may well be the case that few of the lower grades of hotel and catering staff ever qualify for maternity pay, etc., since the turnover of staff in the industry is very high and few staff remain in the continuous employment of one employer for two years.
4 The woman must give notice (normally in writing) to her employer at least 21 days before her absence begins. The notice must contain, in addition to her reason for absence, a statement that she intends to return to work, and should include details of the expected date of confinement.
5 At her employer's request the employee may be required to produce a certificate from her doctor or midwife stating the expected date of confinement.

How does the right to return to work operate? Where an employee has fulfilled the conditions in s. 33 she is entitled to return to work at any time before the end of 29 weeks commencing with the actual week of confinement – s. 45(1) EPCA. When the employee returns to work she is entitled to return to her old job. Furthermore, the terms on which she is employed after her return must not be less favourable than those which would have applied had she not been absent from work. It is clearly set out in the statute that continuity of employment is maintained. The purpose of the provisions relating to return to work following confinement is to preserve the employee's position, i.e. the employee should not lose benefits to which she had been entitled prior to the pregnancy.

How is the right to return exercised? Although a woman has given notice to her employer that she intends to return to work, it is her prerogative to change her mind. This leads to uncertainty, since by giving notice of her intention to return all she has done is to keep her options open. To resolve (to an extent) the uncertainty, ss. 33(3A) and 33(3B) provide that an employer may, after 49 days from the expected week of confinement, make a written request to the employee asking for confirmation that she intends to return to work. The employee will lose her right to return to work unless she gives such confirmation as requested within fourteen days of receiving the employer's request, or as soon as is reasonably practicable thereafter. Even if the woman confirms her intention to return to work, this does not bind her to return. Where the woman concerned does wish to return to work certain procedures are to be followed to facilitate her return. Written notice of her intention to return should be given by her to her employer at least 21 days before the date notified for her return. However, her return may be postponed (s. 47 EPCA), first by the employer, provided he or she notifies her and gives reasons for the postponement, and secondly by the employee, if she is incapable of returning to work owing to ill health.

Under EPCA s. 56, failure to permit a woman to return to work after confinement is treated as dismissal. This provision is, however, excluded in cases specified by s. 56A (added by the Employment Act 1980). This covers two situations:

(a) where the employer employed under five employees and it is not reasonably practicable for him or her to permit return;
(b) where it is not reasonably practicable for the employer to permit the woman to return and he or she offers the woman suitable and appropriate alternative employment which she unreasonably refuses.

Rehabilitation of offenders

A question commonly asked by employers during the recruitment or selection process is whether applicants have ever been convicted of a criminal offence. The Rehabilitation of Offenders Act 1974 provides that certain offences will become "spent" after a specific period of time. The effect of this is that the offender is allowed to treat the spent conviction as never having existed, and if the employer later discovers the existence of the spent conviction he cannot use it as grounds for dismissing an employee or excluding a job applicant from employment.

Rehabilitation periods run from the date of conviction and include the following:

Sentence	Rehabilitation Period
Imprisonment for up to 30 months but more than six months	ten years
Imprisonment for up to six months	seven years
Fine	five years
Conditional discharge	one year
Absolute discharge	six months

Sunday trading

The Sunday Trading Act 1994 gives shop-workers rights in respect of Sunday working. Legally the definition of a shop does not include catering businesses or places of amusement.

If a part of the premises is devoted to retail trade, that part may be defined as a shop and the following rights apply to those employees who were employed prior to the date the Act was enforced. They have the right:
- not to be dismissed for refusing to work on Sunday
- not to be selected for redundancy for refusing to work on Sunday
- not to suffer any other detriment for refusing to work on a Sunday.

Detriment is likely to include: disciplinary action; loss of pay and benefits; failure to promote or offer training, etc. These rights apply to employees irrespective of age, length of service or hours of work, but do not apply to those who have been employed to work only on Sundays.

Employment of children

Children are defined as being under the minimum school-leaving age – i.e. in England and Wales, at the end of the Spring term for those children whose sixteenth birthdays fall between 1 September and 31 January inclusive, and the Friday preceding the Spring Bank Holiday for those whose sixteenth birthdays fall between 1 February and 31 August. (In Scotland school-leaving dates are prescribed by the Secretary of State.)

The Employment of Children Acts 1933-1969 prohibit the employment of children in the following circumstances:
(a) where the child is under 13 years of age; or
(b) before the close of school hours on any day on which they are required to attend school; or
(c) for more than two hours on any day on which they are required to attend school; or
(d) before 7 a.m. or after 7 p.m. on any day; or
(e) for more than two hours on any Sunday; or
(f) where the job requires them to lift, carry or move anything so heavy as to be likely to cause injury to them.

In any event, a permit to employ children must be obtained from the local education authority. This will specify the employment conditions which must be observed. They are likely to:
(a) authorise the employment of children
   (i) under the age of 13 by their parents or guardians in light agricultural or horticultural work;
   (ii) for not more than one hour before the commencement of school hours on any day on which they are required to attend school;
(b) prohibit absolutely the employment of children in any specified occupation;
(c) prescribe
   (i) the minimum age at which children may be employed;
   (ii) the maximum number of hours in each day or week and the times at which children may be employed;
   (iii) meal and rest intervals and holidays to be allowed to them;
   (iv) any other conditions to be observed in relation to their employment;

(d) require employers to keep and furnish records on children they employ or propose to employ.

Employment of young people

Regulations which previously governed young persons' hours of work in certain employment situations are no longer in force. However, restrictions still apply in relation to employment in bars.

9.5 DISMISSAL

It was not until 1971 that the law recognized the right of an employee not to be unfairly dismissed. The only remedy available at common law was for breach of contract on the part of the employer, namely, wrongful dismissal. No compensation was payable for the mode of dismissal. Furthermore, certain forms of dismissal for which the law now provides a remedy were considered lawful practices. The right of an employee not to be unfairly dismissed is now contained in s. 54 EPCA 1978.

Remedies for certain forms of dismissal which are 'unfair' are also covered by the EPCA, e.g. dismissal for pregnancy. 'Unfair dismissal' has a highly technical meaning and should not be thought of in colloquial terms. The purpose of this section is to consider so far as is possible the various legal aspects of dismissal, both at common law and under the EPCA 1978, and, furthermore, to outline the procedural requirements for dismissal, and the procedure to be followed when pursuing a claim before the County Court or industrial tribunal.

Wrongful dismissal

It must first be established that the person whom the employer seeks to dismiss is an employee within the meaning of s. 153 EPCA, as explained through the case law (see section 9.1).

An employer must, when lawfully dismissing an employee, comply with the terms stated in the contract as to dismissal and the various statutory provisions which apply. Outside the provisions which relate to unfair dismissal an employer is required to comply with certain minimum conditions as to notice.

An employer may, when drafting the terms of the employee's contract of employment, make certain conditions of the essence of the contract. The employer may of course state that certain types of behaviour are so grave that they constitute gross misconduct, which entitles the employer to bring the contract to an end without notice. This is known as summary dismissal. Certain kinds of behaviour are normally considered to be gross misconduct:
(a) theft from the employer;
(b) fighting at work;
(c) drunkenness at work;
(d) wilful damage to the employer's property;
(e) disregard for health and safety precautions;

(f) fraudulent recording of time worked;
(g) refusal to carry out the employer's reasonable instructions.
Other forms of gross misconduct might also be appropriate to hotel and catering establishments:
(a) rudeness to customers or guests;
(b) sexual misconduct;
(c) any breach of licensing or excise laws;
(d) sleeping on duty;
(e) inviting unauthorised guests onto the premises e.g. to share a bedroom.
An example from the hotel industry of conduct which may amount to gross misconduct is to be found in the following case.

TRUSTHOUSE FORTE HOTELS LTD v. MURPHY [1977] IRLR 186 (EAT) — Murphy was employed as a night porter at a hotel. Part of his duties was to keep a liquor store so that guests staying at the hotel could have a drink after the bar had closed. He failed to account for a stock deficiency in the liquor, and admitted that he had stolen some of it; he was summarily dismissed. The dismissal was held by the EAT to be fair, the view being taken that 'it would place an unreasonable burden upon employers whose employees had been proved to be guilty of theft of the employer's property entrusted to his care, that the employer should not be entitled to dismiss and to dismiss fairly'.

What of the situation where a hotel or restaurant employee is abusive to a guest or customer? The cases of *Wilson* v. *Racher* [1974] IRLR 114 (CA) and *Pepper* v. *Webb* [1969] 2 All ER 216 (CA) ought to be considered. In both cases the employees concerned were abusive to their respective employers. In *Pepper* v. *Webb* summary dismissal was held to be justified; the abuse and the employee's refusal to comply with the employer's reasonable instruction amounted to gross misconduct. In *Wilson* v. *Racher* the view was taken that 'it requires very special circumstances to entitle a servant who expresses his feeling in such a grossly improper way to succeed in an action for wrongful dismissal'. It is arguable, therefore, that abuse directed towards guests would be similarly treated and be sufficient to justify summary dismissal.

Incompetence or negligence in the way in which an employee carries out his or her tasks is not necessarily gross misconduct sufficient to justify summary dismissal. Gross negligence in exercising professional judgment (e.g. by failing to supervise or intervene) will not itself mean that a manager is liable to summary dismissal. This can be seen from the Court of Appeal's decision in *Dietman* v. *Brent London Borough Council* [1988] IRLR 299.

Where summary dismissal is not justified the employer is required to give the employee notice in accordance with the contract of employment (if this is greater than the statutory minimum), or in accordance with the statutory minimum set out in ss. 49 and 50 EPCA. An employee who has been continuously employed for a period of one calendar month (s. 49(1) EPCA as amended by s. 20 and Schedule 2 Employment Act 1982) is entitled to the following periods of notice:
(a) continuous employment longer than one month but less than two years – a minimum of one week's notice;
(b) continuous employment of two years or more, but less than twelve years – a minimum of one week's notice for each complete year of continuous employment;
(c) continuous employment of twelve years or more – a minimum of twelve weeks' notice.

Section 50 and Schedule 3 EPCA 1978 lay down exact rules as to how the amount of pay to which the employee is entitled during the notice period is to be calculated. Where the employee wishes to terminate his or her contract of employment with the employer a minimum of one week's notice must be given.

Where an employee has been dismissed without notice, and such a dismissal is not justifiable as a summary dismissal (see above), then the employee may claim damages against his or her employer for wrongful dismissal in the County Court. Damages for wrongful dismissal include the following.

Wages. An employee can claim a sum equivalent to the wages he or she has earned to date which remain unpaid. If an employee is dismissed without notice (or with less than the statutory minimum), wages representing the period up until the expiry of the statutory minimum period of notice can be claimed.

Tips and bonuses. If an employee has a contractual right to tips, etc., these will be taken into account in the calculation of damages. This may be of some importance to hotel and restaurant staff, where a considerable percentage of the weekly wage is in the form of such payments.

Fringe benefits. If an employee who works on a 'living in' basis is dismissed without notice and asked to leave his or her living quarters, either immediately or with very short notice, a claim for damages representing this loss of amenity may be established.

Injured feelings, however, are not normally compensated. In calculating the damages to be paid by the employer the County Court will take into account any unemployment benefit received by the employee, as well as any compensation otherwise paid by the employer to the employee for unfair dismissal or for redundancy payments.

The grounds for unfair dismissal

It should be remembered that not all employees are entitled to make a claim for unfair dismissal.

Qualification period

Some employees may not have had the required period of continuous employment in order to qualify and claim unfair dismissal. In order to bring a claim for unfair dismissal, the applicant must have been continuously employed for a period of two years ending with the 'effective date of termination' – see s. 64(1)a EPCA 1978. There are some exceptions to the two-year rule, including dismissal on grounds of race, sex discrimination and trade union membership or activities.

This qualification period is calculated from the beginning of the employee's employment under the relevant contract of employment. This could be earlier than the actual date on which the employee started to perform his or her duties (*The General of the Salvation Army* v. *Dewsbury* [1984] IRLR 222).

Normal retiring age

A person cannot make a complaint of unfair dismissal if, on or before the effective date of termination, he or she has attained the age which, in the undertaking in which he or she works, is the normal retiring age for an employee holding the position which he or she held.

'Normal retiring age' is to be determined from the reasonable expectations of employees holding the position of the applicant at the date of his or her dismissal. The contractual retiring age will usually be the normal retiring age, but this may be departed from in practice – see *Waite* v. *GCHQ* [1983] 2 AC 714, and *Hughes Coy and Jarnell* v. *DHSS* [1985] 2 AC 419.

Where there is no 'normal retiring age', s. 64(1)b EPCA states that men aged 65 and over and woman aged 60 and over may not bring an application for unfair dismissal.

The European Court, in *Marshall* v. *SW Hampshire Area Health Authority (Teaching)* [1986] 2 WLR 780, held that different compulsory retiring ages for men and women infringed the EEC equal treatment Directive 76/207.

Section 3(1) of the Sex Discrimination Act 1986 has followed the *Marshall* ruling and substituted the above provision for a new provision whereby an employer will only be able to rely upon the exclusion resulting from the normal retiring age if that age applies equally to men and women. If there are discriminatory retirement ages or no normal retiring age, then the residual age of 65 will apply to all employees whatever their sex.

An employee over normal retiring age or over 65 can bring a claim for unfair dismissal if it is shown that the reason for the dismissal was 'union-related' (see s. 64(3) EPCA).

Employment overseas

Any employment where, under the terms of the contract of employment, the employee ordinarily works outside Great Britain is outside the scope of unfair dismissal rights: s. 141(2) EPCA.

Prior to considering the grounds on which a claim for unfair dismissal may be based it is important to understand the terminology used by the EPCA and other Acts relating to dismissal.

Continuous employment

Before an employee can qualify for a number of employment rights, including unfair dismissal, it must be established that he or she has been continuously employed for the qualification period (as set out in the Act). The way of calculating continuous employment is complex; the relevant rules are contained in s. 151 and Schedule 13 of the EPCA 1978. Minor amendments have been made by s. 20 and Schedule 2 of the Employment Act 1982; these alter the basis of calculation from a total of weeks to months.

Section 151 EPCA 1978 (as amended by s. 20 and Schedule 2 Employment Act 1982) states:

> *(1) References in any provision of this Act to a period of continuous employment are, except where provision is expressly made to the contrary, to a period computed in accordance with the provisions of this section and Schedule 13; and in any such provision which refers to a period of continuous employment expressed in months or years a month means a calendar month and a year means a year of twelve calendar months.*
>
> *(2) In computing an employee's period of continuous employment any question arising as to –*

(a) whether the employee's employment is of a kind counting towards a period
      of continuous employment, or
(b) whether periods (consecutive or otherwise) are to be treated as forming a
      single period of continuous employment,
shall be determined in accordance with Schedule 13 (that is to say, week by
week), but the length of an employee's period of employment shall be computed
in months and years of twelve months in accordance with the following rules.
(3) Subject to the following provisions of this section, an employee's period of
      continuous employment for the purposes of any provision of this Act begins
      with the day on which he starts work and ends with the day by reference to which
      the length of his period of continuous employment falls to be ascertained for the
      purposes of the provision in question.

The important aspects of continuity of employment for our present purposes are:
1   There is a presumption of continuity of employment – Schedule 13 paragraph
    1(3) EPCA 1978.
2   A week in which an employee is employed for sixteen hours or more will count
    in computing a period of employment – Schedule 13 paragraph 3 EPCA 1978.
    Therefore, an employee must normally work at least sixteen hours per week in
    order to qualify for statutory rights. Any week in which an employee is
    contracted to work sixteen hours but does not, e.g. annual holiday, will still
    count towards that person's period of continuous employment. The 1982 Act
    substitutes for paragraph 8 to Schedule 13 a new paragraph which allows the
    Secretary of State to decrease the requisite number of hours from sixteen by
    means of an order.
3   Where an employee is absent through sickness or injury (or pregnancy –
    Schedule 13 paragraph 9 EPCA) the employee is entitled to add the first 26
    weeks of his or her absence towards continuity.
4   Weeks where there is a 'temporary cessation of work' will not break the
    continuity of employment – Schedule 13 paragraph 9. In the case of *Sillars* v.
    Charrington Fuels Ltd [1988] IRLR 180, the EAT held that a fuel delivery driver
    regularly employed for seven months per year over fifteen years was not
    continuously employed for the qualifying period for an unfair dismissal claim.
    The breaks in his employment were not a 'temporary cessation of work,' such as
    would preserve continuity of employment. If the case had established continuity
    of employment in such a case, this would have had far-reaching consequences for
    the hotel and catering industry, which relies heavily on 'seasonal staff' and in like
    manner provides full-time employment for a fixed number of months of the year
    and thereafter lays off staff, only to seek their services again the following year.
5   Absence from work by arrangement will not break continuity.
6   Strikes do not break continuity.

Change of employer and transfer of undertakings

Rules of considerable importance for the protection of employees' rights upon the
transfer of a business for which he or she was working were introduced by the Transfer
of Undertakings (Protection of Employment) Regulations 1981. These regulations
brought UK law into line with that in the EC, giving effect to EEC Council Directive
77/187.

Where an 'undertaking' is 'transferred' from the ownership of one person (X) to that of another (Y) then:

1   Individuals who are employed by X immediately before the transfer automatically become the employees of Y from the time of the transfer, on the terms and conditions they previously held with X.
2   Y inherits X's rights and liabilities in relation to those individuals.
3   Collective agreements made by or on behalf of X with a trade union recognized by X are inherited by Y.
4   Where X recognizes a union in respect of employees in the undertaking to be transferred and, following the transfer, the undertaking transferred maintains an identity distinct from any other undertaking owned by Y, Y must recognize the union in respect of those employees.
5   X must inform recognized trade unions about the consequences of the transfer, and Y must provide X with sufficient information in this regard.
6   In certain circumstances it may be necessary for X or Y to consult recognized trade unions concerning the transfer.
7   Dismissal of any employee (whether before or after the transfer) for any reason connected with the transfer is automatically unfair except when the reason is 'an economic, technical or organizational reason entailing changes in the workforce', in which case the dismissal is fair if reasonable in the circumstances.

What is meant by a 'transfer' of an 'undertaking'? An 'undertaking' includes any 'trade or business,' but *not* 'any undertaking which is not in the nature of a commercial venture'. Obviously, hotel and catering enterprises come within the scope of a trade or business. There was some doubt as to whether public sector organizations would be classified as 'commercial ventures'. However, in 1994 there was a European Court of Justice decision concerning the Acquired Rights Directive and its impact on the Transfer of Undertakings Regulations. The case concerned a lady who was employed by a bank as a cleaner. She was dismissed when the cleaning was contracted out. It was decided that the decisive factor in determining if a transfer has taken place is whether the business retains its identity, in other words, is the new employer resuming or continuing the same or similar activities? This interpretation did not have regard for the transfer of the assets of the business as stated in TUPE regulations (*Schmidt v. Spar- und Leihkasse der früheren Amter Bordesholm, Kiel und Cronshagen* (1994 IRLR 302).

This case seems to indicate that most contracting out operations will be considered as transfers of business. Subsequent to the *Schmidt* ruling, the Court of Appeal has followed the ruling over the transfer of a contracted cleaning service in the health sector (*Dines* v. (1) *Initial Health Care Services Ltd.* (2) *Pall Mall Services Group Ltd.* (1994 IRLR 336)).

Consequently, contractors who take over such contracts have to cover all the employees on terms and conditions which are no less favourable than before the transfer.

When is an undertaking transferred? An undertaking may be 'transferred' within the meaning given by the regulations where the undertaking is:
(a) sold;
(b) disposed of;
(c) transferred 'by operation of law'.

A transfer is effected only where the business is acquired as a 'going concern'; thus it is in effect the same concern but in different hands.

A number of pointers can be used to determine whether the undertaking has been transferred as a going concern:
(a) the assignment of goodwill from the vendor to the purchaser;
(b) the assignment of the vendor's trade name to the purchaser;
(c) the assignment to the purchaser of the vendor's existing benefits/obligations under contract with customers/suppliers;
(d) a covenant restricting the vendor from competing with the purchaser.

All of these terms and others would be in, for example, a contract for the sale of a pub by a brewery to a licensee purchasing it to run it as a 'free house'. This is a clear example of a transfer of an undertaking. It is generally different from the case of a brewery selling a prime town-centre site for redevelopment, which is clearly not a transfer of an undertaking.

It is most important to note the assignment of goodwill. In a 'people business' like the licensed trade and hotel and catering industry, goodwill is of vital importance. Unlike a manufacturing industry, where there may be considerable investment in stock in trade, the key commodity in a service industry such as catering or hotelkeeping is the goodwill which the business has built up. Otherwise one is looking merely at the sale of an asset (i.e. the premises alone) which has a separate value from, and often a considerably lower one than, the business itself. Goodwill, however, is of little commercial significance where the business is 'running down'.

The assignment of contracts of employment, etc. Regulation 5(1) and (2) provides that those of the vendor's employees:
(a) who were employed by the vendor immediately before the transfer; *and*
(b)   whose contracts would otherwise have been terminated by the transfer
automatically become, from the moment of the transfer, employed by the purchaser on the terms and conditions which they enjoyed with the vendor.

All the vendor's rights and liabilities connected with these employees' contracts are assigned to the purchaser, and anything done by the purchaser prior to the transfer in relation to these employees is deemed to have been done by the vendor.

This regulation applies only to contracts of employment in existence at the time of the transfer – *Secretary of State for Employment* v. *Spence* [1986] ICR 181 (CA).

It can be seen that the purchaser of the undertaking inherits those employees employed by the vendor immediately before the transfer on their existing terms and conditions. The purchaser cannot, without the agreement of the employees concerned, impose any terms other than those inherited from the vendor. It follows that any employee who is transferred cannot insist that he or she be given the benefit of any preferential terms and conditions enjoyed by the purchaser's existing staff.

The date of transfer of an undertaking was recently considered by the EAT in *Brook Lane Finance Co. Ltd* v. *Bradley* [1988] IRLR 283.

Dismissal and the transfer of an undertaking

Where an employee is dismissed:
(a) by the vendor in advance of the transfer of the undertaking by which he or she is employed; *or*
(b) by the purchaser of the undertaking after the transfer,
simply because of the transfer or reason connected with it, the employee may bring a claim for unfair dismissal or redundancy.

Unfair dismissal. In order to claim unfair dismissal the employee must show that he or she has been dismissed – s. 55 EPCA. The transfer of an undertaking cannot itself be taken as a dismissal. However, where the purchaser substantially changes the terms and conditions of employment previously enjoyed by the transferred staff to their detriment, the staff may resign and treat the purchaser's action as amounting to constructive dismissal.

Where an employee is dismissed by either the purchaser or the vendor and the reason for the dismissal is a reason connected with the transfer, the dismissal is automatically unfair unless it qualifies as an 'economic, technical or organizational reason entailing changes in the workforce' of either party to the transfer (regulation 6, see *Litster* v. *Forth Dry Dock and Engineering Ltd* [1989] IRLR 161 (HL)). If it falls within this reason the dismissal will be held to be fair, if the employer acted reasonably in all the circumstances in treating the reason as sufficient to justify the dismissal within s. 57(3) EPCA.

Redundancy. An employee who is dismissed by reason of redundancy is (subject to various qualifying conditions) entitled to a redundancy payment.

An employee whose contract is automatically assigned by reason of the Regulations will not be dismissed by the vendor and cannot therefore become entitled to a redundancy payment unless and until he or she is dismissed by the purchaser by reason of redundancy.

Where:

(a) an employee is dismissed by the vendor in advance of the transfer by reason of the fact that the vendor is to go out of business in the place where the employee was employed, or no longer requires work of the particular kind done by the employee; *or*

(b) following the transfer the purchaser dismisses the employee for either of these reasons

the employee is, *prima facie*, entitled to a redundancy payment.

There would appear to be no reason why an employee should not qualify for a redundancy payment – *Gorictree Ltd* v. *Jenkinson* [1985] ICR 51 (EAT).

Can employers avoid the Regulations? Regulation 12 lays down that any agreement to exclude or limit the application of the Regulations is invalid. The normal commercial practice is for the vendor to indemnify the purchaser for sums payable in consequence of the operation of the Regulations. Of course the cost of such an indemnity is a factor taken into account in negotiation of the purchase price.

Dismissal

'Dismissal' has a technical meaning; in order to claim unfair dismissal the employee must establish that he or she was dismissed within the meaning of the term under the EPCA 1978. Hence, where a contract of employment comes to an end in some way other than within the technical definition of dismissal, no claim for unfair dismissal may be pursued – e.g. *Harvey* v. *Yankee Traveller Restaurant* [1976] IRLR 35. It is essentially a matter of fact whether there has been a dismissal:

FUTTY v. BREKKES LTD [1974] IRLR 130   During an argument between the employee and his foreman the employee was told by the foreman, 'If you do not like the job, you can fuck off'. The employee regarded this as dismissal. He found other employment and sought compensation for his dismissal. It was held that in the context of the workplace (a fish-processing plant) the employee had not been dismissed.

The important point here is the intention of the employer; the words may be mere abuse, though doubtless in some cases (particularly in the decorous surroundings of a hotel!) an employer telling an employee to fuck or piss off may constitute dismissal.

Dismissal for the purposes of the EPCA 1978 is defined in s. 55(2) thus:

> *Subject to s. 55(3) an employee shall be treated as dismissed by his employer if, but only if, –*
>
> (a) *the contract under which he is employed by the employer is terminated by the employer, whether it is so terminated by notice or without notice, or*
> (b) *where under that contract he is employed for a fixed term, that term expires without being renewed under the same contract, or*
> (c) *the employee terminates that contract, with or without notice, in circumstances such that he is entitled to terminate it without notice by reason of the employer's conduct.*

If employees already under notice from the employer give notice themselves to the employer ending their employment on a date earlier than the employer's notice, then they will still be treated as dismissed by the employer's notice. However, the major problems with identifying a dismissal lie in s. 55(2)(c) and constructive dismissal. The early problems have today to a large extent been circumvented by the Court of Appeal's decision in the following case.

WESTERN EXCAVATING (EEC) LTD v. SHARP [1978] 2 WLR 344

The employee was dismissed for taking unauthorized time off work. He appealed through the internal appeals procedure, which substituted a penalty of five days' suspension from work without pay. This the employee accepted, but being in need of money he asked for a £40 advance of accrued holiday pay; his employer refused the request. He then sought a £40 loan from his employer, but this was also refused. The employee then resigned, in order to get his holiday pay, and brought a claim for unfair dismissal, arguing that the employer's conduct amounted to constructive dismissal.

Held: The Court of Appeal took the view that in order to amount to constructive dismissal the employer's conduct must amount to a breach of contract which entitled the employee to treat the contract as at an end and resign. It was said that:

> *The employer must be guilty of conduct which was a significant breach of the contract, going to the root of the contract of employment, or which showed he no longer intended to be bound by one or more of its essential terms; in these circumstances the employee is entitled to treat himself as discharged from any further performance; if he does so then he is constructively dismissed.*

Constructive dismissal

Constructive dismissal may occur, therefore, where the employer tries to impose a unilateral change in the terms and conditions of the employee's contract, e.g. change of job, loss of earnings, etc. The more difficult cases arise where the employee argues that a constructive dismissal arises not because of a breach of an express term of contract by the employer, but because there has been a breach of an implied term, e.g. in *Gardner (FC) Ltd* v. *Beresford* [1978] IRLR 63 (EAT), breach of an implied term not to treat the employee arbitrarily or inequitably with regard to pay. In *Woods* v. *W. M. Car Services (Peterborough) Ltd* [1981] IRLR 347, the Court of Appeal took the view that whether an employer had behaved in such a manner as to repudiate the contract was essentially a question of fact to be determined in each case according to the construction of the contract. The principles of constructive dismissal are conveniently summarized in *Lewis* v. *Motorworld Garages Ltd* [1986] ICR 157 (CA) by Glidewell LJ, where he opines:

> *If the employer is in breach of an express term of a contract of employment, of such seriousness that the employee would be justified in leaving and claiming constructive dismissal, but the employee does not leave and accepts the altered terms of employment, and if subsequently a series of actions by the employer might constitute together a breach of the implied obligation of trust and confidence the employee is entitled to treat the original action by the employer which was a breach of the express terms of the contract as a part – the start – of the series of actions which, taken together with the employer's other actions, might cumulatively amount to a breach of the implied terms.*

Where an employee claims that he or she has been constructively dismissed, the employee must resign in consequence of the employer's breach. If the employee continues to undertake work for the employer, he or she cannot be taken to have been constructively dismissed. There are other ways in which a contract may come to an end which may at first appear to be dismissal but in fact are not.

A common problem where staff have relatives and family overseas is failure to report for work after leave of absence. In *Igbo* v. *Johnson Matthey Chemicals Ltd* [1986] ICR 505, the Court of Appeal held that a provision in an employee's contract of employment which provided for automatic termination of the contract where an employee fails to report for work on a specified date could operate as a dismissal of that employee where he or she did not report for work on the date specified.

Frustration. Where an employee is sentenced to imprisonment and is thereafter dismissed by his or her employer, this has been held not to amount to 'dismissal' within the scope of the EPCA 1978; rather the contract is frustrated – *Hare* v. *Murphy Bros* [1974] 3 All ER 940. Following this decision, there was conflicting opinion as to whether imprisonment could or could not amount to frustration: see, e.g., *Norris* v. *Southampton City Council* [1982] ICR 177 (EAT); *Chakki* v. *United Yeast Co. Ltd* [1982] 2 All ER 466 (EAT). This issue was, however, resolved by the Court of Appeal in favour of the view that imprisonment can constitute a frustrating event: *FC Shepherd & Co. Ltd* v. *Jerrom* [1986] IRLR 358. Note should be made of the continuing question of how long a sentence need be to frustrate the contract, which amounts to a question of fact in most cases.

An employee's illness may frustrate his or her contract of employment – *Eggs Stores (Stamford Hill) Ltd* v. *Leibovici* [1977] ICR 260 (EAT). However, in *Harman* v. *Flexible Lamps Ltd* [1980] IRLR 418 (EAT) it was held that the illness of an employee would not frustrate the contract of employment where the contract could easily have been terminated by notice. The courts are, generally, reluctant to find frustration in the case of sickness.

Self-dismissal. It had been decided that an employee could in effect dismiss himself or herself by reason of his or her own misconduct. The acceptance by the employer of the employee's conduct as bringing the contract to an end was held not to be a dismissal within s. 55(2)a. However, in *Rasool* v. *Hepworth Pipe Co. Ltd* [1980] IRLR 88 (CA) it was decided that the concept of self-dismissal was erroneous. The Court of Appeal took the view that the employer's reaction to the employee's conduct constitutes a dismissal.

Termination by consent. In *Birch* v. *University of Liverpool* [1985] ICR 470 (CA) it was held that an employee who took advantage of an early retirement scheme was not dismissed. Dismissal does not include termination with the consent of both parties.

The effective date of termination (EDT)

Most of the rights under the EPCA depend on the employee having been continuously employed for a stated qualifying period. Therefore, it is necessary to determine the commencement and cessation of employment. The date on which employment ends is not always easy to determine. Section 55(4) lays down rules to determine this ending date, the effective date of termination (EDT):

> ... *the effective date of termination*
> (a) *in relation to an employee whose contract of employment is terminated by notice, whether given by his employer or by the employee, means the date on which the notice expires;*
> (b) *in relation to an employee whose contract of employment is terminated without notice, means the date on which the termination takes effect; and*
> (c) *in relation to an employee who is employed under a contract for a fixed term, where that term expires without being renewed under the same contract, means the date on which that term expires.*

Section 55(5) EPCA (as amended by s. 21 and Schedule 3 to the Employment Act 1982) provides:

> (5) *Where the contract of employment is terminated by the employer and the notice required by section 49 to be given by an employer would, if duly given on the material date, expire on a date later than the effective date of termination (as defined by subsection (4)) then for the purposes of sections 53(2), 64(1)(a), 64A and 73(3) and paragraph 8(3) of Schedule 14, the later date shall be treated as the effective date of termination in relation to the dismissal.*
> (6) *Where the contract of employment is terminated by the employee and –*

(a) the material date does not fall during a period of notice given by the employer to terminate that contract; and

(b) had the contract been terminated not by the employee but by notice given on the material date by the employer, that notice would have been required by section 49 to expire on a date later than the effective date of termination (as defined by subsection (4)),

then, for the purposes of section 64(1)(a), 64A and 73(3) and paragraph 8(3) of Schedule 14, the later date shall be treated as the effective date of termination in relation to the dismissal.

(7) 'Material date' means –

(a) in subsection (5), the date when notice of termination was given by the employer or (where no notice was given) the date when the contract of employment was terminated by the employer; and

(b) in subsection (6), the date when notice of termination was given by the employee or (where no notice was given) the date when the contract of employment was terminated by the employee.

In any case where an employer summarily dismisses an employee with pay in lieu of notice, the EDT is the date on which the employee is told that he or she is dismissed, and not some later date – *Robert Cort & Son Ltd* v. *Charman* [1981] ICR 816 (EAT).

Was the dismissal fair or unfair?

Where it has been determined that the employee was dismissed s. 57 EPCA lays down the grounds on which a dismissal is capable of being fair:

(1) In determining ... whether the dismissal of an employee was fair or unfair, it shall be for the employer to show –

(a) what was the reason (or, if there was more than one, the principal reason) for the dismissal, and

(b) that it was a reason falling within s. 57(2) or some other substantial reason of a kind such as to justify the dismissal of an employee holding the position which an employee held.

(2) In s. 57(1)b the reference to a reason falling within this subsection is a reference to a reason which –

(a) related to the capability or qualifications of the employee for performing work of the kind which he was employed by his employer to do, or

(b) related to the conduct of the employee, or

(c) was that the employee was redundant, or

(d) was that the employee could not continue to work in the position which he held without contravention (either on his part, or on that of his employer) of a duty or restriction imposed by or under an enactment.

(3) Where the employer has fulfilled the requirements of s. 57(1) then, subject to sections 58 to 62, the determination of the question whether the dismissal was fair or unfair, having regard to the reason shown by the employer, shall depend on whether in the circumstances (including the size and administrative resources of the employer's undertaking) the employer acted reasonably or unreasonably in

> *treating it as a sufficient reason for dismissing the employee; and that question
> shall be determined in accordance with equity and the substantial merits of the
> case.*
>
> *(4) In this section, in relation to the employee –*
>
> > *(a) 'capability' means capability assessed by reference to skill, aptitude, health
> > or any other physical or mental quality;*
> >
> > *(b) 'qualifications' means any degree, diploma or other academic, technical or
> > professional qualification relevant to the position which the employee held.*

Whether a particular dismissal based on one (or more) of the four reasons set out in
s. 57(2) or for 'some other substantial reason' as laid down in s. 57(1) will be fair or
unfair is determined in accordance with s. 57(3). We can see, therefore, that there is a
four-stage process in determining whether the case is one of fair or unfair dismissal.

Stage 1. It is for the employee to establish that he or she is covered by the legislation.
This is where rules as to qualification (age, etc.), continuous employment and the
'effective date of termination' all come into play.

Stage 2. It is for the employee to prove that he or she was dismissed in accordance with
s. 55(2).

Stage 3. The employer must then establish that the reason for the dismissal was either
within s. 57(2) or 'some other substantial reason'. If the reason is other than such a
reason, the dismissal will be unfair. The reason required by s. 57 to support a fair dismissal must be in the mind of the employer as the reason when he makes the decision:
Devis v. *Atkins* [1977] ICR 662 (HL).

Stage 4. If the reason established under stage 3 is potentially fair, it is then for the
industrial tribunal to determine, on the basis of the evidence, put to them, whether or
not the employer acted reasonably in treating that reason as a sufficient ground for
dismissal.

An employer must always establish his or her case by means of evidence; general
allegations of incompetence, etc. will not suffice – *Castledine* v. *Rothwell Engineering
Ltd* [1973] IRLR 99.

   It is important to understand the ways in which the industrial tribunals have viewed
the statutory reasons justifying dismissal in s. 57(2) EPCA 1978.

Capability

Capability is further explained in s. 57(4)a (see above), and most of the cases have
related to illness or incompetence of the employee.

Incompetence. To dismiss an employee who is incapable of performing his or her job
to the standard required will be fair provided the employer acts reasonably in all the
circumstances of the case.

EXAMPLE: Gina is unable to do her waiting job properly, and on two occasions she
has dropped food into the lap of the customer whom she was serving. She is also

unable to set tables in the restaurant to the standard required by the restaurant manager. She is dismissed with pay in lieu of notice. Is her dismissal fair?

The dropping of food on customers is obviously a serious matter and (in the absence of accident) shows incompetence on the part of the person serving the food. In *Taylor* v. *Alidair Ltd* [1978] IRLR 82 (CA) it was held, where an airline pilot had landed his aircraft in such a manner as to cause considerable disquiet amongst the passengers and crew on board the aeroplane, that the dismissal after proper investigation was fair. There are some activities which require a high degree of skill, and the potential consequences of not exercising the skill required are so serious that one failure to exercise sufficient skill and care may justify dismissal. However, whilst 'silver service' is undoubtedly a skill, it would be hard for an employer to justify a dismissal following from one such incident. Furthermore, the potential consequences of failing to exercise skill are not in any sense as severe as in *Taylor*'s case. In other words, Gina's employer may not rely simply on one or two incidents of incompetence *per se* as sufficient to justify dismissal. However, if the employee in question had been a chef and his incompetence had caused food poisoning to guests, dismissal would be justified.

General failure to meet the standards required, e.g. laying tables. In *Davison* v. *Kent Meters Ltd* [1975] IRLR 145, an employee assembled a large number of components incorrectly and was dismissed. The dismissal was found to be unfair, since the supervisor had not shown her what to do or duly guided her or corrected her errors. Therefore, if in our example Gina's employer seeks to rely on her general incompetence, he will bear a burden of attributing fault to her; if the true reason why she is not performing to the required standards is lack of supervision, etc., the dismissal may be unfair. An employee who is not working to the required standard should be duly warned of this and given an opportunity to improve prior to any question of dismissal being considered by his or her employer.

Sickness. The nature of the illness is all-important. Is it a long-term or short-term condition? Is the employee likely to recover sufficiently to work effectively in his or her present job? The principles regarding long-term illness are set out in *Egg Stores (Stamford Hill) Ltd* v. *Leibovici* [1977] ICR 260 (EAT). An employer should treat long-term sickness sympathetically and act accordingly. However, the employer is entitled to consider business needs as well as the employee's situation.

EXAMPLE: Ben is the general manager of the Ocean Garden Hotel. He has been employed in that capacity for five years. One weekend he is involved in a serious car accident, sustaining multiple injuries. His mental condition is unaffected and he is likely to make a full recovery, though owing to the injuries he will require in-patient hospital treatment for three months, and physiotherapy, etc. as an out-patient for a further four months. The accident occurs during May at the commencement of the holiday season. Two months after the accident he is dismissed with pay in lieu of notice by his employer. Is this dismissal fair? First we must consider the terms of Ben's contract of employment. Many employment contracts (particularly for staff and management) contain terms which deal explicitly with sickness, time off work and sick pay. If, however, the matter is not covered by the contract of employment, then we must consider the legal principles which govern the matter. Ben, being the general manager, is in a key management position at the hotel and any absence from work (particularly during the season) may cause disruption to the employer's business. The employer should first seek to cover Ben's absence using available staff. If, however, bearing in mind Ben's likely length of absence from work, this is not possible, other measures may need to be taken. However, an employer cannot be expected to go to unreasonable lengths to accommodate a sick employee. What it is reasonable for an employer to do is largely a question of fact in any given case – *Garricks (Caterers) Ltd* v. *Nolan* [1980] IRLR 259. Both the role of the employee and the size of the employer's business organization are important factors in determining whether it would be fair to dismiss the employee.

Qualifications

This is further defined by s. 57(4)b EPCA. If an employee is employed on the basis of his or her qualifications, e.g. he or she is a member of the HCIMA, or has a degree in hotel and catering management, and thereafter it is found that the person is incompetent, the employee may be dismissed for his or her lack of competence (see above). If a person is employed and is competent at his or her work but either (a) it is thereafter discovered that he or she does not possess the required qualifications for the post, or (b) he or she is employed as a trainee and fails to attain the standards required by the examinations for which he or she was training, then if the employee is thereafter dismissed such a dismissal is potentially fair. There are few examples which have come before the courts; however, *Blackman* v. *Post Office* [1974] ICR 151 is a case in point.

Even though it can be shown that the employee lacks the necessary qualification for the job, the employer must still act reasonably in treating that reason as a sufficient ground for dismissal. In *Blue Star Ship Management Ltd* v. *Williams* [1979] IRLR 16, the view was taken that mere lack of qualification is not *per se* sufficient ground for dismissal; the approach is, 'can the employee cope with the job?'.

EXAMPLE: Andy is employed as a management trainee with the ABC Catering Services Company. He has not completed his HCIMA part B examinations, having previously failed a paper. After two years of service with the company and a further attempt at the examinations (which he did not pass), he is dismissed. Is the dismissal fair? Potentially the dismissal is fair for lack of qualification. However, it is open to doubt whether the employer in this example acted reasonably in treating this as a sufficient reason for dismissal as he is required to do by s. 57(3). In *Sutcliffe & Eaton Ltd* v. *Pinney* [1977] IRLR 349, where the employee was dismissed after failing to pass the examinations at the end of his training, it was held that the employers should have allowed him an extension of his training programme so that he could resit the exams and, in failing to do so, they had not acted reasonably within s. 57(3).

Conduct

There are many possible ways in which the conduct of the employee may be sought to be used as a reason for justifying dismissal. Conduct at work is more often given as a reason than conduct outside work. It is open to an employer to state in the employee's contract of employment those forms of misconduct which will entitle the employer to treat the employee's actions as bringing the contract to an end, and summarily dismiss the employee. Misconduct at work (short of gross misconduct provided for in the employee's contract) may be treated by an employer as a reason for dismissing an employee, and such a dismissal is potentially fair. An important qualification is that an employee cannot be ordered to do something unlawful or contrary to public policy; if he or she is dismissed for refusing such an order that dismissal will consequently be unfair: see, e.g., *Riley* v. *Joseph Frisby Ltd* [1982] IRLR 479 (IT). However, the methods adopted by the employer for investigating the misconduct, as well as the means by which the employee was dismissed, must be fair and reasonable. Equally, an employee must be given sufficient warning that such conduct will be treated by the employer as a sufficient reason for dismissal, though such warnings are not required where the employee's conduct amounts to gross misconduct. A useful illustration of the giving of warnings and their relevance to dismissal can be found in *Auguste Noel* v. *Curtis* [1990] ICR 604 (EAT). The previous warnings in that case were unrelated to the substantive issue upon which the employer sought to dismiss the employee. However, the EAT considered that the employer was entitled to look at the substance of previous complaints which gave rise to the warnings 'in reaching his decision to dismiss'. The Advisory Conciliation and Arbitration Service Code of Practice 1 on 'Disciplinary practice and procedures in employment' (Appendix 9), whilst not mandatory, should be complied with in order to ensure that fair procedures when considering disciplinary matters (such as misconduct) are adopted. Examples of misconduct at work are many and various, as shown below.

Dishonesty. See *Trusthouse Forte Hotels Ltd* v. *Murphy* [1977] IRLR 186 and *Tesco* v. *Hill* [1977] IRLR 63. An employee should normally be given the opportunity to explain his or her conduct prior to dismissal. However, this is not an absolute requirement, though a failure to afford such an opportunity may show that the employer has not acted reasonably as he or she is required to do by s. 57(3). It is necessary for an employer to have reasonable grounds for his or her belief that the employee is guilty of misconduct, and an investigation should normally have been instituted. The question is not simply whether the employee is guilty of misconduct, but whether it is reasonable for the employer to dismiss the employee, taking into account all the circumstances and facts known to the employer – *Da Costa* v. *Oftolis* [1976] IRLR 178.

In *Weddel & Co. Ltd* v. *Tepper* [1980] ICR 286, the Court of Appeal approved Arnold J's approach to cases of misconduct in *British Home Stores Ltd* v. *Burchell* [1980] ICR 303, where he stated:

> *What the tribunal have to decide every time is, broadly expressed, whether the employer who discharged the employee on the grounds of misconduct in question (usually, though not necessarily, dishonest conduct) entertained a reasonable suspicion amounting to a belief in the guilt of the employee of that misconduct at that time. . . . First of all, there must be established by the employer the fact of that belief; that the employer did believe it. Secondly, that the employer had in his mind reasonable grounds upon which to sustain that belief. And thirdly, we think, that the employer at the stage at which he formed that belief on those grounds, at any rate at the final stage at which he formed that belief on those grounds, had carried out as much investigation into the matter as was reasonable in all the circumstances of the case.*

It is not uncommon for the police to commence criminal investigations with a view to a prosecution. This procedure may take some time, especially now, since the decision to prosecute is in the hands of the Crown Prosecution Service. Is it proper, therefore, for the employer to conduct his or her own investigations and question the employee? In *Harris and Shepherd* v. *Courage (Eastern) Ltd* [1982] ICR 530 the Court of Appeal took the view that there is no absolute rule that once an employee has been charged with a criminal offence, an employer cannot dismiss him or her for the alleged offence. Employers frequently carry out their own investigations and dismiss the employee before the prosecution process has been completed. However, it should not be forgotten that even if an employee has been charged with a criminal offence he or she must be given an opportunity by the employer to explain his or her actions – *Read* v. *Phoenix Preservation Ltd* [1985] ICR 164.

Uniform or appropriate dress. For an example of refusal to wear uniform or dress appropriate for work (e.g. where an employer insists that female staff wear skirts and not trousers) see *Atkin* v. *Enfield Group Hospital Management Committee* [1975] IRLR 215 (CA).

Sexual behaviour at work. For an example of a case where an employee indulges in sexual relations during business hours see *Newman* v. *Alarmco* [1976] IRLR 45. For examples of cases dealing with sexual behaviour outside work see *Gardiner* v. *Newport County Borough Council* [1974] IRLR 262 (IT) and *Saunders* v. *Scottish National Camps Association Ltd* [1980] IRLR 174 (EAT).

Redundancy, legality and 'some other substantial reason'

Redundancy. See section 9.6 below.

Legality. See *White* v. *British Sugar* [1977] IRLR 121.

'Some other substantial reason'. This can be seen as something of an 'umbrella' section, trying to catch any potentially justifiable reason for dismissal. The types of reason which may come within this section are not quantifiable, since they are potentially very wide-ranging. It covers, for example, personality clashes between employees – *Gorfin* v. *Distressed Gentlefolks Aid Association* [1973] IRLR 290 and *Treganowan* v. *R. Knee & Co. Ltd* [1975] IRLR 112; business reorganization, *Hollister* v. *NFU* [1979] IRLR 238; and refusal by an employee to agree to a change in his terms and conditions of employment, *RS Components Ltd* v. *Irwin* [1974] 1 All ER 41. Under the Transfer of Undertakings (Protection of Employment) Regulations 1981 the dismissal of an employee for economic, technical or organizational reasons which require changes to be made in the workforce can be for 'some other substantial reason'. However, in this case, as in all other cases, the employer must be able to justify the dismissal as being reasonable.

'Union-related' dismissals

Under s. 152, Trade Union and Labour Relations (Consolidation) Act 1992 the dismissal of an employee will automatically be regarded as unfair if the principal reason for it was that the employee:

(a) was, or proposed to become, a member of an independent trade union; *or*
(b) had taken, or proposed to take, part in the activities of an independent trade union *at an appropriate time*; *or*
(c) was not a member of any trade union, or of a particular trade union or of one of a number of particular trade unions, or had refused, or proposed to refuse, to become or remain a member.

'An appropriate time' with regard to an employee taking part in the activities of a trade union means at a time which either:

(a) is outside his or her working hours; *or*
(b) is a time within his or her working hours at which, in accordance with the consent of his or her employers, it is permissible for him or her to take part in such activities.

The dismissal of a person because he does not belong to any or a particular trade union, or because he has been refused membership of any or a particular trade union, will be automatically unfair.

The employee's right to a statement of reasons for dismissal

It is provided by s. 53(1) EPCA 1978 that:

> *An employee shall be entitled –*
> *(a) if he is given by his employer notice of termination of his contract of employment;*
> *(b) if his contract of employment is terminated by his employer without notice; or*
> *(c) if, where he is employed under a contract for a fixed term, that term expires without being renewed under the same contract;*
> *to be provided by his employer, on request, within 14 days of that request, with a written statement giving particulars of his dismissal.*

Did the employer act reasonably? The importance of s. 57(3) EPCA 1978

Section 57(3) EPCA 1978 states:

> *the determination of the question of whether the dismissal was fair or unfair, having regard to the reason shown by the employer, shall depend on whether in the circumstances (including the size and administrative resources of the employer's undertaking) the employer acted reasonably or unreasonably in treating it as a sufficient reason for dismissing the employee; and that question shall be determined in accordance with equity and the substantial merits of the case.*

This question of fairness is judged through the eyes of the reasonable employer. In *Watling & Co. Ltd* v. *Richardson* [1978] IRLR 255, Phillips J took the following view:

> *the fairness or unfairness of the dismissal is to be judged not by the hunch of the particular industrial tribunal, . . . but by the objective standard of the way in which a reasonable employer in those circumstances in that line of business, would have behaved.*

Each case will have to turn on its own particular facts and therefore decisions relating to s. 57(3) are rarely going to set binding precedents – *Bailey* v. *BP Oil (Kent Refinery) Ltd* [1980] IRLR 287 (CA). However, in *Iceland Frozen Food Ltd* v. *Jones* [1982] IRLR 439 (EAT) it was said that the principle that an industrial tribunal should consider was the reasonableness of an employer's conduct (s. 57(3) EPCA) in dismissing an employee; this was a rule of law, a breach of which gave rise to a claim for unfair dismissal. The test for determining reasonableness was held to be one based upon a band of reasonable responses to the employee's conduct; if the decision to dismiss falls within the band of reasonable responses which a reasonable employer might have adopted it will be regarded as fair.

Procedural defects (see ACAS Code of Practice, Disciplinary practice and procedure in employment, Appendix 9) are usually raised in connection with s. 57(3). The reason for dismissal must be the one given by the employer at the time of the dismissal; therefore, any misconduct, etc., discovered by the employer subsequent to the dismissal cannot be used to justify the dismissal, and should not be considered under s. 57(3).

POLKEY v. A. E. DAYTON   The employee was employed as a van driver by the employers
SERVICES LTD [1987] 3 All   from 1978. In 1982 the employers, in order to stem continuing
ET 974 (HL)   financial losses, decided to reorganize their business to reduce
                            overheads by replacing their four van drivers with two van
                            sales reps. The employers formed the view that three of the
van drivers, including the employee, would not be suitable for employment as van sales reps and that they should therefore be dismissed as redundant. Without any prior consultation or warning, the employee was told that he was being made redundant, was handed a redundancy letter and was immediately sent home. The employee complained to an industrial tribunal that he had been unfairly dismissed. The tribunal dismissed his claim, holding that although the employers had failed to observe the requirements of the statutory code relating to consultation the employee would still have been dismissed if there had been consultation. The employee appealed to the Employment Appeal Tribunal and then to the Court of Appeal but both courts dismissed his appeal on the ground that they were bound by authority to do so. The employee appealed to the House of Lords, contending that the failure to consult showed that the employers had 'acted . . . unreasonably in treating [the redundancy] as a sufficient reason for dismissing the employee' and that was sufficient to make the dismissal unfair for the purposes of s. 57(3)a of the Employment Protection (Consolidation) Act 1978, and whether the outcome would have been the same if there had been consultation was hypothetical and irrelevant.

Held: In determining for the purposes of s. 57(3) of the 1978 Act whether the employers had acted reasonably or unreasonably in treating as sufficient their reason for dismissing the employee, the industrial tribunal was required to determine whether the employers had acted reasonably on the facts known to them at the time, and accordingly it was not open to the tribunal to find, on the basis of facts subsequently brought to light after the dismissal, that the dismissal was reasonable because the employee had not in fact suffered any injustice as a result. It followed therefore that the appeal would be allowed and the case was remitted to an industrial tribunal to determine whether, on the facts known to the employers at the time of the dismissal, the employers had acted reasonably.

The House of Lords' decision makes it quite clear that the key question is, 'Has the employer acted reasonably in dismissing the employee?' Lord Mackay LC observed:

> the subject matter for the tribunal's consideration is the employer's action in treat-
> ing the reason as a sufficient reason for dismissing the employee. It is that action
> and that action only that the tribunal is required to characterise as reasonable or
> unreasonable. That leaves no scope for the tribunal considering whether, if the
> employer had acted differently, he might have dismissed the employee. It is what the
> employer did that is to be judged, not what he might have done. On the other hand,

in judging whether what the employer did was reasonable it is right to consider what a reasonable employer would have in mind at the time he decided to dismiss as the consequence of not consulting or not warning . . .

It is obvious that a reasonable employer will normally follow the guidance of the appropriate ACAS Code of Practice. How is an employer to know whether it is reasonable or unreasonable not to follow the normal procedures? Lord Mackay approved the dictum of Browne-Wilkinson J, in *Sillifant* v. *Powell Duffryn Timber Ltd* [1983] IRLR 91, where he stated:

The weight to be attached to such procedural failure should depend upon the circumstances known to the employer at the time of dismissal, not on the actual consequence of such failure. Thus in the case of a failure to give an opportunity to explain, except in the rare case where a reasonable employer could properly take the view on the facts known to him at the time of the dismissal that no explanation or mitigation could alter his decision to dismiss, an industrial tribunal would be likely to hold that the lack of 'equity' inherent in the failure would render the dismissal unfair.

Lord Mackay, in *Polkey*, emphasized:

If the employer could reasonably have concluded in the light of the circumstances known to him at the time of dismissal that consultation or warning would be utterly useless he might well act reasonably even if he did not observe the provisions of the Code . . .

Since the decision in *Polkey* considerable attention has been focused upon whether employers have acted reasonably by reference to the procedures adopted when dismissing employees. Recent case examples include *Stoker* v. *Lancashire County Council* [1992] IRLR 75 (CA) and *Sartor* v. *P&O European Ferries* [1992] IRLR 291 (CA).

A useful illustration of the application of the reasonableness test is to be found in *Denco Ltd* v. *Johnson* [1991] 1 WLR 330 (EAT). In that case the employee was a sheet metal worker and also a trade union shop steward. He was an authorized user of the employers' computer with his own password, which permitted him entry to the menu containing engineering information. He was accused by the employers of using the identity code and password belonging to an employee of the employers' wholly owned subsidiary company, which used the same computer, to obtain access information which could be of use to him in his trade union activities and hostile to the interests of the company. The employee admitted that he had obtained access to unauthorized information but claimed that he had done so by accident. He was summarily dismissed for gross misconduct and on his complaint of unfair dismissal, an industrial tribunal found that the employers were reasonable in concluding that the employee had deliberately gained access to unauthorized information but that they had not given any reasonable ground for their conclusion that this purpose was illegitimate and that his dismissal was therefore unfair.

The employers appealed. Allowing the appeal, it was held that if an employee deliberately used an unauthorized password in order to enter a computer known to contain information to which he was not entitled, that was of itself gross misconduct which *prima facie* would attract summary dismissal. The industrial tribunal had misdirected themselves in law in requiring the employers to show reasonable grounds for believing that the employee had an illegitimate purpose in obtaining access to a particular programme, and the case would be remitted to the tribunal for further hearing.

The EAT considered that unauthorized use of or tampering with computers is an extremely serious industrial offence. However, it is clearly desirable to reduce into writing rules concerning the access to and use of computers and not only to display them but to leave them near the computers for reference.

There are three clear examples of times when consultation would be utterly useless or futile:
(a) an employer who sees an employee stab another in the back – *BP Oil (Kent Refinery)* v. *Bailey* [1980] ICR 642;
(b) a trusted employee who is dismissed after having pleaded guilty to theft from his or her employer – *West Midlands Co-operative Society* v. *Tipton* [1986] 2 WLR 306 (HL);
(c) an employee caught at the factory gate with a pocketful of his or her employer's secrets – *Wells* v. *Derwent Plastics* [1978] ITR 47.
In considering whether the employer had acted reasonably s. 63 EPCA provides:

> *No account shall be taken of any pressure which, by calling, organising, procuring or financing a strike or other industrial action, or threatening to do so, was exercised on the employer to dismiss the employee.*

Dismissals and pregnancy: automatic unfairness

A female employee may have a right to receive maternity pay and return to work. Where an employee is dismissed because she is pregnant the following will apply. By s. 60(1) EPCA it is automatically unfair if the reason or principal reason for the employee's dismissal is that she is pregnant or any other reason connected with pregnancy unless:
(a) at the effective date of termination she is incapable, because of her pregnancy, of adequately doing the work which she is employed to do; *or*
(b) she cannot, after that date and because of her pregnancy, continue to do her work without contravention (by her or her employer) of a duty or restriction imposed by or under any enactment.
Even if (a) or (b) is met, the employee may still be unfairly dismissed if, at the time of the dismissal, there was a suitable available vacancy but the employer failed to offer such employment to her before or on the effective date of termination: s. 60(2). The new work must be 'both suitable in relation to the employee and appropriate for her to do in the circumstances' and 'not substantially less favourable to her than the corresponding provisions of the previous contract': s. 60(3).

The phrase 'any other reason connected with her pregnancy' has been held to include physical ailments such as anaemia (*Grimsby Carpet Co. Ltd* v. *Bedford* [1978]

ICR 975 (EAT)) as well as anticipated physical occurrences connected with pregnancy such as confinement (*Stockton-on-Tees Borough Council* v. *Brown* [1988] 2 All ER 129 (HL)).

HIV, AIDS and dismissal of employees

This highly sensitive area of the law has as yet been notable by its absence from the English courts' reported case law. An interesting insight into the HIV virus and its impact upon the workplace in the USA and UK is provided by Professor Joseph Kelly in an article in the *New Law Journal* of 25 January 1991, p. 88.

With regard to AIDS and dismissal from employment, *Buck* v. *Letchworth Palace Ltd* (1987) (unreported) is one of the few decided cases. In that case an employee was dismissed following his conviction for gay sex offences, when his colleagues refused to work with him. The industrial tribunal concluded that the dismissal was fair, despite the overreaction of the dismissed employee's colleagues and there being no evidence of the alleged HIV infection. The EAT reversed the IT's decision on the basis that the employer had not followed the appropriate procedure – applying the House of Lords' ruling in *Polkey* v. *A. E. Dayton Services Ltd* (see p. 326).

Bringing the claim for unfair dismissal

The claim for unfair dismissal is brought before an industrial tribunal and the procedure is regulated by the Industrial Tribunals (Constitution and Rules of Procedure) Regulations 1993.

Time limit for applications

A complaint to an industrial tribunal must be made by lodging an originating application within three months of the effective date of termination; e.g. if the effective date of termination falls on 1 April 1996 the time limit for lodging a complaint will be 30 June 1996. If it is not reasonably practicable to lodge the complaint within three months then the industrial tribunal may accept a late application provided they are satisfied that it was not 'reasonably practicable' for the complainant to have made the complaint within three months. This is tested by asking the question, 'Had the person just cause or excuse for not presenting his or her complaint within the prescribed time?' – *Walls Meat Co. Ltd* v. *Khan* [1978] IRLR 499 (CA).

The originating application: IT1

The proceedings are commenced by the complainant filling in form IT1 and sending it to the Central Office of Industrial Tribunals (COIT) in London. Upon receipt it is registered.

The notice of appearance: IT3

The ITI, after receipt by COIT and registration, will be copied and a copy will be sent to the respondent and a conciliation officer at ACAS, who is under a duty to seek a resolution of the matter. Within fourteen days of receipt of the IT1 the respondent must complete and return the IT3 if he or she wishes to resist the claim. The IT3 will contain the grounds put forward by the respondent for resisting the claim.

Matters prior to hearing

Pre-hearing assessments. A tribunal may at any time prior to the hearing, upon an application by either party or of its own volition, sit to assess the merits of the claim or any specific point raised by either the applicant or the respondent. This procedure is designed to 'weed out' weak or spurious claims and defences.

Discovery, further and better particulars. These are means by which either party may obtain further information which is necessary for conducting the case.

The hearing

Stage 1 The employee must show that he or she is a qualifying employee in employment covered by the legislation.

Stage 2 The employee must prove the dismissal.

Stage 3 The employer must prove a reason for dismissal falling within s. 57 EPCA 1978.

Stage 4 It is for the industrial tribunal to decide whether the employer acted reasonably within s. 57(3).

The tribunal consists of a legally qualified chairman or chairwoman and two lay-members, one nominated by employers' organizations, the other a representative of employees and trade unions. Evidence is received in the normal way by the tribunal as if it were a court, only the proceedings are less formal and the tribunal will receive certain kinds of evidence, e.g. hearsay, not received by courts.

Costs

Costs will be awarded against a party only if the tribunal considers that in bringing or conducting the proceeding that party has acted frivolously, vexatiously or otherwise unreasonably. Legal aid is not available in the industrial tribunal, though legal advice and assistance are available under the 'green form scheme'.

Review and appeals

An appeal lies on a point of law to the Employment Appeal Tribunal. Reviews are heard by another industrial tribunal and in the main concern procedural matters.

Remedies for unfair dismissal

There are three remedies available where a dismissal has been found to be unfair by the tribunal: reinstatement; re-engagement; and compensation.

Reinstatement

This is provided for by s. 69 EPCA. Reinstatement is an order that the employer shall treat the complainant in all respects as if he or she had not been dismissed; i.e. continuity is maintained. The tribunal, prior to making such an order, must consider:
(a) the complainant's wishes;
(b) whether it is practicable for the employer to comply with such an order if it is made;
(c) the complainant's conduct.
Reinstatement is rarely sought by applicants to the industrial tribunal, since the bringing of an action in the industrial tribunal is often the final stage in a long and unhappy saga which both the complainant and the respondent wish to have brought to an end, rather than be continued in another mode.

Re-engagement

If an order for reinstatement has been considered by the tribunal but thought inappropriate, re-engagement must then be considered. This amounts to re-employment in a comparable position rather than in the complainant's 'old job'. The same criteria are applied by the tribunal in determining the suitability of this remedy as were applied when considering reinstatement.

Compensation

The award of compensation for unfair dismissal comprises two parts: basic award and compensatory award.

Basic award. This is calculated in accordance with s. 73(3) EPCA 1978:

> *The amount of the basic award shall be calculated by reference to the period ending with the effective date of termination, during which the employee has been continuously employed, by starting at the end of that period and reckoning backwards the number of years of employment falling within that period and allowing –*
> *(a) 1½ weeks' pay for each such year of employment which consists wholly of weeks in which the employee was not below the age of 41;*
> *(b) 1 week's pay for each year of employment not falling within paragraph (a) which consists wholly of weeks in which the employee was not below the age of 22; and*
> *(c) half a week's pay for each such year of employment not falling within either of paragraphs (a) or (b).*

A week's pay is to a maximum of £210 (1996) for dismissals.
   The basic award may be reduced in the following circumstances:
1   Where the conduct of the employee before the dismissal was such that it would be just and equitable to do so (s. 73(7B) EPCA).
2   Where the employee has unreasonably refused an offer of reinstatement which would have resulted in his being treated in all respects as though he had never been dismissed, in which case the tribunal may reduce compensation to such an extent as it considers just and equitable (s. 73(7A) EPCA).
3   Where the EDT falls after the employee's sixty-fourth birthday. In these circumstances the basic award is reduced by one-twelfth for each whole month

for which the employee was employed between his or her sixty-fourth birthday and the EDT (s. 73(5), (6) EPCA).

4   Where the employee is dismissed for redundancy and receives a redundancy payment, in which case the payment is offset against the basic award (usually reducing it to nothing).

Compensatory award. Section 74(1) EPCA states:

> *the amount of the compensatory award shall be such amount as the tribunal considers just and equitable in all the circumstances having regard to the loss sustained by the complainant in consequence of the dismissal insofar as that loss is attributable to action taken by the employer.*

The statutory maximum for the compensatory award is £11,300 (1996) for dismissals. The loss sustained by the employee is taken to include:

1   Expenses reasonably incurred by the complainant consequent upon dismissal.
2   The loss of any benefit which he or she might reasonably be expected to have but for the dismissal. This covers: (a) immediate loss of wages; (b) the mode of dismissal where it causes the employee financial loss; (c) future loss of earnings; (d) loss of statutory rights.

An employee is, by virtue of s. 74(4), under a duty to mitigate his or her loss.

Section 74(6) allows for the reduction of the compensatory award where complainants have to any extent caused or contributed to their dismissal by their conduct. The compensatory award may be reduced to nothing in cases where the employees brought the dismissal upon themselves.

It should be noted that where compensation is sought against an employer, and the true reason for the dismissal was pressure placed on the employer by a third party, e.g. a trade union, then s. 76A EPCA 1978 (as provided by s. 7 of the Employment Act 1982) applies. The employer or the complainant may request the tribunal to make that third party a party to the proceedings, and if thereafter an order for compensation is made by the tribunal, it may be made against the third party.

9.6 REDUNDANCY

The purpose of the legislation is to compensate long-serving employees for the loss of employment. To establish a claim for a redundancy payment the employee must first show that he or she is an employee covered by the legislation; that is, he or she has worked in qualifying employment for a period of two years. Dismissal for the purposes of redundancy is defined by s. 83 EPCA, and includes those forms of dismissal covered by s. 55(2) (see the section on grounds for unfair dismissal). In addition, where the employment is terminated by the death, dissolution or liquidation of the employer, or the appointment of a receiver, s. 93 states that these also will amount to dismissal.

For a claim to be made the employee must be dismissed for reason of redundancy. It is for the employee to prove that he or she has been dismissed, but once this has been done a rebuttable presumption then arises that the dismissal is by reason of redundancy. Therefore, the employer must then show that the dismissal was for some reason other than redundancy. This illustrates the importance of the right of an employee to a statement of the reasons for his or her dismissal – s. 53(1) EPCA.

In *Brown* v. *Stockton-on-Tees Borough Council* [1988] IRLR 263 the House of Lords held that a woman who had been selected for redundancy because she would require maternity leave had been unfairly dismissed, in that her dismissal was for a reason connected with her pregnancy within s. 60 EPCA 1978 and therefore deemed to be unfair.

How is redundancy defined?

Section 81(2) EPCA 1978 states:

> *For the purposes of this Act an employee who is dismissed shall be taken to have been dismissed by reason of redundancy if the dismissal is attributable wholly or mainly to –*
> *(a) the fact that his employer has ceased, or intends to cease, to carry on the business for the purposes of which the employee was employed by him, or has ceased, or intends to cease to carry on that business in the place where the employee was so employed, or*
> *(b) the fact that the requirements of that business for employees to carry out work of a particular kind, or for employees to carry out work of a particular kind in the place where he was so employed have ceased, or diminished or are expected to cease or diminish.*

The first way in which there may be a redundancy is where either the business of the firm has ceased, or it is intended that it will cease. This covers both temporary and permanent cessation of business. The second is where the business ceases to be carried on at a particular place, or where at a particular place of work there is no further need for that employee. The last is where the employee is surplus to the requirements of the business.

COWAN v. HADEN LTD [1982] IRLR 225 — A quantity surveyor had accepted a job of divisional contracts surveyor. A term in his contract of employment required him to undertake at the discretion of the company any and all duties which reasonably fell within the scope of his capabilities.

Held: The EAT considered that a redundancy is accepted as having been shown where it is demonstrated that the actual job which the claimant was carrying out had ceased to exist. It was not sufficient in order to establish redundancy to show merely that the requirements of the employers for employees to carry out work of the kind on which the employee was actually engaged had ceased or diminished; it was necessary to show such diminution or cessation in relation to any work that he could have been asked to do. Major changes in job functions, provided they fall within the contractual definition of job duties, do not therefore constitute redundancy.

It should be noted that where an employee is dismissed on the basis of an alleged redundancy and his or her job is thereafter done by another employee, it cannot be

said that the requirements of the business for an employee have ceased or diminished
– *Vaux & Associated Breweries Ltd* v. *Ward* (1968) 3 ITR 385.

Other factors to be considered

Offer by the employer to renew the employee's contract. If, prior to a dismissal
for redundancy, the employer makes an offer to renew the contract of employment
(or offers to re-engage the employee), and such an offer is to take effect either
immediately after the old contract comes to an end or no more than four weeks
thereafter, the employee may lose any right which he or she may otherwise have had
to a redundancy payment. If the employee does not accept the employer's offer
s. 82(3)(5) operates. Provided the offer was of suitable employment, and the
employee has unreasonably refused it, the employee will lose his or her right to a
redundancy payment. If, on the other hand, the offer was unsuitable, then the original dismissal is by reason of redundancy, and the employee preserves his or her
right to a redundancy payment.

If the employee accepts the employer's offer, the termination of the original
contract will not be treated as a dismissal and no claim to a redundancy payment
arises. Continuity of employment is maintained. A four-week trial period in the new
job is provided for. If the new job is unsuitable the employee may leave and claim a
redundancy payment, but only if the new job is unsuitable and his or her refusal of
the new job after the trial period is reasonable.

Change of employers. Schedule 13 paragraph 17 1978 Act provides that where a trade
or business is transferred from one person to another continuity will normally be
maintained. This must be considered in relation to the Transfer of Undertakings
(Protection of Employment) Regulations 1981, which provide that where one person
transfers an undertaking to another, that transfer will not operate as a termination of
the contract of employment. Since there will be no dismissal in such circumstances, no
claim for redundancy can arise.

Misconduct. Misconduct such as would entitle the employer to terminate the contract
of employment without notice will disentitle the employee to a redundancy payment.
This must be read subject to s. 92 EPCA.

Redundancy and unfair dismissal

There are circumstances where a dismissal, albeit for redundancy (which will if established be deemed to be fair by s. 57(2) EPCA), is in fact unfair. If a dismissal falls
within the scope of s. 57(2) it is still open to the tribunal to find that the employer acted
unreasonably in the circumstances in treating this as a sufficient reason to dismiss.
Lack of due consultation prior to the dismissal of employees, or an unfair procedure
of selection for redundancy, may render a dismissal which is by reason of redundancy
unfair. If the employer gives his or her reason for dismissal to be redundancy, and the
employee can prove to the satisfaction of the tribunal that the true reason was not
redundancy, but some other reason, i.e. trade union activities, the dismissal will automatically be unfair within the scope of the legislation – s. 59(a) EPCA. It will suit the
employee monetarily to seek to establish unfair dismissal since greater compensation
is payable.

Handling redundancies

In most cases an employer who fails to consult with employees may be found to have unfairly dismissed them. This became clear from the House of Lords in *Polkey* v. *A. E. Dayton Services Ltd* [1987] (IRLB 503) – '*in the case of redundancy, the employer will normally not act reasonably unless he warns and consults any employees affected or their representatives, adopts a fair basis on which to select for redundancy and takes such steps as may be reasonable to avoid or minimise redundancy by re-development within his own organisation*'.

Notice of dismissal should not be issued until consultation has taken place. The consultation should include the following:

- Explanation of the need for redundancies.
- Explanation of why particular employees have been identified as candidates for redundancy
- Explanation of any selection criteria
- Explanation of why the employer has not been able to offer alternative work

The employees should be allowed to make comments on any of the points.

If an organization recognizes a trade union who represents the category of employees who are being dismissed, there are some statutory time limits set out regarding consultation:

(a) where the employer is proposing to dismiss as redundant 100 or more employees at one establishment within a period of 90 days or less, at least 90 days notice before the first of those dismissals takes effect: or

(b) where the employer is proposing to dismiss as redundant 10 or more employees at one establishment within a period of 30 days or less, at least 30 days notice before the first of those dismissals takes effect.

An employer has to offer suitable alternative employment if it is available. Employers have an obligation to see what alternative vacancies exist not only in their own company, but also in associated companies. Also it should not be assumed that an employee is not prepared to work for less money, or on shorter hours. It is good practice to circulate vacancies to redundant employees and then invite applicants. If employers do not look for alternative employment or make assumptions about what jobs employees may accept, and therefore not offer them, there could be a justifiable case for unfair dismissal (*Nationwide Anglia Building Society* v. *Hooper* (EAT 360/91)). Employees can reject alternative employment if they feel that the alternative employment is unreasonable. Section 82(5) of the Employment Protection (Consolidation) Act 1978 provides that 'if the employee unreasonably refuses a suitable offer of employment, he is not entitled to a redundancy payment'. The question of 'reasonableness' is one that often could only be decided by a tribunal. Staff on maternity leave are regarded as employees if they have stated their right to return to work after the appropriate period of time. Such employees should not be forgotten when looking for suitable alternative employment for potentially redundant employees.

The redundancy payment

Redundancy payment is paid by the employer. The amount is calculated in the same way as for the basic award for unfair dismissal. There is a maximum of 20 years' reckonable service at £210 (1996)/week making a maximum of £6300 (£210 × 20 × 1.5 weeks, being the award for service between the ages of 41 and 60). A claim for redundancy payment, if it has not been paid by the employer, must be made to the industrial tribunal, within the time limit laid down in Section 101, i.e. six months.

Stress at work

The High Court has recognized the liability of an employer for inducing illness through stress at the workplace. In *Walker* v. *Northumberland County Council* [1994] NLJ 1659, it was held that where it is reasonably foreseeable to an employer that an employee might suffer a nervous breakdown because of the stress and pressures of his/her workload the employer is under a duty of care (as part of the duty to provide a safe system of work) not to cause the employee psychiatric damage through the volume or nature of the work which the employee is required to undertake.

This case may turn on its own particular facts. Mr Walker had previously suffered a period of stress-induced illness caused by his workload. As a manager in the social services team of his employer, he had been encouraged to return to work by promises that he would get more staff and support in order to be able to cope more effectively with his difficult case-load (child protection cases). The promises of additional support were not fulfilled and Mr Walker suffered a further breakdown and was subsequently dismissed by his employer on grounds of permanent ill-health. The fact that Mr Walker had previously been unwell made it foreseeable that his return to work without the additional support would cause him psychological harm.

This case is more about the provision of a safe system of work – see Chapter 10 – than it is about individual employment rights. However, where an employer takes on a member of staff knowing that they may be vulnerable, to stress or any other particular risk of injury, the employer may be liable to the employee in damages if the employee suffers injury as a consequence of that foreseeable risk. This is an old established principle of law – see *Paris* v. *Stepney Borough Council* [1951] 1 All ER 42 (page 344 below). The liability of the employer turns on the foreseeability of the risk and the reasonableness of the steps which the employer takes to guard against the risk of injury to the employee – see *Latimer* v. *AEC Ltd.* [1953] 2 All ER 449.

Employers should now guard against not only foreseeable risks of physical harm through manual work but also the risks of psychological harm in a whole range of 'white collar' supervisory and management roles. The police, fire and ambulance services, along with doctors, nurses and other caring professions e.g. teachers, will be those most exposed to the risk of long-term stress-induced ill-health. Other industries such as the railways are likely to see litigation emerging which is based on this principle.

9.7 DISABILITY DISCRIMINATION ACT 1995

By the end of 1996, the main employment provisions of the Disability Discrimination Act 1995 will be in force. Essentially the Act prohibits an employer with 20 or more employees from treating employees and job applicants less favourably than others on account of their disability, unless there is some substantial reason. Disability also covers those with learning disabilities. The Act requires employers to make reasonable alterations to working practices and lay-outs which might otherwise be a non-essential barrier to the employment of disabled persons.

CASE STUDY

Mildred has been employed as a full-time waitress at the Bull Hotel, Wapping, for 30 months. She takes a £5 note from a customer and places it in her own pocket rather than in the money pouch with which she has been provided.

Mildred is seen doing this by Eric, the restaurant manager. He calls her into his office and dismisses her instantly and without pay in lieu of notice.

Mildred was never charged by the police for the theft, and Eric recovered the £5 note when he dismissed her.

Advise Mildred as to any remedies she may have against her employer.

Mildred may seek to claim both wrongful dismissal and unfair dismissal.

Wrongful dismissal. This is an action in the County Court for monies due under the contract of employment where the employer has failed to give the employee notice prior to dismissal or pay in lieu of notice.

Mildred must establish that:
(a) she was an employee (see p. 271).
(b) she was dismissed.
(c) her length of service with the employer entitled her to a notice period which was not given nor pay provided in lieu of notice. Here the requisite notice period would be two weeks; thus Mildred is claiming two weeks' pay in lieu of notice (s. 49 EPCA 1978).
Mildred's employers will seek to argue that it was not necessary for them to give notice to her since her conduct amounted to gross misconduct sufficient to justify instant dismissal (see p. 308).

Since wrongful dismissal does not compensate for the manner of the dismissal, it is merely a question of fact whether or not Mildred's conduct was sufficient to merit summary dismissal (*Trusthouse Forte Hotels Ltd* v. *Murphy*, see p. 309). It is likely that 'theft' will be set out in Mildred's contract of employment as conduct sufficient to merit summary dismissal.

Unfair dismissal. This should be approached in four stages:
1   Has the employee established that he or she is covered by the legislation? It is for Mildred, on the facts of this case study, to show that she is an employee, that she has been employed for the qualifying period (two years) in full-time employment which is covered by the legislation, and that she is beneath the normal 'retiring age'.
2   Has the employee proved that she was dismissed? Mildred must do this in accordance with s. 55 EPCA 1978. Clearly she has been dismissed on the facts of this case study.
3   Has the employer established that the reason for the dismissal was either within s. 57(2) EPCA or 'some other substantial reason'? Mildred's employer will seek to establish that the reason was misconduct, which is within s. 57(2) EPCA. If it can be established the dismissal will be potentially fair.
4   At this stage the industrial tribunal, having satisfied themselves that the reason is potentially fair, must then determine on the basis of the evidence put to them whether or not the employer acted reasonably in treating that reason as a sufficient ground for dismissal (see s. 57(3) EPCA). The industrial tribunal will take account of the procedure followed by the employer. On this point there has been considerable case law. The House of Lords has recently clarified the law in

Polkey v. *A.E. Dayton Services Ltd* (see p. 326). The facts of Mildred's situation compare most closely with those in *West Midlands Co-operative Society* v. *Tipton* [1986] AC 536. It was held by the House of Lords in that case that internal procedures are an integral part of the dismissal procedure and should be taken into account; refusal by an employer to allow an internal appeal may itself be evidence of unfairness.

Having discussed the substantive issues it is important to consider the remedies for unfair dismissal, which are fully discussed on pp. 330–2.

APPENDIX 9

CODE OF PRACTICE

ACAS Code of Practice 1

Disciplinary practice and procedures in employment

Introduction

1 This document gives practical guidance on how to draw up disciplinary rules and procedures and how to operate them effectively. Its aim is to help employers and trade unions as well as individual employees – both men and women – wherever they are employed regardless of the size of the organization in which they work. In the smaller establishments it may not be practicable to adopt all the detailed provisions, but most of the features listed in paragraph 10 could be adopted and incorporated into a simple procedure.

Why have disciplinary rules and procedures?

2 Disciplinary rules and procedures are necessary for promoting fairness and order in the treatment of individuals and in the conduct of industrial relations. They also assist an organization to operate effectively. Rules set standards of conduct at work; procedure helps to ensure that the standards are adhered to and also provides a fair method of dealing with alleged failures to observe them.

3 It is important that employees know what standards of conduct are expected of them and the Contracts of Employment Act 1972 (as amended by the Employment Protection Act 1975) requires employers to provide written information for their employees about certain aspects of their disciplinary rules and procedures.

4 The importance of disciplinary rules and procedures has also been recognized by the law relating to dismissals, since the grounds for dismissal and the way in which the dismissal has been handled can be challenged before an industrial tribunal. Where either of these is found by a tribunal to have been unfair the employer may be ordered to reinstate or re-engage the employees concerned and may be liable to pay compensation to them.

Formulating policy

5 Management are responsible for maintaining discipline within the organization and for ensuring that there are adequate disciplinary rules and procedures. The initiative for establishing these will normally lie with management. However, if they are to be fully effective the rules and procedures need to be accepted as reasonable both by those who are to be covered by them and by those who operate them. Management should therefore aim to secure the involvement of employees and all levels of management when formulating new or revising existing rules and procedures. In the light of particular circumstances in different companies and industries trade union officials may or may not wish to participate in the formulation of the rules but they should participate fully with management in agreeing the procedural arrangements which will apply to their members and in seeing that these arrangements are used consistently and fairly.

Rules

6 It is unlikely that any set of disciplinary rules can cover all circumstances that may arise: moreover the rules required will vary according to particular circumstances such as the type of work, working conditions and size of establishment. When drawing up rules the aim should be to specify clearly and concisely those necessary for the efficient and safe performance of work and for the maintenance of satisfactory relations within the workforce and between employees and management. Rules should not be so general as to be meaningless.

7 Rules should be readily available and management should make every effort to ensure that employees know and understand them. This may be best achieved by giving every employee a copy of the rules and by explaining them orally. In the case of new employee this should form part of an induction programme.

8 Employees should be made aware of the likely consequences of breaking rules and in particular they should be given a clear indication of the type of conduct which may warrant summary dismissal.

Essential features of disciplinary procedures

9 Disciplinary procedures should not be viewed primarily as a means of imposing sanctions. They should also be designed to emphasize and encourage improvements in individual conduct.

10 Disciplinary procedures should:
(a) Be in writing.
(b) Specify to whom they apply.
(c) Provide for matters to be dealt with quickly.
(d) Indicate the disciplinary actions which may be taken.
(e) Specify the levels of management which have the authority to take the various forms of disciplinary action, ensuring that immediate superiors do not normally have the power to dismiss without reference to senior management.
(f) Provide for individuals to be informed of the complaints against them and to be given an opportunity to state their case before decisions are reached.
(g) Give individuals the right to be accompanied by a trade union representative or by a fellow employee of their choice.

(h) Ensure that, except for gross misconduct, no employees are dismissed for a first breach of discipline.
(i) Ensure that disciplinary action is not taken until the case has been carefully investigated.
(j) Ensure that individuals are given an explanation for any penalty imposed.
(k) Provide a right of appeal and specify the procedure to be followed.

The procedure in operation

11 When a disciplinary matter arises, the supervisor or manager should first establish the facts promptly before recollections fade, taking into account the statements of any available witnesses. In serious cases consideration should be given to a brief period of suspension while the case is investigated and this suspension should be with pay. Before a decision is made or penalty imposed the individual should be interviewed and given the opportunity to state his or her case and should be advised of any rights under the procedure, including the right to be accompanied.
12 Often supervisors will give informal oral warnings for the purpose of improving conduct when employees commit minor infringements of the established standards of conduct. However, where the facts of a case appear to call for disciplinary action, other than summary dismissal, the following procedure should normally be observed:
(a) In the case of minor offences the individual should be given a formal oral warning or, if the issue is more serious, there should be a written warning setting out the nature of the offence and the likely consequences of further offences.
    In either case the individual should be advised that the warning constitutes the first formal stage of the procedure.
(b) Further misconduct might warrant a final written warning, which should contain a statement that any recurrence would lead to suspension or dismissal or some other penalty, as the case may be.
(c) The final step might be disciplinary transfer, or disciplinary suspension without pay (but only if these are allowed for by an express or implied condition of the contract of employment), or dismissal, according to the nature of the misconduct. Special consideration should be given before imposing disciplinary suspension without pay and it should not normally be for a prolonged period.

13 Except in the event of an oral warning, details of any disciplinary action should be given in writing to the employee and if desired, to his or her representative. At the same time the employee should be told of any right of appeal, how to make it and to whom.
14 When determining the disciplinary action to be taken the supervisor or manager should bear in mind the need to satisfy the test of reasonableness in all the circumstances. So far as possible, account should be taken of the employee's record and any other relevant factors.
15 Special consideration should be given to the way in which disciplinary procedures are to operate in exceptional cases. For example:
(a) *Employees to whom the full procedure is not immediately available.* Special provisions may have to be made for the handling of disciplinary matters among nightshift workers, workers in isolated locations or depots or others who may pose particular problems for example because no one is present with the

necessary authority to take disciplinary action or no trade union representative is immediately available.

(b) *Trade union officials.* Disciplinary action against a trade union official can lead to a serious dispute if it is seen as an attack on the union's functions. Although normal disciplinary standards should apply to their conduct as employees, no disciplinary action beyond an oral warning should be taken until the circumstances of the case have been discussed with a senior trade union representative or full-time official.

(c) *Criminal offences outside employment.* These should not be treated as automatic reasons for dismissal regardless of whether the offence has any relevance to the duties of the individual as an employee. The main considerations should be whether the offence is one that makes the individual unsuitable for his or her type of work or unacceptable to other employees. Employees should not be dismissed solely because a charge against them is pending or because they are absent through having been remanded in custody.

Appeals

16 Grievance procedures are sometimes used for dealing with disciplinary appeals though it is normally more appropriate to keep the two kinds of procedure separate since the disciplinary issues are in general best resolved within the organization and need to be dealt with more speedily than others. The external stages of a grievance procedure may, however, be the appropriate machinery for dealing with appeals against disciplinary action where a final decision within the organization is contested or where the matter becomes a collective issue between management and a trade union.

17 Independent arbitration is sometimes an appropriate means of resolving disciplinary issues. Where the parties concerned agree, it may constitute the final stage of procedure.

Records

18 Records should be kept, detailing the nature of any breach of disciplinary rules, the action taken and the reasons for it, whether an appeal was lodged, its outcome and any subsequent developments. These records should be carefully safeguarded and kept confidential.

19 Except in agreed special circumstances breaches of disciplinary rules should be disregarded after a specified period of satisfactory conduct.

Further action

20 Rules and procedures should be reviewed periodically in the light of any developments in employment legislation or industrial relations practice and, if necessary, revised in order to ensure their continuing relevance and effectiveness. Any amendments and additional rules imposing new obligations should be introduced only after reasonable notice has been given to all employees and, where appropriate, their representatives have been informed.

TEN

The caterer and the staff II:
Safety and working conditions

Health and safety at work, in recent years, have come to play a vital role in the respons-ibility of the owners and managers of organizations. The hospitality industry is labour-intensive employing many people in a variety of different work situations some of which are relatively safe, others which are surrounded by hazards. Dangers range from the obvious such as boiling fat, sharp knives, powerful mixing and cutting machines through to the less obvious such as dangerously noisy discos, poorly lit and smoke-filled work areas such as bars and the more recently identified hazards such as those associated with working for too long at Visual Display Units (VDUs). Some jobs may lead to diseases such as dermatitis as a result of using detergents, handling flour or heat stress resulting from working in extremely hot, humid conditions. In this chapter we set out to describe the principles underlying the law concerned with health and safety at work and to describe the major statutes affecting employers and their employees. This chapter however, is not intended to be a completely comprehensive statement of the law.

The law on safety at work, like so many other areas, traverses both civil and criminal law. The civil law, principally the law of torts, is designed to compensate the victim of an accident at work, and has grown piecemeal during the late nineteenth and early twentieth centuries. The criminal aspects of health and safety seek to establish and regulate standards of safety at the workplace, in the form of Acts and Regulation legis-lated by Parliament, e.g. the Health and Safety at Work etc. Act 1974. Since much of the safety law today is in statutory or regulatory form, the common law may be regarded as the background in which the statutory law operates.

10.1 CIVIL ASPECTS OF HEALTH AND SAFETY AT WORK

Common-law duties

The common-law duties owed by an employer to his or her employees are primarily to be found in the tort of negligence, and in particular in the area of employer's

342

liability, discussed later. However, much of the common law has been superseded by statute and the victim of an accident at work may sue for breach of the specific statutory duty imposed upon the employer or occupier of the workplace. It should be pointed out that not all persons who may be at the workplace are employees; subcontractors (e.g. window cleaners, service engineers, decorators and repair people) and other lawful visitors (e.g. postwoman, delivery man) may also be present and could sustain injury. It is important, therefore, to consider safety at work in a slightly broader aspect than simply the duties owed by employers to their employees.

Although the law in this area stems from the law of torts it is worthy of note that the contract of employment between the employer and the employee contains an implied term as to safety at work.

SMITH v. BAKER [1891]   Lord Herschell observed: 'It is quite clear, that the contract
AC 325 (HL)   between employer and employed involves on the part of the
                         former the duty of taking reasonable care to provide proper
                         appliances, and to maintain them in a proper condition, and so
to carry on his operations as not to subject those employed by him to unnecessary risk. Whatever the dangers or the employment which the employed undertakes, amongst them is certainly not to be numbered the risk of the employer's negligence and the creation or enhancement of danger thereby engendered.'

Applying this principle it would seem that an employee may sue an employer for breach of an implied term of his or her contract of employment: to take reasonable care to ensure the employee's safety at work.

Negligence liability

At common law an employer is under a duty to take reasonable care to ensure the health and safety of his or her employees. This duty is derived from the general duty owed to one's neighbour, following from the principle enunciated by Lord Atkin in *Donoghue* v. *Stevenson* [1932] AC 562 (HL). The duty enunciated in *Donoghue* v. *Stevenson* is a general duty owed to those persons whom one might reasonable foresee as being injured by one's actions. The scope of the duty owed covers not only employees but also other visitors to the premises. However, if an employee is the person seeking damages for an injury sustained at work he or she will sue for breach of the employer's duty under the principle in *Wilson & Clyde Coal Co. Ltd* v. *English* [1937] 3 All ER 628 (HL). If, on the other hand, the person injured is a lawful visitor to the employer's premises, that person will sue under the Occupiers' Liability Act 1957. Therefore, the simple tort of negligence will not be used.

Employer's liability to employees

This form of tort is derived from the general tort of negligence, though it gives rise to a special form of duty owed by an employer to his or her employees. In the nineteenth century the courts denied employees a right of action against their employers for injuries sustained at work – *Priestley* v. *Fowler* [1835–42] All ER Rep. 449. However, in the twentieth century, since the House of Lords' decision in *Wilson & Clyde Coal Co. Ltd* v. *English* [1937] 3 All ER 628 (HL), such a right of action has been recognized. This duty of care is owed personally by an employer to his or her employees and cannot be delegated to another person, e.g. a manager. The duty is owed by the employer to each employee as an individual, and this gives rise to two issues. First, each individual employee therefore has a potential right of action against the employer for breach of duty. Secondly, the duty owed will vary according to the individual nature of each employee. If an employee is particularly young or inexperienced, or he or she is disabled or has a learning difficulty, the standard of care required of the employer to fulfil his or her duty towards that particular employee may be higher than that required in relation to a 'normal' employee:

PARIS v. STEPNEY BOROUGH COUNCIL [1951] 1 All ER 42 (HL)	The plaintiff, Mr Paris, was employed by the defendant as a garage hand. His job involved general manual work in preparing vehicles for service, dismantling, etc. It was not customary to provide garage hands with goggles to wear in the course of their work. However, Mr Paris was blind in one eye.

In the course of his work he hit a bolt on the underside of a vehicle, causing a metal splinter to fly into his good eye, with the disastrous consequence that he became totally blind. Mr Paris alleged that his employer had breached the duty of care owed to him by failing to provide him with goggles.

Held: The defendants had breached their duty of care towards Mr Paris. Lord Simmonds opined:

> *I will say at once that I do not dissent from the view that an employer owes a particular duty to each of his employees. His liability in tort arises from his failure to take reasonable care in regard to the particular employee and it is clear that, if so, all the circumstances relevant to that employee must be taken into consideration.*

The fact that the duty is a personal one owed by the employer to each individual employee raises two further practical points. An employer who employs a person whom he or she knows to be illiterate will owe that person a higher duty. A mere written notice will not be sufficient to communicate safety procedures, etc.; the employer will have to take further steps. Similarly, where the employee does not have a good command of English, e.g. a non-English-speaking immigrant labourer, the duty owed to such an employee will be higher than that owed to other employees who have a full command of the English language. The only case in this area is *James* v. *Hepworth & Grandage Ltd* [1967] 2 All ER 829 (CA), where the employee was illiterate and unable to read the employer's notice. It was held, however, that the employer had done sufficient to bring the need for safety clothing to his attention. It is of vital importance that the person to whom the duty is owed is an employee of the defendant. If the plaintiff is not an employee no duty is owed and the defendant will have a complete answer to the plaintiff's claim. How one may ascertain whether an individual is the employee of another is a complex issue and is discussed in Chapter 9.

What is the extent of the employer's duty? The employer owes a duty to take such precautions for the safety of his or her employees as would be taken by a reasonably prudent employer in the same circumstances. Therefore, this is not an absolute duty; rather it is one tempered by reasonable foreseeability of injury to the employee. If, therefore, an employer does not know of the danger, and could not reasonably be expected to know of it in the light of current knowledge, or the employer did not foresee a potential hazard and could not reasonably be expected to foresee it, the employer will not be liable to the employee. However, if a danger is appreciated, the employer must take those steps which all reasonably prudent employers would take to protect the employee from the danger – see *Latimer* v. *AEC Ltd* [1953] 2 All ER 449 (HL). In *Smith* v. *Scott Bowyers Ltd* [1986] IRLR 315 (CA) an employer who had provided wellington boots to employees working in slippery conditions, and had explained to them why the wearing of the boots was necessary for their safety, was held not to be under an obligation to go further and instruct the employees that when the tread wore off the boots they should ask for new ones, or to inspect the boots that the employees were wearing to ascertain whether they ought to be replaced. Gibson LJ took the view that the employers would have been liable in negligence if, and only if, they had known, or ought to have known, that the plaintiff was exposing himself to a significant risk of slipping by failing to obtain new boots, and had failed to instruct him to do so.

The duty owed by an employer to employees is said to be threefold, though each element can be said to form part of a single more general duty to take reasonable care of the health and safety of the employee.

Johnstone v. *Bloomsbury Health Authority* [1991] 2 All ER 293 (CA) provides an important illustration of where an employer's interpretation, enforcement and application of the terms of an employee's contract of employment might be argued to be detrimental to the employee and form the basis of an action by the employee against his employer.

In that case the plaintiff was employed by the defendant health authority as a junior hospital doctor under a contract of employment which required him, by para. 4(b), to work 40 hours per week and to 'be available' for overtime of a further 48 hours per week on average. The plaintiff brought an action against the authority alleging breach of the authority's duty as his employer to take all reasonable care for his safety and well-being and seeking a declaration that the plaintiff could not lawfully be required by the defendant to work under his contract of employment for so many hours in excess of his standard working week as would foreseeably injure his health. The plaintiff alleged that he had been required to work intolerable hours with such deprivation of sleep that his health had been damaged and the safety of his patients put at risk, and that he suffered from stress and depression, had been physically sick from exhaustion and had felt suicidal. An application by the authority to strike out the main claim was granted by the master but an appeal against the striking out was allowed by the judge. An application by the authority to strike out the claims based on the 1977 Act and public policy was granted by another judge. The authority and the plaintiff appealed to the Court of Appeal.

It was held by a majority of the Court of Appeal that although the defendant health authority was entitled, under para. 4(b) of the contract of employment by which junior hospital doctors were employed, to require the plaintiff to work overtime of up to 48 hours average per week at its discretion, the health authority had to exercise that power in such a way as not to injure the plaintiff and accordingly it could not require the plaintiff to work so much overtime in any week that his health might reasonably foreseeably be damaged. It followed that if the pleaded facts were established the health authority would be in breach of duty. Accordingly, the main claim should not be struck out and the health authority's appeal would be dismissed.

The High Court has recognized the liability of an employer for inducing illness through stress at the workplace. In *Walker* v. *Northumberland County Council* [1994] NLJ 1659, it was held that where it is reasonably foreseeable to an employer that an employee might suffer a nervous breakdown because of the stress and pressures of his/her workload the employer is under a duty of care (as part of the duty to provide a safe system of work) not to cause the employee psychiatric damage through the volume or nature of the work which the employee is required to undertake.

This case may turn on its own particular facts. Mr Walker had previously suffered a period of stress induced illness caused by his workload as a manager in the social services team of his employer, he had been encouraged to return to work by promises that he would get more staff and support in order to be able to cope more effectively with his difficult case-load (child protection cases). The promises of additional support were not fulfilled and Mr Walker suffered a further breakdown and was subsequently dismissed by his employer on grounds of permanent ill-health. The fact that Mr Walker had previously been unwell made it foreseeable that his return to work without the additional support would cause him psychological harm.

This case is clearly about the provision of a safe system of work, and extends a principle long established with regard to physical harm to a new area, psychological injury. Where an employer takes on a member of staff knowing that he/she is vulnerable to stress, the employer may be liable to the employee in damages if the employee suffers injury as a consequence of that foreseeable risk. This is established principle of law is set out in *Paris* v. *Stepney Borough Council* [1951] 1 All ER 42 (above) with regard to physical injury, *Walker* now extends the principle to stress-related injury. The liability of the employer turns on the foreseeability of the risk of harm to the employee and the reasonableness of the steps which the employer takes to guard against the risk – see *Latimer* v. *AEC Ltd.* [1953] 2 All ER 449 (above).

Employers in the hotel and catering industry should be mindful of the risks of pressure on managers and supervisory staff who may find long hours and management responsibility too much for them. However, a claim will not succeed unless the employee can show psychological injury – not just fatigue or non-clinical depression – *and* that this was caused by his/her work and not by any other cause, for example matrimonial or financial difficulties outside the workplace.

Equipment. There is a duty to take reasonable care to provide employees with safe plant, machinery and tools with which to carry out their work. Therefore, the failure to provide any equipment, or the provision of inadequate or defective equipment, will constitute a breach of the employer's duty towards his or her employees. Hence, if a cook is burned in a hotel kitchen when a defective chip fryer malfunctions, the cook has a potential right of action against the proprietor of the hotel under this principle. However, if an employer purchases equipment from a reputable supplier, and has no knowledge of any defect in it, he or she will have done sufficient to discharge the duty owed to his or her employees – *Davie* v. *New Merton Board Mills Ltd* [1959] 1 All ER 346 (HL). Therefore, if, in the example cited above, the hotel proprietor purchased the chip fryer from a supplier of quality catering equipment and the proprietor has been given no reason to suspect that the fryer is in any way defective, then he or she will have done sufficient to discharge the duty of care which he or she owes to the cook. The employee does, however, have a remedy against the employer by virtue of the Employers' Liability (Defective Equipment) Act 1969, which reverses *Davie* v. *New Merton Board Mills*. Section 1(1) of this Act states:

> *Where ... (a) an employee suffers personal injury in the course of his employment in consequence of a defect in equipment provided by his employer for the purposes of the employer's business; and (b) the defect is attributable wholly or partly to the fault of a third party (whether identified or not), the injury shall be deemed to be also*

attributable to negligence on the part of the employer (whether or not he is liable in respect of the injury apart from this subsection), but without prejudice to the law relating to contributory negligence and to any remedy by way of contribution or in contract or otherwise which is available to the employer in respect of the injury.

Therefore, in circumstances such as the example given above, the injured employee would sue the employer for his or her 'deemed' negligence, and the employer would attempt to recover the amount of damages he or she has paid out to the employee from the third party who was truly at fault.

System of work. There is a duty to take reasonable care to provide a safe system of work for each employee. The employer is responsible for the layout of the workplace, the training and supervision of staff and the methods of working adopted. The employer's responsibilities also cover the provision of protective clothing and instructions for their use where necessary. Whether by taking the precautions which the particular employer has taken, he or she has established a safe system of work is a question of fact in each case. How much must be done by the employer to establish a safe system of work will depend on the risk of injury involved and the likely gravity of the injury which may be sustained.

Staff. An employer is under a duty to provide a reasonably competent staff with whom the employee will be required to work. If an employer engages an incompetent employee whose actions thereafter cause an injury to another employee, the employer will be liable to the injured employee for failing to take reasonable care in the selection of the employee's colleagues. In *Hudson* v. *Ridge Manufacturing Co. Ltd* [1957] 2 All ER 229 the employer was held liable where a fellow employee injured the plaintiff whilst carrying out a practical joke. In such circumstances, and after due warning, the employer should dispense with the services of a practical joker who proved to be a menace to himself or herself and to others, in order to prevent injury being caused to others. The employer should, therefore, at the time of appointing staff, be mindful as to whether the employee's lack of experience, personality, etc. will expose other employees to danger and create a risk of injury. Hence, the employer should always ensure that where inexperienced staff are allocated work which could give rise to danger, either to the employee or to others, the employee is given proper training and is adequately supervised. An employer will therefore be liable for the acts of an employee which are done in the course of his or her employment and which cause injury to another employee.

Limitations on the employer's liability

A primary limitation on the liability of an employer towards his or her employees is that the employer is required to do only that which is 'reasonably practicable' to ensure the safety of the employee. This principle can be most clearly seen in the case of *Latimer* v. *AEC Ltd* [1953] 2 All ER 449 (HL). In that case the employers had done all that was practicable, save to shut down the premises and exclude the workforce. The House of Lords held that the employers were not liable for the plaintiff's injuries. Just what is required of an employer to satisfy the standard of care is a question of degree, to be decided according to the facts of each particular case. Hence, employers may deny negligence on their part simply by establishing that they took those steps which a reasonably prudent employer would take in the circumstances, e.g. *Brown* v. *Rolls-Royce Ltd* [1960] 1 WLR 210 (HL). Equally, employers may argue that the actions which they took were not the cause of the employee's injury, and therefore they are not liable. If the employee has contributed by his or her actions to the injuries which he or she has sustained, the employer may have a defence of contributory negligence based on the Law Reform (Contributory Negligence) Act 1945. If the employee is the sole cause of his or her own injuries, the employer will have a complete defence to the employee's action under the principle of *volenti non fit injuria*. However, this may be extremely difficult to establish.

The employee will be required in each case to prove that the injury was due to the negligence of the employer. In other words, employees must establish first that the employer owed them a duty of care, secondly that the employer acted in breach of that duty, and thirdly that as a result of that negligence they suffered injury. There are a number of rules of evidence which help employees to prove their cases. For instance, to ensure that the full facts are available to the employees so that they can more easily establish their cases, the court may order the disclosure of documents in the employer's possession or an inspection of the premises. A most useful rule of evidence to the employee in establishing his or her case is *res ipsa loquitur* (see above).

Many employers, conscious of the responsibilities laid on them by by s.2 of the Health and Safety at Work Act 1974, now conduct regular health and safety inspections, the results of which and any subsequent actions taken by the employer, might be used in evidence.

Vicarious liability

An employer may be vicariously liable for actions of employee X, done in the course of his or her employment, which cause injury to employee Y. Employee Y therefore has a course of action against both X and their employer for the injury which he or she has sustained.

Two interesting points arise from the case law. First, there is the employer's responsibility, if any, for the actions of an employee who carries out practical jokes on other employees, resulting in injury. In *Harrison* v. *Michelin Tyre Co. Ltd* [1985] 1 All ER 981 the plaintiff sued his employers on the basis that the prankster had been acting in the course of his employment. The employers unsuccessfully denied that they were vicariously liable, contending that the prankster had embarked on a 'frolic of his own'. It was held that the test for determining whether an employee was acting in the course of his employment was to ask whether a reasonable man would say that the incident was part and parcel of the employment in the sense of being incidental to it, albeit unauthorized or prohibited (in which case the employer is liable) or whether it was so divergent from the employment as to be alien to and wholly distinguishable from it (in which case the employer is not liable). Secondly, there is the type of loss for which an employer can be vicariously liable. In *Attia* v. *British Gas PLC* [1987] 3 All ER 455 (CA), the defendant employers were found to be vicariously liable for the actions of one of their service engineers who, when installing a central heating system, created an explosion which caused not only substantial physical damage to the plaintiff's property but also nervous shock. The novelty in the case lies in the nervous shock aspect; here damages were for the first time recoverable for nervous shock relating to damage to property. For present purposes, this case adds a further potential head of damage for which an employer may be vicariously liable.

Statutory duties

Parliament may lay down various duties for a person to perform, e.g. in the Factories Act 1961. The sanction for failure to perform such a duty will usually be in the form of prosecution and thereafter punishment in the criminal courts. A further question arises regarding the breach of such duties; can a person who has sustained injury due to the failure of another to perform the statutory duty imposed upon them bring a civil action for damages based on the other's failure to fulfil the statutory duty? In many cases the answer is yes. The English civil courts recognize a tort of breach of statutory duty. However, there is no automatic presumption that a breach of statutory duty will give rise to an actionable tort. To determine whether a civil claim for damages exists one must examine the statute, what the purposes and objects of the statute are, and whether Parliament intends that the statute should lead to civil liability. This may be done only through careful interpretation of the words of the statute.

Not every breach of statutory duty is actionable in damages – *Cutler* v. *Wandsworth Stadium Ltd* [1949] 1 All ER 544 (HL). An example of how the law operates may be gleaned by considering the statutory duties imposed in relation to the provision of adequate and suitable accommodation for employee's clothing not worn during working hours. This duty is provided for by s. 59 of the Factories Act 1961 and this provision is mirrored by s. 12 of the Offices, Shops and Railway Premises Act 1963. In relation to s. 59 FA 1961, in *McCarthy* v. *Daily Mirror* [1949] 1 All ER 801 (CA) it was held that this could give rise to a civil action on the part of the employee where the employer's failure to fulfil this duty had led to loss of or damage to the employee's clothing.

Section 58 FA 1961 imposes a duty upon employers to provide adequate and suitable facilities for washing (i.e. hot and cold water, soap, towels), and these facilities should be conveniently accessible to employees and be maintained in a clean and orderly manner. It would appear that this duty cannot be enforced *per se* by an employee. An employee will have no civil action against his or her employers simply because they have failed to provide adequate washing facilities. The purpose of the provision is to enforce a standard by means of criminal sanction. However, it would appear that if an employee were to contract dermatitis or some other skin disorder owing to the failure of the employer to provide adequate washing facilities this would be actionable as a civil claim for damages on the part of the employee – *Reid* v. *Westfield Paper Co. Ltd* [1957] SC 218.

It may be said that some of the duties imposed by the Offices, Shops and Railway Premises Act 1963 (see p. 351) give rise to both criminal proceedings to enforce the duty and civil liability in damages to the injured party.

As far as the Health and Safety at Work etc. Act 1974 (see pp. 359ff) is concerned, s. 47 provides that no civil action may be brought in respect of a breach of the general duties and obligations imposed by ss. 2–8 of the Act. However, a breach of health and safety regulations made under the Act shall be actionable in a civil court. We can say, therefore, that the scope of civil liability under the HSWA 1974 is very limited indeed. The statute's primary purpose was to impose and enforce standards of health and safety backed by criminal sanction, not to provide civil remedies for injured or aggrieved employees.

What must a person show in order successfully to establish a civil claim for breach of statutory duty?

1   A person must show that he or she is within the class of persons for whose benefit the duty was imposed. This will depend entirely on the wording of the provision in question.

2   The injury sustained by the person bringing the action must be of such a kind as the statute was designed to prevent.
3   The defendant must be in breach of his or her statutory duty.
The defendant's breach of duty caused the injury sustained by the plaintiff – *McWilliams* v. *Sir William Arrol & Co. Ltd* [1962] 1 All ER 623 (HL).

The Occupiers' Liability Acts 1957, 1984

An employer is an occupier of premises, i.e. the workplace, since it is the employer who has occupational control. Therefore, an employee is owed a duty of care by his or her employer under s. 2(1) of the Occupiers' Liability Act 1957 (OLA 1957). An employee is a lawful visitor whilst he or she is fulfilling the purpose for which they are invited to the premises, namely work. However, if, for example, employees go to a part of the premises they are forbidden to enter, they step outside the purpose for which they were invited to the premises and the employer would not be liable for any injury the employees might thereafter sustain – see *Hillen & Pettigrew* v. *ICI (Alkali) Ltd* [1936] AC 69 (HL). If employees do something which is outside the purpose for which they are invited to the premises they thereafter are trespassers to the premises and are owed a lower duty, the 'duty of common humanity' – *BRB* v. *Herrington* [1972] 1 All ER 749 (HL). It should also be noted that as an occupier an employer owes a duty of care under s. 2(1) OLA 1957 not merely to his or her employees but to all lawful visitors. However, the duty owed to employees may vary because of s. 2(3)b:

> *an occupier may expect that a person, in the exercise of his calling, will appreciate and guard against any special risks ordinarily incident to it, so far as the occupier leaves him free to do so.*

Under the 1984 Act a duty of care is owed even to persons who are not lawful visitors to the premises such as visitors invited onto the premises by staff against the employer's rules (e.g. boyfriends or girlfriends invited against an employer's express instructions into the rooms of living-in staff).

Occupiers cannot exempt themselves from liability for death or personal injury caused to visitors to their premises – s. 2(1) of the Unfair Contract Terms Act 1977. Further discussion of occupiers' liability is to be found in section 3.2.

Fatal accidents

Where employees are killed in the course of their employment an action may be commenced by their personal representatives (e.g. the executors of the deceased's will) for the benefit of the deceased's estate under the Law Reform (Miscellaneous Provisions) Act 1934. Damages may be awarded for the pain and suffering caused to the deceased up to the time of death, the deceased's loss of earnings up to the time of death, and medical and hospital expenses incurred. Another form of action, one which is usually brought at the same time as the above, arises from the Fatal Accidents Act 1976:

> *If death is caused by any wrongful act, neglect or default which is such as would (if death had not ensued) have entitled the person injured to maintain an action and recover damages in respect thereof, the person who would have been liable if death*

had not ensued shall be liable to an action for damages notwithstanding the death of the person injured.

This form of action rests upon the loss to the deceased's dependants, e.g. his wife and children. The wife and children of the deceased have lost his financial support (e.g. *inter alia* wage-earning capacity) and may therefore claim damages in compensation for this loss. How much they will receive in damages is speculative; the general principle is that damages are awarded in proportion to the injury resulting from the death of the deceased to the parties respectively for whom and for whose benefit the action is brought.

State benefit schemes

An employee may make a claim for injuries sustained at work under the provisions of the Social Security Act 1975 (SSA 1975). Such a claim is wholly independent of any other actions which the employee may have, either at common law or under statute. Furthermore, proof of fault on the part of the employer is not required. The purpose of the scheme is to provide compensation for those employees who suffer personal injury caused by an accident occurring in the course of their employment – s. 50 of the Social Security Act 1975. In order to claim benefit the claimant must establish:
(a) that he or she has sustained personal injury;
(b) that the injury was caused by an accident; and
(c) that the accident arose from, and during the course of, his or her employment.

From 1948 until 1982, provision was made in the industrial scheme both for short-term incapacity for work (injury benefit payable for a maximum of six months) and for residual disability (disablement benefit payable when entitlement to injury benefit had expired). Injury benefit was abolished in 1982 (Social Security Housing and Benefit Act 1982), with short-term illness falling within the provisions of sickness benefit. Entitlement to disablement benefit is covered by s. 57 SSA 1975: the claimant must show that he or she 'suffers as a result of the relevant accident from loss of physical or mental faculty'. In addition, benefit is available in respect of industrial disease (s. 76 SSA 1975).

Health and safety

Health and safety in most hospitality premises is covered by the Health and Safety at Work Act 1974 and regulations made under that Act. The Office Shops and Railway Premises Act 1963 (OSRPA 1963) was repealed by the Workplace (Health and Safety and Welfare) Regulations 1992 but many of the old provisions of the OSRPA 1963 were re-enacted until the end of 1996, as schedule 1 to the Health and Safety at Work Act. From January 1997 many of the old OSRPA 1963 provisions are to be contained in regulations made under the Health and Safety at Work Act 1974.

10.2 THE HEALTH AND SAFETY AT WORK ETC. ACT 1974

The Health and Safety at Work etc. Act 1974 (HSWA) was designed as a compre-hensive and integrated legislative framework to ensure the health and safety of those at work. Prior to the HSWA the protection afforded to employees in relation to health and safety had grown in a haphazard and piecemeal fashion. The bulk of the common law concerned compensation for injuries which had already been sustained, whilst various Acts and Regulations provided some preventive powers to enforce health and safety standards at work, e.g. OSRPA 1963. However, in the main the preventive measures were industry-based, e.g. Factories Act 1961. The catering industry was partly covered by OSRPA 1963. A purpose of the HSWA was to consolidate the existing safety provisions in various Acts and provide comprehensive standards applicable to all. This approach required that a number of administrative bodies be established to enable the Act to function properly.

The institutions of health and safety

The HSWA establishes the Health and Safety Commission and the Health and Safety Executive.

Health and Safety Commission

This body was established by s. 10 HSWA. The primary responsibility of the Health and Safety Commission is to administer the law and practice of health and safety at work. The Health and Safety Commission is under a general duty to do such things and make the necessary arrangements to fulfil the general purposes laid down by s. 1(1), which include:

(a) securing the health, safety and welfare of people at work;
(b) protecting people other than those at work against risks to health and safety arising out of or in connection with the activities of people at work.

The specific duties of the Health and Safety Commission are set out in s. 11(2) HSWA, and the powers of the Commission are laid down in s. 13 of the Act. If an accident occurs (or some other occurrence or situation is brought to their attention) the Health and Safety Commission have power under s. 14 HSWA, where they consider it would be expedient to do so, to order an investigation or an inquiry. An inquiry is a formal public investigation, and will usually relate to some matter of public importance, whereas an investigation is a more informal process.

Health and Safety Executive

The Health and Safety Executive was also established by s. 10 HSWA. The Executive comprises a director and two other members (all three appointed by the Health and Safety Commission). The Health and Safety Executive controls the various branches of the Inspectorate whose job it is to enforce the Act and Regulations made thereunder. It is the duty of the Health and Safety Executive to exercise those powers of the Health and Safety Commission which have been delegated by the Commission to the Executive. However, the enforcement of the Act in any particular case is a matter for the Health and Safety Executive alone. It is the decision of the Health and Safety Executive as to how the various statutory provisions are to be applied in individual cases. We can see, therefore, a clear division of labour between these bodies. The Commission is the policy-making organ, whilst the Executive is the enforcement agency, putting the legislation into effect.

Enforcement

The whole tenor of the HSWA is preventive rather than curative. The Act seeks to enforce standards of safety whereby injury shall be prevented, rather than providing recompense after an accident has occurred. However, the Act also has a curative aspect. Where there is danger to health and safety the Act gives powers to require the prohibition of a dangerous practice, etc., to prevent an accident occurring.

Since the Act is primarily a preventive measure, the first approach to enforcement is through the giving of advice and assistance to any employer or other person who is seeking to meet the standards of safety required by the Act. By advice and persuasion the Inspectorate facilitates the observance of the standards of safety required and avoids, to a large extent, the ultimate deterrent of prosecution and punishment. The purpose of the Act is to enforce standards, not to create further classes of criminals.

The enforcement of the Act is by means of an Inspectorate. Section 18 HSWA sets out the various responsibilities of the enforcing authorities and s. 19 provides for the appointment of inspectors. The powers of an inspector are wide-ranging and are set out by s. 20 HSWA. They include *inter alia* the power: (a) of entry to premises at any reasonable time; (b) to make such examination and investigation of the premises as may be required; (c) to question any person who the inspector reasonably believes has such information as may assist the investigation; (d) to require the inspection of documents and machinery. Further powers as to the obtaining of information are provided by s. 27 HSWA.

Actual day-to-day enforcement is shared between the Health and Safety Executive and the local authorities' Environmental Health Departments. For example, educational establishments fall within the scope of the Health and Safety Executive whilst most commercial catering establishments and hotels come within the scope of the environmental health offices of the local authority.

Where after an inspection a breach of the Act or any of the health and safety regulations has been discovered then the matter may be dealt with in either of two ways. First, the inspector may issue an enforcement notice or, where appropriate, seize and destroy the offending equipment. Secondly, a prosecution may be commenced.

Enforcement notices

These are of two kinds: an improvement notice and a prohibition notice. Enforcement notices may be issued by Health and Safety Executive inspectors and environmental health officers, *inter alia*. Improvement notices are provided for by s. 21 HSWA:

> *If an inspector is of the opinion that a person –*
> *(a) is contravening one or more of the relevant statutory provisions; or*
> *(b) has contravened one or more of those provisions in circumstances that make it likely that the contravention will continue to be repeated, he may serve on him a notice ('an improvement notice') stating that he is of that opinion, specifying the provision or provisions as to which he is of that opinion, giving particulars of the reasons why he is of that opinion, and requiring that person to remedy the contravention, as the case may be, the matters occasioning it within such period . . . as may be specified in the notice.*

The notice will not specify a period of less than 21 days, which is the time limit for an appeal to be lodged against the notice. The effect of the improvement notice may be summarized thus: if the Act or regulation requires the doing (or halting) of a certain thing, an inspector, by serving an improvement notice, is requiring that the thing be done (or halted) after the period stated in the notice has passed. However, the fact that a period of grace is permitted does not absolve the person upon whom the notice is served from any criminal (or civil) liability in respect of an occurrence prior to the notice taking effect. Normal practice is for the inspector, pursuant to s. 24 HSWA, to attach to the notice a schedule setting out the steps to be taken by the person to whom the notice is directed to remedy the breach of the statute or regulation.

Prohibition notices are provided for by s. 22 HSWA. Where an inspector is of the opinion that activities are being carried on (or are about to commence) to which the provisions of the HSWA apply (or any regulation made thereunder), which involve, or will involve, a risk of serious personal injury, he or she may serve a prohibition notice. A prohibition notice will state that the inspector is of the opinion that the matter specified in the notice is giving rise, or will give rise, to the risk of serious personal injury. If the matter also involves a contravention of a relevant statutory provision the notice will state the provision and give particulars of the reason why the inspector is of the opinion that the statute has been breached. The notice will direct that the activities to which the notice relates shall not be carried on by or under the control of the person on whom the notice has been served unless the matters specified in the notice (and any associated contraventions of the statute) have been remedied.

Where the inspector takes the view that the risk of serious personal injury is imminent, the prohibition notice will take immediate effect. If it is not imminent the notice will take effect at the end of the period specified in the notice. Such a notice is known as a deferred prohibition notice.

An inspector, before issuing a prohibition notice, need only be satisfied that the activities concerned give risk to a risk of serious personal injury; there need not be any breach of a statutory provision.

A person upon whom an improvement or prohibition notice has been served may appeal to an industrial tribunal within 21 days of receipt. The tribunals may either confirm or cancel the notice. Where such a notice is confirmed, this may be on its original terms, or with such modifications as the industrial tribunal see fit to make. Section 24 HSWA provides for the appeal, and the Industrial Tribunals (Improvement and Prohibition Notices Appeals) Regulations 1974 lay down the procedure to be followed.

Criminal prosecutions

Criminal proceedings brought by the enforcing authority, against a person in breach of the HSWA or Regulations made thereafter are a weapon of last resort. Where the Inspectorate decide to prosecute this normally reflects a past history of non-compliance on the part of the person prosecuted, and a blatant failure of the methods of persuasion. Persistent non-compliance and the gravity of the incident (where one has occurred), as well as public interest, point towards the commencement of a criminal prosecution. The prosecutor is an inspector of the Health and Safety Executive, or, in more serious cases, the office of the Director of Public Prosecutions. Only these two bodies may commence such prosecutions. The proceedings may be brought summarily before the Magistrates' Court or upon an indictment in the Crown Court.

The duties imposed by the HSWA 1974

The duties imposed by the Health and Safety at Work etc. Act 1974 are of two sorts: general duties and specific duties. General duties are imposed by s. 2(1) and s. 7 of the Act. Section 2(1) states:

> *It shall be the duty of every employer to ensure so far as is reasonably practicable, the health, safety and welfare at work of all his employees.*

This is the basic duty outlined by the Act: further duties imposed by s. 2(2) merely illustrate and particularize this general duty. It should be noted that the duty is tempered by the fact that the employer is bound to do only that which is 'reasonably practicable' to ensure the health, safety and welfare of employees. It is not, therefore, an absolute duty. What may amount to the employer having done all that is reasonably practicable is a question of fact in each case. The duty owed by an employer to his or her employees under s. 2(1) is owed only while such employees are acting in the course of their employment. Whilst the section specifically refers to the 'health, safety and welfare' of employees, the Act does not define the meaning to be attributed to these terms. Health can be said to refer to both the physical and mental health of the employees. Safety would seem to refer to the absence of any foreseeable injury. Welfare is a somewhat more wide-ranging term, but could be said to include those matters which relate to the personal comfort of the employee at the workplace, e.g. toilets, washing facilities, the provision of a rest room and refreshment facilities.

Section 7 HSWA imposes certain general duties upon the employee rather than upon the employer:

> *It shall be the duty of every employee while at work –*
> *(a) to take reasonable care for the health and safety of himself and of other persons who may be affected by his acts or omissions at work; and*
> *(b) as regards any duty or requirement imposed on his employer or any other person by or under any of the relevant statutory provisions, to co-operate with him so far as is necessary to enable that duty of requirement to be performed or complied with.*

Certain specific duties are imposed by s. 2(2) following from the general duty contained in s. 2(1) (as outlined above):

> *Without prejudice to the generality of an employer's duty under the preceding sub-section, the matters to which that duty extends include in particular –*
> *(a) the provision and maintenance of plant and systems of work that are, so far as is reasonably practicable, safe and without risks to health;*
> *(b) arrangements for ensuring, so far as is reasonably practicable, safety and absence of risks to health in connection with the use, handling, storage and transport of articles and substances;*
> *(c) the provision of such information, instruction, training and supervision as is*

> *necessary to ensure, so far as is reasonably practicable, the health and safety at work of his employees;*
>
> (d) *so far as is reasonably practicable as regards any place of work under the employer's control, the maintenance of it in a condition that is safe and without risks to health and the provision and maintenance of means of access and egress from it that are safe and without such risks;*
>
> (e) *the provision and maintenance of a working environment for his employees that is, so far as is reasonably practicable, safe, without risks to health and adequate as regards facilities and arrangements for their welfare at work.*

These duties appear to be relatively clear in themselves and require little explanation, though the importance of s. 2(2)(c) cannot be overemphasized. Proper and clear instructions must be given by the employer as to what must be done and what is forbidden. Workers who do routine jobs frequently take little care of their own and others' safety. The monotony of the tasks which they perform may make them careless. The employer must therefore give clear instructions and training to his or her staff as to safety at work. Furthermore, greater care should be taken to ensure that employees who speak and understand little of the English language (and those of limited intelligence) understand and appreciate the rules as to safety at work. Equally, young and inexperienced staff may require further training as to safety.

Safety policies

An employer is required by s. 2(3) HSWA to provide a statement of the employer's policy on health and safety at work:

> *Except in such cases as may be prescribed it shall be the duty of every employer to prepare and as often as may be appropriate revise a written statement of his general policy with respect to the health and safety at work of his employees and the organisation and arrangements for the time being in force for carrying out that policy, and to bring the statement and any revision of it to the notice of all his employees.*

A safety policy statement will, where properly drafted, include:
(a) a general statement as to the commitment of the employer to fulfil standards of safety, etc., at least as high as those required by statute;
(b) the organization and distribution of responsibility within the organization for health and safety;
(c) the arrangements presently in force to ensure compliance with the required standards of health and safety at work;
(d) the maintaining and review of safety policy.
The policy document should be signed by the senior member of the business, so that all employees will recognize the authority and importance of the document. Furthermore, this shows a continuing commitment throughout the organization to the health and safety policy.

General duties owed to people other than employees (s. 3 HSWA) and duties owed by an employer as the controller of premises have been considered in Chapter 3.

A problem sometimes encountered where the workplace is open to the public, or where large numbers of people do not use it as a workplace (e.g. a hotel, works canteen or cinema), is the misuse and interference with equipment provided to ensure health and safety. Instances are the removal of first-aid equipment and the removal of fire extinguishers, etc. Section 8 HSWA creates a criminal offence which deals with this problem:

> *No person shall intentionally or recklessly interfere with or misuse anything provided in the interests of health, safety or welfare in pursuance of any of the relevant statutory provisions.*

Safety representatives

An important innovation brought about by the HSWA is the safety representative. Section 2(4) HSWA empowered the Secretary of State to make regulations for the appointment by recognized trade unions of safety representatives from among the employees. The functions of the safety representative are set out in the regulations and include consultation with the employer on matters of health and safety at work. An employer is under a duty to consult safety representatives. Section 2(6) states:

> *It shall be the duty of every employer to consult any such representatives with a view to the making and maintenance of arrangements which will enable him and his employees to co-operate effectively in promoting and developing measures to ensure the health and safety at work of the employees, and in checking the effectiveness of measures.*

The relevant regulations made under s. 2(4) are the Safety Representative and Safety Committee Regulations 1977 together with an Approved Code of Practice.

A safety representative may be appointed by an independent trade union which is recognized by the employer for the purposes of collective bargaining. It has been argued that the right to appoint safety representatives should be afforded to bodies other than recognized trade unions. It is said that the present approach perpetuates an employer versus trade union forum in an area where this traditional void is inappropriate. Furthermore, in non-unionized areas of employment the statutory requirements as to safety representatives need not be observed. A duly appointed safety representative has the right to be consulted by the employer pursuant to s. 2(6) above. The 1977 Regulations lay down certain other functions of safety representatives. By Regulation 4 their function is:

(a) to investigate potential hazards and dangerous occurrences at the workplace, and to examine the causes of accidents at the workplace;
(b) to investigate complaints made by an employee whom they represent as to health, safety or welfare at work;
(c) to make representations to the employer regarding employee complaints (as in (b) above) of health, safety and welfare at work;
(d) to make representations to the employer on general matters affecting the health, safety and welfare at work of the employees at the workplace;
(e) to carry out inspections of the workplace and of documents;

(f) to represent employees in consultations at the workplace with Health and Safety Executive inspectors (or any other enforcing authority, e.g. environmental health officers);

(g) to receive information from inspectors;

(h) to attend meetings of the safety committee, as a representative in the discharge of the above functions.

A safety representative is entitled to time off work to perform his or her functions as a representative, and to receive the requisite training to fulfil his or her functions as a safety representative in accordance with the provisions of the Approved Code of Practice.

Safety committees

By Regulation 9 the employer must establish a safety committee if requested to do so by two safety representatives in writing. Section 2(7) HSWA lays down the functions of the safety committee as keeping under review the measures taken to ensure the health and safety at work of employees, and such other functions as may be prescribed. The safety committee, as constituted in accordance with the regulations, should meet on a regular basis, according to necessity and the volume of matters with which it is empowered to deal.

What if an employer does not comply with the regulations as to safety representatives and the safety committee? A safety representative may present a complaint to an industrial tribunal on the following grounds: (a) the employer has failed to permit the representative to take time off for the purpose of performing his or her functions as a safety representative, or to permit him or her to go on a training course; or (b) an employer has failed to pay him or her for his or her time off. The enforcement of the other duties arising from the Act and the Regulations is the responsibility of the appropriate enforcing authority, e.g. Health and Safety Executive Inspectorate. A failure on the part of an employer to comply with the duties imposed by ss. 2(4) and 2(7) amounts to a criminal offence.

Health and Safety Information for Employees Regulations 1989 (SI 1988/682)

These Regulations made by the Department of Employment under the Health and Safety at Work etc. Act 1974 came into force on 18 October 1989.

They apply to all employees except:

(a) the Master and crew of a sea-going ship;

(b) where the Health and Safety Executive have granted a written exemption.

An employer must do one of two things to comply with the Regulations:

(a) Display and keep displayed in a readable condition at a reasonably accessible (to employees) place at work and in such a position it can easily be seen and read, a poster provided by the Health and Safety Executive; or

(b) Give each employee a leaflet provided by the Health and Safety Executive and, in the case of new employees after 18 October 1989, give out the leaflet as soon as reasonably practicable after they commence employment.

With the poster or leaflet the employer is required to give information as to the whereabouts of certain public bodies involved in enforcing or advising on health and safety at work.

The Regulations permit the Health and Safety Executive to amend the poster or leaflet from time to time and, consequently, require employers to notify employees as to such amendments.

Where an employee works in more than one location he is treated as working at the premises from which his or her work is administered.

It is an offence under the Health and Safety at Work etc. Act 1974 for an employer to contravene the Regulations unless it can be proved that the employer took all reasonable precautions and exercised all due diligence to avoid committing an offence. In practice this defence will rarely be available.

Health and Safety at Work Regulations

Most workplaces are covered by these regulations. The regulations place responsibilities on employers for their employees and others who may be affected by the work. The regulations include the self-employed. They implement six EC directives on health and safety at work. They cover:

- Health and Safety (General Provisions) Regulations; this includes the assessment of risk and the management of health and safety measures
- Provision and use of Work Equipment Regulations; this consolidates piecemeal legislation placing general duties on employers
- Manual Handling Operations Regulations; this mainly replaces out-of-date law, with a modern, ergonomically based approach
- Workplace (Health, Safety and Welfare) Regulations; this covers workplace conditions such as lighting, ventilation, suitability of seating, at the same time replacing old law such as parts of the Factories Act and the Offices, Shops and Railway Premises Act.
- Personal Protective Equipment at Work Regulations; these lay down the principles for the proper selection of personal protective equipment such as safety footwear
- Health and Safety (Display Screen Equipment) Regulations; these regulations make employers responsible for assessing and reducing risks associated with display screen equipment.

Most of the duties are not new – tending to reinforce earlier health and safety legislation. The emphasis is on effective health and safety management, placing the responsibility on employers to assess risk and to install appropriate safety measures.

10.3 ACCIDENTS AND DANGEROUS OCCURRENCES

There is a requirement to report and notify accidents and dangerous occurrences, following the Reporting of Injuries, Diseases and Dangerous Occurrences Regulations 1985. This applies to all work activities covered by the HSWA 1974. The Regulations deal with four types of incidents: (a) fatal accidents; (b) major injuries; (c) dangerous occurrences; and (d) other accidents. Only (a), (b) and (c) are reportable to the enforcing authority.

Fatal accidents. A fatal accident must be reported when it arises out of or in connection with any work activity, even though the victim was not an employee. Hence if a guest or visitor to a hotel were killed by an accident at the hotel, e.g. a fire or an explosion in the kitchens, this would have to be reported so as to comply with the order.

Major injury. The kind of injuries meant here are fractures to the skull, spinal injuries, loss of limb, etc. This kind of accident must be reported.

Dangerous occurrences. Certain dangerous occurrences must be reported irrespective of injury. Part I of the order lays down those occurrences within this category; they include, *inter alia*, explosion and electrical short circuit which causes fire or explosion.

The employer must report the accident or dangerous occurrence by the quickest possible means to the appropriate authority. In the case of offices and shops, etc. this is the local authority; all other buildings report to the Factory Inspector. Records of all notifiable accidents and dangerous occurrences must be kept by every employer. Schedule III to the order sets out the nature of the record to be kept:

(a) date of accident or dangerous occurrence;
(b) particulars of the person injured, i.e. name, age, sex, occupation and nature of the injuries sustained;
(c) place where the accident or dangerous occurrence happened;
(d) a brief description of the surrounding circcmstances.

The Reporting of Injuries, Diseases and Dangerous Occurrences Regulations 1985 (RIDDOR)

The Regulations impose duties upon those responsible for the activities of people at work and on self-employed people to report accidents resulting in death or major injury arising out of or in connection with work, and to report specified dangerous occurrences.

Additionally the Regulations require certain particulars of accidents at work reported to the DHSS to be sent to the Health and Safety Executive, and require records to be kept.

10.4 PEOPLE AT SPECIAL RISK

The catering industry employs a considerable number of women, as well as a large number of immigrant workers, or workers whose first language is not English. Both groups present additional responsibilities to the employer.

Pregnant women

Since a pregnant woman is carrying a child, regard should be given to the health and safety of the mother and to that of the foetus. If, for instance, an employer requires the pregnant woman to do such work as might injure the foetus, and the foetus is injured, yet thereafter born alive, the employer may be civilly liable to the child for the injuries sustained in the womb. Section 1(1) of The Congenital Disabilities (Civil Liability) Act 1976 states:

If a child is born disabled as the result of such an occurrence before its birth as is in s. 1(2) below, and a person (other than the child's own mother) is under this section answerable to the child in respect of the occurrence, the child's disabilities are to be regarded as damage resulting from the wrongful act of that person and actionable accordingly at the suit of the child.

By s. 1(2):

An occurrence to which this section applies is one which –
(a) affected either parent of the child in his or her ability to have a normal, healthy child; or
(b) affected the mother during her pregnancy, or affected her or the child in the course of its birth, so that the child is born with disabilities which would not otherwise have been present.

Section 1(3) states:

Subject to the following subsections, a person . . . is answerable to the child if he was liable in tort to the parent or would, if sued in due time, have been so; and it is no answer that there could not have been such liability because the parent suffered no actionable injury, if there was a breach of legal duty which, accompanied by injury, would have given rise to the liability.

Hence, an employer is a potential defendant to an action brought under the 1976 Act where it can be shown that by requiring the woman to undertake certain work, injury was caused to the child in the womb. What must be proven is a breach of duty owed to the pregnant woman (e.g. a breach of a statutory duty owed under the OSRPA 1963), yet it is not necessary that the pregnant woman is herself injured.

Where a pregnant woman is employed she has a right not to be dismissed because of the pregnancy – see s. 60 EPCA 1978. The proper course of action for an employer regarding pregnant women on his or her staff whose work is heavy and may potentially cause injury to her or the foetus during the pregnancy (e.g. room-maids) is to offer the pregnant woman suitable alternative employment within the catering establishment which does not expose her or her child to a health risk.

Immigrant workers

Workers whose command of English, and in particular their ability to read English, is very low are at special risk in the workplace. Safety notices and instructions are usually written; therefore special measures must be taken to explain such notices and instructions to these employees. Furthermore, where workers have a limited understanding of English, they may put at risk other workers who work with them. In *Hawkins* v. *Ian Ross (Castings) Ltd* [1970] 1 All ER 180 an employee was injured in part because he was working with an immigrant whose understanding of English was very limited and who misunderstood a shouted warning. The view taken by the court was that in such circumstances the employer owed a higher standard of care to the employees. In other words, following the principle decided by the House of Lords in *Paris* v. *Stepney Borough Council* [1951] 1 All ER 42, a higher duty of care is owed to those who are at special risk.

The fact that there may be a language barrier is not a sound reason to exclude immigrants from employment; rather it is a clear rationale for imposing a stricter duty to care for their safety at work and the safety of others who might be affected by their actions.

10.5 INSURANCE AGAINST INJURIES

The Employers' Liability (Compulsory Insurance) Act 1969 sought to ensure that all employers have valid insurance cover to meet personal injuries claims from their employees. A certificate to this effect must be displayed at the employer's premises.

An employer must take out and maintain, pursuant to the 1969 Act, an insurance policy against liability for bodily injury and disease sustained by employees, and arising out of and in the course of their employment. The policy must provide cover of at least £2 million arising out of any one occurrence. This Act applies to every employer carrying on a trade or business. Hotels, inns and restaurants are all clearly covered by the Act. The insurance covers liability towards employees only. Therefore, independent contractors who are injured at a place of work are not covered; e.g. a cabaret artiste who falls from the ballroom stage is not a person insured under the Act. Any employer who is not insured in accordance with the Act is guilty of a criminal offence, to a maximum penalty of £500 for each day in default.

The mere fact that the employer has a valid policy pursuant to the 1969 Act does not confer an automatic right to compensation for an employee who has sustained injury. The insurance merely provides the compensation monies if the employer is found liable for the injuries caused to the employee. All the Act does is ensure that if an employee succeeds in a civil claim for damages for personal injury against his or her employer, funds will be available to be paid in compensation to the employee.

10.6 CONTROL OF SUBSTANCES HAZARDOUS TO HEALTH REGULATIONS 1988

The Control of Substances Hazardous to Health Regulations 1988 (COSHH) (SI 1988 No 1657) place a duty on all employers to reduce employee exposure to hazardous substances to within, and preferably below, acceptable limits. The emphasis is very much on personal, as opposed to environmental, exposure and consideration especially in catering establishments, should be given to exposure via skin contact/absorption, as well as via inhalation and ingestion.

COSHH does not apply to physical hazards such as flammability.

It is unlikely that catering establishments will be deeply affected by COSHH, although some of the cleaning chemicals will almost certainly fall under its provisions.

Areas such as pastry kitchens may also require consideration due to the flour, sugars, etc. handled (dermatitis) and any dusts generated.

10.7 THE VDU DIRECTIVE

Wrongly, managers and supervisors of staff who perform office-based tasks often ignore the implications of health and safety in the workplace for their staff. However, EC Directive 90/270 on the health requirements for work with display screen equipment addresses the issues of health and safety of the many staff using word processing and VDU equipment. The Directive applies to all equipment put into service after 31 December 1992 and will apply from 31 December 1996 to all equipment installed before the end of 1992.

CASE STUDY

The Sporting Club has a restaurant, and has made an arrangement with Smart Catering that Smart will operate the restaurant. Smart instructs West End Decorators to re-decorate the restaurant. Smart's own employee, Ms Fuse, is to rewire the restaurant and kitchen at the same time.

The Sporting Club's maintenance man, Mr Grey, hovers around while the wiring and redecorating is being carried out; Mr Grey is the only person who knows exactly how the circuit in the restaurant works. On the first day the foreman of West End Decorators turns all the switches off in the restaurant and kitchen. At lunchtime Ms Fuse puts some switches on in order to test her work. She is observed doing this by Mr Grey. Ms Fuse leaves the light switches on, and when Jack, an employee of West End Decorators working on the restaurant ceiling, resumes work he receives a shock from a wire protruding from the ceiling and falls off his ladder, severely injuring himself.

West End Decorators are a very small business; they have not taken out an employer's liability insurance and have no real assets.

Consider the legal liability of the parties.

This case study raises a whole range of different civil actions and the possibility of criminal prosecution under the HSWA 1974.

Jack may commence a number of civil actions to recover compensation for his injuries. As he is an employee of West End Decorators, he is owed a duty by his employers to provide a safe place of work, a safe system of work and a competent staff of people to work with (see *Wilsons & Clyde Coal Co. Ltd* v. *English*). Jack may sue his employers if he can establish a breach of this duty on their part and can show that his injuries arose from that particular breach.

Jack may commence an action in negligence against Smart Catering, who are the employers of Ms Fuse, the person rewiring the restaurant. Such an action is based on the principle of vicarious liability (see p. 348). To succeed it must be proved that Ms Fuse had been negligent by switching the electricity supply back on, and that in consequence of this negligence Jack sustained injury.

It is arguable that Smart Catering are the occupiers (either jointly or solely – see *Wheat* v. *Lacon Ltd*, p. 78) of the premises and Jack may bring an action against them for breach of their duty as occupiers under the Occupiers' Liability Act 1957 (see p. 350).

Jack may wish to commence proceedings in negligence against the Sporting Club, arguing either that they are vicariously liable for Mr Grey's negligence in not preventing Jack's injuries or that they are liable as joint or sole occupiers of the premises.

It should be noted that potential claims exist against Ms Fuse and Mr Grey in person, but since neither is covered by insurance for third party liability, Jack would be ill-advised to seek redress against either of them.

The Sporting Club, Smart Catering or West End Decorators may seek to establish that Jack was responsible either in part or in full for his own injuries by means of the defences of contributory negligence and *volenti non fit injuria* (see p. 348).

Criminal liability may arise from the HSWA 1974. Section 2(1) of the Act creates a general duty of an employer to ensure the health, safety and welfare of his or her staff. Obviously, West End Decorators alone as Jack's employer are covered by this duty. Reference should be made to the particularization of the duty in s. 2(2) of the Act (see p. 355).

Mention can also be made of the need to report the accident and the consequences of a failure to do so under the Reporting of Injuries, Diseases and Dangerous Occurrences Regulations 1985 (see p. 360).

ELEVEN

The caterer and the staff III: The employer, the employee and the trade union

The role and relative importance of trade unions in the hospitality industry vary considerably, dependent upon the sector. Within the public-sector hospitality organizations such as hospitals and school meals services, membership and union influence may well be relatively high and managers will be in constant touch with union members and officials. In contrast, union membership and influence in most commercial sectors such as hotels and restaurants are very low and, in the main, non-existent. However, such distinctions between the public and private sectors are becoming blurred with the development of compulsory competitive tendering within the public sector. This is is, of course, having a big influence long term on union membership and influence in the public sector. Overall union membership within the industry is estimated to be between 5% and 10% of the workforce contrasted with around 30% for the workforce of the UK overall.

The place of trade unions within our society is probably one of the most politicized areas of the law. Within the last twenty years, and particularly under Thatcher governments, trade union law has been the object of major reform. It is not the aim of this book to give a history of trade union law, there are many other textbooks which do that. Instead we set out here to give a brief summary of the law as it affects the relationship of employers, employees and trade unions.

11.1 TRADE UNIONS

Most law concerning trade unions is now contained in the Trade Union and Labour Relations (Consolidation) Act 1992 and the Trade Union Reform and Employment Rights Act 1993. These will be referred to respectively as the 1992 Act and the 1993 Act. Under the 1992 Act a trade union is defined as:

... *an organisation (whether permanent or temporary) which either:-*
(a) *consists wholly or mainly of workers of one or more descriptions and whose principal purposes include the regulation of relations between workers of that description or those descriptions and employers or employers' associations; or*
(b) *which consists wholly or mainly of –*
(i) *constituent or affiliated organisations which fulfil the conditions specified in paragraph (a) above (or themselves consist wholly or mainly of constituent or affiliated organisations which fulfil those conditions), or*
(ii) *representatives of such constituent or affiliated organisations; and whose principal purposes include the regulation of relations between workers and employers or between workers and employers' associations, or the regulation of relations between its constituent or affiliated organisations.*

A trade union may be a corporate body, i.e. registered as a company under the Companies Act 1985, or otherwise incorporated (see Section 1 Trade Union and Labour Relations (Consolidation) Act 1992). However, s. 10 1992 Act gives a trade union a statutory legal personality, empowering it to make contracts, own property, sue and be sued in the courts, etc.

As with all things, the acquisition of 'status' imposes obligations. Trade unions have statutory obligations, which are:
1   To keep accounting records (s. 28 1992 Act).
2   To appoint auditors and make annual returns (s. 35 1992 Act).
3   To compile and keep an up-to-date register of members (s. 24 1992 Act). A member of a union may apply to the High Court or to the Certification Officer for a declaration that this requirement has not been complied with, and the court may additionally make an enforcement order requiring the union concerned to compile or update the register of members.
4   To ensure that voting members of the Executive Committee stand for election at least every five years (s. 46 1992 Act). Such a ballot must, as far as is reasonably practicable, be secret and members entitled to vote must, as far as is reasonably practicable, be given a convenient opportunity to vote by post (s. 51 1992 Act). Government funding has been made available for the conduct of such elections (s. 115 1992 Act). Any person who claims that the union is in breach of the election provisions may apply to the Certification Officer or to the High Court, provided that:
(a)   he or she was a member of the union at the date of the election;
(b)   he or she is a member of the union at the date of the application; and
(c)   the application is made within one year of the date on which the results of the election were announced (s. 54–56 1992 Act).
The Certification Officer or the High Court may make a declaration specifying the provisions with which the trade union has failed to comply. Where it makes such a declaration, the court may also make an enforcement order to secure the holding of an election as specified in the order.
5   S. 73 1992 Act obliges trade unions which have passed a resolution on the application of trade union funds for political purposes (e.g. donations to a political party) to hold ballots at least every ten years, to determine whether the membership wish to continue the application of their funds to those purposes. Funds are available (s. 115 1992 Act) from the Government through the Funds for Trade Union Ballots Regulations for the holding of such ballots. Any member of a trade union who considers that his or her union has failed to

comply with the ballot requirements may apply to the High Court for a declaration to that effect, and the court may make an order requiring the union to hold such a ballot.

A trade union's liability in tort

Trade unions were once in a privileged position: they were to all intents and purposes immune for tortious liability for their actions in pursuance of an industrial dispute. This was provided for under TULRA and was sometimes referred to as the 'golden formula'. Section 15 of the Employment Act 1982 removed this immunity. The immunity which a trade union has against a claim in tort applies to action taken 'in contemplation or furtherance of a trade dispute'. It does not now protect 'secondary action' of trade unions.

A trade union does *not* enjoy immunity from liability in tort for inducing breaches of contract of employment unless its action has the support of a ballot which complies with s. 226 of the 1992 Act.

Trade union recognition

Trade union recognition was once a key issue, but is now of importance only for the notification of redundancies, the disclosure of information for collective bargaining and the information and consultation requirements set out in the Transfer of Undertakings Regulations 1981. Equally, the right to time off for trade union duties and activities applies only to officials of recognized independent trade unions.

An employer may, of course, voluntarily agree to recognize a trade union.

Trade union independence

A list of trade unions is maintained by the Certification Officer. A trade union whose name is entered on the list may apply to the Certification Officer for a certificate that it is independent – see s. 6 1992 Act.

If the union is listed by the Certification Officer this officer will determine whether the union is an independent trade union. An independent trade union is defined in s. 5 1992 Act as:

> *a trade union which –*
> (a) *is not under the domination or control of an employer or a group of employers or of one or more employers' associations; and*
> (b) *is not liable to interference by an employer or any such group or association (arising out of the provision of financial or material support or by any means whatsoever) tending towards such control.*

The factors which are taken into account in assessing independence include:

> (a) *history of the union particularly if the union started with management encouragement and support;*

(b)	membership base and proportion of members concentrated in one employer;

(c)	organisation and structure – the main requirement being that members can play a full part in the decision-making process;

(d)	negotiating record – this will be taken into account when looking at the other factors so that a strong record in negotiations may outweigh other factors which are unfavourable to the union's case.

(Guidance for Trade Unions Wishing to Apply for a Certificate of Independence; published by the Certification Officer.)

The Certification Officer may at any time withdraw a certificate, after giving due notice to the trade union and determining the relevant questions, where he or she is of the opinion that the trade union is no longer independent.

Trade union funds

Section 15 of the 1992 Act imposes restrictions upon the use of trade union funds for indemnifying an individual for unlawful activities for which he or she has been ordered to pay a penalty. Section 15 provides:

(1)	It is unlawful for property of a trade union to be applied in or towards –
    (a)	the payment for an individual of a penalty which has been or may be imposed on him for an offence or for contempt of court,
    (b)	the securing of any such payment, or
    (c)	the provision of anything for indemnifying an individual in respect of such a penalty.

(2)	Where any property of a trade union is so applied for the benefit of an individual on whom a penalty has been or may be imposed, then –
    (a)	in the case of a payment, an amount equal to the payment is recoverable by the union from him, and
    (b)	in any other case, he is liable to account to the union for the value of the property applied.

(3)	If a trade union fails to bring or continue proceedings which it is entitled to bring by virtue of subsection (2), a member of the union who claims that the failure is unreasonable may apply to the court on that ground for an order authorising him to bring or continue the proceedings on the union's behalf and at the union's expense.

(4)	In this section 'penalty', in relation to an offence, includes an order to pay compensation and an order for the forfeiture of any property; and references to the imposition of a penalty for an offence shall be construed accordingly.

(5)	The Secretary of State may by order designate offences in relation to which the provisions of this section do not apply.

Any such order shall be made by statutory instrument which shall be subject to annulment in pursuance of a resolution of either House of Parliament.

(6)	This section does not affect –
    (a)	any other enactment, any rule of law or any provision of the rules of a trade union which makes it unlawful for the property of a trade union to be applied in a particular way; or
    (b)	any other remedy available to a trade union, the trustees of its property or

any of its members in respect of an unlawful application of the union's property.

(7) In this section 'member', in relation to a trade union consisting wholly or partly of, or of representatives of, constituent or affiliated organisations, includes a member of any of the constituent or affiliated organisations.

Section 16 provides a right of redress for a member of a trade union who claims that the trustees of the union's property:

> (a) *have so carried out their functions, or are proposing so to carry out their functions, as to cause or permit an unlawful application of the union's property; or*
>
> (b) *have complied, or are proposing to comply, with an unlawful direction which has been or may be given, or purportedly given, to them under the rules of the union.*

Section 16(2) provides:

(2) In a case relating to property which has already been unlawfully applied, or to an unlawful direction that has already been complied with, an application under this section may be made only by a person who was a member of the union at the time when the property was applied or, as the case may be, the direction complied with.

(3) Where the court is satisfied that the claim is well-founded, it shall make such order as it considers appropriate.

The court may in particular –
  (a) require the trustees (if necessary, on behalf of the union) to take all such steps as may be specified in the order for protecting or recovering the property of the union;
  (b) appoint a receiver of, or in Scotland a judicial factor on, the property of the union;
  (c) remove one or more of the trustees.

(4) Where the court makes an order under this section in a case in which –
  (a) property of the union has been applied in contravention of an order of any court, or in compliance with a direction given in contravention of such an order, or
  (b) the trustees were proposing to apply property in contravention of such an order or to comply with any such direction,
the court shall by its order remove all the trustees except any trustee who satisfies the court that there is a good reason for allowing him to remain a trustee.

(5) Without prejudice to any other power of the court, the court may on an application for an order under this section grant such interlocutory relief (in Scotland, such interim order) as it considers appropriate.

(6) This section does not affect any other remedy available in respect of a breach of trust by the trustees of a trade union's property.

(7) In this section 'member', in relation to a trade union consisting wholly or partly of, or of representatives of, constituent or affiliated organisations, includes a member of any of the constituent or affiliated organisations.

11.2 THE EMPLOYEE'S RIGHTS AS A TRADE UNIONIST

An employee who is a member of a trade union has the following rights in relation to his or her employer.

The employee has a right not to be dismissed for membership of, or taking part in the activities of, an independent trade union. Where he or she is so dismissed, such dismissal is automatically unfair.

The employee has a right not to have action short of dismissal taken against him or her by his or her employer for membership of, or for taking part in the activities of, an independent trade union. Where such action is taken the employee has a right to complain to an industrial tribunal which may award him or her compensation.

The employee, as a trade union member, has the right to time off (unpaid) to take part in trade union activities. Where he or she is a trade union official he or she has a right to take time off (paid) to undertake his or her trade union duties.

Time off work

Employees who are members of an independent trade union (see above) recognized by their employer may take unpaid time off work to take part in trade union activities (other than industrial action) (s. 168 1992 Act). The extent of the time off must be reasonable. Employees who are officials of an independent trade union recognized by their employer may take paid time off to carry out official duties concerned with negotiations or performance of agreed trade union functions, or to undergo industrial relations training relevant to their duties (s. 169 1992 Act). As with s. 168, the extent of time off must be reasonable in the circumstances. Employers and employees should be aware of the ACAS Code of Practice *Time Off for Trade Union Duties and Activities*.

Refusal of employment

Section 137 of the 1992 Act makes it unlawful to refuse employment on grounds related to trade union membership, i.e. because a person is or is not a member of a trade union (s. 137(1)a) or because he or she is unwilling to accept a requirement (s. 137(1)b):

   (i) *to take steps to become or cease to be, or to remain or not become a member of a trade union, or*
   (ii) *to make payments or suffer deductions in the event of his not being a member of a trade union.*

Section 137(2) provides redress for such action by way of a right to complain to an industrial tribunal within three months of the date of the conduct to which the complaint relates. If a complaint is well founded, the tribunal will have the power to make a declaration and order compensation or make a recommendation that the respondent take practicable action to obviate or reduce the adverse effect of such conduct.

Compensation shall be assessed on the same basis as damages for breach of statutory duty and may include compensation for injury to feelings. (s. 140, 1992 Act).

A trade union member's rights in relation to the union
(Trade Union Reform and Employment Rights Act 1993)

Trade union members have been granted a range of rights regarding their union membership under the 1993 Act. The principal rights are:

* not to be refused employment because of his/her union membership or non union membership
* not to be refused the services of an employment agency because of his/her union membership or non union membership
* to belong or not to belong to a trade union
* not to make payments in lieu of union membership subscriptions
* to take part in union activities
* union dues to be deducted by the employer (check-off) only with the written consent of the employee, which must have been given within the last three years.
* at least one month's notice of any increase to the subscriptions to be deducted together with a reminder that the employee may withdraw from the check-off scheme at any time
* not to be excluded or expelled from a trade union (excepting for one of the specified reasons).

The 1993 Act provides a two-stage remedy for an employee who complains that he or she has been unreasonably expelled or excluded. First, he or she can present a complaint to an industrial tribunal within six months of the alleged refusal or expulsion. As with unfair dismissal cases ACAS may seek to settle the dispute through conciliation. The tribunal must then determine whether or not the complaint is well founded. If it is, the tribunal may make a declaration that the refusal or expulsion was unreasonable. The union may appeal to the EAT against such a finding. A four-week period follows the declaration, the purpose of which is to give the trade union the opportunity of admitting or re-admitting the complainant to membership. After the four-week period the complainant may apply to the industrial tribunal for compensation. Where the complainant is admitted or re-admitted, the appropriate tribunal for him or her to seek compensation is the industrial tribunal. Where he or she has not been admitted or re-admitted, the appropriate tribunal is the EAT. Both have considerable powers to award compensation.

Right to a ballot before industrial action (s. 2, 1992 Act)

A member of a trade union may apply to the court for an order where he or she claims that the union has, without the support of a ballot, authorized or endorsed any industrial action in which union members are likely to be or have been induced by the union to take part. Where an application is made to the court under s. 1(1) and the court is satisfied:
(a) that the trade union has, without balloting its members, authorized or endorsed any industrial action;
(b) that members of the union are likely to be or have been induced by the union to take part or to continue to take part in the action; and

(c) that the applicant is a member of the union who has been or is likely to be so
     induced,
the court shall make such an order as it considers appropriate for requiring the union
to take steps for ensuring that there is no, or no further, inducement of members to
take part in the action and that no member engages in any conduct after the making
of the order by virtue of having been induced to do so before the making of the order.

Right not to be denied access to the courts (s. 63, 1992 Act)

The purpose of this section is to ensure that a trade union member cannot have denied
to him or her any right of redress through the courts which may have been excluded
from or denied by the union by use of the union rule book.

Right not to be unjustifiably disciplined (s. 64, 1992 Act)

This is one of the most controversial provisions of the Act, introduced by the
Employment Act 1988 and hailed by some as the 'Scabs' Charter'. Section 64, 1992 Act
prohibits a trade union disciplining a member for, amongst other things, continuing to
work for his or her employer at a time when the union was taking industrial action
against the employer.

Section 66, 1992 Act provides an individual trade union member with a right to complain to an industrial tribunal that he or she has been unjustifiably disciplined and that
his or her right under s. 64 has been infringed.

Right to inspect trade union's accounts

Section 30, 1992 Act gives individual members the right to inspect the union's accounts
and requires the union to maintain their accounts ready for inspection.

Right to require employer to stop deduction of union subscriptions

Section 68 of the 1992 Act provides:

> (1) Where any person ('the employee') has certified to his employer –
>   (a) that there has been or will be, as from a particular date, such a termination
>   of his membership of any trade union as is within the knowledge of the
>   union; or
>   (b) that any notice which he has given to a trade union for the purpose of
>   terminating his membership of that union has expired or will expire on a
>   particular date,
>   the employer shall ensure that no amount representing a payment to the union
>   in respect of the employee's membership after that date of that union is deducted
>   from emoluments payable by the employer to the employee.
> (2) Subsection (1) above does not apply in relation to emoluments paid –
>   (a) before the first day following the giving of the certificate on which it is
>   reasonably practicable for the employer to give effect, in compliance with
>   that subsection, to a variation of the net amount of emoluments payable to
>   the employee; or
>   (b) after the employee notifies his employer that the certificate is withdrawn.

(3) *Notwithstanding anything in any contract between the employee and the employer, or in any agreement or consent signified by the employee, a deduction made in contravention of this section shall in all cases be treated for the purposes of Part I of the Wages Act 1986 as a deduction in contravention of section 1(1) of that Act.*

By reason of ss. 15 and 9 of the 1992 Act trade union members have a right to ensure that trade union funds are not misapplied.

The Commissioner for the Rights of Trade Union Members

The Employment Act 1988 created the office of the Commissioner for the Rights of Trade Union Members. His or her appointment by the Secretary of State is provided for by s. 266, 1992 Act. An individual who is an actual or prospective party to proceedings covered by the Commission can apply to the Commissioner for assistance. The Employment Act 1990 s. 10 lists those proceedings in respect of which such assistance may be provided, and includes: balloting, authorizing or endorsing of industrial action and appointment to or removal from office. The office of Commissioner and the assistance which emanates from the Commission are similar to those of the Commission for Racial Equality in that both are designed to promote the rights of particular groups and to ensure that people from the respective groups have assistance in enforcing their rights by means of legal redress.

11.3 THE CLOSED SHOP

In the past it was common practice, in some industries, for employers and trade unions to agree that all workers, or some specified categories, would have to be members of a specified union or unions, in order to work for the employer. In some cases there were 'pre-entry' closed shops, i.e. a worker had to be a member before starting employment. In other cases there were 'post-entry' closed shops, i.e. the worker had to join within a specified period or upon achieving a certain status. Prior to the Employment Act 1988 dismissal of a non-union member employee was automatically fair where there was a 'closed shop' agreement. The 1988 Act, however, removed such protection from the employer and dismissal on grounds of non-union membership, as written above, is unlawful (s. 137, 1992 Act). As a consequence the 'closed' shop is banned because employers can no longer oblige a worker to join a union.

11.4 TRADE UNION BALLOTS

The 1992 Act makes a number of provisions as to trade union ballots. Before considering these, it is as well to recall perhaps the most important provision on balloting. The Act gives each union member the right to a ballot on any proposal for industrial action.

Election addresses

(1) The trade union shall –
  (a) provide every candidate with an opportunity of preparing an election address in his own words and of submitting it to the union to be distributed to the persons accorded entitlement to vote in the election; and
  (b) secure that, so far as reasonably practicable, copies of every election address submitted to it in time are distributed to each of those persons by post along with the voting papers for the election.
(2) The trade union may determine the time by which an election address must be submitted to it for distribution; but the time so determined must not be earlier than the latest time at which a person may become a candidate in the election.
(3) The trade union may provide that election addresses submitted to it for distribution –
  (a) must not exceed such length, not being less than one hundred words, as may be determined by the union, and
  (b) may, as regards photographs and other matter not in words, incorporate only such matter as the union may determine.
(4) The trade union shall secure that no modification of an election address submitted to it is made by any person in any copy of the address to be distributed except –
  (a) at the request or with the consent of the candidate, or
  (b) where the modification is necessarily incidental to the method adopted for producing that copy.
(5) The trade union shall secure that the same method of producing copies is applied in the same way to every election address submitted and, so far as reasonably practicable, that no such facility or information as would enable a candidate to gain any benefit from –
  (a) the method by which copies of the election addresses are produced, or
  (b) the modifications which are necessarily incidental to that method, is provided to any candidate without being provided equally to all the others.
(6) The trade union shall, so far as reasonably practicable, secure that the same facilities and restrictions with respect to the preparation, submission, length or modification of an election address, and with respect to the incorporation of photographs or other matter not in words, are provided or applied equally to each of the candidates.
(7) The arrangements made by the trade union for the production of the copies to be so distributed must be such as to secure that none of the candidates is required to bear any of the expense of producing the copies.
(8) No-one other than the candidate himself shall incur any civil or criminal liability in respect of the publication of a candidate's election address or of any copy required to be made for the purposes of this section.

Section 49, 1992 Act: independent scrutiny of elections. This section provides a number of requirements for scrutinizing certain ballots. The purpose of this is to ensure that the due process is adhered to.

Section 18 EA 1988. This provides a Code of Practice of Trade Union Balloting.

An employer's obligation on trade union ballots

An employer is obliged, so far as is reasonably practicable, to comply with a request to use his or her premises for the purpose of giving a convenient opportunity of voting (in accordance with the Trade Union Ballots Regulations) to employees who are members of the union making the request.

This obligation arises only where:

(a) the employer, together with any associated employer, employs more than 20 employees;
(b) the trade union is recognized by the employer for collective bargaining purposes.

If an employer fails to comply with a trade union's request the union may present a complaint to an industrial tribunal that it has made a request and that it was reasonably practicable for the employer to comply with it, but that he or she has failed to do so. The complaint must be presented to the tribunal before the end of the period of three months beginning with the date of the failure, or within such further period as the tribunal considers reasonable in a case where it is satisfied that it was not reasonably practicable for the complaint to be presented before the end of the period of three months.

Where a tribunal finds such a complaint well founded, it will make a declaration to that effect. It may make an award of compensation to be paid by the employer to the union of such amount as it considers just and equitable in all the circumstances, taking into account the employer's default and any expense incurred by the union because of the failure. An appeal lies to the Employment Appeal Tribunal on a question of law.

Table of Statutes

Table of EC Law

Table of Regulations and Orders

Table of Cases

Subject Index

PRINCIPLES OF
HOSPITALITY LAW

Other hotel and catering texts available from the publisher:

Hotel and Catering Case Studies – Peter Abbott and John Shepherd
Computer Systems in the Hotel and Catering Industry – Bruce Braham
Hotel and Food Service Marketing – Francis Buttle
Food Service Operations, second edition – Peter Jones
The Management of Hotel Operations – Peter Jones and Andrew Lockwood
People and the Hotel and Catering Industry – Andrew Lockwood and Peter Jones
Strategic Hospitality Management – Richard Teare (ed.)
Managing and Marketing Services in the 1990s – Richard Teare (ed.)
Managing Projects in Hospitality Organizations – Richard Teare (ed.)
Services Management – Richard Teare and Colin Armistead (eds)